Collaboration in Higher Education

Also Available from Bloomsbury

Community-Based Transformational Learning,
edited by Christian Winterbottom, Jody S. Nicholson and F. Dan Richard
Academic Working Lives, edited by Lynne Gornall, Caryn Cook, Lyn Daunton,
Jane Salisbury and Brychan Thomas
Exploring Consensual Leadership in Higher Education,
edited by Lynne Gornall, Brychan Thomas and Lucy Sweetman
Dominant Discourses in Higher Education, Ian M. Kinchin and Karen Gravett
Changing Higher Education for a Changing World,
edited by Claire Callender, William Locke and Simon Marginson
Pursuing Teaching Excellence in Higher Education, Margaret Wood and Feng Su
Locating Social Justice in Higher Education Research,
edited by Jan McArthur and Paul Ashwin
Subjectivity and Social Change in Higher Education, Liezl Dick and Marguerite Müller
Decolonizing University Teaching and Learning, D. Tran
Social Theory and the Politics of Higher Education,
edited by Mark Murphy, Ciaran Burke, Cristina Costa and Rille Raaper
Leadership in Higher Education from a Transrelational Perspective,
Christopher M. Branson, Maureen Marra, Margaret Franken and Dawn Penney

Collaboration in Higher Education

A New Ecology of Practice

Edited by Sandra Abegglen, Tom Burns and
Sandra Sinfield

BLOOMSBURY ACADEMIC
LONDON • NEW YORK • OXFORD • NEW DELHI • SYDNEY

BLOOMSBURY ACADEMIC
Bloomsbury Publishing Plc
50 Bedford Square, London, WC1B 3DP, UK
1385 Broadway, New York, NY 10018, USA
29 Earlsfort Terrace, Dublin 2, Ireland

BLOOMSBURY, BLOOMSBURY ACADEMIC and the Diana logo
are trademarks of Bloomsbury Publishing Plc

First published in Great Britain 2023
Paperback edition published 2025

Copyright © Sandra Abegglen, Tom Burns and Sandra Sinfield and contributors, 2023

Sandra Abegglen, Tom Burns and Sandra Sinfield and contributors have asserted their right under the Copyright, Designs and Patents Act, 1988, to be identified as Author of this work.

Cover design: Grace Ridge
Cover image © stuart bebb / Stockimo / Alamy Stock Photo

This work is published open access subject to a Creative Commons Attribution-NonCommercial-NoDerivatives 4.0 International licence (CC BY-NC-ND 4.0, https://creativecommons.org/licenses/by-nc-nd/4.0/). You may re-use, distribute, and reproduce this work in any medium for non-commercial purposes, provided you give attribution to the copyright holder and the publisher and provide a link to the Creative Commons licence.

Bloomsbury Publishing Plc does not have any control over, or responsibility for, any third-party websites referred to or in this book. All internet addresses given in this book were correct at the time of going to press. The author and publisher regret any inconvenience caused if addresses have changed or sites have ceased to exist, but can accept no responsibility for any such changes.

A catalogue record for this book is available from the British Library.

Library of Congress Control Number: 2023937569.

ISBN:	HB:	978-1-3503-3405-2
	PB:	978-1-3503-3409-0
	ePDF:	978-1-3503-3406-9
	eBook:	978-1-3503-3407-6

Typeset by Integra Software Services Pvt. Ltd.

To find out more about our authors and books visit www.bloomsbury.com and sign up for our newsletters.

Contents

List of Figures	viii
List of Tables	x
List of Authors	xi
Foreword: Collaboration In, Against and Beyond the Neoliberal, Neocolonical, Pandemic University	xxxii
List of Abbreviations	xxxviii

1 Introduction: Why Collaborate? … 1

2 Choose Your Own Collaboration: An Adventure in Academic Time and Space … 7

3 Staff Collaborations to Enhance Teaching and Learning … 33
 Introduction … 33
 Writing Retreats in Social Work: A Disruptive Approach to Facilitating Practice Learning … 35
 Collaboration for Academic Literacies Development and Enriched Inter-professional Relationships … 39
 Co-producing a Skills-based Programme: Peer-to-peer Learning Partnerships in Professional Development … 43
 Bringing Research to Life: Enhancing Research Skills through Collaborative Storytelling … 49
 Approaching Blended Learning through Teaching Team Collaboration: Lessons from an AU Postgraduate Accounting Programme … 52
 Developing Twenty-first-century Skills through Meaningful Cross-institutional Collaborative International Community Service Projects … 57
 Cross-disciplinary Collaborations for Sustainable Futures, and a Vital and Relevant Academic Community … 62

4 Students as Partners … 77
 Introduction … 77
 Enhancing the Wider Postgraduate Experience: Student Partnership in Co-creating Online Learning … 79

	Students as Co-creators of an Inclusive Equality and Diversity Teaching Resource: An Example from Life Sciences	83
	Speaking of Vocabulary: A Socio-material Collaboration with Graduate Students	88
	Staff-student Collaboration across Disciplines: An Academic Literacies Approach	93
	Researching Together: A Collaborative Research Volunteer Scheme and Its Student-staff Partnership Evaluation	97
5	**Collaboration with Stakeholders**	**109**
	Introduction	109
	Tutors, Students and Other Stakeholders at the Roundtable: A Matter of Equal Partnership	110
	Healthcare Scientist Education: Multi-stakeholder Cross-institutional Collaboration to Deliver Excellent Student Experience	115
	Multi-partner Doctoral Training Collaborations: More than the Sum of Their Parts	120
6	**Creative and Digital Partnerships**	**129**
	Introduction	129
	Paper as Teacher: Challenging Dominant Learning Norms in Higher Education through Collaborating in Origami	131
	Upheaval, Creativity and Student Partnerships: A Case Study of Relational, Collaborative Pedagogy	138
	Supporting Collaboration: Transforming the Arts Curriculum in Practice	142
	Connectivity as Transgressive Practice in Doctoral Research: Making the Elephant Dance	146
	Changing the Rules of the Game: A Staff-student Digital Support Network	150
	Enhancing Digital Inclusivity: Powerful Partnership with Students	154
7	**Decolonizing Relationships and Partnerships for Social Justice**	**165**
	Introduction	165
	Coming in Together: Staff-student Collaboration in a 'Decolonizing' Induction Process	167
	Unite and Unrule! Reflections of a Co-created Pedagogy for Transformation	172
	Honest Conversations about 'Race' and Racism: Innovative Decolonizing Practice	177
	Love, Respect, Esteem: Collaborative Student Partnerships for Social Justice	183
	Inclusive Learning and Teaching in Higher Education: Students as Co-creators in Course Re-design	187

	Teaching for Equality and the Politics of Feminist and Decolonial Education: From Polarized Debate to Collaborations for Change	192
8	**Reflections on Collaboration**	**205**
	Introduction	205
	Together: The Story of Collaborating to Create the Open Picture Book	207
	Autoethnography, Academic Identity, Creativity: Transitionary Tales from Practice to Teaching and beyond	212
	Working Together: Reflections on a Non-hierarchical Approach to Collaborative Writing	216
	Humane Relationships: Reflections on Dialogue and Collaboration in a Foundation Art, Architecture and Design Course	220
	Coaching for Collaborative Autonomy: A Reflection on an Inter-university Course	224

Afterword: Collaboration, Community-building and 'Brokering'   234
Index   241

Figures

3.1	Session 1 – Challenges at semester start (Soccio & Tregloan, 2022)	46
3.2	The scope of the SF: Key partners, activities and impacts	65
3.3	Academic observations of the impacts of SF events on students. The x-axis represents the number of responses of academic staff reporting each factor	66
3.4	Motivation of academics to attend the SF events. The x-axis represents the number of responses from academic staff reporting because of each factor	67
3.5	Impacts of academic participation in SF events on academic practices. The x-axis represents the number of responses of academic staff reporting each factor	68
4.1	The nine protected characteristics of the Equalities Act (2010)	84
5.1	Illustration showing which institutions are involved in each of the three DTPs exemplified in this case study	121
6.1	Folding demonstration (Image courtesy of Hao & Pentek, 2021)	133
6.2	Students working on Miura folding (Image courtesy of Hao & Pentek, 2021)	134
6.3	Workshop aims	135
6.4 & 6.5	Supplemental diagrams by Pentek, showing fold points along a piece of paper	135
6.6	Mean scores for the survey question – 'To what extent do you agree with the following statement? The online learning environment and content is accessible': 1 = Definitely disagree, 5 = Definitely agree (n=10,699)	157
6.7	Mean scores for the survey question – 'To what extent do you agree with the following statement? The online learning environment and content is inclusive': 1 = Definitely disagree, 5 = Definitely agree (n=8,917)	157
7.1	Khanga. Anthony Kalume shares the history of the Khanga at Brighton Museum (image credits: Willie Robb)	179

7.2	Khanga exhibit. Anthony Kalume giving a talk on the Khanga exhibit at Brighton Museum (image credits: Willie Robb)	180
7.3	Khanga workshop. Workshop at Brighton Museum using the Khanga exhibit as a source of inspiration for creative work (image credits: Willie Robb)	182

Tables

4.1 A sample of entries of students' contributions 90
4.2 RVS – example project types and degree of potential collaboration 98
6.1 Conceptual framework: Dominant systems vs arts-based practices 132

Authors

Editors

ORCIDs
Sandra Abegglen: https://orcid.org/0000-0002-1582-9394
Tom Burns: https://orcid.org/0000-0003-1280-0104
Sandra Sinfield: https://orcid.org/0000-0003-0484-7623

Sandra Abegglen is Researcher in the School of Architecture, Planning and Landscape at the University of Calgary, Canada, where she explores online education, and learning and teaching in the design studio. Sandra has an MSc in Social Research and an MA in Learning and Teaching in Higher Education. She has extensive experience both as a social researcher and lecturer/programme leader. She has published widely on emancipatory learning and teaching practice, creative and playful pedagogy, and remote education. Find her personal website at: https://sandra-abegglen.com/.

Tom Burns is Senior Lecturer in the Centre for Professional and Educational Development at London Metropolitan University, UK, developing innovations with a special focus on praxes that ignites student curiosity, and develops power and voice. Always interested in theatre and the arts, and their role in teaching and learning, Tom has set up adventure playgrounds, community events and festivals for his local community, and feeds arts-based practice into his learning, teaching and assessment practices. He is co-author of *Teaching, Learning and Study Skills: A Guide for Tutors* and *Essential Study Skills: The Complete Guide to Success at University* (5th Edition).

Sandra Sinfield is Senior Lecturer in Education and Learning Development in the Centre for Professional and Educational Development at London Metropolitan University, UK, and a co-founder of the Association for Learning Development in Higher Education. She has co-authored *Teaching, Learning and Study Skills: A Guide for Tutors* and *Essential Study Skills: The complete Guide to Success at University* (5th Edition). Sandra is interested in creativity as liberatory and holistic practice in Higher Education; she has developed theatre and film in unusual places, and inhabited SecondLife as a learning space.

Contributors

Carol Ainley is Head of Department of Life Sciences at Manchester Metropolitan University, UK, and Director of Manchester Academy for Healthcare Scientist Education (MAHSE). Her interest lies in biomedical/healthcare science education, focusing on the student experience, with publications and conference proceedings in this field. A registered Biomedical Scientist, Carol continues to work with the Health and Care Professions Council and the Institute of Biomedical Science. She is a Senior Fellow of the Higher Education Academy and Fellow of the Leadership Foundation.

Quentin Allan, PhD, SFHEA, is Senior Lecturer and Learning Advisor at Auckland University of Technology, New Zealand. As a member of the Learning Success team within the AUT Library, Quentin uses his knowledge of pedagogy and applied linguistics to develop students' academic literacies, working closely with faculty lecturers from a wide range of academic disciplines.

Pranit Anand is Lecturer in Learning Design at Queensland University of Technology, Australia, where he advises other educators about contemporary learning and assessment design. He has over eighteen years' experience in higher education across several different cultural contexts. It is through this experience that he has developed the empathy to appreciate diversity of students' learning experiences, and therefore ability to design flexibility in learning designs for all students. Some of the research agendas that Pranit is exploring include internationalization of the curriculum, flexible and inclusive assessments, educational technology to emphasize a 'philosophy of care' and equity issues in higher education.

Karen Arm, PhD, is Senior Lecturer in Learning and Teaching at Solent University, UK, leading university-wide enhancement in learning, teaching and assessment, with an emphasis on meeting the needs of students from diverse backgrounds. Her main research interests lie in the field of social justice and equity in higher education. Karen is committed to addressing differentials in academic experience and outcomes of university students and working with learners as partners in the pursuit of educational change.

Ryan Arthur is Learning Development Coordinator at Birkbeck College, University of London, UK. He is a Fellow of the Higher Education Academy and an accredited coach. He has a BA (hons), MA and PhD in the humanities and an MA in Learning and Teaching in Higher Education (MALTHE). He regularly presents his dialogic approach to learning development at international conferences. His research interests include the BAME award gap, decolonizing the curriculum and learning development.

Gordon Asher is an Independent Scholar and Developer, and academic editor/proofreader. He worked previously as a Learning and Curriculum Developer (UWS and University of Strathclyde, UK) and has held teaching roles across adult, community and higher education. He has most recently published on 'critical academic literacies' in the book he co-edited – *Friendship, Critical Pedagogy and Revolutionary Hope: A Festschrift with and in Honour of Joyce Canaan*. Much of his work and publications focus on linking critical educational theories and practices within the university, with radical education across struggles and movements outwith the academy. He can be found on Academia.edu and Facebook.

Tamara Ashley, PhD, is Senior Lecturer in Dance at the University of Bedfordshire, UK with an ongoing research interest in dance and environmental change, the intersections between embodiment and climate action.

Cybele Atme is a PhD candidate at the Department of Law, Society and Crime at the Erasmus University, Rotterdam, the Netherlands. She holds an MSc at the University of Amsterdam, the Netherlands, in International Development Studies, where she was involved as a student and a teacher in several co-created initiatives around equality in education. Two of these initiatives are cases in this book, CDDE and Teaching for Equality. In addition to her interests in practising social justice in education, her research interest intersects the anthropology of money and migration studies. Her current research focuses on the impacts of financial restrictions on humanitarian work in Lebanon.

Lydia Bales is Learning and Teaching Librarian at The Open University, UK. She enjoys exploring creative ways to engage students in research and referencing. In her previous role at Staffordshire University, she created a unique induction exercise for Forensic students. 'Body in the Library' required students to solve information literacy riddles, the answers to which prompted players to physically access the library, in order to solve the mystery and complete the induction. Combining her school library background with the academic world, she is particularly interested in reading for pleasure and the effect on student well-being and module understanding and retention.

Laura Barclay is Learning Development Tutor in the School of Area Studies, History, Politics and Literature at the University of Portsmouth, UK. She is currently undertaking a Doctorate in Education with a focus on the application of playful learning in higher education. Her project will investigate the student experience of engaging with the French language through musical theatre.

Manuela Barczewski is Senior Lecturer at the School of Art, Architecture and Design at London Metropolitan University, UK. She was sponsored to study towards her Postgraduate Certificate in Education (PGCert) which she was awarded with distinction in 2020. In her teaching she focuses on the link between creative practice and pedagogy with a dedication to humane, democratic and socially engaged practice. Manuela has an expanded practice as a visual artist and musician, having performed and exhibited in the UK and internationally. She holds a Diplom II in Fine Art Photography from Folkwang Universität der Künste and an MA in Fine Art from Central Saint Martins.

Geoff Barrett is a Newly Qualified Teacher working in the primary sector in Renfrewshire Council, UK. He completed his BA (hons) at Glasgow Caledonian University, UK, before embarking on a successful career in retail. He sold his business after fifteen years to pursue a teaching career. He worked with a number of projects in Glasgow, supporting young people who had disengaged from education before working for Kibble Education and Care in their social enterprise. He ran several activity clubs for children with Additional Support Needs (ASN). In 2019 he undertook his PGDE (Primary) at University of Glasgow with placements in primary schools in Renfrewshire.

Keith Beckles is Lecturer at London Metropolitan University, UK. He completed a BA in Furniture and Product Design at London Metropolitan University in 2016. In 2016 Keith started as an Associate Lecturer at London Metropolitan University, teaching Critical and Contextual studies at Level 4 for two years. He then joined Foundation Art, Media and Design where he was able to implement his knowledge of drawing and photography, and contribute to decolonizing the curriculum. In his spare time, Keith regularly attends classes at the Royal Drawing School. Keith was awarded Fellowship of Advance HE in 2019 and continues to study towards his MA in Learning and Teaching.

Ed Bickle, PhD, has been Lecturer in Learning Development at Bournemouth University, UK, since 2017. He has extensive experience in widening participation research and his primary interests lie in the lived experiences of widening participation students, and phenomenological research methodologies.

James Bishop, PhD, is a Chartered Building Engineer, Fellow of the Chartered Association of Building Engineers, Senior Fellow of the Higher Education Academy and course leader for the construction management degrees at the University of Bedfordshire, UK.

Silvina Bishopp-Martin has been Learning Developer at Canterbury Christ Church University, UK, since joining the institution in 2012. She is a fellow of the Higher Education Academy and an ALDinHE Certified Leading Practitioner. She has worked on the development of online learning materials, peer-mentoring schemes and embedding academic literacies in academic programmes. She has research experience on academic literacies, critical EAP and Learning Development professionalism and identity.

Sharon Bittner is Assistant Faculty Librarian for Humanities, Law, & Criminology at the University of Portsmouth, UK, teaching research skills to all levels of university students and staff, but primarily to students enrolled in humanities, social sciences and law courses. She has two MAs from the University of Missouri-Columbia, USA, and an MSc from the University of Portsmouth, UK. Sharon has a keen interest in promoting digital newspaper archives to students due to using microfilmed newspapers to research bicycle racing in late nineteenth-century Missouri.

Jennie Blake is Head of Teaching and Learning Development at the University of Manchester Library, UK, and Academic Lead for Student Success for the University of Manchester Institute for Teaching and Learning, UK. She has been working in education for over twenty-five years in the United States and UK and led on the development of the Library's multi-award-winning My Learning Essentials. She is a National Teaching Fellow of the Higher Education Academy, has an MA in Education from the University of California at Berkeley, USA, has published widely on student engagement and student success and focuses her work on advocating for, supporting and allying with underrepresented groups.

Pauline Bon is a Programme Coordinator in the human rights field. After the successful completion of the research master's in international development studies at the University of Amsterdam, the Netherlands, she has been working as the Shelter City programme coordinator at the Urgent Foundation. She assisted human rights defenders from high-risk countries by providing them with temporary resettlement in the Netherlands and personalized support for the development of their professional projects. Her conviction is that by strengthening principles of solidarity and social justice underlying development policies and education, it is possible to build stronger democracies and communities of care.

Kevin Brazant is Learning Development Practitioner at London Metropolitan University, UK. He is a Fellow with the Higher Education Academy (FHEA) and a Certified Practitioner (CeP) with the Association of Learning Developers in Higher Education (ALDinHE). His research interests include BAME attainment and the application of Anti Racist and Critical Pedagogies, as part of learning and teaching practice in Higher Education.

Mieke Lopes Cardozo, PhD, is Senior Lecturer at the University of Amsterdam, the Netherlands. Within the Bachelor and Master International Development Studies, her teaching, supervision and research focus on the potential of education in processes of peacebuilding, social and gender justice and inclusive, regenerative development. As an engaged educator, in her co-created teaching collaborations with students and colleagues she brings her experience as an international scholar, regenerative development practitioner, yoga teacher and reiki practitioner.

Paul Chin, PhD, PFHEA has worked in Higher Education for nearly thirty years, working across both learning development and educational development roles. Paul is Head of Learning and Teaching in the Centre for Learning and Teaching at University of Bath, UK, having previously worked at Hull and the former Higher Education Academy. Paul's research interests include online peer learning and assessment.

Helen Connolly, PhD, is an Educator at the University of Bedfordshire, UK whose teaching incorporates critical education for democracy, social justice and transformative experiential learning, with a focus on peace pedagogies, forced migration and trafficking, linked to SDG 16.

Adam Cooke is Widening Participation Officer at the University of Manchester Library, UK. He is an experienced teacher for over ten years at secondary schools and now leads on the development of the Library's widening participation and social responsibility contributions. This included shaping the Library's response to the Covid-19 pandemic and the award-winning Library Peer Network. He has an MA in Educational Leadership from the University of Manchester, UK, and is interested in how education can tackle social inequality including how the sector can widen access for students and educators to research and socially just best practice.

Tess Czerski, MSc, is Junior Lecturer (untenured) at the Bachelor for Political Science at the University of Amsterdam, the Netherlands, teaching courses in academic writing, law & politics and gender & sexuality studies. Her research interests focus on the intersection in gender, race, media and inclusive education. After working in local government and NGOs, she is currently teaching the 'Teaching for Equality?' course that the chapter is based on and is the main co-author of this chapter.

Mila Luca Romee De Graaf is currently writing her thesis on LGBTI activism in Namibia in order to finish a Research Master's in International Development Studies at the Graduate School of Social Sciences of the University of Amsterdam, the Netherlands. She has taken a mental health break for two years and worked outside of academia during that time. She works as an office manager for training and coaching bureau AtPresent and as a bartender. Besides that, she volunteers for the LGBTI buddy project at De Regenboog Groep in Amsterdam.

Amanda Egbe is a Senior Lecturer in Media Production and a practising artist at the University of West England, UK. Her practice and research concerns archives, new technologies, race and activism.

Jana Finke, MSc, is a PhD Candidate at the department for Human Geography and Spatial Planning at Utrecht University, the Netherlands. Formerly, she taught as a junior lecturer at the University of Amsterdam, in the Bachelor for political science and the minor gender & sexuality studies. She initiated the creation of the course *Teaching for Equality?: The Politics of Feminist and Decolonial Education* that the chapter in this handbook is based on, and is main co-author of the chapter. Next to her passion for designing and practising social justice education, her research focuses on migration into rural areas and learning.

Sonya Frazier is currently working as an Associate Medical Writer at McCann Health Medical Communications. She recently passed her PhD viva, after successfully defending her thesis *Investigating Placental MicroRNAs and Optimizing a Gene Therapy Strategy for Targeting the Placenta*. She spent the summer of 2020 writing up her thesis as well as working with an amazing team on the Life Sciences Diversity project.

Martha Gardiner is an MRes Sociology and Research Methods graduate from The University of Glasgow, UK, and a BA(Hons) Sociology graduate from Abertay University, UK. Martha served as Abertay University's Sociology Programme Ambassador and Board Member of the School of Social and Political Science's Student Experience Forum at the University of Glasgow. Her research interests include gender-based violence, young people's sexual and reproductive health and creative participatory methodologies. Participating in the research scheme allowed her to gain practical research experience within a cross-disciplinary team as well as explore the use of film as a creative research output, producing a short film documenting findings.

Emma Gillaspy is Reader in Creative and Collaborative Learning, National Teaching Fellow, #creativeHE host, academic developer and executive coach based at the University of Central Lancashire. Emma activates the passions of learners and empowers them to reach their potential through a unique blend of appreciative inquiry-based coaching, heutagogy and social learning. Emma works holistically, incorporating learners' lifewide experiences, not just their working identities. Emma uses creative materials and non-linear learning technologies to support this approach which enables non-verbal ways of knowing to emerge, leading to congruent development aligned with learners' core values and beliefs. Connect with Emma on Twitter @egillaspy.

Alke Gröppel-Wegener, PhD, is a National Teaching Fellow and Associate Professor of Creative Academic Practice at Staffordshire University, UK, where her teaching focus is on Animation Studies. Her research interests include regenring, experience design and exploring the links between creative and academic practice, and she has developed a number of visual analogies and creative activities to help students understand 'hidden' academic practice, which have been collected in *Writing Essays by Pictures*, a workbook for students, as well as a board game and a series of postcards. She blogs about her work at www.tactileacademia.com.

Ewan D. Hannaford is Research Assistant at the University of Glasgow, UK, working on the AHRC-funded *Our Heritage, Our Stories* project, and a Graduate Teaching Assistant in LEADS. He also teaches on various courses within the English Language & Linguistics department at the university, with his research background primarily in linguistics. His research interests focus on discourse analysis, health communication and media discourse, with his PhD examining changing representations of health conditions in the UK and US press.

Guangbo Hao is Senior Lecturer in the School of Engineering and Architecture at University College Cork, Ireland. He is a Fellow of ASME. His research interests focus on design of compliant mechanisms and robotics and their applications in precision engineering, energy harvesting and medical devices. He is serving as the Editor-in-Chief of *Mechanical Sciences* and an Associate Editor of *ASME Journal of Mechanisms and Robotics*, of *IEEE Robotics and Automation Letters* and of *Mechanism and Machine Theory*. He has won some accolades including the 2017, 2018 and 2022 ASME Compliant Mechanisms Awards. He has published over 170 peer-reviewed papers. He is the chair of ASME IDETC-CIE 2022 46th Mechanisms & Robotics Conference.

Scott M. Hardie heads the Division of Sport and Exercise Sciences at Abertay University, Scotland, and is a Senior Fellow of the Higher Education Academy with 26+ years' HE teaching experience. Published work covers 30+ articles spanning primate behaviour, handedness, individual differences and mental health. A Chartered Psychologist and Associate Fellow of the British Psychological Society, Scott served on their Psychology Education Board and chaired the Scottish Branch. Along with Lynn Wright, co-founded Abertay's Research Volunteer Scheme and was delighted it was a runner up in Sparqs' (student partnerships in quality Scotland) Shaping the Curriculum Award in 2019.

Daniel Haudenschild is a PhD candidate at the Department for Development and Postcolonial Studies at the University of Kassel, Germany. He has been involved in the CDDE collective at the University of Amsterdam for several years, working on co-creative and anti-oppressive pedagogies. His current research interest is the political ecology of extractive infrastructure development, and he investigates the environmental conflict over the Autobahn A49 in Hessen, Germany.

Katherine Herbert is Lecturer in Blended Learning in the Faculty of Business, Justice, and Behavioural Sciences at Charles Sturt University, Australia. Her role involves providing stakeholders across the faculty with evidence-based and -informed advice, coaching and mentoring around learning and teaching in current and emerging learning environments. She has a Master of Education in Knowledge Networks and Digital Innovation and is currently undertaking her doctoral studies. Her research focus is the continued development of learning and teaching practice in higher education, which incorporates the use of data analytics to empower teaching academics' further capability building.

Vikki Hill is Educational Developer: Attainment (Identity and Cultural Experience) in the Academic Enhancement Team at University of the Arts London (UAL), UK. A Senior Fellow of the HEA, Vikki works with staff to support equitable outcomes and experiences for students. Vikki's research is focused on educational development, compassionate assessment, pedagogies and policies through arts-based and posthuman approaches. She is project lead for the QAA Collaborative Enhancement Project 2021 – *Belonging through Assessment: Pipelines of Compassion* and is co-author of the website *Belonging through Compassion:* https://belongingthroughcompassion.myblog.arts.ac.uk/.

Debbie Holley is Professor of Learning Innovation at Bournemouth University, UK. An inspirational educator, she is a National Teaching Fellow and her national work developing strategic educational themes with mobile learning, augmented, virtual and mixed realities saw her being awarded a principal fellowship of AdvanceHE. She has led the Research Excellence Framework submissions in Education at two UK universities, contributing papers and mentoring and championing the work of others. Her research interests are in Digital Competence Frameworks, digital health and well-being and the ways in which hybrid pedagogies can bridge the gaps between formal/informal and work-based learning. Debbie influences national policy through her published work, keynote addresses and policy articles. You can follow Debbie on twitter @debbieholley1.

Monika Hrebackova, PhD, leads language, intercultural and social competence courses to BSc and MSc students at School of Business of the University of Chemistry and Technology in Prague, the Czech Republic. She runs a number of Erasmus projects, namely CORALL on autonomous learning and Learn2Change on collaborative digital storytelling for sustainable change. She publishes on the topics of innovative teaching and learning. Her publications include 'Teaching intercultural communicative competence through virtual exchange.' *Training, Language and Culture*, 3(4) 2019.

Nahid Huda is Learning Developer at London Metropolitan University, UK. Her research interests are in academic reading and embedding academic literacies practices within the taught curriculum. Nahid is a Fellow of the Higher Education Academy and an accredited coach. She has twenty-seven years of teaching experience, mainly in the secondary school sector and was Head of Design and Technology in a London community school. Nahid draws on her teaching experience and principles of design to inform her approach when creating and delivering interactive learning sessions on academic literacies.

Anna Hunter, PhD, is Programme and Student Lead for the PGCHE/PGDipHE/MA in Education at the University of Law, UK. A #creativeHE host with a background in literature, the humanities and creative approaches to teaching and learning, Anna has research interests in academic identity, autoethnography and creative research methods. In previous roles she has led academic development around teaching, learning and assessment for staff across a range of roles and career stages. Anna works closely with new academics to support their development as teachers, championing visual methods and the use of metaphor as a vehicle to explore fragmented, often contradictory identities.

Susanna Ison has gained extensive knowledge of PGR funding, recruitment and training via several roles supporting the postgraduate research community at the University of Nottingham, UK. She contributed to the funding application to the Arts & Humanities Research Council (AHRC) to expand Midlands3Cities Doctoral Training Partnership into the multi-institutional consortium Midlands4Cities Doctoral Training Partnership, which she now manages. Susanna draws on previous experience in Human Resource roles with large commercial organizations, SMEs and charities where she was involved with screening, recruiting, training and project management.

Nima Javanbakht is currently pursuing his PhD studies at the Industrial Systems Engineering and Management department, National University of Singapore, Singapore. His research interests include Enterprise Architecture, Decision-making Systems, Enterprise Modelling and Digital Transformation. Nima, from a systems thinking perspective, believes the key to master any knowledge is connecting the dots and recognizing relationships between contents, which can be facilitated through collaborative learning.

Ian Johnson has been Learning Development Tutor at University of Portsmouth, UK since 2015. His main research interests are in the value and professionalism of Learning Development, on which he is currently completing a Professional Doctorate in Education. Ian has also published on the effects of written feedback on students' work. Ian founded the ALDinHE research Community of Practice in May 2020, and has coordinated it since. Ian is also a Fellow of the Higher Education Academy.

Eleanor Johnston is a Librarian and Skills Tutor at Staffordshire University, UK, working with the School of Digital, Technologies and Arts. Eleanor is particularly interested in the relationship between information literacy and how students find and share information. Eleanor loves to collaborate with other information professionals, university students and especially with academics from a range of disciplines. She works with students to increase their knowledge of peer-reviewed resources, reading lists and excellent academic practice. Eleanor loves burritos, quizzes and pubs, which, coincidentally, also appear in Choose Your Own Collaboration!

Anna Maria Jones, FHEA, FSEDA, is Teaching Fellow at Imperial College London, UK, has worked to support enhancement of learning and teaching in Higher Education, with particular focus on postgraduate biomedical and clinical contexts, alongside teaching at undergraduate and postgraduate levels within her own disciplinary context of anatomy. Working with student collaborators and other staff colleagues, Anna Maria led on the design, development, delivery and evaluation of an online course entitled Adapt to Postgrad to support Imperial students in their transition to postgraduate taught study, which is further expanded upon as a case study within this book.

Anthony Kalume Dip. PGCert. MA is Chair of Diversity Lewes, UK, an Unincorporated Community Interest Group formed in 2010 to create awareness on all things discriminatory. He is also a member of the Sussex Police Independent Advisory Group, consultant on race, Chief Negotiator for the Mijikenda Tribe of the Coastal region of East Africa for the return of the *Vigango*, performing artist, film producer, Image Curator for the Obsidian Collections and Obsidian U.K. Lead manager. Anthony graduated from the MA Curating Collections and Heritage, University of Brighton, UK, in February 2022.

Ralitsa Kantcheva, PhD, SFHEA, has been a Study Skills Advisor at Bangor University, Wales since 2016. She has experience supporting students through both subject specific and generic provision of academic literacy skills. Her primary research interest is students' understanding of threshold concepts embedded in academic writing and in scientific research procedures.

Holly Kerr is a current PhD student at the University of Edinburgh, UK, as part of the first cohort of the Welcome Trust's new programme: *One Health Models of Disease: Science, Ethics and Society*. After graduating with a degree in Genetics from the University of Glasgow, she spent the summer of 2020 working at the Lighthouse Lab testing for Covid-19 alongside working for the Life Science Diversity project.

Jack Knowles is now a Senior Scientist, working for the UK Health Security Agency. Whilst working on the Life Sciences Equality and DIversity project in 2020, he completed a research Master's in Biomedical Sciences at the University of Glasgow, UK, and later worked at the Glasgow Lighthouse Lab in national Covid-19 testing.

Max Korbmacher is a neuroscience PhD student at the Western Norway University of Applied Sciences, Norway, with a background in psychology and sociology. His research on large-scale neuroimaging data focuses on finding biomarkers of ageing and health. Additionally, he is interested in meta-science, science communication and education. Participating in the research volunteer scheme helped him personally to feel more included in the research community and particularly enabled him in his communication with other researchers. Currently he is leading an international study on students' research practices and collaborating in a range of projects across the globe involving both students and senior academics.

Danielle L. Kurtin is a PhD student of Computational Neuroscience at the University of Surrey, UK, in partnership with Imperial College London, UK. She was an MSc Translational Neuroscience student when she joined the Adapt to Postgrad (ATP) team (discussed within this book as a case study) as a student partner during its pilot phase. She influenced the structure of and created content for the course's pilot, evaluated and improved aspects of ATP's pilot, and communicated the results of the pilot internally and externally. Danielle is currently investigating the neuromodulatory effects of brain stimulation on neural networks underpinning cognition.

Tianshu Liu studied MSc Health Data Analytics and Machine Learning at Imperial College London, UK, from 2020 to 2021. With the transition from undergraduate to postgraduate study being hard, the Adapt to Postgrad course (discussed as a case study within this book) helped Tianshu a lot during this process and so decided to join its evaluation and development team to contribute back. Tianshu is currently a Population Health PhD student at University of Oxford, looking into the prediction power of polygenic risk score on heart diseases.

Daron Benjamin Loo is Senior Lecturer at Universiti Malaysia Sabah, Malaysia. Previously, he was an academic writing lecturer at the Centre for English Language Communication (CELC), National University of Singapore (NUS), Singapore, where he had taught the co-authors of their book chapter contribution. Daron has published in the areas of written corrective feedback, intercultural education, English teacher and student identity, as well as language learning ecology of university students.

Byron Tsz Kit Lui has been a lecturer in the sub-degree sector in Hong Kong since 2008. Educated in Taiwan and Hong Kong with a background in computer science and information technology, Byron has developed a keen interest in multimedia and education technology. Currently, he is devoted to exploring how to enrich both the online and offline teaching and learning environments in the sub-degree sector by leveraging various technologies and pedagogies.

Julia Lynch is the Head of School of Business at Charles Sturt University, Australia. She has a PhD in Economics and has taught in the areas of microeconomics, microeconomic policy, banking and finance, financial regulation and financial markets. Her research interests are focused on government regulation and policy in both the agricultural and finance sectors. She has a passion for student learning, engagement and success. Her role now allows this to be fostered on a School wide basis, and the blended learning project with CSU's partners Study Centre has been a particular professional achievement.

Alina Georgeta Mag is Lecturer in the Teacher Education Department inside Social and Human Sciences Faculty, from University 'Lucian Blaga' of Sibiu, Romania, where she teaches early childhood education, educational psychology, inclusive education and pedagogy. She has a PhD in Educational Sciences and her research interests are focused on Early Childhood Education, Teacher Training and Academic Education. She participated in several national and international conferences, publishing so far five books and many articles to share her research work. Alina was involved as a trainer and educational expert in national and international projects, and she is the Romanian coordinator for the European Early Childhood Education Research Association. As a person with real passion for the pedagogical field, she enjoys working with people and she continues to develop her research interests.

Simone Maier, FHEA, is Associate Lecturer at London Metropolitan University, UK. She holds a BA Arts (English & Visual Performing Arts) and a BA Fine Arts (Hons). Her creative practice explores the boundaries between poetry and sculpture. In 2019, Simone became the inaugural recipient of *The Cass Scholarship in Creativity and Diversity* that sponsored her to study towards a Post Graduate Certificate in Education (PGCert) which she was awarded with distinction. Since then, Simone has taught on the Foundation art, architecture and design course, with a social constructivist pedagogy.

Robyn McWilliams, FHEA, is Senior Lecturer and Learning Advisor at Auckland University of Technology, New Zealand. As a member of the Learning Success team within AUT Library, Robyn works closely with faculty lecturers in the disciplines of Health and Education to develop a range of resources to support students' academic literacies.

Melina Merdanovic is currently an Innovation Research Executive at a global market research agency called Kantar. In the past, she worked at War Child Holland, University of Amsterdam and THNK School of Creative Leadership. Her career path is mainly led by her passion for societal issues, transformative education and research. Through her formal education, she obtained a degree in International Relations and Development Studies that has broadened her view on education systems around the world. Her non-formal education involved working with diverse communities such as yoga teacher training, volunteering experiences with teachers in Myanmar.

Jess Moriarty is Principal Lecturer at the University of Brighton, UK, where she is Course Leader on the Creative Writing MA and Co-director for the Centre of Arts and Wellbeing. She has published widely on autoethnography and pedagogy in writing practice. Jess works on engaging students in community projects and using innovative and personal writing to challenge traditional academic discourse. Her focus is on developing student's confidence with their creativity and her new book (available from March 2022) is called *Walking for Creative Recovery*.

Humayun Murshed currently holds the position of Leading Education Professional at the UNSW (University of New South Wales) Global, Australia. Humayun has worked in diverse leadership roles, and expands into areas encompassing education, programme management and evaluation and delivery. His previous experience includes, among others, working as an Associate Professor at Murdoch University, Australia, and Charles Sturt University (CSU), Australia, where he led the delivery of accounting and business programmes in three study centres. He holds a PhD in Accounting from the University of Manchester, UK. Humayun also worked for the World Bank, and consulted for the projects for the Asian Development Bank, and UNDP.

Chrissi Nerantzi is Associate Professor in the School of Education at the University of Leeds, UK. She is an open practitioner and researcher and has initiated with many other educators a wide range of open, collaborative and cross-institutional professional development initiatives such as #creativeHE and the #LTHEchat. Through her doctoral studies she has developed a cross-boundary collaborative learning framework. Chrissi is interested in the intersection of creativity, openness and collaboration and her practice and research are in these areas. She is a National Teaching Fellow 2015, ALT Learning Technologist of the Year 2017, a GO-GN Fellow 2020, and won the following team awards: OEGlobal Open Innovation Award 2021 and the Collaborative Award for Teaching Excellence 2022.

Julia Ngadi completed her master's in Global Crime Justice and Security at Liverpool John Moores University (LJMU), UK, after her Criminology degree at Abertay University, UK. Julia's research interests include conflicted-related sexual violence, gender-based violence, transnational organized crime, race, racism and policing. Julia is an advocate for equality at university; she was elected as a Bame officer at JMU where she founded the Bame Student Network and spearheaded many projects that voiced concerns and addressed issues faced by Bame students. Julia took part in the RVS to improve her research skills and work collaboratively with academics and fellow students.

Jasmine Nisic is a member of the Library Student Team at the University of Manchester Library, UK. She graduated from the University of Manchester, UK, with a Distinction and First Class with Honours in her MSc in Applied Mathematics and BSc in Mathematics. Passionate about breaking down barriers to education she has made a significant contribution to widening participation work both as a student and after her graduation. Whilst at Loreto Sixth Form Jasmine received a scholarship from the Dick Camplin Education Trust for overcoming significant barriers to her education and continues to support current scholars to tackle imposter syndrome and lift aspirations.

Jane Nodder has worked in higher education in the UK for over twenty years as a research supervisor, senior lecturer and course director for both under- and postgraduate programmes. She is currently studying for the award of PhD in Technology Enhanced Learning and E-Research at Lancaster University, UK. Jane's research interests focus on using activity theory and formative interventions such as the Change Laboratory to promote learning and development in online academic communities.

Eleonore Nouel is a social science researcher and activist based between France and the Netherlands. She presented her findings on educational policy at international conferences such as UKFIET 2019, Oxford and ICEDC Conference 2019, UCL. Eleonore uses her research on decolonial and alternative pedagogies to help prevent sexual violence on French university campuses. She co-founded *Sexe et Consentement*, a French organization which uses arts and dialogue to educate about sexual consent in higher education and beyond. Eleonore is also passionate about finding solutions towards the circular economy. When she is not working, you'll likely find her volunteering on urban farms.

Monica Catherine O'Brien is Effective Learning Advisor for international students in Student Learning Development (SLD) at the University of Glasgow, UK. In this role she supports students in developing their academic literacies and skills. Previously, Monica was a Postdoctoral Fellow at the Herzog August Bibliothek, Wolfenbüttel, Germany, as well as a Graduate Teaching Assistant in SLD and a wide range of subject areas in the College of Arts, University of Glasgow, UK. Monica has a PhD in History and her research explores medical, social and emotional responses to epidemics in the early modern world.

Siobhán O'Neill is Research Support Officer in the Insight Centre for Data Analytics (formerly of the Centre for the Integration of Research, Teaching and Learning) and a PhD candidate in the School of Applied Psychology, University College Cork (UCC), Ireland. She is an experienced researcher, having worked on a wide range of research projects including curriculum and intervention design. Her PhD work explores daily life experiences and psychobiological well-being which frames her research practices. Her current research interests include the exploration of innovative and creative approaches to teaching, learning and assessment with a focus on Universal Design for Learning and inclusive assessment frameworks.

Donna Palmer is Doctoral Training Programmes Manager in the Researcher Academy at the University of Nottingham, UK. She currently manages the portfolio of programmes funded by the Economic and Social Research Council (ESRC) and is the Training Lead for the Natural Environmental Research Council (NERC) Envision DTP. After completing her PhD, Donna worked in industry and gained significant project management, line management and collaborative research experience managing UK- and EU-funded collaborative research and development projects. Since moving to the higher education sector, she has developed expertise in supporting doctoral researchers, their training and development, funding and recruitment.

Victoria Paterson, PhD, is Lecturer in Animal Biology at the School of Biodiversity, One Health and Veterinary Medicine at the University of Glasgow, UK, with main research interests in wildlife epidemiology and the impacts on pollinators. Victoria is also a Co-chair of SoLS Athena SWAN and one of the founders of the Equality & Diversity teaching resource at the School of Life Sciences.

Alex Pentek completed a research-based MFA at NCAD in 2022; his gallery work has been exhibited in Ireland, the UK, Germany, the United States and Australia, exploring the fold as a site of transformation. Introducing complex origami surfaces and ideas of 'non-knowledge' that must be experienced directly allows him to think and communicate in this way. This trans-disciplinary approach offers endless collaborative possibilities in a range of fields including sculpture, design, robotics, architecture, dance, skateboard performance and sound. Co-authoring a number of papers around this subject, folded origami surfaces continue to inspire his work on a range of visual, scientific and philosophical levels.

Diana J. Pritchard, PhD, is an educator and Principal Fellow of the Higher Education Academy, UK, and the founder and coordinator of the Sustainability Forum at the University of Bedfordshire, UK. She works to develop anti-discriminatory and inclusive practices and education for sustainability and is an international higher education evaluation consultant. Her research explores higher education practices which develop twenty-first-century competences.

Declan Prosser graduated from the University of Glasgow, UK, in 2020 with a degree in Anatomy. He now works as a Commercial Assistant for Babcock International in their Scottish Rail Department and is currently undertaking a Masters in Quantity Surveying at Glasgow Caledonian University, UK.

Hélène Pulker is Senior Lecturer in French in the School of Languages and Applied Linguistics at the Open University, UK. She has extensive experience in designing, authoring and delivering undergraduate courses for distance and online language learning. Her research focuses on open, online and distance education and teacher training with a particular interest in the reuse of OER for online language teaching. She has been involved in several collaborative OER projects and has received awards for the online course '*Learning to (re)use OER*' in 2016 and the '*Moving your language teaching online*' toolkit in 2020.

Victoria Rafferty, PhD, has worked in learning development roles for a number of years in both Further and Higher Education settings. Her doctoral research is an in-depth exploration of 1-1 learning development discussions from students' perspectives, capturing the complexity of learning relationships between students and learning developers. Victoria is currently Senior Lecturer at Arden University, UK.

Sue Raleigh is Senior Lecturer in the School of Public Health and Interdisciplinary Studies at Auckland University of Technology, New Zealand. As well as teaching and coordinating a second-year undergraduate course on human anatomy and physiology, from 2022 teaching includes direct entry Master of Nursing students studying applied pathophysiology. Sue works with Learning Advisors to develop a range of tools that help students navigate learning and assessments. These students are health professionals from many disciplines, including nursing, midwifery, paramedicine and medical laboratory science. Sue is a recipient of three teaching awards, including the Vice Chancellor's Teaching Excellence Award.

Anne-Kathrin Reck is an Academic Skills Tutor for international students and those whose first language is not English in the Faculty of Creative and Cultural Industries, University of Portsmouth, UK. She is an FHEA and member of the International Visual Literacy Association. Anne has an MA in English and Russian Studies (Leipzig) and previously worked as an HE lecturer in German and Russian, EFL teacher as well as Dyslexia specialist. Her interests range from critical reading, mindsets and visual note-taking to onomastics/names research. During the recent lockdowns she discovered macramé and yoga to justify sitting around in a mindful way.

Gabriella Rodolico is Lecturer in Science Education at the School of Education (SoE), University of Glasgow (UoG), UK. She has a PhD in the Pharmacological Science and Physiopathology of the Respiratory System, with several publications in this sector. In 2013 Gabriella gained the Biology with Science Secondary School teaching qualification in Scotland. In 2019 Gabriella joined the SoE equipped with strong expertise to bridge the gap between schools and universities. Her main interests are STEM Education, Virtual Reality application in Initial Teacher Education courses, as well as Transnational Education, with several scholarship outcomes available on her UoG profile page https://www.gla.ac.uk/schools/education/staff/gabriellarodolico/.

Zhiqing Rong is currently working as a journalist in China after completing her master's degree in Southeast Asian Studies at National University of Singapore (NUS), Singapore. Through her experience of learning foreign languages like English and French, Zhiqing believes that linguistic acquisition should be continuous development, spurred by one's own motivation. The development could also be forged gradually through collaborative learning, which encourages learners to think independently while interacting with peers.

Paul Rowinski, PhD, is a journalist, former foreign correspondent and expert in political and intercultural communications, currently writing a book about our culture wars. He works at the University of Bedfordshire, UK.

Lara Ryan graduated from the University of Glasgow, UK, in 2020 with a degree in Neuroscience and Psychology and is currently a PhD student at the Einstein Centre for Neurosciences Berlin, Germany. While at the University of Glasgow, Lara was a member of the School of Life Sciences Athena SWAN student self-assessment team and was involved in organization of events for International Women's Day, which also inspired her to become involved with the Diversity Project.

Mohamed Saeudy, PhD, is Director of the Research Centre for Contemporary Accounting, Finance, and Economics (Res CAFE), UK, teaches and researches sustainable accounting and finance at the University of Bedfordshire, UK.

Ayesha Shahid completed her BSc (Hons) Psychology degree at Abertay, UK, in 2019. She actively participated in the Research Volunteer Scheme during her final two years of study and used the opportunity to broaden her CV.

Uzma A. Siddiqui, FHEA, is Senior Lecturer in Health at London Metropolitan University, School of Social Sciences and Professions, UK. She's a qualified Medical Doctor with almost thirty years' experience and expertise in Global Health, Public Health, Health and Social Care, Medicine and Research.

Deborah Simpson is a Primary School Teacher working within East Ayrshire, Scotland. In 2002 she completed her BSc (hons) Psychology at University of Stirling, UK, before taking up a post within the Diplomatic Branch of the Foreign and Commonwealth Office in London. After spending three years there she pursued a career in Policing for fifteen years, where she mainly worked within community policing roles. She also ran the Safe Highlanders event for all Primary 7 children in the Caithness area of Scotland. In 2019 she undertook her PGDE (Primary) at the University of Glasgow, UK, with placements in primary schools in East Ayrshire.

Jessica Slotte is a first-class honours BA (Hons) Design for Art Direction graduate (2020) from University of the Arts London (UAL), UK, who created the resource pack *Supporting Collaboration,* in her third year of the course. She has an interest in developing sustainable collaborative practices and in how that could help the learning environment of higher education students. Furthermore, she strongly believes collaboration to be a cornerstone in making design and society more inclusive, efficient and sustainable.

Philippa (Pippa) Soccio, PhD, is Lecturer in Teaching and Learning with ABP Built Environments Learning + Teaching (BEL+T) group at the University of Melbourne, Australia. Pippa is passionate about how indoor environment quality impacts learning. Her current research is an investigation into the pedagogy used to teach students about acoustics, air quality, thermal comfort and lighting. She previously worked with the Learning Environments applied Research Network (LEaRN) managing the *Towards Effective Learning Environments in Catholic Schools* project (2018). This is the largest known study to have evaluated the relationships between the built environment and the practices, activities and behaviours of students and educators.

Alisia Southwell is a Global Master of Public Health student in the Faculty of Medicine at Imperial College London, UK. Her previous educational background includes Psychology and Big Data Analytics, and her professional background is in clinical research, focusing on stroke and neurodegenerative diseases in Toronto, Canada. As a student partner for a case study discussed within this book, Alisia assisted in quantitatively and qualitatively evaluating the first iteration of the Adapt to Postgrad course and providing feedback for future iterations.

Martin Štefl holds a PhD in English Philology, works at the UCT School of Business in Prague, Czech Republic, and teaches courses in ESP and skills training, in particular critical thinking; he researches into philosophy of business, critical thinking and ELT. His publications include Pfingsthorn J. et al. 'Interculturality and Professional Identity' in *Interculturality and the English Language Classroom* (2021); Štefl, M. 'The Human/Machine: Science Fiction as a Primer for Critical Thinking' in *Mapping the Imaginative I. Anglistik & Englischunterricht 92* (2020).

Andrew Struan is Head of Student Learning Development at the University of Glasgow, UK. He has worked across the globe in academic literacies and in political history. His role at Glasgow is in developing students' academic literacies, and he leads an award-winning, multi-disciplinary team. Andrew convenes several courses at undergraduate and postgraduate level, ranging in topic from the History of Argumentation to the linguistics of academic text. His research investigates the implementation of active blended approaches to academic literacies pedagogies. His PhD is in political history: he researches the linguistic history of parliamentary debate and the role of language in shaping ideologies.

Kiu Sum is a Doctoral Researcher in nutrition in the School of Life Sciences at the University of Westminster, UK. Her research interest focuses on workplace nutrition, public health nutrition and behavioural sciences. Kiu also recently joined Solent University, Southampton, UK, as Lecturer in Nutrition. She has a broad interest in pedagogy research and student engagement and is a Registered Associate Nutritionist with the Association for Nutrition. Kiu also previously contributed to the RAISE Network as a Student Officer and now co-convenes the Engagement Assessment and the Early Career Researchers Special Interest Groups.

Briony Supple, PhD, is Senior Lecturer in Design Thinking Pedagogy and Praxis at the School of Education, University College Cork (UCC), Ireland. She has worked for several years in academic development and has published extensively on inclusive, learner-focused approaches to teaching, learning and assessment and innovations in learning spaces. Briony's current practice includes creative, hands-on approaches to teaching and learning in Higher Education through facilitating Lego Serious Play workshops and collaborative applied rigid origami practices.

Annamária Szelics is a fourth-year Neuroscience student at the University of Glasgow, UK, with an interest in neuroimaging and biomedical image analysis. Annamária spent the summer of 2020 working at the Lighthouse Laboratory testing for Covid-19 alongside working for the Life Science Diversity project. She is currently undertaking a twelve-month industrial placement within the In-Vivo Bioimaging Team at GSK, Stevenage, UK.

Louise Taylor (AFHEA) is Senior Lecturer in Academic Support at University of the Arts, London (UAL), UK. As a learning developer, her practice focuses on the intersection of education and social justice, student transition to university, and peer learning. She has a background in documentary photography and academic practice. Additionally, she has an interest in visual and participatory research methodologies, with a particular focus on photography.

Stuart J. Taylor, PhD, FHEA, is Lecturer in Academic Practice in the Department of Learning and Teaching Enhancement at Edinburgh Napier University, UK, where he teaches on Blended & Online Education (MSc) and Teaching & Supporting Learning in Higher Education (PgCert) programmes. Previously, Stuart was a Graduate Teaching Assistant in LEADS, Widening Participation, and English Literature at the University of Glasgow, UK. Stuart's PhD (English Literature, University of Glasgow, UK) analysed mathematical structures in the encyclopaedic novel.

Rhiannon Parry Thompson is Learning Development Tutor in the Faculty of Humanities and Social Sciences at the University of Portsmouth, UK, and an Adult and Community Education Tutor in Sussex, UK. She has been a secondary school teacher, language school tutor and university lecturer. She has a long-standing interest in oral storytelling for environmental stewardship. A keen student of Celtic cultures, a Welsh speaker and Cornish language learner, she delivers Welsh and Cornish taster classes at the University of Portsmouth.

Dee Tracey, qualified Social Worker and Associate Lecturer in Social Work (FHEA), is the Social Work Practice Development Lead in a London Authority where she leads on the development of practitioners; she is passionate about the learning and development of others with the outlying focus of providing excellent quality of care for people that use local authority services.

Kate Tregloan, Associate Professor, leads the Built Environment Learning + Teaching (BEL+T) group at the University of Melbourne, Australia. She focuses on design education and its contributions to interdisciplinary impact, the built environment and addressing community need. She explores the interplay of exploration and judgement, such as through decisions and values influencing creative work, and interactive tools that offer new ways to engage with praxis and production. Examples include the internationally award-winning RIPL POE evaluation framework and panoramas (2015); MyHomeSpace, a VR gamespace exploring housing design for people with disability (2018); and Multiple Measures, a searchable online library of interdisciplinary assessment design (2018).

Rachel Van Krimpen currently works in the Researcher Academy at the University of Nottingham, UK, as Manager of the Nottingham BBSRC DTP. Experienced in doctoral training partnership management and multi-institutional collaboration, she has significant expertise in equality, diversity and inclusion in the postgraduate space, through the development of successful interventions for recruitment and active work on widening participation to postgraduate study via the National Education

Opportunities Network (NEON). She regularly contributes to the development of doctoral training funding bids and is a member of the UK Council for Graduate Education (UKCGE) Executive Committee.

Nicola Veitch, PhD, is Senior Lecturer in Infection Biology at the School of Infection and Immunity at the University of Glasgow, UK. Her scholarship interests are in the use of innovative digital technologies to support Bioscience teaching, and she is an active member of the Athena Swan Committee. Nicola is one of the founders of the Equality & Diversity teaching resource at the School of Life Sciences.

Tanja Vesala-Varttala, PhD, is Principal Lecturer in Marketing and Communication at Haaga-Helia University of Applied Sciences, Research Unit of Entrepreneurship and Business Regeneration, in Helsinki, Finland. Her research interests focus on digital marketing storytelling, Education for Sustainable Development (ESD) in higher education, multi-stakeholder collaboration and co-creation, and collaborative autonomous learning. She has published on narrative ethics, multi-cultural business communication and autonomous learning. Her most recent publication is a refereed article on ESD: 'Fostering Sustainability Competencies and Ethical Thinking in Higher Education: Case Sustainable Chocolate' (2021).

Xun Wang has a Master's degree from the National University of Singapore, Singapore. In 2021, she took the graduate English writing module taught by Dr Daron Benjamin Loo (the first author of the co-authored chapter) at NUS. During her studies, Wang Xun developed an understanding of the importance of collaborative learning with students from other disciplines to facilitate language and writing learning at the graduate level.

Karen Welton is Learning Development Advisor at Arts University Plymouth, UK. Within this creative environment she supports students, many of whom are neurodivergent, with breaking down barriers to learning, building confidence and developing their academic skills. She is passionate about raising awareness of neurodiversity and co-facilitates the ALDinHE Neurodiversity and Inclusivity Community of Practice. As a member of the ALDinHE Research Community of Practice she recently co-authored a publication for the *Journal of University Teaching and Learning Practice*: 'Emerging from the third space chrysalis: Experiences in a non-hierarchical, collaborative research community of practice' (2021).

Stewart White, PhD, is Senior Lecturer in the School of Biodiversity, One Health & Veterinary Medicine at the University of Glasgow, UK, with main research interests in the ecology of neotropical rainforest birds and the foraging behaviour of damselflies. Stewart is also a co-chair of BOHVM Athena SWAN and one of the founders of the Equality & Diversity teaching resource at the School of Life Sciences.

Nicholas Worsfold, PhD, is an ecologist and environmental educator and Reader (Education) in Environmental Sciences at Brunel University, UK.

Lynn Wright is Senior Lecturer and Programme Leader in Psychology at Abertay University, Scotland. She has a background in Behavioural Science and a PhD in Psychology. She is a chartered member and Associate Fellow of the British Psychological Society, and a Senior Fellow of the Higher Education Academy. Lynn has over twenty years of higher education teaching experience and has regularly been shortlisted for Student Led Teaching Awards. Her main research interest is laterality, and she is also interested in student well-being and the student experience. She co-founded the Research Volunteer Scheme with Scott Hardie at Abertay University.

Jana Zvěřinová, MA, is Lecturer at the School of Business of the University of Chemistry and Technology Prague, Czech Republic. She teaches courses in English and Spanish with the focus on communication and competence development. In collaboration with an international team of language and content HE teachers, she runs a course of Global Virtual Teams focusing on specific aspects of online teamwork and communication in an interuniversity project. She has also actively participated in several Erasmus+ projects. She publishes on the topics related to her teaching and projects in academic journals and presents at international conferences.

Foreword: Collaboration In, Against and Beyond the Neoliberal, Neocolonical, Pandemic University

Gordon Asher

In this Foreword, Gordon Asher offers a highly theorized and theoretical account of what collaboration might mean and what it offers to an increasingly neoliberal HE Sector. As such, it provides a stimulating and challenging contextualization of and opening for the book as a whole. Asher's lens is that of critical theory and critical pedagogy/popular education and offers a 'realist' account – this is the chapter to dip into for your literature review when building an academic argument for and justification of collaboration in higher education.

Introduction

Collaboration in Higher Education focuses on co-creation and cooperative partnerships in HE. This apposite collection includes contributions from educators, in the widest sense, in and engaging with HE institutions across the world. It includes examples of collaborative practice between staff members, staff and students, across institutions, and institutions working with external communities and organizations.

The book explicitly frames its collaborative content – which integrates theoretical perspectives and contemporary practices – as in opposition, and as providing alternatives to the highly individualistic and alienating competitive culture that dominates HE under neoliberal globalization (Giroux, 2019). It speaks to both the necessity of harnessing existing and creating new opportunities for critical collaboration within institutional contexts, where time, space and latitude for cooperative work are increasingly foreclosed, and navigating the inevitable resistances to and challenges of doing so.

Collaboration in Higher Education is aimed at an international audience, with the kind of critical collaboration it espouses speaking to the vital boundary and border crossing (Giroux, 2005) that builds movements for eco-social justice, whilst appreciating the variability, including the penetration of neoliberalism, between and within national contexts with respect to education sectors and wider society. As such, it speaks to the urgent need to develop a broad, critical educational movement across and beyond HE that can address the crisis of the university (Bacevic, 2017; Hall, 2018) alongside contributing to wider struggles against the compound crises facing humanity.

Locating itself within this critical paradigm serves to emphasize important ontological and epistemological dimensions of *critical* collaboration and co-creation. *Collaboration in Higher Education* consciously sets out to assist readers to discover and develop positionalities and opportunities for critical collaborative practice – to collectively locate and create, work within, expand and connect, the 'cracks' (Holloway, 2010) in the neoliberal domination of the university and wider society.

Contemporary Higher Education and the Crisis of the University

Neoliberal practices are intensifying and accelerating across society, with processes of 'deep neoliberalistion' (Canaan, 2013) permeating academia. At the root of HE's contemporary crisis are decades-long processes of continual restructuring of the public university, driven by conjoined processes of corporatization, privatization and outsourcing; marketization, consumerization and competition; and commercialization, commodification and financialization, delivered through the imposition of the human capital model of 'new managerialism', the 'organisational form of neoliberal governance' (Lynch, 2014). 'The University is being explicitly restructured for the production, circulation and accumulation of value, materialised in the form of rents and surpluses on operating activities' (Hall, 2020, 830). This is reflected in the predominance of neoliberal narrativizing (Morrish & Saunston, 2020; Themelis, 2021), which serves to shut down criticality, social agency, imagination and alternatives.

Formal education's systemic role has always been, in large part, to (re)produce what and whom the dominant powers in society have afforded value (Chomsky, 2004). Furthermore, universities are not mere victims of local and global pressures in their 'restructuring [...] as "competing capitals"' (Hall, 2013), the university is also neoliberalizing of itself – and of all who labour within it – as well as of wider social relations it increasingly serves to shape (Asher, 2015). However, beyond repressive hierarchical processes, the contemporary university is also shaped through processes of resistance and struggle from below and to the left, occupying a long-contested terrain of liberatory possibilities as a social and public good (Giroux, 2019).

The nature of contemporary HE means it is increasingly difficult to find the time and space; the embodied and cognitive abilities; and the consent to engage in critical collaboration or other forms of critical educational work. Consequently, a central question of our praxis is how to individually and collectively navigate such positions of tension and contradiction and develop understandings of the risks involved and of the inevitable responses to critically oriented forms of collaboration – from discouragement, resistance and 'othering', to outright hostility, while attending to the collective self-care necessary in such immiserating contexts.

Collaboration in Higher Education provides valuable examples and resonant lessons for navigating such tensions, and for appreciating and resisting the ever-present danger of co-option or appropriation of empowering work, especially when collaboration at one scale or location is folded into competition at another scale and with other locations. These understandings foreground the need to locate hope in what may seem like increasingly hopeless contexts and times (Hall, 2021; Holloway, 2022).

Responding to Crises: Building Movements and Locating Hope

Collaboration in Higher Education provides rich material and inspiration for educators, students, universities' external constituencies and community partners, seeking to come together to work critically (with)in, against and beyond the constraints and imperatives of the increasingly crisis-torn university. The book provides guidance to enable readers to locate themselves and their work in ways that reject the conceptualization of an atomistic, entrepreneurial self and resist the alienating subsumption of academic labour within HE.

Collaboration and cooperation speak powerfully to how we might build and evolve connections between educators and students (often isolated and alienated within institutions and disciplinary silos), and between critical theories, practices and projects within and outwith HE. As such, contributing to building and evolving the kind of critical networks and movements that are so urgently needed, to address both the exacerbated crisis of the 'new normal' university (Asher, 2022; Fleming, 2021) and the wider, manifold, intersecting and cascading social, economic, political, cultural and ecological/environmental crises, within which this unfolds (Chomsky & Waterstone, 2021). Yet, with respect to HE, as elsewhere across society, dominant policy responses are not just failing to address these crises, they are, through their naturalizing pursuit of further neoliberalization, intensifying them (Seymour, 2019).

This entails working interconnectedly towards more compassionate, emancipatory forms of education practice and attendant relations, and the emergence of a more equitable, radically democratic, de-colonized, post-capitalist, post-nation state world, where humans are harmoniously entangled with nature and those we share the planet with. An emancipatory politico-pedagogical project that understands liberation/emancipation as necessarily concerning both self-and-social transformation, in dialectical relationship formed through dialogical praxis, to transcend the oppressive, repressive and exploitative social relations and identitarian categorizations of capitalism.

Appreciating Dinerstein's (2021) exposition of 'hope as a category of praxis' should inform our doing so. Foregrounding the affective and embodied nature of critical hope as collective/collaborative – as located in and between us, as a constituent aspect of our being and becoming with each other and with the world – facilitates an understanding of it as both informing and emerging through struggle and praxis – as educated hope. Hope then is essentially a pedagogical issue, '[i]t is a question of learning hope' (Bloch, 1995, 1).

Education is Dialogic Collaboration: An Argument for Eco-Social Justice

It is neither possible nor desirable for education to be neutral, objective or apolitical, despite mystificatory and manipulative rhetoric to the contrary that serves in consequence, if not always intent, to support the evolving (neoliberal) status quo. Education is at heart a *collaborative* and deeply political pursuit – one 'that requires ways of exercising power, of organising a collective, of building a community' (Kohan, 2021, 7). Cooperation is, for humanity, an ontological vocation (Freire, 1998), as per the concept of ubuntu – I am because you are; that 'we are who we are through others' (Ramose, 1999). A vital aspect of such collaborative processes is an attention to not just the cognitive and behavioural, but the affective, the embodied – what occurs in and between people.

A critical conception of dialogue (Asher, 2018) is also key, as prefigured by the dialogical processes involved in the production of this volume. The book and its content are dialogical in essence and intended as the foundation for further dialogue. Indeed, it explicitly sets out to open up cascading processes of dialogue with readers, as actual or 'potential collaborators'. Dialogue is understood as collective exploration, the co-creation or co-production of knowledges and relations, and vitally, as focused on an orientation to praxis for liberation – for it is only through dialogue grounded in a deep sense of love for each other and the world that we can achieve transformational change (Darder, 2017). This is what the critically collaborative focus of the book speaks to – empowerment, as both agentic possibility (*power*) and orientation (*will*), necessary to make meaningful contributions to personal and social transformation, where dialogue is key.

In pedagogical terms, the provision of a focus on co-writing, co-researching, co-teaching and co-learning stands as cooperation-in-waiting, inviting participation by readers in the co-creation/production of knowledges that are inter/multi/trans/meta/supra-disciplinary. *Collaboration in Higher Education* embodies an understanding of education as *collectively* evolving our understandings of ourselves, others, the word and the world – and the relationships between them. This is allied to an appreciation of our individual and *collective* agency and an orientation to act in and on the world to transform it in the interests of a life-affirming praxis of eco-social justice.

The book provides wide-ranging examples that can inform such an urgently needed, broader, critical educational project that places collaboration and cooperation at the heart of all we do. Given the individualized, isolating and competitive compulsion of capitalist social relations, focusing on such collaboration can in itself be transgressive, serving to break down national, institutional and sectorial barriers and boundaries, including the disciplinary silos of HE. Critical collaboration speaks to the radically different ways of democratically doing things which are vital to prefigurative resistances to oppressive processes of neoliberalization and to the building of emancipatory alternatives to them – through the embodying and modelling of transformative relations, in the present.

Sandra Abegglen, Tom Burns and Sandra Sinfield provide us with an invaluable and wide-ranging collection of critically collaborative practice case studies from around the world and, through doing so, dialogically and prefiguratively open up a most welcome process of mutual learning and knowledge co-production – for collaborating in, against, and beyond the neoliberal, neocolonial, pandemic university (Asher, 2015; 2022) and, more widely, the capitalist and nation-state system that is the root cause of the integrated crises we face today (Holloway, 2016). To paraphrase the Zapatistas in foregrounding our collaboration for achieving prefigurative, transformational change, we make the road by walking and by asking questions together. *Collaboration in Higher Education* courageously takes on this task, whilst calling us to embrace the power of collaboration for emancipatory social change.

References

Asher, G. (2015). Working in, against, and beyond the neoliberal university. Paper, presented at Standing Conference on University Teaching and Research in the Education of Adults (SCUTREA), 2015. https://www.academia.edu/13925922/Working_in_against_and_beyond_the_neoliberal_university

Asher, G. (2018). Critical dialogues for learning and technology: In, against and beyond the neoliberal university. *Open Review of Educational Research, 5*(1), 144–9. DOI: 10.1080/23265507.2018.1547950

Asher, G. (2022). Working, in, against and beyond the neoliberal university: Critical academic literacies as a pedagogical response to the crisis of the university. In G. Asher, S. Cowden, A. Maisuria, & S. Housee (Eds.), *Critical pedagogy and emancipation: A festschrift in memory of Joyce Canaan*. Oxford: UK, Peter Lang.

Bacevic, J. (2017). Why is it more difficult to imagine the end of universities than the end of capitalism, or: Is the crisis of the university in fact a crisis of imagination? *Jana Bacevic: Internal conversation, eternal emigration*, 17 October 2017. https://janabacevic.net/2017/10/11/is-the-crisis-of-the-university-in-fact-a-crisis-of-imagination/

Bloch, E. (1995). *The principle of hope*. MIT Press.

Canaan, J. (2013). Resisting the English neoliberalising university: What critical pedagogy can offer. *Journal of Critical Education Policy Studies, 11*(2), 16–56. http://www.jceps.com/archives/426

Chomsky, N. (2004). *Chomsky on miseducation*. Rowman and Littlefield.

Chomsky, N., & Waterstone, M. (2021). *Consequences of capitalism: Manufacturing discontent and resistance*. Hamish Hamilton.

Darder, A. (2017). *Reinventing Paulo Freire: A pedagogy of love*. Routledge.

Dinerstein, A. C. (2021). Decolonising critique: Reconnecting critical theory with radical praxis. Centre for Urban Research on Austerity (CURA), Annual Lecture, 14 April 2021. https://cura.our.dmu.ac.uk/annual-lecture-2021/

Fleming, P. (2021). *Dark academia: How universities die*. Pluto Press.

Freire, P. (1998). *Pedagogy of freedom: Ethics, democracy and civic courage*. Rowman & Littlefield.

Giroux, H. (2005). *Border crossings: Cultural workers and the politics of education* (2nd ed.). Routledge.

Giroux, H. (2019). *Neoliberalism's war on higher education* (2nd ed.). Haymarket Books.

Hall, R. (2013). It is time to stand up for collective forms of higher education and contest the enclosure and commodification of the university. *LSE Blogs*, 4 May 2013. https://blogs.lse.ac.uk/politicsandpolicy/it-is-time-to-stand-up-for-collective-forms-of-higher-education-and-contest-the-enclosure-and-commodification-of-the-university

Hall, R. (2018). *The alienated academic: The struggle for autonomy inside the university*. Palgrave MacMillan.

Hall, R. (2020). The hopeless university: Intellectual work at the end of the end of history. *Postdigital Science and Education, 2*, 830–48. https://link.springer.com/article/10.1007/s42438-020-00158-9

Hall, R. (2021). *The hopeless university: Intellectual work at the end of the end of history*. MayFly Books.

Holloway, J. (2010). *Crack capitalism*. Pluto Press.

Holloway, J. (2016). *In, against, and beyond capitalism: The San Francisco lectures*. PM Press.

Holloway, J. (2022). Hope in hopeless times: An interview with John Holloway. *ROAR*, 21 January 2022, https://roarmag.org/essays/hope-hopeless-times-holloway-interview/
Konan, W. O. (2021). *Paulo Freire: A philosophical biography*. Bloomsbury.
Lynch, K. (2014). 'New managerialism' in education: The organisational form of neoliberalism, *OpenDemocracy*, 16 September 2014. https://www.opendemocracy.net/en/new-managerialism-in-education-organisational-form-of-neoliberalism/
Morrish, L., & Saunston, H. (2020). *Academic irregularities: Language and neoliberalism in higher education*. Routledge.
Ramose, M. B. (1999). *African philosophy through Ubuntu*. Mond Books.
Seymour, R. (2019). Misanthropecene. *Richard Seymour*, 22 March 2019. https://www.patreon.com/posts/25552145
Themelis, S. (Ed.) (2021). *Critical reflections on the language of neoliberalism in education: Dangerous words and discourses of possibility*. Routledge.

Abbreviations

AU　　Australia
CA　　Canada
CZ　　Czech Republic
FI　　Finland
DE　　Germany
HE　　Higher Education
HK　　Hong Kong
LMS　　Learning Management System
NGO　　Non-Governmental Organisation
NL　　The Netherlands
NZ　　New Zealand
PD　　Professional Development
RO　　Romania
SG　　Singapore
STEM　　Science, Technology, Engineering and Maths
UK　　United Kingdom
VLE　　Virtual Learning Environment
WP　　Widening Participation
Q&A　　Questions and Answers

1

Introduction: Why Collaborate?

Sandra Abegglen, Tom Burns and Sandra Sinfield

We, the Editors of this book, would like to invite you, the reader, to take a moment before you delve into the pages of this collection to reflect on the context you are situated within. In CA, this includes the acknowledgement of Indigenous presence and land rights. In the UK, this means a recognition of a colonizing past. If we take these territorial acknowledgements as sites of reconciliation, they can be transformative acts that can bring people together. It is in this spirit that we would like to show honour and respect to those past, present and future – to move forward in a good way, co-creating together.

Welcome: Come on In

This collection articulates and demonstrates the value of collaboration in, through and beyond the university. The case studies included illuminate the opportunities and challenges of 'real' collaboration in action – with examples, contexts, methods and reflections to aid the reader with thinking through collaborative projects of their own. Our overarching narrative challenges the competitive, elitist and individualistic HE status quo whilst augmenting understanding of the potential of a collaborative university that facilitates the humane, 'backstage' and 'third spaces' in which all academics – staff, students and partners – can 'be' their authentic selves (Burns et al., 2019). Drawing on our own collegiate transgressive practice as 'outsider' academics (Walkerdine, 2020) who research and write together, we have gathered case studies that operate 'against the grain' to outline what might enable isolated and marginalized voices to be heard. There is liberatory potential in these spaces of solidarity, collaboration and trust – to challenge the repressive structures within which we work and study.

Collaboration Stories

Academia is a Babel of voices and our stories are shaped by our diverse contexts – the urban, the rural, the national and international – that constitute our various 'tribes' (Roxå & Mårtensson, 2009). Within this 'babble', there are different 'constellations' of speakers (Benjamin in Gilloch, 2013): those who speak with authority and drive the academic discourse; those that are listened to and those that are not; those that act and those that are acted upon (see Foucault, 1970). There are the authorized conversations that determine, surveille and manage disciplinary praxes, and the personal and informal conversations that occur when people work together; the emergent, phatic and messy conversations between faculty, students and partners especially at the 'margins' of our practice. These are the 'authentic' personal dialogues that allow for an 'educational imagination' (Eisner, 2001) to emerge: new 'Communities of Practice' (Lave & Wenger, 1991), new ways of seeing and doing. *Collaboration in Higher Education* embraces those stories that talk about the bringing together of people and institutions in education: collaborations between staff, between staff and students; collaborations between universities and with those outside academia.

As lecturers and workers in HE, collaborating and 'being with' (Nancy, 2000; Wise, 2022) our students and our colleagues create and sustain a more humane HE (Spence et al., 2022; see also *Foreword* by Gordon Asher and *Afterword* by Debbie Holley). Through conversation and dialogue we can create a pedagogy and practice of hope to explicitly challenge an individualistic, competitive, marketized HE driven by metrics, isolation and unfeasible workloads (Giroux, 2018). In our daily interactions (formal and informal) as academics – and as people – we are all constructing and restructuring the stories that build the larger narratives of who we are, what we do and how we live. We speak and we write and we become: '... language is the privileged medium in which we "make sense" of things ...' (Hall, 1997, 1). It is through our stories of collaborative practice that we construct meaning, ourselves and a more socially just HE. This collection brings together those voices, purposefully showcasing examples of what is possible when people come together and work in partnership.

Collegiality itself has power and value – as do the spaces it creates for those 'backstage' moments where 'talk in HE' and 'talk about HE' take place among academics, between students and academics, and between all of us involved in HE. These dialogic spaces (Bakhtin, 1981) are vital: for reflection, growth and the development of a humane and 'just' education in both theory and practice. It has never been more important to involve the heteroglossia in this dialogue: to listen to the voices of those of the margins, those experiencing the most 'churn' and most affected by our competitive, marketized conditions (Giroux, 2014). However, it is those very widening participation students, busy juggling their busy lives, alongside 'outsider' academics, with heavy teaching loads and precarious work contracts, that have little time or space for these vital conversations (Abegglen et al., 2020a). There is dwindling space and place for the trivia, the risky, the emergent and the creative: because staff rooms, student canteens and corridor benches have been lost; because personal workloads allow no time for these informal exchanges; because spaces and places for truly democratic collaborative and collegiate practice, those spaces and places where vulnerability is possible, always have to be fought for.

It is the collaborative venture and its 'backstage' conversations that amplify the voices of the marginalized (see Bhabha, 2004, for reflections on culture) that create spaces of coming together and of becoming. In this sense, and in this book, we seek to build hope and voice in a context which seeks to diminish both. *Collaboration in Higher Education* is collaborative talk that constitutes both transgressive behaviour (hooks, 1994) and the opportunity for radical thought and action (Freire, 1970), in research and writing and also in teaching practice. We want to celebrate and promote what is often seen as 'distracting' anti-elitist practice – collaborative partnerships within and across the academic space. For it is 'outsider talk', that talk by those at the margins, that represents and enables a more empowered engagement in academia by those that would normally be sidelined or silenced. With this book we seek to create an epistemological space – an emergent ecology of collaborative practice – rhizomatic connections of stories, heritages, narratives and conversations, of and for 'action'. We present diverse journeys within and towards the strange, mysterious and often hostile land of academia, a 'mapping' to better understand the ways in which together we can subvert the individualistic, authoritarian academy and seek out spaces for mutual support and solidarity.

Backstage Conversations: Voices from the 'Wings'

Collaboration in Higher Education offers over thirty case studies from 100 diverse contributors that are all boundary crossing and life affirming in one way or another: working across teams, across disciplines, across institutional and national borders, and across staff/student boundaries – and beyond. The case studies were selected to showcase variety and breadth. They are not systematic research papers but examples of 'real' practice. Thus the book acts as a reference source, mapping the terrain, offering thumbnail sketches and stories to navigate. As such we open with *Choose Your own Collaboration: An Adventure in Academic Time and Space* which mirrors the call to adventure and the myriad ways that you can successfully traverse the collaborative journey – and this book.

We follow with current case studies that explore how staff worked together on curriculum design and delivery across departments and disciplines to enhance student learning and success: *Staff Collaborations to Enhance Teaching and Learning*. The second set of case studies outlines how staff and students co-created together: *Students as Partners*. *Collaborations with Stakeholders* focuses on cross-institution collaboration where whole institutions and individuals have partnered up with external parties, and *Creative and Digital Partnerships* explores how partnerships were established within creative and virtual settings, and how these partnerships were supported and sustained to challenge dominant norms to achieve a common goal. The fifth set of case studies focuses on cross-boundary working: *Decolonising Relationships and Partnership for Social Justice*, where curriculum, pedagogy and practice are reimagined to create an inclusive and 'socially just' education. The sixth and final set of case studies helps us rethink relationships and connections to deterritorialize and humanize academia: *Reflections on Collaboration*.

Each set of case studies is introduced by us, the editors, to frame and contextualize the work presented, and to highlight key issues and opportunities of and for collaboration in a particular area. The case studies are further complemented by a *Foreword* and *Afterword* that provide additional, personal accounts of the power of collaborative practice and as such act as a further springboard for dialogue and thought.

The selected case studies and opening/closing commentaries are not prescriptive accounts but suggestions that will speak differently to different readers. Education and HE are in flux – no singular definition of collaboration – no one example – is totally paradigmatic. However, in this collection we argue that we do adequately cover the emergent terrain (including through and post-pandemic, Covid-19) of what is useful and generalizable to the reader's own context.

Outro: Make Collaboration Fly

Every man, by nature, has an impulse toward a partnership with others.
(Aristotle in Duvall & Dotson, 1998, 1253a29)

Humans are social, inter-dependent beings, needing to be and communicate with each other to grow and develop, to create a sense of self and identity. As the 'new' HE context continues to exclude and sideline some voices and positions (for the UK, see, for example, Office for Students, 2022, latest 'crackdown'), as it constrains and removes spaces and places for formal collegiate practice and those crucial informal conversations between and among staff and students, we seek to amplify marginalized voices for hope. Together we have the opportunity to see ourselves in new lights, to construct new questions in the search for new answers, to tear down and rebuild our stories and narratives, and to create new worlds. Collaborative practice can make spaces and create places for academics, students and partners to raise their voices and find their authentic selves – to join (often more hostile) conversations in their respective academic, disciplinary and professional communities with power and agency.

With *Collaboration in Higher Education* we aim to work out loud, sharing and telling the stories of 'being with', to highlight the 'fissures and cracks' (Deleuze & Guattari, 1987/2005) in the hegemony of academia that allow us to come together and co-create. Through our relations (Bingham & Sidorkin, 2004) we acknowledge each other – and others – with compassion and empathy, and we challenge the characteristics of an increasingly individualistic and competitive academia.

Only if we embody emancipatory practice in all our work practices can we create 'safe' spaces for risky backstage conversations, to listen to those at the periphery and empower those from the margins to speak. We hope that in *Collaboration in Higher Education* we have created that trusted space that allows us to actively and attentively speak with and listen to each other, and subsequently to all our students and colleagues. Voices need to be heard, truly heard, before they can be engaged with and responded to.

In a supercomplex world (Abegglen et al., 2020b) with ever-increasing urgent challenges it is only 'authentic' conversation and collective action that can give voice to hope. In this collection, we celebrate the different partnerships created by our authors, where the very act of co-working, co-researching and co-writing creates a more humane and just academia.

References

Abegglen, S., Burns, T., Middlebrook, D., & Sinfield, S. (2020a). Outsiders looking in? Challenging reading through creative practice. *Journal of University Teaching & Learning Practice, 17*(2). https://ro.uow.edu.au/jutlp/vol17/iss2/7/

Abegglen, S., Burns, T., Maier, S., & Sinfield, S. (2020b). Supercomplexity: Acknowledging students' lives in the 21st century university. *Innovative Practice in Higher Education, 4*(1), 20–38. http://journals.staffs.ac.uk/index.php/ipihe/article/view/195

Bakhtin, M. (1981). *The dialogic imagination: Four essays*. University of Texas Press.

Bhabha, H. K. (2004). *The location of culture*. Routledge.

Bingham, C., & Sidorkin, A. M. (2004). *No education without relation*. Lang Publishers.

Burns, T., Sinfield, S., & Abegglen, S. (2019). Third space partnerships with students: Becoming educational together. *International Journal for Students as Partners, 3*(1), 60–8. https://doi.org/10.15173/ijsap.v3i1.3742

Deleuze, G., & Guattari, F. (1987/2005). *A thousand plateaus: Capitalism and schizophrenia*. University of Minnesota Press.

Duvall, T., & Dotson, P. (1998). Political participation and Eudaimonia in Aristotle's Politics. *History of Political Thought, 19*(1), 21–34.

Eisner, E. W. (2001). *The educational imagination: On the design and evaluation of school programs* (3rd ed.). Pearson.

Foucault, M. (1970). *The order of things*. Pantheon Books.

Freire, P. (1970). *Pedagogy of the oppressed* (MB Ramos, Trans.). Continuum.

Gilloch, G. (2013). *Walter Benjamin: Critical constellations*. John Wiley & Sons.

Giroux, H. (2018). *The new Henry Giroux reader: The role of the public intellectual in a time of tyranny*. Myers Education Press.

Giroux, H. A. (2014). *Neoliberalism's war on higher education*. Haymarket Books.

Hall, S. (Ed.) (1997). *Representation: Cultural representations and signifying practices*. Sage & Open University Press.

hooks, b. (1994). *Teaching to transgress*. Routledge.

Lave, J., & Wenger, E. (1991). *Situated learning: Legitimate peripheral participation*. Cambridge University Press.

Nancy, J. L. (2000). *Being singular plural*. Stanford University Press.

Office for Students (2022). Sets out plans to crack down on poor quality courses. https://www.officeforstudents.org.uk/news-blog-and-events/press-and-media/ofs-sets-out-plans-to-crack-down-on-poor-quality-courses/

Roxå, T., & Mårtensson, K. (2009). Significant conversations and significant networks – exploring the backstage of the teaching arena. *Studies in Higher Education, 34*(5), 547–59. DOI: 10.1080/03075070802597200

Spence, R., Rawle, F., Hilditch, J., & Treviranus, J. (Eds.) (2022). *Learning to be human together: Humanizing learning*. Pressbooks. https://ecampusontario.pressbooks.pub/onhumanlearn/

Walkerdine, V. (2020). What's class got to do with it? *Discourse: Studies in the Cultural Politics of Education, 42*(1), 60–74. DOI: 10.1080/01596306.2020.1767939

Wise, S. (2022). *Design for belonging: How to build inclusion and collaboration in your communities*. Ten Speed Press.

2

Choose Your Own Collaboration: An Adventure in Academic Time and Space

Alke Gröppel-Wegener, Eleanor Johnston and Lydia Bales

- Collaboration can be chaotic, random and unpredictable, which makes it rich, because it potentially extends your individual expertise, skills and abilities through combining them with others.
- Collaboration is also difficult to plan and rarely a straightforward linear process.
- This case study allows readers to reflect on this process by taking on the role of a university librarian in a choose-your-own-adventure style piece.
- The reader (YOU!) is presented with a number of choices and paths, and it is up to you to decide which route to take.
- Note that some options are randomized (e.g. flip a coin or throw a dice) to represent the importance of chance in any real life situation and reflect the nature of the collaborative process. But in contrast to real life, you can start again to change your fate.

Introduction and Rationale

The process of collaboration is usually complex, and rich, and can be very emotional – potentially ranging from utter frustration to seemingly unlimited joy. The richness and plurality of this experience make it difficult to describe collaboration in a way that replicates the emotional experience itself and to reflect upon it. No matter how you try to tell the story, you will always have to go through a process of reduction and simplification to try to bring a certain point across. When we, as colleagues, collaborated across the divide of 'the academics' and 'the library support staff' at our university, we decided to examine and reflect on our experiences of working together. We considered this supercomplexity and the emotional implications both of participating in collaboration and of reflecting on it as important factors – aspects that are hard to find in the traditional academic literature. Because really, you need to experience it to get a sense of what happened. The prescriptive structure of academic papers, such as peer-reviewed journals or research reports, are familiar to (academic) readers, but we wanted to achieve more than those constraining genres allow. We wanted to take you – our readers – on a journey, a quest, where you experience similar emotions and thoughts as us, when we engaged in our processes as collaborators. We did not just want you to read it, we wanted you to be able to engage with it at another level, and be able to also be subject to the feeling of not quite being in control of both process and outcomes, as other people's decisions and random events end up having a big impact on these.

This chapter was inspired by a virtual escape room project that was started during the first lockdown of the Covid-19 pandemic. It was a way to rethink content delivery and collaboration, as we were not able to meet in person. It inspired us to really consider how we interact with academic materials and communicate with each other, as well as engage with a larger/broader audience – something we wanted to continue in the consideration of this collaboration. Just as the escape room collaboration gave us a fun work project to look forward to, the writing of this chapter did as well, and we hope that you will have fun reading it, as well as taking it as an opportunity to reflect on how you collaborate with colleagues and who you collaborate with, and how you could improve your practice.

We chose the *Choose your own Adventure* format to put you into our shoes and ask you to make the sort of decisions we practically made in creating this online escape room. We hope to illustrate how collaboration is essential to success and what the steps are to achieve a truly collaborative and constructive team effort. All along our collaborative journey, there were points where the objective would fall out of sight, or where the support and motivation to create something together were missing. Luckily, we were able to come together and produce an outcome that we were happy with, but it is these detours that inform the structure of this chapter, which we hope may add to the audience's understanding of the complex business of collaboration.

It may seem that not writing a text in a traditional manner is frivolous – an easy way out or showing a lack of academic or theoretical rigour. Be assured that research has gone into this, as we considered not only our own experiences and reflections of designing the virtual escape room and of other collaborations we were part of, with each other and in other contexts, but also previous literature on collaboration. This informed strands and paths within the adventure you might encounter as a reader, but it (purposefully) is not presented in the traditional form of in-text citations and references (although these are still included if you wish to explore further). The chosen format meant a different approach to creating the content – not linear but branching, considering all the potential paths to take and the possible effects of each of those decisions. That brought a refreshing challenge to us as academic authors, as we felt empowered to step off the structured path of a traditional chapter or article, but it also provides an adventure for the reader.

As authors, the paths we set allowed us to consider what decisions others could take and what improvements we could make in future collaborations. Colleagues, lecturers and staff within the library were willing to test the paths of the chapter. This feedback gave us the opportunity to improve our future collaborative practice as we developed the chapter itself. Indeed, we found that the format provided us with a fantastic opportunity to reflect on our own practice and how we can become better educators and collaborators. It opened a discussion of what collaborative practice is and how it can be successfully facilitated. It spurred our curiosity to look at research findings and related literature, helping us understand the broader context and each other's points of view – the realization of how different the university system works for people who work in different parts of it, even if they are at the same institution! We hope it will do the same for our readers, that it will bring a new perspective to you.

We hope you don't just read this once – depending on your choices and chance this might end up a very short read indeed – but rather that you reflect on your journey, retrace your steps and also consider what you would have done differently. You could be reminded of a different experience from that which we put forward, and we welcome that. In a way we are putting forward options that we thought of as typical, but really, they are meant as starting points for reflection and discussion. We hope that it will also encourage you to challenge assumptions of the traditional ways of doing things within academia, whether that be researching or teaching or any other role you might have.

Interested in going on this adventure? – start reading Section 1.
Not quite your bag? – find the next chapter in this edited collection.

The Adventure

1

'I just came across the idea of a virtual escape room on Twitter, and thought this might work really well to test students on their library skills ... is that something that already exists? Or if not, would you be interested in helping me build something like that?' You look again at the email that just popped up in your inbox from Alex, a young colleague who recently joined the library team. A virtual escape room for the library?

- You immediately hate the idea – go to section **68**
- You are intrigued, but not really sure what an escape room is, even less the 'virtual' part – go to section **61**
- You love the idea and definitely want to be part of this – go to section **38**

2

Based on the research you have already done on virtual escape rooms, you compose an email laying out the potential benefits for the students and send it to your line manager.

- Either – go to section **50**
- Or – go to section **79**

3

You start emailing back and forth about your ideas for the virtual escape room, but progress is quite slow. Whenever you do meet, you all have a great time, but you notice that the discussion of the actual escape room project becomes less and less. At some point Alex takes you to one side saying how disappointed they are that you haven't really gotten anything together.

- Do you want to try to establish clearer rules to restart the project – go to section **69**
- Have you sort of lost interest in the project yourself – go to section **16**

4

Over the next two days you get replies from your colleagues, but seemingly only other librarians are up for it. No matter, you set up a meeting so that you can introduce Alex to your new team.

- Go to section **58**

5

You agree to send out the link to each of the subject areas you promote and to advertise it on the university pages, as well as promoting it via the library social media channels. You also each agree to host the link on your subject support pages.
Flip a coin.

- If it's heads – go to section **76**
- If it's tails – go to section **62**

6

Over the next two days, a number of academics get back to you! Three academics want to help create the rooms. This is amazing! They are clearly up for making time for this project and can contribute subject experience from across the entire university. Set up a meeting so that you and Alex can get to know your new team.

- Go to section **14**

7

As it turns out, everybody is completely fine with arranging regular online meetings, so you do just that and can now press on with coming up with some objectives for your virtual escape room.

- Go to section **63**

8

Now that you know a bit more about the virtual escape room idea ...

- You want to continue with the project – go to section **38**
- You need to do more research – go to section **39**
- You decide that this isn't really for you – go to section **75**

9

You come clean at the next meeting, telling the team that you are struggling making this work. Some others say that they are not surprised, because they have had trouble with this software in the past, and they admit how happy they were when you volunteered for this task ... Somebody suggests you share your screen, and you figure the steps out together. While it takes a while, the team really helps make sense of the instructions and you manage to put the content into the file.

- Go to section **80**

10

Somebody in the team volunteers for this task and by the next meeting they have shared a file that includes all the room content you had come up with.

- Go to section **80**

11

Most members of the team seem to prefer communicating via email, as well as having the occasional meeting in the burrito bar or down the pub.

- You agree with this strategy – go to section **18**
- You think maybe you need a more structured approach – go to section **47**

12

You get stuck in a colleague's room. How embarrassing! And also, if you get stuck, how likely is it that students can solve this?

- Go to section **67**

13

Over the next two days, you don't hear back from anybody. Even though you double-check, and the message really did go out and it really did include the right spelling of your email address. A few days later you have received a few apologies and even some induction requests, which you 'share' with Alex.

- Do you try a more personal approach and get in touch with some of the academics you know? – go to section **22**
- Clearly the academics are not interested or too busy, so you and Alex will have to go it alone – go to section **57**

14

You arrive at your meeting, but not everyone shows up … Maybe the other's interest in the project wasn't that great after all? A bit disheartened, you suggest making a start when you get an email from one of the academics saying that they were embarrassed to admit that they went to the old site of the library … another one didn't find the right room (although it sounds like at least they were in the right building). Maybe you've been here so long you didn't consider where other people work and just assumed they would be as familiar with the location as you are. Does choosing the library as a meeting venue make this a library-led project rather than a true collaboration?

You decide to reconvene to the pub – everybody knows where that is …

- Go to section **58**

15

Hi Alex, on the topic of asking some of the academics to collaborate with us: I'm just reading this piece, which fits in nicely: 'We should resist the temptation of adopting stereotypical depictions that contrast the monkish habits of sole-author book-publishing humanities scholars with the assumed sociability of multi-authored article-publishing scientists' (Lewis et al., 2012, p.694 – in case you are interested). In the same way it's probably not healthy for us to assume that the academics won't want to work with us 'lowly librarians'. There must be so much pressure on them with all the bids they have to write on top of all the teaching and admin … but maybe some of them really want to join this project. So, we should give them the opportunity to take part. What do you think would be best, to send out a message for everybody on the university intranet, or shall we each make a list of the lecturers we work with and approach them?

- Either – go to section **26**
- Or – go to section **19**

16

You realize that this project is going nowhere, but hey, the loyalty card for the burrito bar wouldn't have filled up all by itself, and you did start a regular evening at the pub with some nice colleagues. This should surely count as a collaborative effort!

The End.

17

You have an email exchange with Alex and you both agree on a deadline and make a plan of how much time you can spend on it every week. Then you forward this carefully considered breakdown to your line manager, emphasizing the relatively short time you'll spend on it (only one hour per week each), the deadline (it'll be ready for the students coming back in September) and potential benefits (student engagement, but also showing the library team off as innovative). Clearly you did a great job, because you immediately get a positive response and now can crack on.

- Go to section **45**

18

Throw a dice

- If you throw anything from 1 to 5 – go to section **3**
- If you throw a 6 – go to section **41**

19

The next morning you receive a reply from Alex. 'Hi, in a way I think it would be better to approach people we know, but because I am so new, I don't really know anybody yet. Do you think you have enough contacts to make this work?'

- Go to section **22**

20

As you open the last paper you want to read before finally deciding whether to actually commit to this project or not, you realize it was written by X and some collaborators discussing the very successful virtual escape room project they designed and implemented at your university. Unfortunately, you missed taking part in it, because you were too busy reading about the theory. It's interesting that you seemed to prefer reading about the project rather than actually collaborating with people …

The End.

21

You take Alex out for a pint and explain to them that at your institution the academics really just work on their own stuff and that you can't really think of anybody who would even get back to you if approached. Some of the frustrations of being considered a 'supporter' rather than a collaborator on equal footing might slip out, too. For example, librarians never really get funding to do any research … It's a long night but you end up bonding over an involved comparison of the advantages of real ale versus cocktails.

- Are you Team Cocktail? – go to section **57**
- Are you Team Real Ale? – go to section **78**

22

Hi Alex, I really think the personal approach is the way to go – I know of some really committed academics and library staff who I think will put in the time and effort – and have amazing individual expertise that we can utilise. I don't want to pester staff who are already super busy. Why don't I put together a message and see whether any of those 'usual suspects' would be up for helping us? I know an excellent tutor in animation who I am sure could come up with some amazing scenarios ….

You compose some emails to the people you think are likely to be up for this, sit back and wait … and flip a coin

- If it is heads – go to section **4**
- If it is tails – go to section **6**

23

At your next meeting you all agree that you think that your virtual escape room is now finished. Yay! You are all really proud of what you have achieved. The next step, of course, is to put it out there and encourage students to actually play it (and hopefully learn something).

- If your team was of librarians only – go to section **5**
- If your team consisted of both librarians and academics – go to section **37**

24

You end up with a list that is very specific to the subjects of the academics in your team … and it quickly becomes so specific that it doesn't feel like a collaboration anymore.

- Do you just leave the academics to do it themselves, after all they each know what the students actually need – go to section **53**
- Do you suggest taking a step back and trying to find a way to make it more generally applicable – go to section **32**

25

Hi Alex, thanks for sending that paper over. Really interesting stuff. The issue of considering the environment that Mattesich identified really chimed with me. I think he means the institution's history of previous collaborations and political and social issues at work inside an institution are important. I am sure your experience of working in a University Library will be fascinating compared with mine, so maybe we can have a chat about those previous experiences? Fancy meeting for a cup of tea and having a chat about this?

- Go to section **35**

26

The next morning you receive a reply from Alex.

> Hi, I totally think we should be asking as many academics as possible – I'm new and really want to find out who may reply – I've literally no idea! Could we ask comms to add a message onto our staff intranet and weekly newsletter asking for volunteers? I think we should ask for people who'd like to contribute in the long term – in so far as creating the escape rooms and adding their expertise, in terms of their subject knowledge. I currently don't really know that much about the subjects outside my school, so I am intrigued to hear what resources they want to highlight and push to their students. I suspect there will be loads of things I have never even heard of! What do you think? Best, Alex.

- If you agree – go to section **44**
- If you disagree – go to section **22**

27

Flip a coin

- If it's heads – go to section **82**
- If it's tails – go to section **10**

28

Everybody in the group seems to agree – one even remarks how strange it is that while you are all librarians, some of your work is still so specifically different depending on what subject you are working with, that it is easy to forget what the basics are that most students will need! With this new focus on your collaboration the next meeting is filled with good ideas that would work for most, if not all, of the students at the university.

- Go to section **49**

29

The instructions you have work like a dream, and you are happy to make a good contribution to the team – you had been wondering whether you were actually pulling your weight.

- Go to section **80**

30

Hi there, so funny that you mentioned maybe doing some research on collaboration, because I have started doing just that! I came across a short paper by Mattesich that is well worth checking out – you can find it here (https://shelterforce.org/2003/05/01/can-this-collaboration-be-saved/). He basically identified 20 factors that significantly contribute to the success of a collaborative group, so maybe these could be helpful when going forward. Best, Alex

- Go to section **25**

31

You easily go through all of them – this is great, you basically feel that you have a really solid draft already.

- Go to section **67**

32

At your next meeting you have a great discussion about the different topics you could include in your virtual escape room, specifically building something that would work for as many students as possible. You agree to make this not about a library induction, but rather as a refresher for returning students, but to link some resources in a 'Help' section that would allow students to look up how to do something and make sure they won't get stuck in rooms. One of the things you realize is that you and your academic colleagues are using different terminologies for some things – no wonder that students can be confused when different members of staff use different terms! – so you decide to definitely include something on academic jargon. But what also comes up is that some subjects use different referencing systems and ask the students to use different resources – these are things you could not really cover in a generic escape room. How do you proceed?

- You try to find a way to also include some subject-specific info – go to section **77**
- You decide to only include information that would be useful to students of all subjects and get rid of anything too specific – go to section **52**

33

Now that you have some good content, you'll need to think a bit more about how to actually deliver this – how can you turn it into a virtual escape room (especially considering that you don't have a technical wizard on your team who could build a professional website)?

When looking at examples, you find some simple ones that just seem to use a Form format – a bit of text (and sometimes an image) that ends in a multiple-choice question. But that seems a bit basic. One of your teammates finds instructions written by Dr Emma Thirkell that explain how to build a virtual escape room using OneNote – and after everybody on the team has read that, you all agree to give that a try.

- If your team thinks one person should be in charge of building the web version – go to section **27**
- If your team decides to all work on a shared file – go to section **65**

34

You receive an email from one of your testers: 'Hi there, I tested out your escape room. I think the concept is great, but I got stuck in a room for 40 minutes and could not progress with the rest of the puzzle. I think students might find this too difficult and it maybe needs a rethink.' You discuss this with the team and come to the following conclusion:

- You are all confused how someone could get stuck in that room which includes a really basic puzzle and decide to ignore the feedback as you know that the students will understand it – go to section **64**
- You appreciate the feedback but feel you shouldn't change things just based on one opinion – go to section **46**
- You can see you need to look at this again – go to section **71**

35

You meet Alex for a cup of tea and have a chat about the institutional collaboration environment. And one of the important things is that you tell them all about their new colleagues. During the conversation you really try to highlight the strengths of some of the amazing academics and support staff in your institution, in order to build trust in this community for Alex, as a relatively new colleague. You also plan to make sure that you'll meet up with as many colleagues interested in the virtual escape room project as possible, so that these important links can be made and everybody can get to know the individual skills people bring to the project as well as be able to define the intentions of a newly formed group.

- Go to section **15**

36

You get a short reply from your line manager sarcastically remarking that you obviously don't have enough work if you want to take part in what can surely only be considered a gimmick.

- If you try to persuade them – go to section **2**
- If you decide to work on this anyway, even if you might have to do it outside of your work hours – go to section **45** to commit to the project straight away.

37

You and all your librarian colleagues make sure that the virtual escape room link gets promoted and advertised on the library website, as well as via the library social media channels. Your academic colleagues start using the link as a refresher activity for their students, as well as telling their colleagues about it.

In fact, the outcomes of this collaboration build to something so popular that most students do the escape room at least once while they are students, and they send back some amazing feedback. You are inundated by requests to talk about not the escape room itself, but rather about collaborating with academic colleagues – good thing you managed to get some on the team, because you don't think the project would have been as successful if you had ended up as an insular team.

The End.

38

You'll need clearance from your line manager, so you write them a short email to explain the potential collaboration and ask whether you can take some of your time to take part in it.

- If you are reading this in the am – go to section **36**
- If you are reading this in the pm – go to section **55**

39

You decide to do your own research on escape rooms. Start by reading Taraldsen, Haara, Lysne, Jensen and Jenssen's 2020 'A review on use of escape rooms in education – touching the void' from *Education Inquiry*.

- Go to section **48**

40

The team replies with most members wanting regularly timetabled online meetings. This is exactly what you wanted to hear. You feel that you are naturally falling into the leadership role, but maybe this is something to further discuss with colleagues, so you set up a first meeting to discuss roles and responsibilities. During that meeting everybody seems happy for you to facilitate the project and you are able to agree on a time for regular meetings.

- Go to section **63**

41

Most people in the team seem fine with you scheduling regular online meetings, but it turns out that they don't really have the time, as you hardly ever have the whole team at these meetings. So, most of the work gets stuck with you and Alex, but at least you have some collaborative input.

- Go to section **63**

42

One person gets back to you stating they only joined the group to support their school and cannot be doing something generic for different students, so they drop out. You plough on ahead with a reduced team, but although the loss of a team member has affected morale a bit, you are able to rally and come up with some unique room ideas that would work for most, if not all, of the students at the university.

- Go to section **49**

43

As you continue to work on turning the library induction into a series of rooms for your project, it becomes clear that the academics become somewhat disenchanted by the project, after all they are not librarians and don't know the ins-and-outs of your subject material that well, which is ironic, because they tend to know their subjects in so much detail. But not the library approach … so it really seems to be the librarians that contribute most. But at least you have some reliable testers for your puzzles. (Although you sometimes wonder why you did approach them to collaborate since now they bring so little to the project.)

- Go to section **49**

44

You email the comms peeps and put the message out there, Here's hoping!
This 'choice' is not yours … flip a coin!

- If it is heads – go to section **6**
- If it is tails – go to section **13**

45

After you replied to Alex that you are on board, they get back to you asking whether you maybe should ask other people as well to make it a larger collaboration. Maybe trying to get some of the academics that you support on board might not be a bad idea? On the other hand, they always seem to write their own stuff, so would they be interested in this little project, that is more teaching than research focused – and then not necessarily fit with their subject either?

- You dismiss the idea of approaching academics, because in your experience they work alone (or with each other) – go to section **21**
- You agree that you should at least try to get some academics on board – go to section **15**

46

The team agrees that it would be helpful to know if more people find this particular room difficult, so you reply to the email thanking your colleague for the feedback and particularly look out for mentions of this room from your other testers.

- Either – go to section **70**
- Or – go to section **71**

47

While it is certainly useful to spend some time in social situations with people, you have a hunch that in order to achieve a goal, it can be helpful to set time aside in a more formal setting. While you are trying to find a way to diplomatically communicate this in an email, you all receive a reply from Alex.

> Dear team, I'm so excited that you are all interested in collaborating to put together a virtual escape room. However, I'm a bit worried about doing this just via email and the occasional meeting in the pub. As you know I am still fairly new to my role, and there is so much going on at the moment, that I'm afraid that if our working processes are too fuzzy, they might get lost. Having set times for meetings will also increase my motivation to get tasks done on time! Would you maybe reconsider scheduling regular meetings? It would really help me out!

You're glad at least one person agrees with you!

- If your first name is up to four letters long – go to section **7**
- If your first name is five or longer – go to section **41**

48

- If you feel you have done enough research and want to join the project – go to section **38**
- If you feel you have done enough research, but don't want to join the project – go to section **75**
- If you feel you need to do some more research – go to section **73**

49

Now that you have agreed on what topics your rooms will have, you allocate each room to a member of the team and let them come up with content and puzzle(s) for it. Before your next meeting everybody shares the content and puzzles; they have drafted to give everybody else the time to go through them before you get together.
Throw a dice.

- If you throw a 1 or 2 – go to section **31**
- If you throw a 3 or 4 – go to section **59**
- If you throw a 5 or 6 – go to section **12**

50

Unfortunately, your line manager is not convinced and not prepared to make some time in your workload. However, you decide to work on this anyway, even if you might have to do it outside of your work hours.

- Go to section **45**

51

You receive a message from Alex that admits that while they really enjoyed meeting all the new people, they are a bit nervous when it comes to going forward with a collaboration. It sounds like they had some really bad experiences of working with others as part of their education … You reply:

> Hi Alex. I understand your hesitancies, collaborations always seem tricky to get right. But I'm glad you invited me to do this project with you and that you are part of this process. It is worth stepping back and thinking about this, especially if you are a bit nervous about the whole thing. I did a unit on collaboration recently as part of some CPD, so I've been reading quite a bit about this, and that was really helpful. But, to be honest, not as helpful as actually working with people! I really believe that the membership and 'who's who' of a group are key to our success. As members we need to understand how this collaboration will benefit us and help us

to accomplish our personal goals. I think I'll learn a lot from others and be able to be part of creating something entirely new.

- If you want to check out some of the reading, check section 83, and then continue by going to section **72**.

52

At your next meeting you take the preliminary list of room subjects and go through them one by one discussing with the whole team whether each is targeted at all students, or just at a specific subject. You keep only the ones that are for everybody and get rid of the others. This results in a much leaner list, so immediately the project becomes less daunting – you had had a lot of room ideas before.

- Go to section **49**

53

The project moves forward.

A few months into the work, you talk to Alex and reflect on how much more comprehensive what is being produced now is, but also that there is no real collaboration anymore. Everybody is working on their own subject-specific rooms, and it will be difficult to turn them into one coherent experience for the students. But then maybe this isn't necessary anyway, because none of the students will want to do all the different rooms anyway – why learn about approaches to the approaches to the library that aren't linked to their subject area, after all? So really what you are all producing are not one massive virtual escape room, but rather everybody is building their own for their own subject.

While Alex is, of course, happy to have inspired this flurry of activities, the sharing of skills and collaboration that were both hoping for unfortunately hasn't happened. But in the end you both have built some generic rooms, which your colleagues seem keen to build as introductory sections into their subject-specific rooms, so at least the work was not for nothing.

The End.

54

While the instructions seem really clear, you quickly realize that you are clearly struggling with this.

- If you share your difficulties with the team at the next meeting – go to section **9**
- If you are too embarrassed to let the team know (after you volunteered for the task) and instead find some OneNote training – go to section **56**

55

You get a reply from your line manager asking you to explain why you should spend your time on developing something you have no experience of and that might not even work in supporting students. What do you think is the biggest problem for your line manager?

- They don't know what a virtual escape room is, and need to be made aware of the potential benefits – go to section **2**
- They are not sure how much time this will take away from your other duties – go to section **17**

56

Luckily the university offers training in all sorts of software, so you manage to sign up to a OneNote session, and after that it is all much clearer, and you manage to put the content into a file.

- Go to section **80**

57

The two of you start working on your virtual escape room alone. You put a lot of work into building something that is as useful as possible from a librarian's point of view, and are really proud of the result once it goes live.

Unfortunately, not many students ever play it (although you always point them to it in any sessions you do with them). A few years later you ask one of the lecturers you work with about their opinion on the virtual escape room and they say that they did try to play it once, but the things that were asked for were so obscure they seemed not really targeted at their students, so they never promoted it any further. In fact, they themselves got stuck in the third room, so never finished it! Maybe, in hindsight, collaborating with somebody from the academic side would not have been such a bad idea?

The End.

58

In order to make this exchange of experiences a bit less formal, you decide to meet for a pub quiz. Playing as a team in an informal environment allows you to get to know each other better, and the time between rounds is taken up by sharing skills, knowledge and experiences. You are able to discover some complementary skills that will come in really handy for working on the virtual escape room – and any other future projects.

- Go to section **51**

59

You find all the rooms challenging, but in a good way, and with a few tweaks you think you have a good draft.

- Go to section **67**

60

The group gets together and decides that your aim is to create a virtual escape room for returning students that tests and refreshes their skills in using basic library skills. All the team members then put forward ideas for different rooms and what sort of puzzles you could include, so there are a lot of possibilities on the table. However, you realize that while you are all librarians, you all support different subject areas and are concerned with slightly different issues – and whenever there is a discussion, there is a lot of allegiance to the different subject areas.

- You decide to raise this issue in order to create something that is more generic and can be used by the maximum number of students – go to section **66**
- You think that if your colleagues feel they need to include a lot of subject-specific information, then clearly this is what should be done – go to section **53**

61

You reply to Alex asking for more information, and soon get the following reply:

> Hi there, so glad that you are intrigued. I'm not a huge expert either, but recently at the Association for Learning Development in Higher Education Conference 2021 there were two sessions and a poster talking about this, so it is definitely already being done in HE. The main idea is to present engagement through puzzles and a story, so that the learners are actively exploring. The 2017 EscapED article by Samantha Clarke and colleagues seems to be a key text – you can check this out here: http://journal.seriousgamessociety.org/index.php/IJSG/article/view/180 for more info. So overall this is a development of the whole gamification in education trend – making stuff more accessible and engaging by introducing a playful (and possibly also competitive) dimension. What do you think? Worth a try?

- Go to section **8**

62

Different members of the team seem to get different responses – from no responses at all, to academics who seem to love this initiative and send their students to the link every year. One or two of them even get in touch with you to ask whether you could help them build something similar that is more subject specific.

Maybe there is a new collaboration on the horizon.

The End.

63

The group is throwing out some ideas for what to put into the different rooms.

- Does your team consist of only librarians? – go to section **60**
- Does your team consist of both librarians and academics? – go to section **81**

64

You risk not changing the activity and choose to send the virtual escape room out to students as is. However, as it turns out, quite a few students do end up getting stuck at that point, give up and give this library initiative bad feedback because they got so frustrated as they were not able to complete the room. Maybe in the future you need to be more careful to take feedback into consideration.

The End.

65

Alex volunteers to start a file and then shares it with everybody. After some small hiccups about making sure that everybody has editing permissions, this seems to work well and team members are adding their room content by the next meeting.

- Go to section **80**

66

You send out an email:

> Dear team, Thanks for the last meeting, I think we came up with some really good ideas. However, I am conscious that we are veering a bit towards the subject specific. I am concerned this might mean we lose some students because it becomes a more subject focused exercise rather than the more basic induction/refresher that we had agreed on. I think in order to make this as useful to as many students as possible, we should think of more 'generic' ideas for our next meeting.

Flip a coin.

- If it's heads – go to section **42**
- If it's tails – go to section **40**

67

At your next meeting you all swap feedback regarding the rooms. Some clearly need to be made easier ... You also realize that while you have a lot of variety in your rooms, there is also a certain lack of cohesion, for example, the passwords that are the solutions are all in different formats, some just seemingly random letters, some numbers, some a combination of the two. In order to not overcomplicate things, you agree on a consistent format – each room should lead to a five-letter word – and brainstorm which passwords you could use. Then everybody tweaks 'their' room based on the feedback.

- Go to section **33**

68

Hi Alex, I don't think we have anything like it, and to be honest, I don't think this would work. After all, the students are here to learn and not to play silly games, I really don't like the idea of dressing everything up as 'fun' activities ... And I really don't have the time for extra work at the moment. Best wishes

You sign off and send your reply, happy that this is not one of the things you will have to collaborate on!

The End.

69

You arrange an ad hoc meeting for everyone and review the progress you have made on this project (not much). Then you and Alex convince the rest of the team to start scheduling regular online meetings.

- If your first name is up to four letters long – go to section **7**
- If your first name is five or longer – go to section **41**

70

The other feedback you got indicates that most testers did complete the room in question and that it didn't take them particularly long. So, it seems like some have found the room too hard and some found it fine (and one person when asked states they found it too easy). You decide as a team to keep the puzzle the same but adjust some of the instructions to make it more clear what you want the players to do. You also make sure that there is enough information in the Help section to allow people who get unstuck if necessary.

- Go to section **23**

71

Once you start looking at the feedback properly, and also getting back to some of the testers to ask them about this room particularly, it becomes clear that this room gave pretty much everybody some difficulties, so you take this feedback on board and completely redesign that puzzle. You then send the new puzzle out for 'retesting', and this time it gets positive feedback.

- Go to section **23**

72

Alex seems to be more confident in going forward with a collaboration now but seems to be happier if you start to get the ball rolling properly. Thinking back to the Mattesich article, you realize it is important for the group to decide on roles, responsibilities and purpose, so you decide to kick things off by sending an email to everybody asking for ideas on how best to get together and how often to catch up.
Throw a dice.

- If you throw an odd number – go to section **40**
- If you throw an even number – go to section **11**

73

You continue your own research on escape rooms, gamification, play in learning, game-based learning, active learning and other key words that come to mind.
Roll a dice.

- If you roll 1 – go to section **20**
- If you roll 2–6 – go to section **48**

74

> Hi Alex, I'm sorry, I was probably just feeling a bit negative the other night. You make some great points, without reaching out to other people we would lose all that experience and perspective that is beyond us – I think it is a great idea to get academics and support staff from across the whole university involved. Especially since I think that us librarians sometimes feel a bit 'outside' the traditional research at universities – we just don't have the subject expertise that people reach out to. Well, not in the same way academics do anyway. It's just that sometimes I feel like I am really not being taken seriously by that 'other side' and it is so frustrating. Maybe there is some research on collaboration we could do in order to get this right?

- Go to section **30**

75

You write a polite email back to Alex letting them know that this isn't really your thing, and you don't want to collaborate on this, but wish them good luck with it.

The End.

76

While the link is heavily promoted and hosted across the library website, there seems to be a real lack of buy-in – maybe because you don't have any academics on the team to promote it to their students directly? So, while your collaboration was a success, maybe a less insular approach would have come up with a more popular project.

The End.

77

At your next meeting you have a look at all the different room ideas you have, and sort them into two piles – the ones that would be useful for all students, and the ones that are more subject specific. You decide to definitely keep the ones useful for all students. The rooms that include information that is really targeted at only one subject are more problematic. Specific resources for each subject, for example, don't make sense to share, but the academics on your team argue that they are going to be very useful indeed. You decide that the players should be able to choose between them, and that you could start with making rooms for the subjects the members of your team teach, but then provide some instructions on how to build new ones based on different subject, so that other subject teams can build their own in future to include in this resource. The academics from each subject volunteer to take a lead on 'their' subject room(s).

- Go to section **49**

78

In the next few days, you get an email from Alex.

> Thank you for the great evening the other day. Really fun to go out and socialise a bit. And I totally understand where you are coming from, it is sometimes hard to tell whether academics are actually interested in working with us, or whether they just see us as people they can get to cover a session if they need a day off or just don't feel like teaching the reference systems! However, at my previous institution I had some really good relationships with some and they were great to work with. So maybe we would be missing a trick here if we don't at least try to get some on board – after all, collaboration is really a social activity that takes place within institutional contexts. I've just read this piece by Bozeman and some other people from 2001 where they say the important thing about collaboration is that

it includes the researchers' tacit knowledge, craft knowledge and know-how – and academics might differ from ours, so let's get in touch with some and see what they say. Maybe one or two are really up for it? Could you recommend some that you have worked well within the past, maybe?

- You are not convinced and insist you go it alone – go to section **57**
- You see their point, after all you don't really lose anything by asking – go to section **22**
- You're unsure – maybe a bit of research on collaboration would help? – go to section **74**

79

You receive a favourable response and can now go ahead and start planning.

- Go to section **45**

80

Now that you have a draft of your virtual escape room that the team is happy with, you decide that it is time to ask some people from outside of the team to test it. You ask everybody on the team to send the link to the escape room out to three to five people and ask them to playtest it for you and send some feedback before your next meeting.

- Go to section **34**

81

You meet as a group and start thinking about the topics you could make the individual rooms about. You and Alex come prepared with what the standard library induction teaches – surely that would be a great starting point? However, one of your academic colleagues suggests making a list of the issues that students seem to often struggle with. How do you decide to proceed as a team?

- You stick with the standard library induction, after all that is tried and tested – go to section **43**
- You ask your academic colleagues to make the suggested list and focus on those issues – go to section **24**
- You all make lists to then discuss together – go to section **32**

82

You decide to volunteer for this task; you've always wanted to do a bit more in OneNote.

- If you have experience working with OneNote – go to section **29**
- If you don't really have experience working with OneNote – go to section **54**

83 **References**

Bordogna, C. M. (2019). The development of social capital between operational academics delivering transnational collaborative programme partnerships. *Studies in Higher Education, 45*(11), 2298–310. DOI: 10.1080/03075079.2019.1605502

Bozeman, B., Dietz, J. S., & Gaughan, M. (2001). Scientific and technical human capital: An alternative model for research evaluation. *International Journal of Technology Management, 22*(7–8), 716–40. DOI: 10.1504/IJTM.2001.002988

Cable, E. (2021, 16 April). *Games jam: Create a literary escape room* [video]. YouTube. https://www.youtube.com/watch?v=ozyIBfQf-ws&list=PLkero3eEEZV_gkK_-Dvu5uVxkHr2sqoZ6&index=7&ab_channel=LeedsLibraries

Clarke, S., Peel, D. J., Arnab, S., Morini, L., Keegan, H., & Wood, O. (2017). EscapED: A framework for creating educational escape rooms and interactive games for higher/further education. *International Journal of Serious Games, 4*(3), 73–86. DOI:10.17083/ijsg.v4i3.180

Coulson, K., Rice, P., & Bywater, J. (2021, 7–9 April). *Using an escape room approach to induct new students* [paper presentation]. Association for Learning Development in Higher Education Conference 2021. https://aldcon.co.uk/

Deiglmayr, A., & Spada, H. (2010). Developing adaptive collaboration support: The example of an effective training for collaborative inferences. *Educational Psychology Review, 22*(1), 103–13. DOI: 10.1007/s10648-010-9119-6

Ertmer, P. A., Newby, T. J., Liu, W., Tomory, A., Yu, J. H., & Lee, Y. M. (2011). Students' confidence and perceived value for participating in cross-cultural wiki-based collaborations. *Educational Technology Research and Development, 59*(2), 213–28. DOI: 10.1007/s11423-011-9187-4

Gröppel-Wegener, A., Johnston, E., Bales, L., & Hall, S. (2021). *Unlock the library – developing a virtual escape room to test online library skills for returning students* [poster presentation]. Association for Learning Development in Higher Education Conference 2021. https://aldcon.co.uk/

Holley, D., Buckley, C., & Coulson, K. (2021, 7–9 April). *Breaking the chains of videoconferencing: The possibilities of educational escape rooms* [paper presentation]. Association for Learning Development in Higher Education Conference 2021. https://aldcon.co.uk/

Jin, G., Sperandio, S., & Girard, P. (2019). Selection of design project with the consideration of designers' satisfaction factors and collaboration ability. *Computers & Industrial Engineering, 131*, 66–81. DOI: 10.1016/j.cie.2019.03.032

Lewis, J. M., Ross, S., & Holden, T. (2012). The how and why of academic collaboration: Disciplinary differences and policy implications. *Higher Education, 64*(5), 693–708. DOI: 10.1007/s10734-012-9521-8

Mattessich, P. (2003). *Can this collaboration be saved? Twenty factors that can make or break any group effort*. Shelterforce Online. https://shelterforce.org/2003/05/01/can-this-collaboration-be-saved/

Mattessich, P. W., Murray-Close, M., & Monsey, B. R. (2001). *Collaboration: What makes it work* Amherst H. Wilder Foundation.

Taraldsen, L. H., Haara, F. O., Lysne, M. S., Jensen, P. R., & Jenssen, E. S. (2020). A review on use of escape rooms in education – touching the void. *Education Inquiry*. DOI: 10.1080/20004508.2020.1860284

Thirkell, E. (2020). *OneNote escape rooms. A 10 step guide*. https://digitalhandbook.wp.derby.ac.uk/wp-content/uploads/sites/14/2020/06/Escape-Room-Guidance-1.pdf

Wise, H., Lowe, J., Hill, A., Barnett, L., & Barton, C. (2018). Escape the welcome cliché: Designing educational escape rooms to enhance students' learning experience. *Journal of Information Literacy, 12*(1), 86–96. DOI: 10.11645/12.1.2394

Acknowledgements

This chapter is based on a real – though highly fictionalized – collaboration of academic members of staff with library staff at Staffordshire University. The authors would like to thank Sarah Hall, for going on this adventure with us, our line managers, for allowing us to embark on this adventure in the first place, and all staff and students who played *Unlock the Library*, for following in our footsteps.

3

Staff Collaborations to Enhance Teaching and Learning

Introduction

Collaboration, as its Latin roots suggest – labouring together – is the action of working with one or more people to produce or create something or to achieve a common goal. For collaborative projects to work, there must be a shared vision and commitment to the collaborative project – and to the team itself. A Community of Practice (Lave & Wenger, 1991) must emerge that learns how to act and be together. Within this, trust, empathy, tolerance and communication are important: the genuine interest in the other that promotes bonding, belonging and dialogue. Thus, collaboration in education could be defined as a reciprocal, mutual activity in which problems are identified and solutions are developed collectively, and where contributions are equally valued and respected. This is different from top-down, hierarchical approaches where one party has the expertise or the answer – the power to make decisions. In a humane HE that is resisting the coercion and abjection of these neoliberal times (Hall, 2018, 2021), true partnerships and relationships in education are therefore vital (Bingham & Sidorkin, 2004). By enacting 'community' and co-creating, we can confront difficult and shifting realities, finding new solutions as actors and agents in our own processes. And, it is only through experiencing and enacting true collaboration that academic staff can model and enable this for their students. Staff need positive interpersonal interactions to enrich their practice for 'action' (Freire, 2007, 1998), the building of authentic curriculum spaces that catalyse true partnership, with each other and with students to create a HE of hope.

This section of the book presents inspirational examples of peer-to-peer collaborations to improve teaching and learning, outlining collaborative workings between discipline and professional staff within and across departments. The case studies reveal how academics 'broke out' of their silos, working together to create powerful learning spaces for their students which increased awareness of each other's roles and epistemological practices. Together, they navigated the supercomplexity of academia as they created and modelled what a humane, collegiate HE could look like.

The Case Study Chapters

In *Writing Retreats in Social Work* Kevin Brazant and Dee Tracey demonstrate what is possible when a learning developer and a discipline academic come together to interrogate student issues in disciplinary assessment. Together they developed a six-step writing retreat programme that could be developed for and integrated within any disciplinary context. They outline how to design and deliver meaningful free writing and peer-review activity where students co-create assessment understanding and develop self-efficacy.

Another such collaboration in Health Sciences – *Collaboration for Academic Literacies Development and Enriched Inter-professional Relationships* by Quentin Allan, Robyn McWilliams and Sue Raleigh – outlines how work between faculty staff and academic literacy tutors led to the identification of a gap in student engagement with assessment. They developed active and interactive writing resources to facilitate sessions with students, using authentic writing exemplars to make transparent otherwise opaque academic forms and processes. All participants recognized the impact of the initiative not just on student learning, but on the PD impact of the collaborative endeavour itself.

With *Co-producing a Skills-based Programme* Pippa Soccio and Kate Tregloan develop the notion of collaboration for PD even further, outlining how 'Silver Sessional' staff were drawn into the staff PD unit to develop, deliver and reflect on dialogic PD workshops for staff across the Built Environments Faculty. The lessons learned focused not just on the ethical and effective nature of such a collaborative venture, but that as a result sessional staff felt more agentic, included and valued.

In *Bringing Research to Life* Laura Barclay, Sharon Bitter, Anne-Kathrin Reck and Rhiannon Parry Thompson discuss how they used their shared interest in the power of storytelling to generate an intriguing extra-curricular 'research skills' session for students. The initiative approached research differently, harnessing the power of narrative to make research and research outcomes more meaningful for students while shaking up notions of what research can be and how it can be used.

In *Approaching Blended Learning through Teaching Team Collaboration* Katherine Herbert, Julia Lynch and Humayun Murshed reveal the power of a large-scale, multi-site cross-state collaboration to develop a holistic blended learning experience to foster self-directed study in students who typically do not see themselves as active learners. They tease out the complexity of the issues they wanted to address and the power of cross-team working, even when those teams have differing academic and professional capital, and are located on different campuses.

Developing 21st Century Skills through Meaningful Cross-institutional Collaborative International Community Service Projects by Pranit Anand and Byron Tsz Kit Lui outlines a truly inspirational approach to authentic group work in a transnational project. Educators and students from two different universities in two different countries came together to develop solutions for NGOs situated in a third country, demonstrating how creative collaboration between staff teams can create even more creative collaborative experiences for students.

Diana J. Pritchard, Helen Connolly, Amanda Egbe, Mohamed Saeudy, Paul Rowinski, James Bishop, Tamara Ashley and Nicholas Worsfold make a case for *Cross-disciplinary Collaborations for Sustainable Futures, and a Vital and Relevant Academic Community*. In their case study they outline their boundary crossing project where they pooled their interest in ethical education for sustainable futures to bring together multi-disciplinary teams from within and outwith the university to create mass 'learn-in' events to explore contemporary issues through multiple lenses for 'real' social and academic outcomes. Not only did their project break academic isolation, it seeded management buy-in to transform practice for the long term.

Writing Retreats in Social Work: A Disruptive Approach to Facilitating Practice Learning

Kevin Brazant and Dee Tracey

- This case study describes a co-designed writing retreat designed to support students with the synthesis of theory and practice through writing.
- It models decentring power by switching from transmission to a dialogic pedagogy.
- It offers a six-step model to develop metacognition, critical thinking and analysis as part of assessment practices.
- Promoted in the chapter are free writing and peer review to co-create meaning.
- We recommend writing retreats to develop writing and written discourse.

Introduction: Collaborating to Support the Learning of Social Work Students

This chapter presents a case study of a collaboratively designed writing retreat intervention seeking to support critical and creative capacities among Social Work students on a practice learning module. The goal is to develop students as actors with agency within 'the dominant framework of higher education' (Bellinger & Kagawa, 2012). The authors are aware of the wider challenges to UK Social Work education, its constraints, financial and cultural, and the impact on teaching practices in HE (Maclachlan, 2007) where the pressure can be to 'teach to the test' rather than in ways that are liberatory and empowering for the student. To combat some of these points, a joint collaboration was formed between a learning developer (academic mentor) and a qualified Social Work practitioner (subject tutor) with the purpose of supporting the authentic learning and development of Social Work students.

This case study also addresses the dichotomy of teaching for an employment environment of increased regulation and targets based on political imperatives, yet still requires Social Workers to have creativity and problem-solving skills (Jordan & Jordan, 2000). Adopting a dialogic, social constructionist methodology, the authors circumvent didactic, transmissive and monologic teaching approaches (Stewart & McClure, 2013) – reframing learning as dialogic, disruptive, engaging and collaborative, with positive implications for interdisciplinary learning and teaching practice.

Our Contested Context

Social Work programmes across universities are designed in a similar manner, with a blend of academic theoretical learning alongside practical work placements. In academic terms, the first element of learning is classroom based with the primary focus being based upon the learning (the development) of Social Work skills, knowledge, values, theories and methods. This forms the 'grounding' basis for the student's preparation to enter their Social Work practice placements. In designing our project, we thought about 'how' to fully prepare a student for the reality of Social Work practice when the programme is set within an academic HE structure which does not always fit with the realism of the profession, with the university processes at times being limited and not always matching the professional standards and expectations.

Critical Social Work

When considering preparation for the Social Work role, critical reflection and analysis are harnessed for the development of Social Workers, whether qualified or unqualified. This is recognized as of significant importance when linking theory to practice: for qualified Social Workers it is an essential tool for critical decision making (Thompson, 2018). Mantell and Scragg (2018) and other academics recognize the importance of high-quality Social Work education in developing future-qualified Social Work practitioners. Foremost for a profession which is seen as highly charged, reflective practice can help to integrate theoretical learning into practice, giving the student the tools, capacities and platform to be 'ready for practice'.

Social Work England is the regulatory body for Social Work along with another prominent body, the British Association of Social Work (BASW). In the UK, they recognize that

> critical reflection encourages social workers to examine their approach, judgements, decisions and interventions [and acknowledges that] when applying critical reflection, thinking and analysis it helps social workers formulate a treatment plan or intervention for working with a client.
>
> (Social Work England, 2020)

Therefore, it is essential for students to begin to understand and use the process of critical reflection and analysis as early as possible in their careers, recognizing the importance that it holds, especially to ensure unbiased, anti-discrimination, anti-oppression and anti-racist practice (Tedam, 2021). Based on this importance, we designed our project and teaching sessions to prepare students for their placement and to articulate the experiences of their placements in the form of a practice case study assignment, using techniques for critical reflection and dialogue.

What We Did

The role of the educator is to facilitate the learning process by designing sessions that will help students learn and discover, to wrestle with ideas and 'emergent' knowledge. This was the main aim for this project – to not limit the student in their creativity, but to let them explore and find answers, whilst reflecting on their previous life skills and knowledge. A number of theorists and psychologists, such as Bruner, Dewey and Ausubel, held the view that the purpose of education is not to just impart knowledge, but instead to facilitate thinking and problem-solving skills which can then be transferred to a range of situations. With students using their own past experiences and prior knowledge as part of their learning, this approach sits well with the demographics of Social Work students that attend our programme and who come with life skills, prior experience and can relate these experiences to their current learning (Bates, 2019).

As part of active, collaborative learning, 'Dialogic Pedagogy' (Alexander, 2010) shifts the emphasis from the transmission of knowledge by the lecturer to the achievement of learning by the students, through creating conducive learning environments. Our curriculum design approach to these practice learning sessions was to create dialogic instances throughout the writing retreat, using six strategies as follows:

1. Students engaged in a free writing activity upon a case study assignment to stimulate ideas and reflections and to take ownership of their learning. The task was to identify a family or client group with whom they worked and explore the reasons for the choice and how this met the assessment brief.
2. In smaller groups students annotated the assessment criteria, familiarizing themselves with assignment expectations, exploring these with peers and strategizing on how they will meet learning objectives and outcomes.
3. They then produced a draft reflective case study and a subsequent plan to address any gaps in current knowledge.
4. Then they engaged in a peer-sharing exercise of their (draft) case studies harnessing critical thinking by questioning and assessing the work of their peers as a preface to the self-appraisal of their own work.
5. Using a bespoke toolkit of resources and worksheets to assess criticality in their Practice Study, they built on their reflections and were encouraged to share further tips with peers to bolster their learning strategies.
6. Using a writing retreat style activity, they drafted their actual practice study and gained further feedback from their peers through peer appraisal.

Throughout, students were encouraged to collaborate, cooperate and discuss their learning, their processes, their thinking and their draft work. These processes enacted and modelled learning as the collaborative co-construction of knowledge.

Discussion

This approach was cognisant of the interplay of power (Bakhtin, 1999; Stewart & McClure, 2013) disrupting the monologic discourse of traditional forms of teaching. As illustrated above, the learning developer and practice lead planned and scaffolded the retreat but stepped back from intervening in the dialogic solution of problems; instead, activities were constructed to provoke solutions from and between peers. The facilitation of learning was modelled by a flexible and compassionate style by both lecturer and learning development practitioner, creating a conducive learning environment for social learning (Gilbert 2017; Rogers & Freiberg 1994). Given the emancipatory ideas found in Social Work, we sought to frame a discourse in the retreat space that inspired real action in the world as part of student placements, with their overall experiences articulated through their practice case study assignment (Shor & Freire, 1987).

From a constructionist perspective we sought to model an interpretivist epistemology that co-constructs knowledge and took opportunities to mediate understanding of the curriculum and task at hand between novice, able learners and academics (Vygotsky, 1962). Based on the feedback from students they all agreed unanimously that the thing of greatest value to them was to share their placement experiences with their peers and being given the time to think about their chosen clients for the purposes of their practice study assignment as illustrated below:

> I have learned how to use the feedback of my colleagues to think about my practice and to use this constructive criticism to also form part of my own self-analysis and critique.

> The small group discussions amongst my peers was very helpful to learn about different approaches to knowledge and to apply this to my practice study.

> I had written my practice study but after listening to my peers and lecturers through this workshop I will go back and restructure as I think my work appears more descriptive than critical and I believe this would enhance my grade for this assignment.

Conclusion

In conclusion, with a learning developer and discipline academic undertaking this joint venture, we brought together the 'academic' element of the learning and the practical experience of Social Work learning, whilst integrating learning strategies (developing metacognitive dispositions and study skills) within the collaborative study space. We were able to devise and design a six-step scaffolded framework and use tools to co-teach, meaning that we were able to cooperate to bring a more fulfilling enrichment to the student learning. Our co-delivery used both of the author's skills, disciplinary and interdisciplinary knowledge sets to enhance student learning.

Group work is often fraught with tensions and conflict between students. However, we believe we created space for a collaborative community of practice to emerge that united the students in their endeavours and obviated the normal tensions of (inauthentic) group work. Given the positive feedback from the project, we believe this presents a cogent case for the further development of scaffolded, cooperative, writing retreats as part of assessment preparation, overtly acknowledging peer appraisal as part of this process. Not only did this develop critical thinking as intended but fostered student learning communities and self-efficacy.

Collaboration for Academic Literacies Development and Enriched Inter-professional Relationships

Quentin Allan, Robyn McWilliams and Sue Raleigh

- This case study outlines a collaborative academic literacies development project in a biological sciences setting.
- The key argument is that such development requires close collaboration between faculty lecturers and learning advisors.
- The project promotes a staged approach to interactive engagement with exemplar texts.
- Collaborations between discipline and literacy staff for student development also provide rich professional development, and writing opportunities.
- A next step would be to work with students as partners in future literacies development projects.

Introduction

In this chapter, we argue that academic literacies' development in a university environment ideally involves close collaboration between faculty lecturers (FLs) who are subject experts in their discipline and learning advisors (LAs) whose expertise in applied linguistics informs their academic writing guidance. This chapter has been co-authored by two LA colleagues and one FL. The subject context in this case is biological sciences with a focus on human anatomy and physiology; the linguistic guidance is informed by the 'genre approach', as outlined by foundational writers in the field of educational linguistics (Martin & Rothery, 1993; Swales, 1990). This approach is characterized by a focus on helping students identify salient features of different assignment types. In practical terms, this involves careful deconstruction of exemplar texts that have been produced by students in authentic assessments (Rose & Martin, 2012). Through observation of student writing, and recent interactions with faculty lecturers, the LAs have been inspired to move beyond a 'best-practice model' of embedding academic literacies development as outlined in McWilliams and Allan (2014), to something more collaborative: working together to tackle student study, learning and communication issues. One important way in which we have extended the original model is through the use of exemplar texts as the point of departure, specifically the genre short answer questions. We were interested in exploring the effectiveness of co-developing teaching materials derived from a careful deconstruction of exemplars.

This case study starts by identifying two key themes from the literature: institutional awareness and use of exemplar texts. It moves on to summarize the experiences of an FL who requested LA support and how this developed into a partnership for learning. Next is a discussion of FL awareness of embedding academic literacy practices followed by an examination of the importance of student exemplar texts. The case study concludes with a consideration of how the collaboration has enhanced student learning, followed by recommendations.

Lecturer Awareness Relating to the Value of Embedding Academic Literacy

Collaborative, embedded literacy practices have become more widespread across faculties and disciplinary programmes in recent years (Devereux et al., 2018). To reflect these developments, a number of useful models or frameworks of embedded practice approaches have been developed (e.g. McWilliams & Allan, 2014; Charlton & Martin, 2018; Maldoni, 2018). This focus on discipline-specific practices has raised lecturers' awareness of the linguistic features and rhetorical conventions of particular assessment types (Purser, 2011) and the value of student exemplars in illuminating them (Wingate, 2018). The value here resides in lecturers' ability to draw students' attention to salient textual patterns that are associated with the assignment type and the 'work' that those features accomplish in the text. In a teaching environment, whether online or in a classroom, it is also possible to generate productive discussions with students about learning in general, and academic writing in particular – including the possibilities of writing to learn, as distinct from learning to write (Abegglen et al., 2021).

Importance of Student Exemplar Texts

The use of student exemplar texts has become central to developing effective literacy materials to support students when completing assessments (Dixon et al., 2020; Hawe et al., 2021). Whilst some research suggests that the use of exemplars can be overwhelming for some students (Hendry et al., 2011), the dominant view is that their use is beneficial for improving the quality of student writing. In terms of motivation, providing students with tools to examine their own writing enhances self-efficacy and self-regulation (Hawe et al., 2021). These tools are complemented by lecturer feedback on formative assessments which includes comparisons between exemplar texts and students' own writing (Carless & Boud, 2018).

The Collaboration between Learning Advisors and Faculty Lecturers

In a busy university setting, many interactions between staff members end up being merely transactional and non-dialogic; in contrast, in this case, the interaction between LAs and FL is characterized by a richly dynamic and ongoing relationship that has at its heart student success and retention. From the FL's perspective, one of the primary objectives is to scaffold students in their understanding of the complexities of biological science. This starts with the classroom content and is linked to real-life examples with an awareness of the relevance to future practice in their respective health fields. The focus then tends to be on subject content rather than writing. However, students can experience difficulties with writing about this type of subject and showcasing their learning through writing. These difficulties include concise paraphrasing of complex physiological processes, using appropriate terminology but also familiarizing themselves with subject-specific genres.

The collaboration in this case emerged from a request by the FL for multiple individual student consultations. This request was not feasible given the LA team's limited staff resources and the large student cohort (Semester two, 2019, $n = 572$; Semester two, 2020, $n = 676$). For the assessment tasks in this paper, a number of writing challenges were presented (distinctive structure, purpose and language features) for which there had not been any previous tailored support.

The collaboration here was initiated by the FL with respect to helping students' structure responses to short answer questions. The LAs consulted firstly with students who had been identified as needing support, then with the FLs to understand from the teachers' perspective the sort of problems students were encountering. The next step was to jointly develop a series of academic writing workshops to address the unique writing challenges of this assessment. The objective was to develop sustainable resources for a large cohort that could be transferred from one semester to the next, indefinitely. A key aspect of the LA approach is the use and systematic analysis of authentic exemplar texts to highlight and scaffold the learning required. An exciting development has been the integration of emerging technologies to create text animation to emphasize salient features of exemplars.

The close partnership between the FLs and the LA enabled the coming together of different epistemological approaches and practices, developing mutual understanding and cooperation for the benefit of increased student engagement with their learning.

The teaching and learning materials and classroom activities emerged from this ongoing dialogue:

- Firstly, students were asked to identify key words in a sample question.
- Then students' attention was drawn to linguistic exponents for particular language functions, e.g. language for describing anatomical structures, and language for explaining physiological processes and neurological pathways.
- Students were then shown an exemplar text which had been deconstructed and annotated to highlight key textual features.
- Finally, students were provided with opportunities to practise writing – with formative feedback.

How Did This Collaboration Enhance Student Learning?

The impact on student learning is encouraging. Informal feedback from students who attended targeted writing workshops indicates that they are aware of developing a more nuanced understanding of academic writing, via the explicit pedagogical focus on text structure, purpose and language choices – and especially through opportunities to discuss aspects of their writing with classmates, ALs and FLs.

Furthermore, FL feedback suggests that the embedded literacies focus has resulted in students achieving higher grades; results compared with the previous year indicate improved pass rates from 64 per cent in 2019 to 85 per cent in 2020.

Further, the coming together of FLs and LA in this project produced a cache of annotated, animated exemplars that the students themselves could return to as part of their self-directed learning. A conscious decision was made to provide unlimited access to this growing suite of self-access videos for the duration of their degree, fostering continuous learning support and exchange about writing.

Conclusions

For us, collaboration has enhanced professional development and enriched interprofessional relationships. The FL noticed a heightened sense of linguistic awareness and a greater confidence to talk about text in practical ways with students. Of particular value was the developmental, ongoing and organic collaborative process as the materials were generated, trialled, critiqued and re-worked.

Staff collaborations such as this are designed to enhance teaching and learning. The value of such collaborations is well attested in the literature (McWilliams & Allan, 2014) and our approach was informed by solid pedagogic principles, including the developmental use of exemplar texts. This approach takes the guesswork out of managing the writing demands of a content-rich paper. From an LA perspective, the objective was to establish an approach that is effective and enduring. Sustainable academic literacies support is enhanced with good relationships enhanced by multimodal approaches. Certainly, when FL and LA work together, we have observed positive change in students' performance over time.

Indeed, feedback from students has been overwhelmingly positive; however, in terms of materials development, the student voice has been somewhat backgrounded. In future, it would be desirable to better integrate students as partners, including in post-course feedback development, exploring how students had used the resources and how they had helped in the understanding and ability to articulate their new learning.

The focus of this case study has been on the growing relationship between FL and LA colleagues. With students' development at the heart, such collaborations unfold over time and, in retrospect, can be seen to exhibit a number of dynamic dimensions, including catalysing reflection and promoting creative approaches to student support and writing. Such relationships at their best are dynamic, meetings ongoing, even when the initiating objective has been met.

Reflecting on this case study has inspired us to rework the original model (McWilliams & Allan, 2014) with the student exemplar text occupying a more central role in the collaborative process. Even more so, it has inspired us to continue our partnership and work closely, LA with FL, to develop students' academic literacies. This is co-learning and co-teaching in action.

Co-producing a Skills-based Programme: Peer-to-peer Learning Partnerships in Professional Development

Philippa Soccio and Kate Tregloan

- Sessional staff make a valuable and significant contribution to built environment education, and enrich their teaching with research and industry experience.
- Support for the PD of this high-turnover casual workforce is a complex challenge, raising pragmatic as well as ethical issues.
- Collaborative peer-to-peer learning partnerships were trialled through this project to support PD of this group.
- Findings from the project identify key factors for effective support of sessional staff, such as recognition of personal value, inclusion and agency, and the enduring impact of social learning approaches.

Introduction

Sessional (adjunct, casual, part-time) staff account for more than 60 per cent of the teaching workforce in Australian Schools of Architecture (Maroya et al., 2019). These staff typically come from professional practice or are graduates undertaking Research Higher Degree study. Despite the significant impact they will have on student learning, most sessional teachers have little or no formal training in pedagogy (Sutherland, 2002). The following case study describes a collaborative developmental project by a teaching and learning group at a large comprehensive Australian university. The project supported selected experienced sessional staff to co-produce a skills-based PD programme suitable for their less experienced colleagues, but relevant to all teaching staff.

Context

The Built Environment Learning and Teaching (BEL+T) group was established in 2018 at the University of Melbourne, located in Melbourne, Australia. The group works with staff and students of the Faculty of Architecture Building and Planning (ABP) to improve teaching and learning, developing and sharing resources through the BEL+T website at https://msd.unimelb.edu.au/belt. A targeted discipline-specific PD approach is central to the support of the 400 new and returning sessional staff who are hired each semester in ABP programmes. Together, sessional and tenured teachers work with 3,500 students studying Architecture, Landscape Architecture, Urban Design, Urban Planning, Construction Management, Urban and Cultural Heritage, and Property.

The BEL+T group delivers PD for all staff to improve teaching quality and student engagement through ongoing development of built environment pedagogy. This PD draws on creative problem-solving and design-led approaches, evidence-based research methodologies, and project-focused consultancy. In addition to induction programmes for new staff, 'BEL+T Sessions' typically focus on current issues each year and have included Teaching for Inclusive Learning; Collaboration vs Collusion; Moving Online; and Using the Microstudio to date.

Sessional Staff Engagement (SSE) has been identified as a priority within ABP's Strategic plan, and an SSE Survey was developed by BEL+T to inform this work. Since 2020 the SSE Survey has shifted its focus to understanding bigger challenges through longitudinal data, such as the changed experiences of sessional staff during the Covid-driven shift to online teaching, and a deeper understanding of teaching practice support needs. One opportunity identified was tailoring in-semester PD for sessional staff: a challenge widely recognized in the literature (see Hitch et al., 2018, for a review of thirty-seven related papers published since 2006). The SSF Framework (funded through the Australian Government Office for Learning and Teaching) defines provision of 'a structured, systematic and accessible professional development programme' as a priority for supporting sessional staff (Harvey, 2013, 2). Our vision was for dialogic PD to take place through collaborative projects, and this case study outlines that.

Aim

Results from the SSE survey suggested enthusiasm for PD opportunities in which staff could engage directly with their sessional peers. In contrast to the formats for previous BEL+T Sessions, such as roundtable discussions or focused workshops, this project aimed to celebrate, support and enrich the expertise of sessional teachers through the collaborative design of a dialogic PD programme. BEL+T staff worked with experienced sessional staff to co-design the programme, aiming to encourage a sense of ownership of the initiative, including the freedom to revise sections of the course design based on their lived experience. Review of the programme, with institutional Human Research Ethics Committee approval, investigated What Works?: Peer-to-peer Learning (P2P) Partnerships Informing Staff PD.

How We Approached the Collaboration

P2P partnerships are 'voluntary, reciprocal helping relationships between individuals of comparable status' (Eisen, 2000, 5). While mentoring and coaching are typically one-on-one directive relationships (Parker, et al., 2008), P2P partnerships are themselves a collaboration. Discussion and interaction between participants 'favour the construction of knowledge and help to develop reflective skills and a sense of "togetherness"' (Guldberg, 2008, 46) and draw upon the qualities of social learning spaces such as 'knowing as practice' and 'knowing as identity' (Wenger, 2011, 195) that form part of Communities of Practice for learning (Lave & Wenger, 1991),

As 'discussion' forms the basis of P2P partnerships, experienced sessional staff were recruited early. BEL+T shortlisted experienced sessional candidates to submit expressions of interest. Four staff with twenty combined years of sessional teaching experience were selected, collectively named 'Silver Sessionals', and paid to contribute to four planning and review meetings and to the three conversation events. The *ABP Teaching Tricks and Tips* events programme included: Starting the Semester Right by establishing good staff-student relationships; Giving Students Quality Feedback/Feedforward and Assessment; and Ending the Semester Well through teaching reflection. The programme and the expertise of the Silver Sessionals were promoted through the BEL+T News and Opportunity webpages, Faculty weekly newsletter and the sessional teaching community site on the LMS.

A series of planning meetings underpinned the collaborations. In the first of these, BEL+T presented a loose framework for the programme – this was refined by the Silver Sessionals according to their reflections on their own lived experience. Subsequent meetings explored topics for each event, and drew on BEL+T analysis of SSE survey responses. Silver Sessionals shared related experiences, explored each other's strategies and speculated about alternatives. Key challenges were identified as prompts for each event. Figure 3.1 presents an example – this and other session prompts can be found via https://figshare.com/s/f28b09805ee54ed417c6. Planning meetings also offered time for debriefing of previous events: Would we have changed anything? What did we learn? During these hour-long discussions, the group also planned a structure for the following event. BEL+T confirmed event plans by email with a running sheet highlighting key ideas and strategies.

"Session 1: Challenges when starting the semester right"

Mastering the technology	Building rapport	Encouraging interaction	Effective communication
• How do I overcome my technical challenges? • How do I help students overcome their technical challenges (dropping out / time lag / inexperience)? • How do I use Canvas? • Help! Students don't know how to use online tools (like Miro)!	• How do I get to know the whole group… what works? • How do I help students to feel like they are part of a group committed to learning? • What is the right balance between being friendly, and maintaining professional boundaries?	• How can I fill any awkward silence? • Where will I find the right online tools that help me run learning activities that students will enjoy? • How can I make theoretical content interesting (and engaging)? • How do I encourage discussion amongst students?	• Help! I can't understand the student and/or they can't understand me! • How can I encourage my students to turn their cameras on? • How to I gauge what students are thinking (when online) without access to non-verbal cues like body language?

Self-doubt / inexperience	Return to Campus (Covid 19)	Being inclusive	Student wellbeing
• Am I experienced enough? • What is I can't answer a student's question?	• Where on campus can I run an online class? • How do I maintaining engagement while respecting social distancing? • How do I help students feel at ease on campus after a challenging year? • Help! My students are online + campus. Is this 'dual delivery'?	• How can I pace my teaching in order to bring all students along? • How do I recognize different student needs (diverse learning needs, cultural/social backgrounds)? • How can I include students with access to fewer online resources (limited data / no home printer)?	• Help! Students are not interested • Help! Students are unmotivated • Help! One of my student regularly misses assessment deadlines • Help! A student appears distressed / emotional (online or on campus) • Help! I've just been told about a personal issue impacting a student's academic performance

Figure 3.1 Session 1 – Challenges at semester start (Soccio & Tregloan, 2022).

The PD Events in Action

In all three events, the Silver Sessionals led the discussion facilitated by BEL+T. Half of each event was dedicated to Q&A between Silver Sessionals and attendees. The high levels of interaction were encouraging as all events were held online due to Covid-19 restrictions. The number of participants varied across each event with the highest attendance (nineteen people) at Session 1. Events were recorded for review, and BEL+T summarized key takeaways, confirming these with the group before publication to a Faculty Teaching LMS site. Site analytics indicate that this LMS page of resources was viewed sixty-eight times over the semester. An end-of-project survey distributed via the LMS found that participants valued the initiative, but struggled to attend due to conflicting time commitments. BEL+T has speculated that payment of participants may have improved attendance further.

At the conclusion of the project, an additional debrief meeting with Silver Sessionals provided a focused opportunity to comment on the approach taken across the programme and inform the evaluation of the project. The group consented to recording discussions for the purposes of research and publication; these were transcribed verbatim. BEL+T researchers analysed the data to identify emergent themes in relation to the focus questions:

1. What was attractive about this ABP Teaching Tips and Tricks opportunity?
2. How would you describe your role in the sessions?
3. Did you feel as though you were part of a collaboration?
    a. (If yes) What specific actions helped you to feel you were part of a collaboration?
4. What did you gain from your involvement in Teaching Tips and Tricks?
5. Were there any surprises?

How the Participants Experienced Collaboration

While feedback about the project was very positive, it also highlighted that sessional staff are rarely included as collaborators in teaching and learning discussions, despite their unique perspectives and experiences with students (AUTC, 2003). Participants made it clear that they felt included in the project, and that this was unusual. As an example,

> absolutely, and very much that, when you do ask a question, you are really genuinely listening to the answers, and taking that on board. There are so many instances outside of this space where that isn't the case. So it's really, really lovely to be ... I keep using the word 'embraced' by the community here, and to feel very much part of it in this space.

While the structure for each event was flexible and the conversations quite organic, the value of the planning meetings was highlighted as supporting a sense of agency:

> I think the planning sessions ... (were) really instrumental in helping us develop a sense that we're a community putting this together rather than BEL+T just telling us what we should be answering ... You had a broad idea of what could happen, but you were also entirely open to the conversation flowing and seeing how that might mean that the direction of a particular session was moulded in a different way.

One participant described a perception that there were a series of 'invisible collaborators' who were also contributing:

> The word 'conduit' came to mind for some reason, and I think we're all kind of standing here and we're not just a product of our own. We have all these wonderful life experiences, wonderful teachers who might not necessarily be tutors and yet somehow they influenced us in a way ... in many ways, we don't stand alone in isolation. Everyone (is) together.

The discussion also highlighted how P2P partnership can foster bi-directional learning through joint reflection (Eisen, 2000):

> It's been really valuable listening to other people's teaching ideas and experiences and thinking about ways to adopt them .... Learning and teaching, it's very much a two-way thing ... Or six ways in this case [pointing to four Silver Sessionals and two BEL+T members].

Individual learning was also described:

> Finding a way to articulate what we are doing has been great. Because I think all of us are instinctively, intuitively teaching and doing things, and reinventing

ourselves every single day, and these sessions helped us to learn some language around what we're doing. ... Just finding more ways to articulate these things has been really really valuable.

Small actions that made these participants feel important and valued were also highlighted, reinforcing a commitment to the collaborative process. When asked about what attracted them to the opportunity, one participant remembered the recruitment invitation: 'You had me at the email title. It says, "BEL+T chooses you". It's like, of course, yes ... I'll say "Yes!"'

Conclusion

The Teaching Tips and Tricks and PD project is an example of a P2P partnership focused on co-design of learning experiences for others – in this case for sessional colleagues – but has also highlighted to BEL+T the crucial value of such collaborative partnerships, and the opportunities these offer to members of an inclusive HE landscape. There are ambitions to extend the programme in future semesters, and to highlight the rich experiences of sessional colleagues, by involving them in collaborative PD responses to more subject-specific teaching challenges.

Review of the design and delivery of the ABP Teaching Tips and Tricks pilot has identified some key contributing factors we need to maintain for successful collaborative partnerships with sessional colleagues: ensuring a sense of being valued; supporting inclusion; and recognizing personal agency. It is sobering to acknowledge that these describe atypical experiences for sessional teachers. The central importance of collaboration to learning in HE emerged through participants' reflections, and the development of shared languages, nuance and understandings. The recognition of 'invisible collaborators' – the previous teachers and mentors who contributed to this work through their influence – highlights the enduring impact of social learning and the lessons that can be passed on to others through quality collaboration for PD and learning.

Acknowledgements

BEL+T would like to acknowledge the contribution of our four Silver Sessionals: Dr Anna Hooper, Dhanika Kumaheri, Joel Benichou and Katie Skillington, who have given permission for their names to be included in this case study. Without their important contribution to the collaborative process, this work would not have been possible.

The authors would like to thank the Faculty of Architecture, Building and Planning for its continued support of research into best practice teaching and learning for built environments disciplines.

Bringing Research to Life: Enhancing Research Skills through Collaborative Storytelling

Laura Barclay, Sharon Bittner, Anne-Kathrin Reck and Rhiannon Parry Thompson

- Storytelling as a shared interest and used as a catalyst for this collaborative project.
- We used storytelling to foster students' development of research skills by uncovering local stories to create narratives.
- Storytelling offers a place where students and staff can come together to deepen team working via a creative, non-assessed task.
- For us it enhanced staff understanding of different support roles within the institution.
- It raised student awareness of local historical personalities and the University's place and context – providing students with a deeper sense of belonging.

Prologue

Collaborations are beneficial to all participants, from designers of an activity to the peer groups that participate (Crookendale, 2020; Fox et al., 2011; Montgomery & Miller, 2011). In September 2019, three Learning Developers at the University of Portsmouth hosted a staff-facing symposium on 'Storytelling in Learning Development' to members of the wider Association for Learning Development in Higher Education (ALDinHE) community. This event arose from a shared interest in using storytelling in professional practice. Inspired by the symposium, the Learning Developers collaborated with an Assistant Faculty Librarian to create the student-facing *Bringing Research to Life* workshop. This is an extra-curricular, non-assessed, research skills workshop designed to demystify the research process and encourage student engagement with non-traditional materials and digital historical resources. Students were invited to find evidence to create short, personal narratives of historical figures with connections to the local area.

Our work was grounded in our belief that storytelling is a powerful tool for generating and exploring questions, accessing different kinds of knowledge and helping us to understand the world and our place within it. As Tahir Shah (2008, 152), in *Arabian nights: A Caravan of Moroccan Dreams*, so astutely observed, 'stories are a communal currency of humanity'. Furthermore, the use of storytelling 'frees' the student from the conventions of academic writing, but still encourages research skills, logic, criticality and simply writing. Since our students had not been instructed in storytelling for academic purposes per se, we applied the simple 4 P principle. The stories constructed revolved around historical personalities (=people) with a connection to Portsmouth (=place), were evolved according to what students found in their research (=plot) and served our overall goal (=purpose) of enhancing the participants' engagement, sense of belonging, critical and creative skills in a third space setting for learning development.

This case study highlights the benefits of collaborative working with colleagues to improve student outcomes. For us it contributed to staff understanding of different support roles within the institution, as well as offering a place where students could come together to deepen knowledge of research and team working within a creative, non-assessed task.

Once upon a Time …

Whilst our work practices differ owing to the requirements of our respective cohorts, the process of co-planning, co-implementing and co-evaluating this workshop has allowed us to find synergy in our approaches to facilitating student learning (Montiel-Overall, 2005). With our personal relationships already established through previous collaborative work, we felt that we could work together effectively (Pham, 2019) and explore new ways to address issues that we had noticed in relation to students' approaches to academic writing and use of sources in their academic work.

In early planning meetings, we distributed the workload to allow each person to contribute to an integral part of the workshop, whilst ensuring that work was not duplicated. The content and structure of the workshop were then devised and delivered as a whole group.

From Ivy to Helen & John

The premise of the workshop was inspired by an imaginative narrative about the life of Ivy Williams, written by Professor Matthew Weait, former Dean of the Faculty of Humanities and Social Sciences at the University of Portsmouth. Set at the end of her life, *Imagining Ivy Williams* (Weait, n.d.) presents Ivy reflecting on her life and reminiscing about her numerous achievements. The details woven into Weait's narrative were gathered from sources including photographs, personal correspondence and official documents such as Ivy's last Will and Testament, and referenced via footnotes throughout. At the start of *Bringing Research to Life*, students were given a page from *Imagining Ivy Williams* and asked to comment on what could be learnt about Ivy, and to identify the source of the information. This presented students with an example of the type of personal narrative that we aimed to create later in the session.

In the workshop, students were given the choice of researching one of six people, each of whom had a connection to Portsmouth or the wider local area and chosen also for the potential links to students' academic subject areas:

- Nancy Astor – the first woman in the UK to take her seat in the House of Commons
- Arthur Conan Doyle – goalkeeper for Portsmouth Association Football Club
- Helen Duncan – last person to be imprisoned under the Witchcraft Act 1735
- Katharine Furse – director of the Women's Royal Naval Service
- John Jea – believed to have founded the first Black majority church in the UK
- John Pounds – inspired the creation of Ragged schools

In addition to helping students develop their research and teamwork skills, this activity would provide students with the opportunity to learn about the local area so as to enhance their sense of belonging within the civic and academic community.

We sited the workshop in the library, the heart of the University community, to entice students to use non-traditional materials and digital historical resources for their research. To facilitate the research phase of the workshop, we produced a resource pack in order to give students a starting point for their explorations. The range of sources suggested was based upon the librarian's professional experience and included primary source and newspaper archives, art, architecture and photographic resources, statistics, maps, government documents, legal resources, and paper book stock. The pack was made accessible to attendees via a shared Google document, with clickable links to the online resources.

The Workshop: Inter-disciplinary and Collaborative

Students from our respective faculties were invited to participate in the workshop and could undertake the research portion of the session individually, in pairs or in small groups. Then, for the storytelling element, groups were combined based on the characters chosen. This led to inter-disciplinary groups working towards a shared goal of creating a narrative through weaving together disparate pieces of information found by the group members. Group work allowed students to see how they had approached the task from different angles and gave them the opportunity to develop essential team working and communication skills (Carruthers, 2021).

During the students' discussions, we each worked with a group to help students find ways to incorporate the diverse information into a coherent creative text. For example, a student who researched Helen Duncan discovered where she lived and conducted her seances, and used the library's Special Collections Map Library to find a map of this area during the time that Helen occupied the property. The map revealed that a school was in the same area, which was then incorporated into a narrative where Helen could hear the school children playing in the playground whilst she was preparing for a seance.

The narratives that students created were presented to the rest of the group, creating a sort of feedback loop of exchange. The stories presented ranged from bullet-pointed lists and spider diagrams, to full prose. In each case, we encouraged students to include appropriate references and to explain the range of sources that had been generated by their research and harnessed in their creative stories.

And in the End …

In hindsight, it is apparent that clearer direction during the story creation phase would be helpful. At first, students tended to report information rather than create a narrative that included details. Therefore, in future it could be helpful to suggest a specific moment in the subject's life as a starting point and provide students with a narrative structure.

However, we successfully managed to apply the 4 Ps to our workshop setting. The historical personalities formed the initial hook, created interest and were linked to our locality, Portsmouth. The participants found out key information and put together a creative plot that they presented. Overall, the workshop served a strong purpose of bringing students together in a powerful place to enhance their research skills and introduce them to a plethora of resources valuable for their future academic work. It also brought us, as a team, closer together.

Epilogue

Our collaboration not only brought together colleagues from different faculties but also utilized the knowledge base of our academic librarians. Creating this workshop has broadened the practitioners' knowledge base by working with colleagues and across areas of the institution that were previously unfamiliar. Through participating in this project, we have developed a clearer understanding of each other's role in supporting students, as well as forming new and closer working relationships, which places us in a good position to identify and pursue further inter-faculty collaboration opportunities.

We believe that the key to a successful collaboration is to work with colleagues who share a common interest. Our commitment to using storytelling in our work will continue, with the development of a workshop where students will use items from the Library's Special Collections to reflect on their experience as members of their academic and civic communities. It is hoped that this will help students to cultivate a sense of belonging to both these communities. We are looking forward to the next chapter of using storytelling in our diverse roles to strengthen the support of student learning.

Approaching Blended Learning through Teaching Team Collaboration: Lessons from an AU Postgraduate Accounting Programme

Katherine Herbert, Julia Lynch and Humayun Murshed

- This study showcases the importance of a collaborative approach within teaching teams to successfully engage with both domestic and international students to create a holistic learning experience for all.
- The subject teaching teams, like any team-based collaborative group, are a prime example of the challenges of balancing cohesion of ideas and experiences based on the varying levels of teaching and industry experiences within the team.
- The teaching approach taken and the integration of the learning resources developed helped build blended learning experiences that fostered self-directed learning.

Introduction

The focus of this case study is the intentional collaborative practices in teams teaching across multiple locations, in blended mode and with a largely international cohort (Ali et al., 2015; Heng, 2019; Huang & Turner, 2018; McKenzie et al., 2020). This study is an example of how this context is being addressed in a postgraduate programme at an AU university.

Our investigation looked closely at subject teaching teams whose team members teach in multiple locations, working together in terms of subject knowledge and classroom delivery. The questions addressed were:

1. What insights can be drawn from the collaborative nature of the teaching teams to better understand the community of learning practice that exists in the international on-campus cohorts?
2. How can these insights inform the blended learning design that includes spaces and opportunities to ease international students into their new learning context?

The Programme

Developed to satisfy the academic requirements of the professional accounting bodies in AU and NZ, the Masters of Professional Accounting (MPA) is an accredited programme that allows students to transition into the profession from either a non-accounting undergraduate qualification or an overseas accounting degree not recognized in AU or NZ. As such, international students were primarily enrolled into this programme. At our university, the programmes are run across seven campuses spread across three states. The subjects consist of fundamental accounting principles, compliance and regulatory knowledge, as well as industry-specific skills. These subjects are delivered both online and on campus, with subject materials designed to cater to both modes of delivery. All subject materials are provided through the university's LMS, Blackboard.

In 2018, the internal course review identified areas of the programme needing improvements focused on the need to deliver subject content that optimized development of subject knowledge and skills. It also sought to enhance learning experiences by motivating on-campus students to effectively and efficiently use both online and classroom spaces. Furthermore, it was necessary to address students whose first language was not English, to create inclusive learning that eases international students' transition into a new learning environment and satisfies the accreditation requirements for the profession. Therefore, the teams teaching the programme collaborated to design successful blended learning experiences across the subjects that made up the programme.

The Subject Teaching Teams

The programme consists of twelve subjects and therefore twelve subject teaching teams were involved in designing and delivering the learning. Each team in this programme was made up of two to five members drawn from academics from multiple campuses.

In our institution, there is a minimum expectation of engagement and communication within subject teaching teams. The lead teaching academic, the Subject Convenor (SC), coordinates the teams, the learning activities, resources and topics to be covered in the subject. Sessional staff are then brought in based on location and number of students. While the make-up of the subject teaching teams appears transitory, the reality is many of the sessional teaching staff have taught at the university for quite some time and have an established working relationship with each other.

The decision was made that the challenges faced by the students enrolled in this programme would benefit from a disruption of this hierarchical pyramid, to draw on the voices and expertise of the many experienced practitioners involved. Whereas previously, the SC would take a lead role, here they were encouraged to become more of a facilitator, initiating discussion and conversation – bringing teams together to discuss the overall programme and subject design. A more collaborative work ethic and practice developed through which authentic steps towards implementing the design would be intentional and cooperative. A more holistic picture of the strengths and needs of the students emerged alongside the surfacing of opportunities for effective blended learning.

Team members are made up of transnational academics with various teaching and industry experiences in AU and overseas. In most cases, the academics who teach in the programme are graduates from the programme itself; have come from non-English speaking backgrounds; and have worked in accounting and finance in AU and overseas. The diverse make-up of the subject teaching teams afforded us the opportunities to utilize multiple perspectives, particularly from those, in the city-based campuses, who teach international students on campus.

The Learners

Students enrolled in this programme predominantly came from Asian countries with English as a second language. English as the teaching language was not the only hurdle in transitioning into an AU university and PG programme where the terminology used for the accounting profession in AU and NZ varied significantly to those used in the students' home countries. Students from this demographic typically prefer to have structured guidance and instructor-led information that feeds into assessments, and may need further encouragement to engage in self-directed learning. At the same time, all students need additional motivation – an understanding of 'what's-in-it-for-me' – to engage actively with subject content and resources, online and in class (Heng, 2019). This often poses challenges in motivating students to apply the principles of critical thinking and self-directed learning in their learning process. It was important that the subject design addressed this.

Therefore, two key challenges faced the teaching teams in this programme. The first one was to enable international students to transition into the AU university context due to the language barrier and a sense of not belonging (Ali et al., 2015; Huang & Turner, 2018). Second, there was evidence that students were not actively engaging with subject materials and self-directed learning activities unless directly covered in the synchronous classroom arena online or on campus. This phenomenon has been found in other universities across the globe especially where students are accustomed to coming to class and expect an expert to stand in front of the classroom delivering information (Heng, 2019).

To address these issues, the teaching teams developed a blended learning project.

The Blended Learning Project

Blended learning generally refers to the delivery of learning through a combination of online and face-to-face (Castro, 2019) teaching and materials. Furthermore, blended learning has come to encompass high-impact quality learning and teaching practices through intentional design of learning experiences (McKenzie et al., 2020; Prion & Mitchell, 2018). A three-phase strategy was developed under the Blended Learning Project to harness the multiple perspectives of the subject teaching teams to enhance student learning and engagement. The project aimed to capture in three phases:

1. insights from the subject teaching teams to understand the community of learning practice that exists among on campus students;
2. strategically designed online resources and tools that will remove on-campus (both domestic and international) students' resistance to completing self-directed learning activities; and
3. opportunities for international students to ease into and transition successfully into the AU HE context.

The Collaborative Teaching Model

Teaching in HE provides many opportunities for collaboration (Walsh & Kahn, 2009). In our case, we acknowledged that a more collaborative teaching model and a more direct collaboration within the teaching teams were important and therefore co-working and co-creation would be intentionally built into this project.

The key to seeing any success in Phase One of the project was to harness the experiences and knowledge of the members of the subject teaching teams who already had a process of reflecting on and discussing preparations for their subjects' next delivery. We decided to build on this process. As part of the course review tasks and actions, we organized focus group discussions on each campus, acknowledging that expertise and experience reside implicitly within individuals (Walsh & Kahn, 2009). These spaces were our opportunity to capture the expertise and experiences explicitly by gathering all teaching team members to discuss the course review outcomes and expected actions. Each member was asked to share their experiences, and report on strategies that worked and did not work. The responses collated provided us with key themes and points about subject delivery feedback, as well as online resources design and use in multiple delivery modes. The result of this was the development of a whole programme approach which focused on strategic use of online resources and tools that complemented on-campus, synchronous classes.

In Phase Two of the project, the subjects first encountered by all students in their first year on the programme would incorporate more fundamental learning experiences, while the succeeding subjects would then build students confidence with self-directed learning and application of skills through workshop-type learning activities. The first four subjects studied incorporated induction activities, such as the exploration of the Blackboard space, signposted as activities to engage with before on-campus or online meetings would occur. To encourage participation, students were provided with online access to their textbooks for free. It was revealed during the focus group discussion that many international students would not purchase the textbook due to cost. User analytics for eBook access showed that this intervention led to high numbers of downloads, with students showing evidence of engaging with readings prior to coming to class.

In Phase Three of the project, learning activities were deliberately designed to explicitly guide students' learning in-class and online. Each resource and learning activity were embedded in each subject based on the characteristic of the content and the context of our learners, so that students had a purpose for engaging with the resource. It was explicitly explained to students that resources provided could be accessed at any time, and multiple times which sought to encourage them to learn outside the scheduled classes. This enabled a blended learning experience where online and face-to-face content were integrated and complemented each other.

Outcomes

While we accepted that the students might have been expecting to have an expert 'talk at them', we needed the subject teaching teams to reinforce the students' role in their own learning. We achieved this by removing unambiguous content, clear signposting and directions with respect to readings, resources and activities which needed to be engaged with before the next class (Prion & Mitchell, 2018). This was reinforced by teaching team members through online discussion boards and announcements.

In the synchronous classes, whether in online meetings or on-campus classes, workshop activities were actively promoted and integrated. Students would work together on problems based on their readings and asynchronous activities. These would then be discussed with the 'expert' to satisfy those students that wished for more teacher-led input. Thereby, we did not completely remove the expectation that the teaching academic is the expert, but we provided opportunities for students unfamiliar with this more dialogic type of learning to see how they can build their self-directed learning skills. Taking a more collaborative teaching approach and with a renewed focus on the blended learning experience with a consistent message across the programme enabled students together to take advantage of self-directed learning.

Conclusion

Many students fail to see 'the point' of self-directed learning, due to various educational and cultural experiences and expectations. Studies in the UK (Huang & Turner, 2018) and in the United States (Heng, 2019) point particularly to the cultural context of learning for students who come from more transmissive systems as the main reason international students find it challenging to transition into Western or English universities. We chose to address these interlinked challenges collaboratively and creatively.

The subject teaching teams, like any team-based collaborative group, are a prime example of the challenges of balancing cohesion of ideas and experiences based on the varying levels of teaching and industry experiences within the team. This balancing act is essential to achieving a unified and fulfilled teaching team, creating a coherent and purposive learning experience for students who can equitably engage with the learning activities on offer (Minett-Smith & Davis, 2020). In our case, the coming together of the different teams and joint approach to redesign the programme led to a more integrated learning experience for students.

Recommendations for Practice

This case study showcases the power of collaborating to design a blended learning model which encouraged students, who perhaps do not position themselves as agents in their own learning, to engage in self-directed learning as part of a holistic curriculum designed to aid transition into and through a professional course and a Western university. Our unified approach encouraged students to see the purpose of those blended activities and thus also facilitated a change in mindset, so that students started to see the teaching academic move from 'expert' to 'facilitator'. Future work in this area would be in moving towards students becoming active partners in, and co-constructors of, their learning, building on the opportunities to collaborate with the facilitator-teaching academics.

Developing Twenty-first-century Skills through Meaningful Cross-institutional Collaborative International Community Service Projects

Pranit Anand and Byron Tsz Kit Lui

- This case study shares a collaborative learning activity that was developed between two institutions in AU and HK.
- The group work involved students from AU and HK working together on social projects for NGOs located in a third country.
- The case study highlights challenges and makes suggestions for other educators interested in developing similar initiatives such as addressing the differences that exist between educators, students and institutions across social, cultural, linguistic and geographic boundaries.
- Based on our experience and research, we suggest identifying collaborative institutional partners with similar intent, and being flexible to accommodate differences in timelines, expectations, assessment protocols and compliance requirements.

Background and Context

Collaboration, teamwork and intercultural competencies are widely accepted as important twenty-first-century transformative skills (Martin, 2018; OECD, 2018) and group work is acknowledged as an important part of HE pedagogy. However, designing group work activities in HE that engage and motivate can be challenging. Common challenges identified by both students and educators around group work involve 'free-riding', unequal allocation of workloads, lack of leadership and dominating group members (Davies, 2009; Jaques, 2007; Robinson, 2013). Group work activities become even more complicated when the classes include diverse cultural groups with significant differences in expectations, familiarity with language and other academic conventions and influences (Davies, 2009). These challenges are compounded even further when group work involves assessment. These differences can lead to unwanted consequences such as resistance and non-cooperation to withdrawing from HE altogether.

However, the issue is not just that students resist group work and group assignments. Assessment processes in HE tend to be very 'dualistic' (Crawford et al., 2020), that is, they tend to favour certain rational, individualistic and disembodied ways of thinking that in themselves mitigate against peer-to-peer learning. Universities typically have very strict policies and procedures around assessments, often as a requirement from external accreditation bodies (Dawson, et al., 2013), leaving little room for innovations particularly around cross-institutional collaborative assessments. Furthermore, most assessments tend to focus on very specific learning outcomes with little emphasis on developing the whole student within a globalized workplace (Clifford & Montgomery, 2017). Consequently, many university students do not get the opportunity that group work can provide to engage with diverse ideas and challenges, and ways of solving these challenges through intercultural interactions.

This case study presents the outcomes of a cross-institutional collaborative international community service project that aimed to help students gain real-world experience working with social service organizations and appreciate the challenges of working across social, cultural, linguistic and geographically dispersed groups.

Cross-institutional Collaborative Learning Activity

A collaborative 'assessment for learning' activity was developed between UOW College AU and the Community College of the City University of HK (now UOW College HK). Students from each of the institutions, located in AU and HK, respectively, were brought together to form transnational groups tasked to work together to identify, develop and deploy a social media solution (e.g. increase audience participation) for an NGO located in a third country. The separate geographical locations of the group members and the NGO that they worked for, as well as the task of working with a 'real' organization, provided students with a challenging yet authentic learning experience as they had to negotiate various spatial, technological, cultural, communicative, creative and linguistic challenges while developing a real-life solution for a real 'client'.

The students collaborated with each other across time and space to identify an NGO that they could support. One member of each group was required to contact the organization to discuss their needs and requirements and articulate a 'brief'. The group then worked on the problem presented by the NGO and divided the workload among themselves to complete the task. Although the types of tasks that students worked on were diverse between groups, typical things would involve developing social media strategies and the mock-up sites, marketing and promotional plans, etc. The final solution was then submitted to the NGO for approval, deployment and handover. All this was done using relevant communication technologies negotiated between the students and the NGO.

Each group submitted a portfolio of their work to their host institution, i.e. HK students to their tutors in HK and AU students to their tutors in AU for evaluation. This portfolio included annotations of all their work, all communications between the students, the work submitted to the organization and a link to the outputs they created, feedback from the organization and a comprehensive personal reflection about their engagement in this activity including challenges and learnings. As part of the submissions students also had to do an in-class presentation explaining their work, and students from AU and HK had to participate, either via a live stream or (as it occurred more often) as a pre-recorded video as part of the presentation. That is, students from HK recorded a video for their group members in AU to use in their presentation in AU and vice versa.

The students' portfolios were marked using a set of common criteria such as:

- relevance and appropriateness of communication tools used;
- collaborative endeavour;
- identification of relevant information needed to solve real-life problem;
- evaluation and analysis of information obtained; and
- presentation of information to NGO and within portfolio.

Evaluation Voices

The feedback from the NGOs was extremely positive and shown in the sentiments in the following statement:

> Dear <group>, I want you to know how grateful I am for your devotion to our project, especially our media sites and fanpage. It is good to find such kind volunteers, and your dedication and hard work are greatly appreciated.
> (NGO located in Vietnam)

Similarly, the students enjoyed the opportunity to work with students from a different country and valued the experience. Many of their sentiments are reflected in the following statement:

> It is a pleasure for us to work with an overseas student. He (student name) helped us a lot in doing our project. The most interesting thing is that he can already share his work related to the NGO with us and we include his work in our report as well. His work is quite effective and useful for us which shows that our group members are hardworking and responsible students. We are very thankful to him for helping us a lot.
>
> (Student from HK)

Overall, the collaboration was deemed a success, with positive feedback from all those involved; yet, some challenges were encountered along the way.

Challenges Encountered

Authentic, collaborative cross-institutional projects, especially ones that involve students located in different countries, are uncommon within HE. Projects that also require students to work with external NGOs on real-life problems are even more rare. There were two main categories of challenges encountered in this project: first were the challenges that the educators faced while designing the learning activity across the two institutions, and second, the challenges the students had to face while engaging in the learning experience.

For the educators the major challenge was the fact that the two cohorts of students from the different institutions were studying two different courses. The educators needed to work and communicate well among themselves to refine the common elements of the two courses to let both students from AU and HK fully achieve the expected learning outcomes.

Due to the nature of this project there were some expected challenges for students, for example, working productively and harmoniously within their cross-cultural, cross-national teams to meet a real client brief. However, the depth and breadth of the students' work revealed that providing such authentic group work experiences actually negated some of the more 'usual' problems – the resistance, the complaints, the stress. Further, there were challenges that could not be predicted, but this was all part of giving students as much authentic experience as possible within a safe, structured learning environment.

Recommendations

For other educators interested in designing similar collaborative, cross-cultural learning experiences for their students, it would be recommended to find partner institutions and educators with similar ideas and goals. The educators involved need to develop close working relationships and 'calibrate' their thinking and expectations well before the task is presented to the students and explore any potential challenges that may arise. In our case we used Google Docs to share all important files and worked on those together, synchronously and asynchronously. All discussions were conducted via phone and emails, and issues addressed in a collegial way.

Significantly both parties should be willing to be flexible in their approaches and willing to make changes to suit the schedules of other parties. In our experience these included negotiating start and end dates between AU and HK as the semester start and end dates were very different. Both educators had to make changes to their assessment schedules to ensure start and end times were somewhat aligned, and also ensure their students had ample time to prepare for the project as they worked across their different time zones and programme schedules.

Further, there also had to be negotiation around the assessments and common marking criteria. In our experience it worked well to have some important common criteria, but also provide flexibility to the individual institutions to expect certain things from their own students based on local curriculum and policy requirements.

Conclusion

Projects of this nature are challenging to get off the ground. In the first instance, identifying institutional partners who are willing to collaborate on cross-institutional projects for students can be challenging. Also, getting both parties to agree on common goals and criteria requires a significant amount of flexibility, understanding and cooperation. In many ways, once the teaching team is able to demonstrate these qualities, it becomes easier to transfer these experiences to the students.

The activity enabled students to be involved in the design of the activity, deciding the different roles of the group members, the types of communication tools and channels they preferred to use, the organization they wanted to work with, and then all the processes involved in the negotiation of the task and the decisions as to what the solutions should be. Engaging in this project the students collaborated together to identify needs and provide solutions: a social media strategy which the NGO can continue to use long after the students have completed their projects with them.

This rich collaboration obviously develops students' ability to communicate and negotiate across cultures; it involves them in authentic, collaborative project management; it builds confidence to undertake challenging tasks, with significantly nuanced appreciation of diverse ways of thinking and doing things. Students have also reported building life-long friendships with students from different countries. Many of the processes that students engage with through these cross-institutional, international projects help them develop many of the OECD (Martin, 2018; OECD, 2018) identified twenty-first-century skills.

Cross-disciplinary Collaborations for Sustainable Futures, and a Vital and Relevant Academic Community

Diana J. Pritchard, Helen Connolly, Amanda Egbe, Mohamed Saeudy, Paul Rowinski, James Bishop, Tamara Ashley and Nicholas Worsfold

- A cross-disciplinary group of academics joined forces to design opportunities to engage students in understanding and addressing locally relevant environmental, economic and social challenges.
- Our model can develop the relevant skills, knowledge and values that universities must foster if they are to prepare students for fast changing communities and workplaces, while supporting the communities they serve to transition towards sustainable futures.
- We harnessed our creativity in our autonomous 'community of practice' to organize university-wide events that comprise holistic, experiential and interactive pedagogical approaches.
- We created rich 'social learning' environments for students enhanced by the inclusion of municipal, community and business representatives who shared their expertise and created community-based learning.
- Through evaluation using complementary tools and methods we evidenced the impacts of the events, generating buy-in and resulting in the strategic adoption of our model.

Introduction

The challenges of our rapidly changing climate, environments, cultures, populations and labour markets require HE to 'recognise, own, and engage with the most difficult and intractable issues of our times' (Sterling, 2019, 61; Pritchard, forthcoming). This contrasts with prevailing practices that typically perpetuate paradigms of individualism, inequalities and unsustainability and the exploitation of the environment and people (Tilbury, 2011; Wals, 2015).

Reflecting the distilled features promoted by advocates for education for sustainability, UNESCO (2020) calls for provision that is *holistic, envisions change and achieves transformation* while *building solidarity*. This case study highlights how such education provision can be created and become embedded through staff-led, informal collaborations of a multi-disciplinary group operating outside formal governance structures. Our group, the Sustainability Forum (SF), is based at an English university and eight of us have contributed text or ideas which are reflected in this chapter.

We hope to contribute to discussions on collaboration by demonstrating the significance of cross-disciplinarity, respect for autonomous academic spaces, and the involvement of external organizations to achieve transformative outcomes that engage students, staff and communities in change.

Our SF practices take place at the University of Bedfordshire which is a WP and regional university and is characterized by a high proportion of students who are the first in the family to go to university, are mature and work part-time, while 60 per cent students are from Black, Asian and minoritorized ethnic groups.

Our Sustainability Forum

At our teaching-led institution, a group of us sharing concerns for climate chaos, environmental degradation, social injustice, human rights violations and conflict came together informally, across four faculties, to establish the SF in 2014. We are based in Performance, Art and Design, Media, Sociology, Biology, Sports Science, Business, Accounting and Construction and in professional services. The SF has included between twelve and fifteen academics (numbers fluctuating over the years), at different levels of seniority. Crucially, there is no formalized membership: we each define our degree of involvement.

By connecting with like-minded colleagues, we created a 'domain of interest' (Wenger, 1998) and overcame our isolation in our respective departments. We became energized socially and intellectually. Our early decision that the SF's primary aim would be to engage students in learning about sustainably galvanized us across the discipline spectrum. Specifically, we agreed to organize day-long university-wide events that focus on local manifestations of key global challenges. We have run these since 2016 and in this case study describe our ongoing and voluntary dedication to develop student learning.

Pooling Efforts to Hold Community-based Learning Events on Campus

For each event we selected a theme in which we have collective expertise, namely climate change, human rights and migration, peace and justice, and health and well-being, with a view to model practices which advance not just education *about* sustainability, but education *for* sustainability. This requires facilitating student learning about changes in the real world, developing their agency to identify creative solutions to problems and effecting changes in themselves and the wider world.

We achieved this by stirring our creativity and drawing on our pedagogic experience to design and pilot at the events a series of dynamic and immersive learning activities, underpinned by the concept of 'horizontal learning' (Freire, 2005) characterized by student partnership and co-creation. We included simulations, role-play and workshops which were delivered in plenary or parallel sessions to deliver curriculum, to identify project and community action projects and create networking opportunities.

Importantly, we pooled our contacts to invite representatives of relevant community, civic and business organizations to these events, effectively rendering our events 'mass-learn-ins' whereby everyone learnt from each other. These practitioners shared their experiences and perspectives, generating information of value for the curriculum and as topics for authentic student projects, assessments or research. This also created rich 'social learning' environments and, more specifically, a variation of 'community-based learning'. Elsewhere such approaches have been demonstrated to develop academic learning and competences relevant for sustainability and the twenty-first century (Kuh, 2008; Wals, 2012).

While our events primarily served the students of SF members, we encouraged participation by students and staff from the wider institution. Our events have involved up to 200 people each time. Working alone, none of us individually could have achieved this scale of event, nor felt able to be so innovative or risk-taking: together, responsibility is spread.

Our Holistic Approach to Enhance Sustainability

The epistemological diversity represented in our SF enabled us to foster understandings of interrelated social, environmental and economic complexity. Consequently, our events were essentially holistic, nurturing learning – for students, staff and other participants – which is more than the sum of individual disciplines. Integrating disciplinary perspectives creates new transdisciplinary understandings of and responses to complex issues.

For example, at the event on modern-day slavery, the combination of students and staff from social sciences, media and construction led to wider understanding of potential violations of human rights on construction projects. This resulted in the expansion of awareness of project ethics as a core aspect of the taught curriculum. Likewise, we co-taught some sessions, for example, combining Biology and Sociology students to learn about the multiple and interrelated consequences of climate change for migration: both human and non-human. Further, we used our event spaces to exhibit work prepared by Art and Design students and showcase performances and media productions.

We curated all our events to envision change by offering presentations on historical trends. With a view to nurture competences that enable students to take action in the creation of alternative futures, we were able to harness academic, civic and practitioner expertise to provide background knowledge and understandings of past, present and projected future changes such as relating to increases in global temperatures or forced migration flows.

The heterogeneity of our event participants also served to lay the foundations for students to 'deal critically and creatively with reality and discover how to participate in the transformation of their world' (Freire, 2000, 34). Specifically, this mix served to leverage collective intelligence in the co-construction of sense-making of the challenges and the identification of feasible actions to address local problems (Markova, 2015). It also inspired change and increased the probability, as indicated elsewhere by research, that the solutions identified will be followed through with tangible change-making action (Peter & Wals, 2013).

We also created the contexts to enable students to identify where they can contribute through projects, research or voluntary work, or what authentic assessments academics could set by examining existing strategies and plans at different levels, such as the UN Sustainable Development Goals, relevant civic strategies or campaigns of local NGOs.

Collaborative Evaluations and Research

Although the principal activity of our SF was the organization of these events, our collaborations have extended, as represented in Figure 3.2, to include the evaluations of the short- and long-term impacts and outcomes of our events. We have captured these from digital feedback during the events, follow-up student and staff surveys, detailed analysis of student grades, interviews with students, including upon their graduation, and audits of course and module enhancements.

Figure 3.2 The scope of the SF: Key partners, activities and impacts.

Findings: Achieving Education Transformations

Our results suggest the ways in which our events comprised transformative education for students (Mezirow, 1991). Many reported on the intense nature of the learning experience, one stating that 'this is the most [she had] ever had to think in [her] life!' on account of being required to engage with complexity, shift from being a passive to an active learner and gain new perspectives.

Students enthusiastically reported that their subjects 'came alive', while academics noted in our survey (Figure 3.3) that their students became more engaged in their studies, took increased ownership of them. Students also pursued activities of direct relevance to their degrees, future careers, gaining (and following up) tangible ideas for applied research projects or placements which reflect their inspiration to become

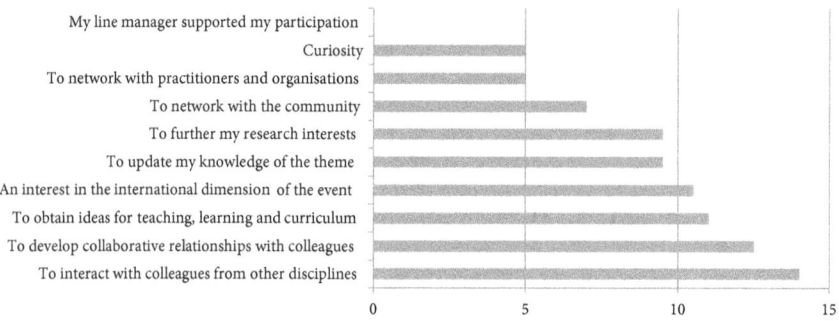

Figure 3.3 Academic observations of the impacts of SF events on students. The x-axis represents the number of responses of academic staff reporting each factor.

part of the solution. Academics also observed that students gained in confidence: a fundamental aspect of empowerment and a consequence of the social mix and ethos of co-production where students acknowledge that they were 'treated as equals when offering [their] ideas'. Importantly, students and staff reported they had 'serious fun' at the events, despite the weight of the existential threats that the events focused on and felt part of a vital community of learning.

As for academic staff, they both were motivated to attend the event and appreciated them because they facilitated connecting with colleagues from other subject areas, developing collaborative relationships and networking with external organizations (Figures 3.4 and 3.5).

Our events, as collective endeavours, recover for academics what Holmwood et al. (2016) identify as their loss of autonomy and collective influence over the direction of universities. The same staff survey also revealed longer-term education changes they had made, including curriculum changes, in at least twenty courses. This resulted in academics incorporating event themes and materials into modules, the design of authentic assessments and the creation of new modules.

This well-evidenced success was recognized which shortlisted us for a nationally prestigious Award for Teaching Excellence 2017. Our evidenced impact also secured university executive buy-in: our 'grand challenge model', community-based pedagogies and professional development approaches have all been incorporated into the university's new education and sustainability strategies.

Conclusion

Our SF work demonstrates the powerful contributions that collaborative practices can make to authentic curricula and powerful student learning. Through unleashing creativity and solidarity, our SF generated learning fit for our time of rapid continuous change. It offers a transferable model of practice indicative of what real-world learning could look like to develop students' understanding and embed education for sustainability. For academics, such collaboration provides relief from the feeling of disempowerment and isolation that they increasingly experience (Fazackerley, 2019).

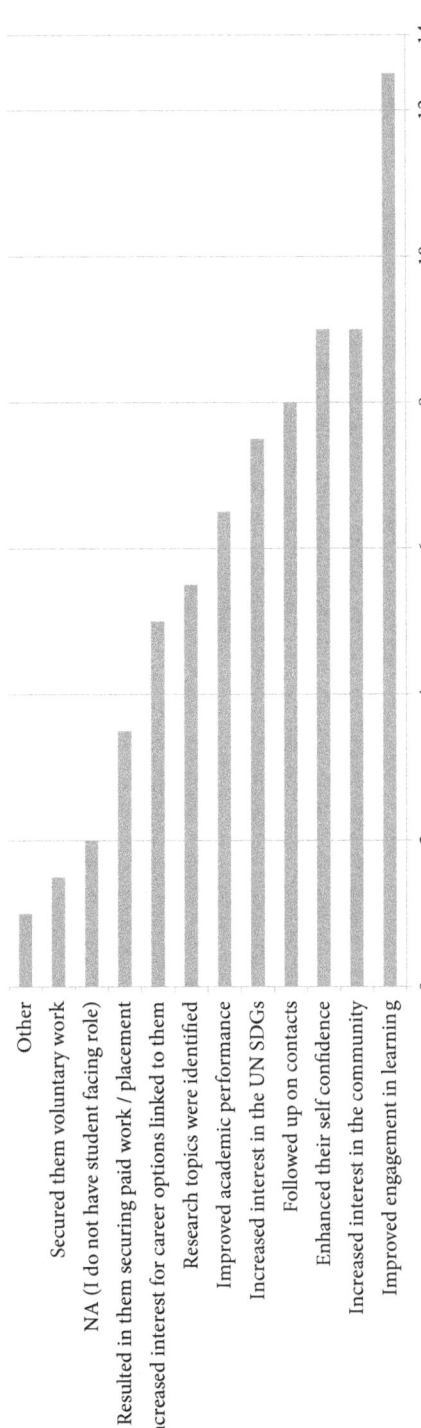

Figure 3.4 Motivation of academics to attend the SF events. The x-axis represents the number of responses from academic staff reporting because of each factor.

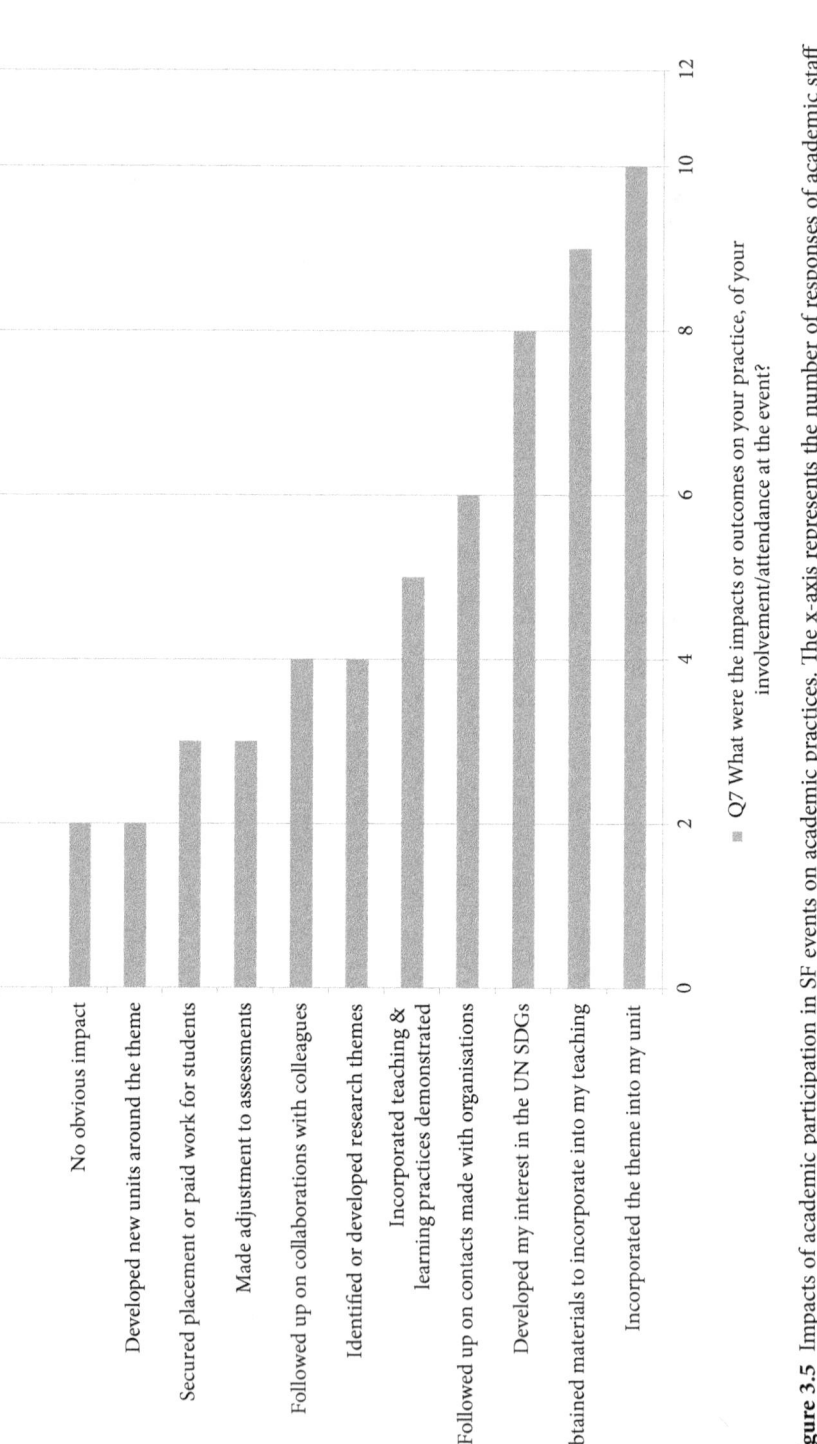

Figure 3.5 Impacts of academic participation in SF events on academic practices. The x-axis represents the number of responses of academic staff reporting each factor.

We consider our collaborative practices, a *hallmark* of a vital academic community, generating agency and contributing to the primary mission of HE: the social good, and – in the context of increasing crises – averting 'systemic global dysfunction' (Lotz-Sisitka et al., 2015). These collaborations also appear to relieve anxieties: there is something about being in a team where the burden of knowledge and creation of solutions are shared. Given the context of the Covid-19 pandemic and the Black Lives Matter movement, which spotlight the importance of relational well-being facilitated by such staff-student and collegial interactions (Singh, 2020), this approach gains even greater significance.

Although our work has had strategic impacts at our university, such collaborative practices and education for sustainability remain marginal. Despite sector frameworks incorporating cross-disciplinarity and sustainability into standards and expectations for HE (QAA/Advance HE, 2021), it retains subject silos and perpetuates administrative and bureaucratic systems that reward singular individual outcomes and curtail pedagogical transformations. The support, celebration and reward for collaborative practices have never been so urgent.

References

Introduction

Bingham, C., & Sidorking, A. M. (Eds.) (2004). *No education without relation.* Peter Lang.

Freire, P. (1998). *Pedagogy of freedom: Ethics, democracy and civic courage.* Rowman & Littlefield.

Freire, P. (2007). *Pedagogy of the oppressed.* Continuum.

Hall, R. (2018). *The alienated academic: The struggle for autonomy inside the university.* Palgrave MacMillan.

Hall, R. (2021). *The hopeless university: Intellectual work at the end of the end of history.* MayFly Books.

Lave, J., & Wenger, E. (1991). *Situated learning: Legitimate peripheral participation.* Cambridge University Press.

Case Study: Writing Retreats in Social Work

Alexander, R. (2010). *Dialogic teaching essentials* [lecture]. University of Cambridge. www.robinalexander.org.uk/dialogicteaching.htm

Bakhtin, M. M. (1999). *Problems of Dostoevsky's poetics, Vol. 8.* University of Minnesota Press.

Bates, B. (2019). *Learning theories simplified* (2nd ed.). Sage.

Bellinger, A., & Kagawa, F. (2012). Learning beyond compliance. A comparative analysis of two cohorts undertaking a first year social work module. *Journal of Pedagogic Development, 2*(1), 40–50. https://www.beds.ac.uk/jpd/volume-2-issue-1/learning-beyond-compliance-a-comparative-analysis-of-two-cohorts-undertaking-a-first-year-social-work-module/

British Association of Social Work (2020). *Professional capabilities framework: Critical reflection and analysis*. BASW. https://www.basw.co.uk/professional-development/professional-capabilities-framework-pcf/the-pcf/social-worker/critical-reflection-and-analysis

Gilbert, T. (2017). When looking is allowed: What compassionate group work looks like in a UK university. In P. Gibbs (Ed.), *The pedagogy of compassion at the heart of higher education* (pp. 189–202). Springer International Publishing.

Jordan, B., & Jordan, C. (2000). *Social work and the third way: Tough love and social policy*. Sage.

Knight, P., & Yorke, M. (2003). *Learning, curriculum and employability in higher education* (1st ed.). Routledge. DOI: 10.4324/9780203465271

Lishman, J. (2018). *Social work: An introduction*. Sage.

Maclachlan, K. (2007). Learning for democracy in undemocratic places: Reflections from within Higher Education. *Concept, 17*(3), 8–12. https://www.i-develop-cld.org.uk/pluginfile.php/4419/mod_folder/content/0/Covers%20and%20Appendices/R-Z/The%20Edinburgh%20Papers.pdf?forcedownload=1

Mantell, A., & Scragg, T. (2018). *Reflective practice in social work* (Transforming Social Work Practice Series). Sage.

Millwood, R. (2013). *A new learning landscape: Learning theory* [blog]. Richard Millwood. https://blog.richardmillwood.net/2013/05/10/learning-theory/

Rogers, C., & Frieberg, H. J. (1994). *The freedom to learn* (3rd ed.). Prentice-Hall Publishing.

Shor, I., & Freire, P. (1987). What is the dialogical method of teaching? *Journal of Education, 169*(3), 11–31. DOI 10.1177/002205748716900303

Social Work England (2020). *Home*. https://www.socialworkengland.org.uk/

Smith, M. K. (2002, 2009). *Facilitating learning and change in groups' in the encyclopaedia of informal education*. www.infed.org/mobi/facilitating-learning-and-change-ingroups-and-group-sessions/

Stewart, T. T., & McClure, G. (2013). Freire, Bahktin, and collaborative pedagogy: A dialogue with students and mentors. *The International Journal for Dialogical Science, 7*(1), 91–108. https://ijds.lemoyne.edu/journal/7_1/IJDS.7.1.08.Stewart_McClure.html

Tedam, P. (2021). *Reflecting for action: Why it's time to take anti-racist practice seriously in social work education and practice* [presentation]. https://www.socialworkengland.org.uk/social-work-week/social-work-week-programme/keynote-speakers/why-it-s-time-to-take-anti-racist-practice-seriously-in-social-work-education-and-practice/

Thompson, N. (2016). *Anti-discriminatory practice: Equality, diversity and social justice* (Practical Social Work Series) (6th ed.). Palgrave Macmillan.

Thompson, S., & Thompson, N. (2018). *The critically reflective practitioner* (2nd ed.). Palgrave Macmillan.

Vygotsky, L. S. (1962). *Thought and language*. MIT Press.

Case Study: Collaboration for Academic Literacies Development

Abegglen, S., Burns, T., & Sinfield, S. (2021). *Supporting student writing and other modes of learning and assessment: A staff guide*. University of Calgary.

Carless, D., & Boud, D. (2018). The development of student feedback literacy: Enabling uptake of feedback. *Assessment & Evaluation in Higher Education, 43*(8), 1315–25. DOI: 10.1080/02602938.2018.1463354

Charlton, N., & Martin, A. (2018). Making the invisible visible. *Journal of Academic Language and Learning, 12*(1), A286–A300. https://journal.aall.org.au/index.php/jall/article/view/540

Devereux, L., Wilson, K., Kiley, A., & Gunawardena, M. (2018). The proof of the pudding ... analysing student written texts for evidence of a successful literacy intervention. *Journal of Academic Language and Learning, 12*(1), A239–A253. https://journal.aall.org.au/index.php/jall/article/view/525

Dixon, H., Hawe, E., & Hamilton, R. (2020). The case for using exemplars to develop academic self-efficacy. *Assessment & Evaluation in Higher Education, 45*(3), 460–71. DOI: 10.1080/02602938.2019.1666084

Hawe, E., Dixon, H., & Hamilton, R. (2021). Why and how educators use exemplars. *Journal of University Teaching & Learning Practice, 18*(3), 1–13. https://doi.org/ro.uow.edu.au/jutlp/vol18/iss3/010

Hendry, G. D., Bromberger, N., & Armstrong, S. (2011). Constructive guidance and feedback for learning: The usefulness of exemplars, marking sheets and different types of feedback in a first year law subject. *Assessment & Evaluation in Higher Education, 36*(1), 1–11. DOI: 10.1080/02602930903128904

Maldoni, A. M. (2018). 'Degrees of deception' to degrees of proficiency: Embedding academic literacies into the disciplines. *Journal of Academic Language and Learning, 12*(2), A102–A129. https://journal.aall.org.au/index.php/jall/article/view/408

Martin, J., & Rothery, J. (1993). Grammar: Making meaning in writing. In B. Cope, & M. Kalantzis (Eds.), *The powers of literacy: A genre approach to teaching writing* (pp. 137–53). University of Pittsburgh Press.

McWilliams, R., & Allan, Q. (2014). Embedding academic literacy skills: Towards a best practice model. *Journal of University Teaching and Learning Practice, 11*(3), 1–20. http://ro.uow.edu.au/jutlp/vol11/iss3/8

Purser, E. (2011). Developing academic literacy in context: Trends in Australia. In M. Deane, & P. O'Neill (Eds.), *Writing in the disciplines* (pp. 30–45). Macmillan International Higher Education.

Rose, D., & Martin, J. R. (2012). *Learning to write, reading to learn: Genre, knowledge and pedagogy in the Sydney School*. Equinox. [Swedish translation, 2013. Skriva, lära (Writing, reading, learning)]. Hallgren & Fallgren.

Swales, J. M. (1990). *Genre analysis: English in academic and research settings*. Cambridge University Press.

Wingate, U. (2018). Academic literacy across the curriculum: Towards a collaborative instructional approach. *Language Teaching, 51*(3), 349–64.

Case Study: Co-producing a Skills-based Programme

Eisen, M. J. (2000). Peer learning partnerships: Promoting reflective practice through reciprocal learning. *Inquiry: Critical Thinking across the Disciplines, 19*(3), 5–19. https://philpapers.org/rec/EISPLP-4

Guldberg, K. (2008). Adult learners and professional development: Peer-to-peer learning in a networked community. *International Journal of Lifelong Education, 27*(1), 35–49. DOI: 10.1080/02601370701803591

Harvey, M. (2013, September). *BLAAST report: Benching leadership and advancement of standards for sessional teaching – sessional staff standards framework*. Office for Learning and Teaching. http://blasst.edu.au/docs/BLASST_framework_WEB.pdf

Hitch, D., Mahoney, P., & Macfarlane, S. (2018). Professional development for sessional staff in higher education: A review of current evidence. *Higher Education Research & Development*, 37(2), 285–300. DOI: 10.1080/07294360.2017.1360844

Lave, J., & Wenger, E. (1991). *Situated learning: Legitimate peripheral participation*. Cambridge University Press. DOI: 10.1017/CBO9780511815355

Maroya, A., Matthewson, G., & Wallis, L. (2019, December). *Architectural education and the profession*. Architects Accreditation Council of Australia (AACA). https://www.aaca.org.au/wp-content/uploads/Architectural-Education-and-The-Profession-in-Australia-and-New-Zealand.pdf

Parker, P., Hall, D., & Kram, K. (2008). Peer coaching: A relational process for accelerating career learning. *Academy of Management Learning and Education*, 7(4), 487–503. DOI: 10.5465/AMLE.2008.35882189

Rice, M. (2004). Discomfort at the coalface: Issues for sessional tutors teaching in online enhanced learning environments. In R. Atkinson, C. McBeath, D. Jonas-Dwyer, & R. Phillips (Eds.), *Beyond the comfort zone: Proceedings of the 21st ASCILITE Conference* (pp. 798–801). ASCILITE. https://www.ascilite.org/conferences/perth04/procs/pdf/rice.pdf

Soccio, P., & Tregloan, K. (2022). *ABP teaching tips and tricks – images*. University of Melbourne. DOI 10.26188/19111634

Sutherland, K. (2002, July). *Maintaining quality in a diversifying environment: The challenges of support and training for part-time/sessional teaching staff* [conference paper]. Higher Education Research and Development Society of Australasia (HERDSA) Conference. Perth, Western Australia. http://citeseerx.ist.psu.edu/viewdoc/download?doi=10.1.1.126.5616&rep=rep1&type=pdf

Wenger, E. (2011). Social learning capacity. In A. Boddington, & J. Boys (Eds.), *Re-shaping learning: A critical reader: The future of learning spaces in post-compulsory education* (1st ed., pp. 193–210). Sense Publishers. https://brill.com/view/book/9789460916090/BP000016.xml

Case Study: Bringing Research to Life

Carruthers, R. (2021, September 6). Developing transferable skills as a university student. *Times Higher Education*. https://www.timeshighereducation.com/student/advice/developing-transferrable-skills-university-student?utm_source=newsletter&utm_medium=email&utm_campaign=student-newsletter&mc_cid=ad6a2a5778&mc_eid=eac0ef1cd0

Crookendale, C. M. (2020). The art school and the library: A case study exploring disciplinary differences. *Art Documentation: Journal of the Art Libraries Society of North America*, 39(1), 114–35. DOI: 10.1086/709816

Fox, R., Carpenter, C., & Doshi, A. (2011). Cool collaborations: Designing a better library experience. *College & Undergraduate Libraries*, 18(2–3), 213–27. DOI: 10.1080/10691316.2011.577699

Montgomery, S. E., & Miller, J. (2011). The third place: The library as collaborative and community space in a time of fiscal restraint. *College & Undergraduate Libraries*, 18(2–3), 228–38. DOI: 10.1080/10691316.2011.577683

Montiel-Overall, P. (2005). Toward a theory of collaboration for teachers and librarians. *School Library Media Research*, 8. https://files.eric.ed.gov/fulltext/EJ965627.pdf

Pham, H. T. (2019). The application of structuration theory in studying collaboration between librarians and academic staff in universities in Australia and Vietnam. *Information Research*, *24*(3). https://files.eric.ed.gov/fulltext/EJ1229378.pdf

Shah, T. (2008). *In Arabian nights: A caravan of Moroccan dreams*. Bantam.

Weait, M. (n.d.). *Imagining Ivy Williams*. https://www.academia.edu/169684/Imagining_Ivy_Williams

Case Study: Approaching Blended Learning through Teaching Team Collaboration

Ali, F., Zhou, Y., Hussain, K., Kumar Nair, P., & Ari Ragavan, N. (2015). Does higher education service quality effect student satisfaction, image and loyalty? A study of international students in Malaysian public universities. *Quality Assurance in Education*, *24*(1), 70–94. DOI: 10.1108/QAE-02-2014-0008

Castro, R. (2019). Blended learning in higher education: Trends and capabilities. *Education and Information Technologies*, *24*, 2523–46. DOI: 10.1007/s10639-019-09886-3

Heng, T. T. (2019). Understanding the heterogeneity of international students' experiences: A case study of Chinese international students in US universities. *Journal of Studies in International Education, 23*(5), 607–23. DOI: 10.1177/1028315319829880

Huang, R., & Turner, R. (2018). International experience, university support and graduate employability – perceptions of Chinese international students studying in UK universities. *Journal of Education and Work, 31*(2), 175–89. DOI: 10.1080/13639080.2018.1436751

McKenzie, S., Hains-Wesson, R., Bangay, S., & Bowtell, G. (2020). A team-teaching approach for blended learning: An experiment. *Studies in Higher Education*, 1–15. DOI: 10.1080/03075079.2020.1817887

Minett-Smith, C., & Davis, C. L. (2020). Widening the discourse on team-teaching in higher education. *Teaching in Higher Education, 25*(5), 579–94. DOI: 10.1080/13562517.2019.1577814

Prion, S., & Mitchell, M. (2018). Content considerations for blended learning experiences. In J. Keengwe (Ed.), *Handbook on research on blended learning pedagogies and professional development in higher education* (pp. 102–21). IGI Global. DOI: 10.4018/978-1-5225-5557-5.ch0006

Walsh, L., & Kahn, P. (2009). *Collaborative working in higher education: The social academy*. ProQuest Ebook Central.

Case Study: Developing Twenty-first-century Skills

Clifford, V., & Montgomery, C. (2017). Designing an internationalised curriculum for higher education: Embracing the local and the global citizen. *Higher Education Research & Development, 36*(6), 1138–51. DOI: 10.1080/07294360.2017.1296413

Crawford, N., Kift, S., & Jarvis, L. (2020). Supporting student mental wellbeing in enabling education. In A. Jones, A. Olds, & J. G. Lisciandro (Eds.), *Transitioning students in higher education: Philosophy, pedagogy and practice* (pp. 161–70). Routledge.

Davies, W. (2009). Groupwork as a form of assessment: Common problems and recommended solutions. *Higher Education, 58*(4), 563–84. DOI: 10.1007/s10734-009-9216-y

Dawson, P., Bearman, M., Boud, D. J., Hall, M., Molloy, E. K., Bennett, S., & Joughin, G. (2013). Assessment might dictate the curriculum, but what dictates assessment? *Teaching & Learning Inquiry: The ISSOTL Journal, 1*(1), 107–11. DOI: 10.20343/teachlearninqu.1.1.107

Jaques, D. (2007). *Learning in groups: A handbook for face-to-face and online environments* (4th ed.). Routledge.

Martin, J. (2018). *Skills for the 21st century: Findings and policy Lessons from the OECD survey of adult skills*. IDEAS Working Paper Series from RePEc.

OECD (2018). *The future of education and skills: Education 2030*. OECD. https://www.oecd.org/education/2030/E2030%20Position%20Paper%20(05.04.2018).pdf

Robinson, K. (2013). The interrelationship of emotion and cognition when students undertake collaborative group work online: An interdisciplinary approach. *Computers and Education, 62*, 298–307. DOI: 10.1016/j.compedu.2012.11.003

Case Study: Cross-disciplinary Collaborations for Sustainable Futures

Fazackerley, A. (2019, 21 May). 'It's cut-throat': Half of UK academics stressed and 40% thinking of leaving. *The Guardian*. https://www.theguardian.com/education/2019/may/21/cut-throat-half-academics-stressed-thinking-leaving

Freire, P. (2000). *Pedagogy of the oppressed* (30th anniversary ed.). Continuum.

Freire, P. (2005). *Education for critical consciousness*. Bloomsbury.

The Futures of Education Initiative (2022). Reimagining our futures together. *United Nations*, 1–158. United Nations. DOI: 10.18356/9789210012102c019

Holmwood, J., Hickey, T., Cohen, R., & Wallis, S. (2016). The Alternative white paper for higher education: In Defence of public higher education – knowledge for a successful society. Convention for Higher Education.

Kuh, G. (2008). *High impact education practices: What they are, who has access to them and why they matter*. Association of American Colleges and Universities. https://provost.tufts.edu/celt/files/High-Impact-Ed-Practices1.pdf

Lotz-Sisitka, H., Wals, A.E., Kronlid, D. & McGarry, D. (2015). Transformative, transgressive social learning: Rethinking higher education pedagogy in times of systemic global dysfunction. *Current Opinion in Environmental sustainability, 16*, 73–80.

Markova, D., & McArthur, A. (2015). *Collaborative intelligence: Thinking with people who think differently*. Random House.

Mezirow, J. (1991). *Transformative dimensions of adult learning*. Jossey-Bass.

Peter, S., & Wals, A. (2013). Learning and knowing in pursuit of sustainability: Concepts and tools for trans-disciplinary environmental research. In M. Krasny, & J. Dillon (Eds.), *Trading zones in environmental education: Creating trans-disciplinary dialogue* (pp. 79–104). Peter Lang.

Pritchard, D. (forthcoming). *Higher education practices for 21st century learning: A scoping review*. Foreign, Commonwealth and Development Office.

Pritchard, D. J., Connolly, H., Egbe, A., Saeudy, M., Rowinski, P., Bishop, J., Ashley, T., & Greenbank, A. (2021). *Multi-disciplinary event for community-based learning and action for the UN SDGs*. Advance HE/QAA. https://s3.eu.west2.amazonaws.com/assets.creode.advancehe-document- anager/documents/advance-he/AdvHE_QAA_ESD_practice_guide_Bedfordshire_Uni_1637679520

QAA/Advance HE (2021). *Education for sustainable development guidance: Executive summary*. The Quality Assurance Agency for Higher Education and Advance HE.

Singh, G. (2020, May 5). *Covid-19 does discriminate – so we should tackle its impact on BAME students*. WONKHE. https://wonkhe.com/blogs/covid-19-does-discriminate-so-we-should-tackle-its-impact-on-bame-students/

Sterling, S. (2019). Planetary primacy and the necessity of positive dis-illusion sustainability. *The Journal of Record, 12*(2), 60–6. DOI: 10.1089/sus.2019.29157

Tilbury, D. (2011). Higher education for sustainability: A global overview of commitment and progress. In Global University Network for Innovation (GUNI) (Ed.), *Higher education in the world 4 higher education's commitment to sustainability: From understanding to action* (pp. 19–28). Palgrave Macmillan. http://www.guninetwork.org/files/8_i.2_he_for_sustainability_-_tilbury.pdf

Wals, A.E. (2012). Full-length report on the UN Decade of Education for Sustainable Development. UNESCO, Paris, p. 114.

Wals, A. (2015). Social learning-oriented capacity-building for critical transitions towards sustainability. In R. Jucker, & R. Mathar (Eds.), *Schooling for sustainable development in Europe* (pp. 87–107). Springer International Publishing.

Wenger, E. (1998). *Communities of practice: Learning, meaning and identity*. Cambridge University Press.

4

Students as Partners

Introduction

Working with students as partners in research and in the design, delivery and evaluation of course programmes redistributes power and decision making across all participants in ethical and liberatory ways (Bullock et al., 2022). This is a humane and holistic 'Participatory Design' (Muller, 2007) approach that enhances the experience, and the outcomes, of those projects – for staff and students alike. This represents a move from student consultation to activity that is rooted in genuine and meaningful co-creation and co-production (Harrington et al., 2021). This empowers students to be agents of change, influencing all levels of institutional activity and working as equals reimagining education.

The positives of such relationship-rich education (Felten & Lambert, 2020) are demonstrated across the case studies here, and underscored by the literature: see Burns et al. (2019), Healey et al. (2016), Harrington et al. (2021) and Mercer-Mapstone (2017). Such partnerships are designed to increase student engagement, developing agency, self-confidence, self-efficacy, belonging, purpose and success, with the goal that students feel heard and listened to.

For such partnerships to be successful, they have to be taken seriously by institutions as well as by the academics involved. There needs to be space created to work together with students on authentic projects – with attention paid to due reward for labour, monetary or otherwise. Student engagement as part of a course or module or as part of paid employment not only helps ameliorate workloads, but helps diminish power imbalances. Student partners become more than 'customers'; they become active participants with valuable expertise to contribute to shaping learning, teaching and assessment. This also benefits staff, helping in the development of new and better teaching and curriculum materials as well as teaching and learning provisions and support. As stated by Cook-Sather et al. (2014, 6–7):

> A collaborative, reciprocal process through which all participants have the opportunity to contribute equally, although not necessarily in the same ways, to curricular or pedagogical conceptualisation, decision-making, implementation, investigation, or analysis.

In this section we have examples of students as collaborative partners in the production of courses, resources and research projects for personal and professional development as well as the wider enhancement of the university.

The Case Study Chapters

Enhancing the Wider Postgraduate Experience by Anna Maria Jones, Danielle L. Kurtin, Tianshu Liu and Alisia Southwell outlines how staff and students have worked together in the design, delivery and evaluation of an interactive online, pre-arrival course for incoming postgraduate students. In the delivery, the partnership and student contributions were foregrounded which increased the relatability and relevance of the course. The staff and student authors recommend that projects such as these require adequate funding and enthusiastic dedication to succeed.

Students as Co-creators of an Inclusive Equality and Diversity Teaching Resource co-written by a staff and students collaborative – Annamaria Szelics, Sonya Frazier, Holly Kerr, Jack Knowles, Declan Prosser, Lara Ryan, Victoria Paterson, Nicola Veitch and Stewart White – provides insights into the development of an equality, diversity and inclusion teaching resource that became a part of the undergraduate life science curriculum at the University of Glasgow. The case study highlights the positive effects the jointly developed resource has on both the team members involved in creating it and the students encountering it in their studies.

Speaking of Vocabulary co-written by Daron Benjamin Loo and students – Nima Javanbakht, Zhiqing Rong and Xun Wang – outlines a collaborative, socio-material approach to the creation of a meaningful vocabulary phrasebank by students that was further developed by the tutor into authentic English for academic purposes tasks. The case study demonstrates that such collaborations are an essential part of 'grounded' pedagogy, creating trust relationships between tutor and students that in the process develop student agency, capital and self-efficacy.

In *Staff-student Collaboration across Disciplines*, Andrew Struan, Monica Catherine O'Brien, Ewan D. Hannaford and Stuart J. Taylor provide an inspirational example of a Learning Development team that integrated early career academics – specifically Graduate Teaching Assistants – through authentic collaborative projects. They harnessed an academic literacies approach both to staff development itself, and to the courses, resources and projects they cooperatively produced for the undergraduate students with whom they worked.

In *Researching Together*, Lynn Wright, Max Korbmacher, Martha Gardiner, Julia Ngadi, Ayesha Shahid and Scott M. Hardie outline a university-wide programme that brings together staff and undergraduate students in co-research projects. They argue that successful student-staff partnerships require a structured approach, clear communication about expectations and roles and due care taken with respect to power imbalances. If done successfully, programmes like this increase competence and confidence aiding students now, and in the future.

Enhancing the Wider Postgraduate Experience: Student Partnership in Co-creating Online Learning

Anna Maria Jones, Danielle L. Kurtin, Tianshu Liu and Alisia Southwell

- Partnership with students can significantly enhance quality in HE but requires investment of staff time.
- Student partners should receive sufficient financial compensation to allow them to effectively participate and feel valued.
- Staff-student partnership offers a unique developmental experience for staff and students.
- All partners should have influence over the nature of the student-staff collaboration in recognition of power dynamics.
- Student-staff partnership should be prioritized and funded appropriately at institutional level.

Introduction

Within the Faculty of Medicine at Imperial College London (ICL), UK, a student-staff team have collaborated in the design, delivery and evaluation of an interactive online, predominantly pre-arrival course entitled *Adapt to Postgrad* (ATP). The course is designed to support prospective students in their transition to Master's study through active learning, in the light of the fact that preparedness for postgraduate-taught (PGT) study is an increasingly recognized challenge in the UK (Macleod et al., 2019; McPherson et al., 2017). The literature expresses the importance of early preparation and the 'setting of expectations' to support this transition (Bamber et al., 2019; Evans et al., 2018). In this case study, we propose that the collaborative nature by which the course was developed significantly enhanced the effectiveness of its reach and impact.

The *Adapt to Postgrad* Project

> It has been a completely new experience for me to be working with not only students but also support staff.
>
> (Tianshu Liu, Student Partner)

The *Adapt to Postgrad* (ATP) course is a non-compulsory online, interactive course which was piloted in September 2020 with the purpose of supporting the student transition to PGT study. In its launch year, the course engaged over 600 students and received an overwhelming amount of positive feedback from students who undertook the course, many expressing feelings of increased preparedness and change of thinking. We as the ATP development team feel that this reception not only suggests success of the course itself, but points towards successful collaboration throughout this project. Whilst it is critical to note that the ATP course has gratefully had input from a large number of students and staff from across the institution, in this case study we will be specifically exploring the nature of our closest and most extensive collaboration: our student-staff partnership.

Funding via Imperial's StudentShapers scheme allowed the ATP development team to recruit four paid student partners to work alongside its staff partners (an Academic Developer, Senior Learning Designer and Project Manager). Whilst student partners were current or ex-Master's students within ICL's Faculty of Medicine, all were students of different PGT programmes of study, and had entirely different amounts (and nature) of experience with collaboration. Three of the four were international students, which may well be reflective of Imperial's high proportion of non-UK students. Due to the Covid-19 pandemic, much of this partnership has been conducted in an entirely remote manner, and as we write this chapter there is a seven-hour time difference between us! Whilst this has required some navigating together, we feel that another indicator of the effectiveness of this collaboration is the extent to which we as students and staff have valued working together in this diverse team. The authors of this case study believe our collaboration serves as a model of student-staff collaboration; for reasons we will discuss further in the sections below.

How It Went: Reflections and Lessons Learnt

Working with staff on the ATP project has been valuable – it's been refreshing to see how open staff have been to input and suggestions throughout and it has been good feeling genuinely useful as part of the process of improving the ATP course.
(Alisia Southwell, Student Partner)

Perhaps this is partly due to the fact that I'm in my early career, but it is almost strange for me to use the label of 'student partners' – they are such integrated and effective members of the team that I simply view them as colleagues.
(Anna Maria Jones, Staff Partner)

Our aim was to collaborate in a manner authentic and reflective of the professional workplace, without ignoring areas where student partners required extra support to contribute effectively. Both students and staff were involved in all key stages of course development, including design and evaluation.

Student Partner Reflection

As implied by our case study title, as student partners we very much appreciated being involved in a meaningful project, the ability to influence decisions, having a specific end goal and seeing recommendations being implemented in real time. This, in combination with being paid members of the team, led to us feeling like genuinely useful and valued partners. For one of us who had not had the chance to experience working life before this partnership, this collaboration provided the chance to experience how work differs from study, and resulted in improvement of communication skills and confidence. We also valued the opportunity to see how the institution functions 'behind the scenes': being able to understand the workload involved when developing and maintaining a course, how projects are carried out and funded. We are not sure where else we would learn this!

Staff Partner Reflection

From the staff perspective, it is very difficult to briefly express all that the student partners brought to this collaboration, but perhaps the most standout characteristic of them all was their unwavering enthusiasm. This could be attributed to their positive working mentalities and the fact that this was a special and temporary opportunity, which they certainly made the most of. They were excellent colleagues who further enhanced the diversity of the team due to their unique perspectives and the variety of their lived experiences and skillsets.

Participant Feedback

Students who engaged with completing the ATP course also valued the student-staff partnership behind the design of the course. Throughout ATP we ensured that our partnership was transparent, so that the insights of our student partners formed content that users engaged with. The feedback consistently stated how much participants valued this, and how it enhanced perceptions around relatability and relevance of the course.

Meta-reflection

In the spirit of true reflection, what could we have done better? One of our student partners recently expressed frustration regarding the barriers of remote working, the lack of spontaneity and more 'casual' conversation. During the Covid-19 pandemic I (Anna Maria, Staff Partner) continually encouraged teaching colleagues to facilitate more 'informal', additional learning in order to enhance a sense of virtual community (Peacock et al., 2020), and yet until this comment I had not thought about creating similar spaces in the collaborative context.

Recommendations for Student-staff Collaboration

> [Staff partners require a] desire to understand the student mindset. If one wants to use students to complete tasks, that's all right, but then the student is not a partner, they are a subordinate. If a staff member truly wants to partner with a student, they will then seek to understand and utilise the mindset of a

student … To prospective staff partners I'd encourage them to ask themselves 'do I have the time and inclination for this responsibility?'

(Danielle Kurtin, Student Partner)

Characteristics for a good student partner are, in my opinion, someone who is eager to learn and get involved … Other characteristics can be taught and reinforced but enthusiasm and genuine interest will make the collaboration much smoother.

(Erin Simpson, Staff Partner/Project Manager)

Interestingly, we are all in agreement that not all students nor all staff would make effective partners in a collaboration similar to ours. Dedication is essential for all participants, and staff must be willing to not only support and guide, but also learn from students and recognize that student input is highly valuable (Bovill et al., 2016; Cook-Sather, 2014) – sometimes more so than staff perspectives! Effective collaboration requires investment and should not be sought by the time-poor, with student partners supported and incentivized through sufficient financial compensation (Burns et al., 2019; Mercer-Mapstone et al., 2017) if possible.

We also emphasize the importance of addressing the power dynamics inherent in these collaborations (Mihans et al., 2008). One of our student partners noted that in other instances where this power dimension had not been adequately addressed, they felt isolated and unsupported. There must be transparency and conversation regarding 'form and format' from the initiation of the partnership to its conclusion, so that all have influence over the nature of the collaboration and continually review its effectiveness together, as colleagues would (Matthews et al., 2018). Practicalities should not be overlooked, including agreeing joint ways of working, collaborating and communicating remotely, and ensuring that all have manageable workloads.

Concluding Thoughts

Student-staff collaboration is incredibly important to higher education – both for staff development and student growth … not only are these practices sustainable, they're vital to continue to make the university experience one that allows students to develop their knowledge and skills as well as gain practical experience for post-university life.

(Erin Simpson, Staff Partner/Project Manager)

Having been deeply engaged in a relatively small student-staff team, we are unconvinced of the scalability of such committed partnership, and this certainly raises the question of how, without the commitment of adequate funding for salaries, all HE students might be provided the opportunity to be involved in meaningful student-staff collaboration. However, despite questions around scalability, we feel that student-staff collaboration is sustainable if prioritized (and it should be!), and this requires sufficient staff and students to be willing. Further, to do this in an inclusive manner, institutional funding for such partnerships must continue (Mercer-Mapstone et al., 2017).

Acknowledgements

We gratefully acknowledge the input and support of all the following individuals/funding schemes of Imperial College London: Erin Simpson (Project Manager), Georgia Simmons (ex-Student Partner), Katie Stripe (Senior Learning Designer), Dr. Sophie Rutschmann (PG Medicine Academic Lead), StudentShapers, Teaching Fellow Development Fund, Medical Education Research Unit, Dr. Mike Streule, Dr. Monika Pazio and, last but certainly not least, all other students and staff across the Faculty and Institution who have had input into the course design and delivery.

Students as Co-creators of an Inclusive Equality and Diversity Teaching Resource: An Example from Life Sciences

Annamaria Szelics, Sonya Frazier, Holly Kerr, Jack Knowles, Declan Prosser, Lara Ryan, Victoria Paterson, Nicola Veitch and Stewart White

- In this chapter, an example of a successful student-staff partnership is presented with a detailed description of the working approach that can be applied in various fields.
- It provides insights into the development of an equality, diversity and inclusion teaching resource that became a part of the undergraduate life science curriculum at the University of Glasgow and might serve as an example for other institutions.
- The chapter highlights the advantages of problem-based learning and how this teaching method might support educators in empowering students.

Introduction

The Equality and Diversity (E&D) project in the School of Life Sciences (SoLS) at the University of Glasgow (UoG) addresses issues prevalent in inclusive education. A key aim of the E&D project is to raise awareness about E&D issues within life sciences and beyond: to highlight barriers to entry and participation. This is important because 20 per cent of ethnic minority students have been racially harassed in the UK (Equality & Human Rights Commission report, 2019) and STEM disciplines rank among the lowest among subject areas when including LGBTQ+ experiences into the curricula (NUS, 2020).

E&D can be taught using various approaches (Carrington, 1999): from using more ethnically and culturally diverse examples within teaching practice to tackling prejudice and exclusion directly. The E&D project decided to construct case studies of exclusion, harnessing real voices and experience via a social constructionist approach, where the individual context is highly relevant. This teaching technique avoids lists of definitions and characteristics to provide explanations for group cultures (Deloney et al., 2000), but encourages students to think of each person as an individual whose own understanding of the world makes them unique (Dogra et al., 2016). To create resources that encouraged students to think for themselves, we adopted a collaborative way of working with students as partners, as this best encapsulated our approach and our goal of a more collegiate and inclusive, HE.

Setting

SoLS secured funding from the Welcome Trust in November 2019 to embed the values of E&D into Level 1 and Level 2 Life Science courses as part of the curriculum. The idea was to create resources that highlighted issues of inclusion and exclusion for the approximately 1,000 participating Level 1 and Level 2 undergraduate Biology students. The educational materials were built around the nine protected characteristics embedded in the Equality Act, 2010 (Figure 4.1).

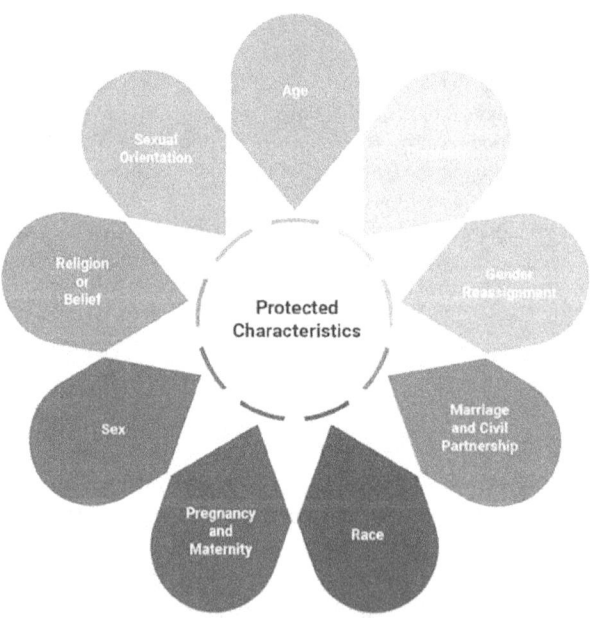

Figure 4.1 The nine protected characteristics of the Equalities Act (2010).

The aims of the resources were:

- Raise awareness of E&D issues and the problems that people face within the Life Sciences and beyond.
- Equip Life Science students with tools that will help them to overcome barriers they may face during their studies and careers.
- Improve equality of access to research degrees by improving student understanding of opportunities and related barriers.

Collaborative Method Adopted

The E&D resources were co-created by six student interns and three staff members. Working with students in the development of educational materials has proven to have long-term benefits for the learners directly involved, including improved research skills, heightened sense of responsibility and enhanced employability attributes (Brew, 2003; Healey, 2005). The student-staff collaboration has also been shown to support mutual learning, effective knowledge acquisition and active engagement (Maunder, 2015). Moreover, embedding the student voice into a course structure was empowering for learners (Boston Advisory Council, 2012; Campbell et al., 2009; Toshalis & Nakkula, 2012). Henneman, Lee and Cohen (1995) and Schuman (2006) suggest that for successful student-staff collaboration a clear structure of common aims is needed, and high levels of commitment, trust, respect and patience are required to ensure meaningful partnership between the two parties. These principles were embedded within the group dynamic, and students were given broad, flexible aims and mainly worked independently within their groups, supported with weekly team meetings.

The Working Approach

Student interns worked in two groups creating materials for Level 1 and Level 2 Biology students. The two teams worked separately, but there was a close collaboration between them. Some of the interns with previous experience in designing educational resources and creating videos assisted others to master these skills. Due to the Covid-19 pandemic, the working process and the resources were moved to a VLE. Both teams had one-hour weekly meetings with the three staff members via Zoom, who provided them with support, advice, feedback and guidance. Besides the three staff members, students received support from various UoG stakeholders including the Learning Enhancement and Academic Development Service, Careers Manager, Race Equality Group member/PhD student and a School of Medicine representative with expertise in PBL. Additionally, the interns were provided with digital support by an E-learning Officer, a Web Designer and an App developer.

The educational materials created by the student interns consisted of case studies, role model interviews and quizzes. Each student intern was responsible for creating a case study where a protected characteristic is explored in a real-life situation with a linked set of tasks and external resources, such as websites and articles. Prior to developing the case studies, the student interns agreed on a set structure for these educational materials. Each case study had intended learning outcomes, a linked set of questions and further resources about the topic covered. The role model section consists of eight interviews, in which interns asked under- and postgraduate students and external research scientists about the barriers they faced throughout their studies and careers and the strategies they used to overcome these obstacles.

The Teaching Approach

The E&D project resources were designed to be integrated into Collaborative ProblemBased Learning (PBL) workshops for the Biology students. PBL was chosen as a student-centred pedagogical approach with reiterative and reflective learning cycles of domain-specific knowledge which improve knowledge acquisition efficiency in students (Dunlap, 2005). Further advantages of PBL include improved academic results (Wahyu & Syaadah, 2018), increased learning motivation (Kang et al., 2016), structural and psychological empowerment (Siu et al., 2005) and high self-efficacy (Dunlap, 2005). Learners were encouraged to find creative solutions for specific issues (Kek & Huijser, 2011) via discussion of concepts, concerns and topics related to E&D. PBL sessions were facilitated in small groups under the supervision of tutors, enabling learners to freely express their opinions on potentially sensitive topics in a safe environment (Phungsuk et al., 2017). The mobile app is available to download: https://play.google.com/store/apps/details?id=com.gla.diversity.

Evaluation of the Materials Developed

To assess the outcomes of the project (ethics approved by MVLS Ethics Committee), students completed a questionnaire before and after engaging with the E&D resource. The responses showed that on completion of the course, students were significantly more aware of how and where to report discrimination at UoG and in the workplace; how to ask for E&D support at UoG and elsewhere; and the role of Athena SWAN within SoLS. Goodness of fit statistical tests revealed that a significant number of the participating students agreed that the E&D resource:

- made them reflect on their behaviour and how they interact with other students and staff members;
- supported their learning;
- made them feel better equipped to challenge inappropriate behaviour at the UoG and elsewhere;
- reinforced their existing knowledge on E&D issues; and
- taught them something new with regard to E&D issues.

Evaluation of the Process

Student interns were hired part-time for six months. Afterwards, five of the student interns graduated from UoG, while the remaining student intern continued to work on the E&D project for an additional nine months. She had the opportunity to present the E&D project at various conferences along with staff members, which improved her presentation and communication skills. In addition, the student intern also led the preparation of the work for publication.

The interns highlighted that this experience was unique and empowering, allowing them to create a conversation about E&D in the Life Sciences that is fully integrated in the curriculum for students at the UoG.

The interns developed their research, writing and video production in the process of developing the resources. The interns reported that student-staff collaboration enabled insight into constructing and evaluating teaching materials. In particular, staff sensitivity and care created a safe space for open and honest discussion throughout the whole process which increased their confidence.

One of the interns working on the E&D resources provided the following feedback about the project:

> Working on this project was a unique experience. I have always had an interest in the issues science faces in terms of diversity, equality, and inclusion. As an undergraduate in a science degree, it is difficult to feel any power to instill change in these causes I am passionate about. It can often feel that we are on the bottom rung of academia and have little time or accessibility to the kind of decision-making processes that help or hinder marginalised groups within science. However, the project with the School of Life Sciences empowered us students to create the conversation about EDI in the Life Sciences that is now part of the curriculum for students at Glasgow.

Conclusion

This project demonstrated that this student and staff partnership was successful in developing Life Science E&D learning resources. Statistical analysis of the survey data demonstrated a positive change in the awareness and behaviour of the students who used the resources. This will be described in more detail in a future publication. Staff and students engaging with the resource reported having a rich experience by being involved in the development and delivery. An additional benefit of this project was that it developed a pathway to discuss social inequality within a science context, as during the usual life science curriculum, there is little room for this.

Senior staff members involved reported that working collaboratively with student interns supported their scholarship and career development. Student interns involved reported that working collaboratively and with agency within the SoLS E&D team was a unique and empowering experience since as students they were given the experience of collegiate working and the trust to develop educational resources, boosting their confidence and career prospects.

Due to the success of this co-curriculum design approach, Dr Paterson, Veitch and White will continue this work to embed E&D values into the curriculum of honours life science students. This work will feed into a wider curriculum design of E&D teaching resources within MVLS; it will link into the process of decolonizing the Life Science curriculum, and will support Athena Swan applications within MVLS.

Speaking of Vocabulary: A Socio-material Collaboration with Graduate Students

Daron Benjamin Loo, Nima Javanbakht, Zhiqing Rong and Xun Wang

- Learning is shaped not only through interactions between teacher and students, but with inanimate objects as well (Actor Network Theory).
- Materials for an academic writing module were co-produced with students' contributions of words.
- Students' contributions shed light on their learning ecology.

Keywords

co-producing material; English for academic purposes; informal learning; university ecology

Introduction

This case study is co-authored by and reports a socio-material (Gravett, 2020) collaboration between lecturer and students in an academic writing module. This approach affirms the Actor Network Theory, which recognizes the networks created through the interactions between human and non-human entities (see MacLeod et al., 2019). In an educational setting, the socio-material approach recognizes the ecology of students' learning experiences as essentially collaborative and cooperative; relationships between social entities (students, lecturers, administrators, the public) and materials (academic texts, teaching and learning tasks, the HE environment, etc.). These relationships illustrate meaningful networks between actors, from where knowledge and critical dispositions towards teaching and learning may be created (Gourlay, 2017). This case study provides an illustration of what university educators can do to understand how students may learn outside the classroom setting, and collaborate creatively with each other and the study materials.

Context: The Academic Writing Module

The teaching and learning activities illustrated here are from an academic writing module offered by the Centre for English Language and Communication to graduate students at the National University of SG. This module aims to help graduate students prepare for thesis or journal article writing. The module is taught as tutorials, with lessons typically comprising short lectures on language points (grammar, syntax) or writing features (use of cohesive devices), followed by writing tasks.

A Socio-material Approach for Collaborative Vocabulary Learning

To ensure the relevance of this module to the students' needs, a socio-material approach was taken to enhance the teaching and learning materials. This approach recognizes students' interaction with social and material entities in the larger university ecology. These interactions can subsequently complement learning in the formal classroom (see Kumpulainen & Kajamaa, 2020). It also legitimizes students' informal learning experiences as being valuable (Gourlay, 2017). In short, a socio-material approach recognizes that students learn in diverse manners, and that learning does take place not only in a formal classroom setting but also in the informal and in-between spaces of learning.

The recognition of students' interaction with socio-material entities and each other thus became the foundation for collaborative vocabulary learning in this module. A socio-material approach at the graduate level is suitable, given that various studies have reported the significance of teachers having to work closely with graduate students in identifying and designing suitable materials to create meaningful dialogic learning opportunities, instead of referring to ready-made materials found in commercial textbooks that may be irrelevant to the needs of their students (Casal & Lu, 2021; Durrant, 2016; Towns, 2020). In addition, there is a recognition that students can benefit and learn from peers (see literature on peer mentoring, peer learning). Vocabulary knowledge, especially for graduate students, is a vital capital for academic literacy and success in the wider world (Winkle-Wagner & McCoy, 2016).

Teaching and Learning Activities

In this module, students were invited to contribute vocabulary useful for graduate-level conceptualization and writing on an online Excel file. This approach valued students' interaction with outside materials: contributions could be of any words the students themselves thought useful, without restrictions. The vocabulary could be a single word, or even short phrases. Students also included the context of appearance (the sentence where the vocabulary was used), the source of the text, the contributor's name (removed from this case study) and the date of contribution (Table 4.1).

Table 4.1 A sample of entries of students' contributions. Note: EFC stands for emotion-focused coping.

Word or phrase	Context (sentence or paragraph where word or phrase appears)	Source (doi number; URL; title of source)	Date of contribution
salient + impetus	EFC can reduce the saliency of a threat and therefore the impetus to take protective actions might not be as salient.	https://doi.org/10.25300/MISQ/2019/14360	21-Aug
delineate	Our classification of EFC helps to more precisely delineate the role of different types of EFC.	https://doi.org/10.25300/MISQ/2019/14360	21-Aug
concrete+ obfuscation +specious+ inconsistent	For those researchers who are talented writers, having a concrete model may prevent obfuscation of specious or inconsistent arguments.	http://doi.org/10.2307/2393788	22-Aug
nuanced	With more practice and more nuanced language comes more of the originating insight.	http://doi.org/10.2307/2393789	22-Aug
resemble + retention	In doing so, their activities resemble the three processes of evolution: variation, selection and retention.	https://doi.org/10.5465/amr.1989.4308376	22-Aug
postulated	This has not been true in the case of other postulated moderators.	http://doi.org/10.1037/0021-9010.66.2.166	23-Aug
taxonomy	We introduce a taxonomy that reflects the theoretical contribution of empirical articles along two dimensions.	http://doi.org/10.5465/AMJ.2007.28165855	23-Aug
exogenous #: endogenous	Social scientists often estimate models from correlational data, where the independent variable has not been exogenously manipulated.	https://doi.org/10.1016/j.leaqua.2010.10.010	24-Aug
stereotype	Many scholars have observed the common stereotypes of experiments – particularly ones that are conducted in the laboratory.	https://doi.org/10.1177%2F1094428107300396	26-Aug

Students contributed from August to November 2020, with a total of 277 entries. The contributed vocabulary was processed with a free online software, VocabProfilers (Cobb, 2021), and a majority of the vocabulary were highly specific disciplinary words, which are also referred to as 'off-list' words. Almost all contributions came from academic sources, such as research papers, with a few from non-academic sources, such as online news sites, online forums, and websites. The main source for contributions being academic texts affirmed that graduate students interacted closely with academic materials to become more familiar with disciplinary epistemological and discursive processes (e.g. Badenhorst, 2018). Through the process, students made their learning visible and shared their learning with others. In further collaborative dialogue with the students, and based on the contributed vocabulary, the lecturer created language tasks to facilitate students' understanding of these words.

Reflection

Collaboration in this module may not be comparable to conventional student groupwork where impact is confined mostly to the students of a group. Here students played an active role in providing materials to each other and the lecturer, who then curated learning experiences for the benefit of all students. The use of students' contributions as and within meaningful learning materials underscored students' legitimacy: they were co-producers of their learning, engaged and active members of the class and wider learning community. This maintains and increases student motivation (see Wilby, 2020).

This was reflected by the student co-authors of this case study. Nima understood collaboration as a way to develop and reinforce one's understanding of vocabulary; Xun understood collaboration as a way to enrich one's vocabulary pool; while Zhiqing understood collaboration as a way to enrich one's understanding of different meanings of a word. These understandings may be gleaned from the student co-authors' reflections:

> I believe to activate and engage long-term memory, collaboration is needed, in any form including assignment and class discussion; otherwise, it would be too difficult to master them by only checking the dictionary. Metaphorically, improving vocabulary is a 'journey', similar to moving from one point of the city to another. We can use an Uber with GPS (dictionary) to go there, but we certainly would forget how to get there. However, if you walk, discuss, and even go wrong, and correct it (collaboratively), then you will master it and can go in the next times by yourself. In short, learning new words is a 'process' and the collaborative approach can be the 'method' to review and leverage the process in a more entertaining manner.
>
> (Nima)

> I think it can, especially through collaboration among students from different disciplines. As a non-native speaker, I find my vocabulary pool concentrates on the words of my field. Collaborative learning with students from other majors can help enrich my vocabulary pool.
>
> (Xun)

> In my experience, how to precisely select vocabulary for different contexts is the hardest part for me in my higher education studies. Although there are many

vocabulary with the same meanings, they might not apply to the same context due to subtle differences between implications or connotations they might contain.

(Zhiqing)

Recommendations for Practice

A collaborative socio-material approach encouraged students to notice words beyond this module to curate for use by all the students on the module. It also fostered a form of collaboration where students were acknowledged to have a meaningful impact on the classroom. Based on these experiences, some recommendations are:

- In any learning setting (not just language), knowledge or skill development should be treated as a developmental process (see Ozdem-Yilmaz and Bilican on Bruner's notion of Discovery Learning, 2020). By doing this, there will be opportunities for trust to be nurtured between students and their lecturer (Jeyaraj & Harland, 2019). This will also render the learning experience more personal, meaningful and long-term oriented.
- Collaboration in a teaching or learning setting should be shaped by the context, guided by the lecturer's practical wisdom (Biesta, 2012). Caveat: to ensure that the lecturer is not overwhelmed by contributions, the lecturer could clearly determine the learning outcomes as well as assessment criteria for students' contributions. This was a limitation of this current practice.

Further Considerations

Based on our case study, there are some research opportunities for future consideration. First, it might be useful to capture the scope of students' engagement with materials beyond the classroom. This may provide an emic insight into how students enact independent learning and share learning. Second, as seen in the students' contributions, students mainly looked at academic texts as their source for vocabulary learning: How can this be leveraged to help graduate students improve competency or vocabulary usage? Third, the lecturer might explore tasks that are optimal for vocabulary learning, especially in a class with students from different disciplines. Fourth, to understand students' learning ecologies, lecturers might gauge students' motivation for their collaboration and their contribution, which may help in the planning or improvement of learning materials.

Finally, as the lecturer of this module, leveraging my students' contribution to enhance classroom materials allowed me to occupy an intermediary space. This enabled students to view me and my module as relevant support for the development of their academic communication needs. What I did in my class also illustrated how an English for academic purpose setting can be flexible and cognisant towards language materials found in students' broader environment, thus approaching language development in a more critical and reflexive manner (Loo & Sairattanain, 2021; Tietjen et al., 2021).

Staff-student Collaboration across Disciplines: An Academic Literacies Approach

Andrew Struan, Monica Catherine O'Brien,
Ewan D. Hannaford and Stuart J. Taylor

- Working collaboratively, permanent staff and Graduate Teaching Assistants (PhD tutors) can create meaningful, impactful academic literacies development for students.
- Academic literacies teaching is an essential part of promoting student success, and collaboration between staff and students (at all levels) is key to enabling this success.
- Multi- and interdisciplinary teaching, research and pedagogic development are crucial to providing twenty-first-century graduates with the essential skills, knowledge and capabilities to succeed.
- Collaboration across subject areas, and between staff and students, should be a central part of engaging students in their academic development.

Introduction

Learning or Academic Developers in the UK context are those 'third space' professionals who typically work directly with students to help them better understand HE and its codes and conventions – its mysteries. Typically, this work is seen as focusing either on 'skills', 'socialization' or 'literacies' (Lea & Street, 2006) with the latter seen as the most liberatory approach. More recently, Learning Development (LD) and the focus on academic literacies development are increasingly central components of the global HE sector (Boyle, Ramsay & Struan, 2019; Hill, 2010). LDs are essentially collaborative, working with students to build understanding of, and confidence and attainment in, academic study, academic research and academic writing. The academic literacies model creates a partnership between LD and student that encourages students to actively participate in their development of the specific practices of their subject areas (Bury & Sheese, 2016; Lea & Street, 1998, 2006). As seen in the examples presented in this chapter, this model encourages LDs to work in multi-disciplinary/ interdisciplinary modes and foreground 'the variety and specificity of institutional practices' (Lea & Street, 2006, 376) and to work together with colleagues and with students in demystifying and detangling these practices.

This chapter discusses the successful integration of Graduate Teaching Assistants (GTAs), who are employed to teach while they undertake their PhD studies, into the collegiate team of LDs at a Scottish research-intensive institution. GTAs come from all subject backgrounds across the institution, but instead of subject-specific teaching, the GTAs teach academic writing, academic study and researcher development to broad, multi- and interdisciplinary groups of undergraduate and postgraduate students.

These GTAs take on a variety of teaching, course- and curricula-design activities, one-to-one meetings with students, assessment and resource creation. All GTAs are active researchers within their own diverse subject areas, ranging from creative writing to astrophysics, with most aiming to go into either academic careers in their discipline or into LD upon completion of their studies. As a result, the role of the GTA is designed as a career development opportunity into the broader world of learning and teaching practice in HE. The role and development of GTAs across HE have been discussed widely, but such discussion has focused on subject-based or subject-specific teaching (Gaia et al., 2003; Hey-Cunningham et al., 2021; Huffmyer & Lemus, 2019; Prieto & Altmaier, 1994; Ryker & McConnell, 2014). There has been little discussion of the role of a multi-disciplinary team of GTAs working to enhance students' academic literacies.

This chapter uses two examples to demonstrate how strong collaboration across the team, between the team and students and across subject areas enables the successful deployment of an academic literacies-based approach to LD. This case study, written jointly by a permanent LD staff member and GTAs, consequently highlights the ways in which collaboration acts as a guiding force within the department.

Composition of the Team and Collaboration Principles

The team is large: there are roughly thirty-six GTAs working with a team of eight permanent LD staff from across the disciplines, and together they assess and teach approximately 16,000 students per academic year (Boyle et al., 2019; Struan, 2021). While many GTAs have extensive experience of subject teaching, practice in and understandings of academic literacies-based pedagogies may be more limited. As a result, the LD department looks to embrace and embed collaborative practice at the heart of its development of GTAs. GTAs work hand-in-hand with permanent members of LD staff to develop, enhance and deploy a variety of initiatives, programmes of study and courses, as described in the first example. The second example illustrates how this collaborative practice takes the form of GTAs, LD staff and students working across multiple disciplinary boundaries.

Working Together: GTAs and LD Staff

The ethos of collaboration is at the heart of the department's structure and organization. GTAs and permanent staff from all disciplinary backgrounds work together to create and deliver all of the department's resources and classes. Meanwhile, students undertaking undergraduate and postgraduate courses at the university shape the departments' focus and teaching through their continual feedback and participation in the flipped- and blended-classroom approach.

At the organizational level, GTAs collaborate across the team, through open and ongoing communication, regarding approaches to pedagogy, course organization and structures. The LD team were early adopters of the university's collaborative platform *Microsoft Teams* and piloted its initial use at their institution. The 'conversational' format of the platform helped the team to maintain free-flowing conversations, enabled group and individual collaboration to emerge independently, and supported the rapid sharing and co-creation of documents/materials. The Covid-19 pandemic did not disrupt normal routes of communication and instead further solidified this open, digital form of departmental communication, discussion, and collaboration as the norm. The early adoption of *Microsoft Teams* allowed for a seamless transition to entirely online work at the start of the pandemic; the use of these instant, collaborative forms of communication is central to the team's ethos and the priority of ongoing debate and discussion.

The department's collaboration was exemplified by the development of new suites of courses to engage undergraduate students in the enhancement of their academic literacies at the peak of the Covid-19 pandemic, through live, interactive study of subjects of interest (Yu, 2020). Courses ranged in topic from 'History of Argument', 'Let's Play with Academia!' and 'Introduction to Creative Writing' to 'Rationality in Scientific Debate' and 'Learning from the Great Scientists'. Courses were vastly over-subscribed – there were several hundred students across the variety of courses, with almost 300 on waiting lists for free spaces. GTAs and permanent members of staff worked together to design and deliver the courses (Huffmyer & Lemus, 2019; McVitty & Andrews, 2021; Park & Choi, 2009). The GTAs and permanent LD staff members collaborated on all elements of course design: from topic, through class-by-class discussion points, to assessment and co-delivery of teaching.

Student feedback was overwhelmingly positive about the development of their academic literacies. We feel that the success of these projects is a direct result of the way that the GTAs and permanent members of staff worked together to design and build new courses with new pedagogical approaches to academic literacies teaching – with GTA bringing their research background to the LD community and with a permanent member of LD staff bringing experience in the pedagogical approaches (Abegglen et al., 2019; Chan & Luo, 2021; Donovan & Erskine-Shaw, 2020). Moreover, through this engagement in all areas of new course design, the GTAs involved have been able to develop knowledge and experience in course design from start to finish.

Furthermore, the collegiate approach to course design allowed GTAs to develop independence and a sense of self-efficacy in learning and teaching, an element often missed in their career development (Auten & Twigg, 2015; Ridgway et al., 2017). Importantly, GTAs were offered freedom in their approach to course design, resource creation and topic, and were encouraged to work together to develop ideas. This 'crowd-source' approach to course design allowed for innovation, fresh perspectives and interdisciplinary approaches to be foregrounded in this new provision. Collaborative 'best practices' were co-developed by GTAs drawing on the unique experiences and knowledge of their respective disciplines. The department's development of a free-flowing and comfortable space in *Microsoft Teams* saw daily collaboration between GTAs and LDs, and the space allowed GTAs and LDs to easily circulate and test ideas with their multi-disciplinary colleagues, and receive feedback and advice. Before the pandemic, collaboration also involved meetings of varying sizes for the department's projects. Zoom meetings substituted here, and while timing could be challenging, recordings and *Teams* ensured everyone remained up-to-date and involved in the conversations.

Working across Subjects: An Interdisciplinary Team

One of the main focuses of the LD department is the encouragement of inter- and multi-disciplinary approaches to study and research. The model of academic literacies relies on effective understanding – often co-built between student and staff member – of academic practice and norms across a variety of subjects. This broad subject discussion has resulted in the LD department creating and hosting a unique annual undergraduate research conference and research journal (Bownes et al., 2020).

In this work, GTAs act as mentors for undergraduates from radically different subject backgrounds to their own. This collaboration supports students' development of their communication skills to speak to wide audiences in academia and their future workplaces. The external perspective on their work provided by the GTA also enhances students' critical reflection. The GTAs work one-on-one with the undergraduates in the development of a public research talk or a piece of written research for a multi-disciplinary audience. Through a process of active collaboration between GTA and undergraduate, a truly multi- and interdisciplinary piece of research communication is created.

In this role, GTAs act as mentor, guide, tutor and subject outsider. GTAs and students work together to refine research questions, draft presentations/articles and perfect multi-disciplinary communication. The results are pieces of undergraduate work that have been shaped through working and collaborating with GTAs (Stamp et al., 2015). Through this activity, GTAs bring their own experiences and subject knowledge to a new discussion; pairings have included, for example, historian GTAs working with undergraduate medical science students. Through a process of active – and quite intensive – collaboration, these projects encourage undergraduates to consider the broader implications of their research. From working collaboratively with the GTAs, the undergraduates also gain an understanding of different subject approaches and important experience and understanding of multi-disciplinary approaches that may otherwise be absent from their degree. These projects provide GTAs' valuable experience of working with students from across a variety of subject areas; the GTAs engage actively to develop their skills as mentors, interdisciplinary researchers and teachers (Craney et al., 2011; Gennis et al., 2020; Mariani et al., 2013).

Conclusion

The academic literacies model demands that LDs 'collaboratively investigate the range of genres, modes, shifts, transformations, representations, meaning-making processes, and identities involved in academic learning within and across academic contexts' (Lea & Street, 2006, 376). This model is one that applies directly to the role of GTA: through work with the LD department, GTAs are encouraged, through collaboration with staff and students, to explore the range of genres, identities, modes and processes involved in their own career development as educators, and in the academic development of the students with which they work.

The key takeaway elements from this collaborative practice, then, are:

- the importance of multi- and interdisciplinary development in liberatory learning and teaching practice for early-career academics;
- the significance of a standardized, easy-to-use platform for instant communication and dialogue, where that is then utilized for collaborative, cooperative and collegiate working practices;
- the impact of multi- and interdisciplinary communication as an essential part of the twenty-first-century student's studies and of academics' practice; and
- the ongoing relevance of the academic literacies model in developing students and staff at all levels.

Researching Together: A Collaborative Research Volunteer Scheme and Its Student-staff Partnership Evaluation

Lynn Wright, Max Korbmacher, Martha Gardiner, Julia Ngadi, Ayesha Shahid and Scott M. Hardie

- A 'student as partners' approach successfully underpins our undergraduate research volunteer scheme.
- Successful partnerships require a structured approach, with clear communication about expectations and roles.
- Student 'partners in research' learn from the collaborative co-construction of knowledge.
- Research projects enabling a greater degree of co-creation were seen to provide the greatest mutual benefits.

Introduction

Engaging students in research programmes is beneficial; students gain valuable experience, develop core skills and form collaborative working practices with staff and with each other (Madan & Teitge, 2013). The Research Volunteer Scheme (RVS), a collaborative research initiative for students and staff, has run at Abertay University, Scotland since 2006 and at the time was not typical in the UK sector. The RVS continues to successfully run and has expanded over the last fifteen years covering all academic schools in the University. Increased participation by staff and students across the years demonstrates this to be a robust and enduring collaborative activity. Initially conceived by two colleagues in Psychology, it continues to be self-managed by academic staff, working with undergraduates. It is open to all academic staff across the

Table 4.2 RVS – example project types and degree of potential collaboration.

Type	Student role	Degree of potential partnership/collaboration
Students as partners: Staff/students collaborate to achieve the project	Students and staff are co-investigators, collaborating on all aspects of the project	Full partnership potential (see Cook-Sather et al., 2014)
Assistance/collaboration: Problem/area defined by supervisors but actual project to be co-designed by student participants	Researching specific areas, generating ideas, more aligned with the PG student model	Research team member, possibly akin to a junior researcher role, more autonomy than the previous projects
Dissemination: Science Fair Demonstrators	Co-worker, acting with staff members and/or in student teams	Design of task and implementation is usually collaborative
Research Data Generation: Data Collection, Lab tasks	Carrying out tasks, may or may not be directly supervised but usually trained and supported	Limited a lot of the time but there may be some choices, and some supervisors ask the student to research the area and present alternative methods, etc.
Specific Task Undertaken: Review literature, Transcription, Coding	Conducting the review – some autonomy on topic/search possible	May be limited, often chosen by students returning home during the summer, contact periodically via email

University who want to take part and involves students across all years of study. Each year, staff advertise research opportunities/projects to students to launch the scheme, and students apply for specific collaboration opportunities from a list proposed by staff (see Table 4.2 for examples). While we assume the usual benefits of participation (see John & Creighton, 2011), we wanted to further explore the nature of the collaboration and its meaning for participants in the scheme. Central to this exploration was the staff-student partnership we specifically created to do this. This case study outlines the scheme itself and the findings from our partnership project.

RVS for Students at Abertay University

The current iteration of the RVS involves a tried and tested format. There is an RVS coordinator who oversees the scheme and completes the associated administration. Within subject areas, individuals coordinate a local version of the scheme and contact staff to solicit relevant projects. Templates for project descriptions are provided (title, staff, brief details/tasks, approximate contribution), along with completed exemplars. Projects are collated and evaluated for suitability, and ethical approval is gained. Once collated, projects are advertised to students who are invited to apply. Applications involve students ranking project choices, and crucially involve a 300-word statement outlining their motivations to take part. Student applications are evaluated and students are assigned to projects based on their interests. Upon completion, they receive certification and a profile of experience (outlining, for example, specific training, experience and skills gained).

The RVS hosts a variety of collaborative projects, ranging from a typical research assistant model (where students assist staff with specific tasks) through to co-working, acting as co-researchers (see Table 4.2 for example).

The RVS Team at Abertay University

In our RVS model, collaboration is essential: throughout our careers we have valued working with others acknowledging collaboration as a powerful way of harnessing the potential of individuals, creating new and exciting synergies. Key to our ethos is the decision that this scheme would be one of partnerships for mutual benefits. Research has highlighted the issue of power and hierarchy within a university setting, especially between staff and students (e.g. Marquis et al., 2019), and we were careful to create a structure with clear expectations and guidelines (see Table 4.2). This included term time limits – and ensuring that skills learned and work carried out were formally recorded on students' Higher Education Achievement Record (HEAR) which accompanies their degree certificate.

A recent collaborative project involved an evaluation of the RVS itself. Our team developed, designed and conducted the evaluation project and analysed the data together. Frequent informal meetings allowed us to exchange ideas, discuss the project and prepare to disseminate the information. Meeting regularly as a group and brainstorming ideas allowed us to get to know each other and work much more collaboratively.

Method

The aim of our evaluation was to investigate perceptions of working together within the RVS project from both student and staff perspectives. Four student researchers and two staff members worked on the project. The students designed two interview schedules based on previous empirical research on student research experience (see, for example, Davidson & Lyons, 2018). Questions asked to students and staff included motivation for participating in the RVS, what they hoped to gain from participation and reflections on working with staff/students. Participants were recruited via an advert on the University's intranet, and through meetings with other staff and students participating in the RVS.

Eleven students and four staff were interviewed face-to-face, and seven staff and eight students completed interview questions online. All participants had experience of the RVS. Interviews were transcribed verbatim and analysed thematically using Braun and Clarke's (2006) six steps. The research team read through all transcripts, making coding notes. Initial codes were examined, reflected upon, combined and refined, and thematic maps were developed and consolidated in an iterative process. In this case study, we focus on the 'Working Together' theme. The other themes not directly related to collaboration (e.g. enhancing employability, developing research skills, increasing confidence) will be discussed elsewhere.

Findings: Working Together

'Working Together' covers aspects of collaboration, mutual benefit and perceptions of what students and staff gained from their partnerships, whatever form their research projects took.

Overall, the RVS was seen by participants as authentic collaboration from its inception, and this is summed up by *Staff 3* who reflects the cooperative ethos:

> Examples in other institutions with research volunteers … where I suppose students were taken advantage of, so students were perhaps keen and naïve and would do lots and lots of stuff sometimes to the detriment of their own work. [RVS] was going to be supportive and also be useful for the student and for the staff member so that both parties were winning.

This view was shared by *Staff 4* and *Student 19* as something more than the experience gained:

> It's a real two-way thing, students get experience and staff get help and support with research projects.

> It did influence me as a team member as I learnt to collaborate with different people and to share responsibilities and tasks according to everyone's strengths and limits.

This also reflects the view that there was a clear sense of partnership, chiming with Cook-Sather et al.'s (2014) definition of SaP. This is supported by *Staff 2*, illustrating that the RVS enables the sort of breaking down of barriers suggested by Bovill (2017):

> I felt I was part of the team. It wasn't just that they were joining working with me, I was joining working with them. So, we were a team …

This was also highlighted across many student interviews, where participation created a sense of inclusion, community and involvement, confirming participants' identities as collaborators within the team, making them partners in their own education rather than mere consumers (Gravett et al., 2020). The opportunity to co-construct knowledge and engage in authentic aspects of university academic practices empowers students' academic development and identity.

This transformation was outlined by a number of students describing how they felt part of a collaborative team and community, and this is summed up by *Student 3*.

> There's more of an understanding in a collaborative sense and I feel from working with supervisors … that it's more of a relationship you have with them, that it's working together with them on a project, not they're going to tell you what to do …

The collaborative nature of their RVS project also helped increase their confidence:

> Confidence would probably be the right word, to have ownership of a project and … collaborate with other people and do it together ….
> (Student 3)

Whilst on the whole the experiences were positive there were responses that suggested 'students did not participate fully' or that staff email communication was not engaging. This emphasizes the need for a meaningful partnership to have mutual effort, good communication and clarity of roles (Martens et al., 2019). It is also essential to address issues and power imbalances early on and establish a strong community for a sustainable and successful partnership (Healey et al., 2014). We feel that our open but structured approach to true partnership has been central to this; good practice is to set out the parameters for cooperation at the start and create an ongoing dialogue between partners.

Conclusion and Recommendations for Practice/Praxis

The RVS is a robust and long-lasting co-curricular programme that is academically focused and collaborative; that facilitates the formation of valuable partnerships between staff and students; and is scalable and portable. As reinforced by our evaluation, it has a positive impact not only relating to research skills and experience, but it also enhances competence and confidence aiding students now, and in the future. A vital component for this is the enactment of SaP principles, namely that students and staff work together in a mutually beneficial collaborative relationship. To quote one staff member, where students are co-creators and co-constructors of the study, 'that works especially well' which represents the higher end of Bovill and Bulley's (2011) ladder and epitomizes key elements of a successful approach.

References

Introduction

Bullock, S., Shobrook, E., Macfarlane, M., Robertson, K., Hill, E., Brown, S., Pemberton, E., Scott, L., & McWilliams, L. (2022). Students as co-creators. *Phoenix*, 164. https://issuu.com/agcas_00/docs/phoenix_issue_164_february_2022?ff

Burns, T., Sinfield, S., & Abegglen, S. (2019). Third space partnerships with students: Becoming educational together. *International Journal for Students as Partners, 3*(1), 60–8. DOI: 10.15173/ijsap.v3i1.3742

Cook-Sather, A., Bovill, C., & Felten, P. (2014). *Engaging students as partners in learning and teaching: A guide for faculty.* John Wiley & Sons.

Felten, P., & Lambert, L. M. (2020). *Relationship-rich education: How human connection drive success in college.* Johns Hopkins University Press.

Harrington, K., Sinfield, S., & Burns, T. (2021). Student engagement. In H. Pokorny, & D. Warren (Eds.), *Enhancing teaching practice in higher education* (2nd ed., pp. 106–24). Sage.

Healey, M., Flint, A., & Harrington, K. (2016). Students as partners: Reflections on a conceptual model. *Teaching & Learning Inquiry, 4*(2), 8–20.

Mercer–Mapstone, L., Dvorakova, S. L., Matthews, K. E., Abbot, S., Cheng, B., Felten, P., Knorr, K., Marquis, E., Shammas, R., & Swaim, K. (2017). A systematic literature review of students as partners in higher education. *International Journal for Students as Partners, 1*(1), 1–23. DOI: 10.15173/ijsap.v1i1.3119

Muller, M. J. (2007). *Participatory design: The third space in HCI* (2nd ed.). CRC Press.

Case Study: Enhancing the Wider Postgraduate Experience

Bamber, V., Choudhary, C. J., Hislop, J., & Lane, J. (2019). Postgraduate taught students and preparedness for master's level study: Polishing the facets of the master's diamond. *Journal of Further and Higher Education, 43*(2), 236–50. DOI: 10.1080/0309877X.2017.1359502

Bovill, C., Cook-Sather, A., Felten, P., Millard, L., & Moore-Cherry, N. (2016). Addressing potential challenges in co-creating learning and teaching: Overcoming resistance, navigating institutional norms and ensuring inclusivity in student-staff partnerships. *Higher Education, 71*, 195–208. DOI: 10.1007/s10734-015-9896-4

Burns, T., Sinfield, S. F., & Abegglen, S. (2019). Third space partnerships with students: Becoming educational together. *International Journal for Students as Partners, 3*(1), 60–8. DOI: 10.15173/ijsap.v3i1.3742

Cook-Sather, A. (2014). Student-faculty partnership in explorations of pedagogical practice: A threshold concept in academic development. *International Journal for Academic Development, 19*(3), 186–98. DOI: 10.1080/1360144X.2013.805694

Evans, C., Nguyen, T., Richardson, M., & Scott, I. (2018). Managing the transition from undergraduate to taught postgraduate study: Perceptions of international students studying in the UK. *Research in Post-compulsory Education, 23*(2), 249–65. DOI: 10.1080/13596748.2018.1444386

Macleod, G., Barnes, T., & Huttly, S. R. A. (2019). Teaching at masters level: Between a rock and a hard place. *Teaching in Higher Education, 24*, 493–509. DOI: 10.1080/13562517.2018.1491025

Matthews, K. E., Cook-Sather, A., & Healey, M. (2018). Connecting learning, teaching, and research through student-staff partnerships: Toward universities as egalitarian learning communities. In V. Tong, A. Standen, & M. Sotiriou (Eds.), *Shaping higher education with students: Ways to connect research and teaching* (pp. 23–9). University College of London Press.

McPherson, C., Punch, S., & Graham, E. (2017). Transitions from undergraduate to taught postgraduate study: Emotion, integration and belonging. *Journal of Perspectives in Applied Academic Practice, 5*(2), 42–50. DOI: 10.14297/jpaap.v5i2.265

Mercer-Mapstone, L., Dvorakova, S. L., Matthews, K. E., Abbot, S., Cheng, B., Felten, P., Knorr, K., Marquis, E., Shammas, R., & Swaim, K. (2017). A systematic literature review of students as partners in higher education. *International Journal for Students as Partners*, *1*(1). DOI: 10.15173/ijsap.v1i1.3119

Mihans, I. I., Richard, J., Long, D. T., & Felten, P. (2008). Power and expertise: Student-faculty collaboration in course design and the scholarship of teaching and learning. *International Journal for the Scholarship of Teaching and Learning*, *2*(2), 16.

Peacock, S., Cowan, J., Lindesay, I., & Williams, J. (2020). An exploration into the importance of a sense of belonging for online learners. *The International Review of Research in Open and Distributed Learning*, *21*(2), 18–35. DOI: 10.19173/irrodl.v20i5.4539

Case Study: Students as Co-creators of an Inclusive Equality and Diversity Teaching Resource

Boston Student Advisory Council (2012). We are the ones in the classrooms – ask us! – Student voice in teacher evaluations. *Harvard Educational Review*, *82*(1), 153–62. DOI: 10.17763/haer.82.1.t3lu73624p0p31w2

Brew, A. (2003). Teaching and research: New relationships and their implications for inquiry-based teaching and learning in higher education. *Higher Education Research and Development*, *22*(1), 3–18. DOI: 10.1080/0729436032000056571

Campbell, F., Eland, J., Rumpus, A., & Shacklock, R. (2009). *Hearing the student voice: Involving students in curriculum design and delivery*. Edinburgh Napier University.

Carrington, S. (1999). Inclusion needs a different school culture. *International Journal of Inclusive Education*, *3*(3), 257–68. DOI: 10.1080/136031199285039

Deloney, L. A., Graham, C. J., & Erwin, D. O. (2000). Presenting cultural diversity and spirituality to first-year medical students. *AcademicMedicine*, *75*(1), 513–4. https://pubmed.ncbi.nlm.nih.gov/10824784/

Dogra, N., Bhatti, F., Ertubey, C., Kelly, M., Rowlands, A., Singh, D., & Turner, M. (2016). Teaching diversity to medical undergraduates: Curriculum development, delivery and assessment. *Medical Teacher*, *38*(4), 323–37. DOI: 10.3109/0142159X.2015.1105944

Dunlap, J. C. (2005). Problem-based learning and self-efficacy: How a capstone course prepares students for a profession. *Educational Technology Research and Development*, *53*(1), 65–83. DOI: 10.1007/BF02504

Equality and Human Rights Commission (2019). *Racial harassment inquiry: Survey of universities*. Research Report No. 130. Equality and Human Rights Commission. https://www.equalityhumanrights.com/sites/default/files/racial-harassment-inquiry-survey-of-universities.pdf

Gibson, S. (2015). When rights are not enough: What is? Moving towards new pedagogy for inclusive education within UK universities. *International Journal of Inclusive Education*, *19*(8), 875–86. DOI: 10.1080/13603116.2015.1015177

Healey, M. (2005). Linking research and teaching to benefit student learning. *Journal of Geography in Higher Education*, *29*(2), 183–201. DOI: 10.1080/03098260500130387

Henneman, E. A., Lee, J. L., & Cohen, J. I. (1995). Collaboration: A concept analysis. *Journal of Advanced Nursing*, *21*(1), 103–9. DOI: 10.1046/j.1365-2648.1995.21010103.x

Kang, S. J., Kim, E. J., & Shin, H. J. (2016). Convergence study about problem-based learning and self-directed learning ability, problem solving skills, academic self-efficacy, motivation toward learning of nursing students. *Journal of the Korea Convergence Society*, *7*(2), 33–41. DOI: 10.15207/JKCS.2016.7.2.033

Kek, M. Y. C. A., & Huijser, H. (2011). The power of problem-based learning in developing critical thinking skills: Preparing students for tomorrow's digital futures in today's classrooms. *Higher Education Research & Development*, *30*(3), 329–41. DOI: 10.1080/07294360.2010.501074

Maunder, R. (2015). Working with students as partners in pedagogic research: Staff and student experiences of participating in an institutional bursary scheme. *Journal of Educational Innovation, Partnership and Change*, *1*(1), 2055–4990. DOI: 10.21100/jeipc.v1i1.162

National Union of Students (2020). *Education beyond the straight and narrow – LGBT students' experiences in Higher Education*. https://www.nusconnect.org.uk/resources/education-beyond-the-straight-and-narrow-lgbt-students-experiences-in-higher-education

Phungsuk, R., Viriyavejakul, C., & Ratanaolarn, T. (2017). Development of a problem-based learning model via a virtual learning environment. *Kasetsart Journal of Social Sciences*, *38*(3), 297–306. DOI: 10.1016/j.kjss.2017.01.001

Schuman, S. (2006). *Creating a culture of collaboration*. Jossey-Bass.

Siu, H. M., Laschinger, H. K. S., & Vingilis, E. (2005). The effect of problem-based learning on nursing students' perceptions of empowerment. *Journal of Nursing Education*, *44*(10), 459–69. DOI: 10.3928/01484834-20051001-04

Toshalis, E., & Nakkula, M. J. (2012). *Motivation, engagement and student voice*. Jobs for the Future.

Wahyu, W., & Syaadah, R. S. (2018). Implementation of problem-based learning (PBL) approach to improve student's academic achievement and creativity on the topic of electrolyte and non-electrolyte solutions at vocational school. *Journal of Physics Conference Series*, *1013*(1), 012096. https://iopscience.iop.org/article/10.1088/1742-6596/1013/1/012096

Case Study: Speaking of Vocabulary

Badenhorst, C. (2018). Citation practices of postgraduate students writing literature reviews. *London Review of Education*, *43*(2), 263–75. DOI: 10.18546/LRE.16.1.11

Biesta, G. J. (2012). Giving teaching back to education: Responding to the disappearance of the teacher. *Phenomenology & Practice*, *6*(2), 35–49. DOI: 10.29173/pandpr19860

Casal, J. E., & Lu, X. (2021). 'Maybe complicated is a better word': Second language English graduate student responses to syntactic complexity in a genre-based academic writing course. *International Journal of English for Academic Purposes: Research and Practice*, *1*(1), 95–114. DOI: 10.3828/ijeap.2021.7

Cobb, T. (2021). *VocabProfilers*. https://www.lextutor.ca/vp/comp/

Durrant, P. (2016). To what extent is the academic vocabulary list relevant to university student writing? *English for Specific Purposes*, *43*, 49–61. DOI: 10.1016/j.esp.2016.01.004

Gourlay, L. (2017). Student engagement, 'learnification' and the sociomaterial: Critical perspectives on higher education policy. *Higher Education Policy*, *30*(1), 23–34. DOI: 10.1057/s41307-016-0037-1

Gravett, K. (2020). Feedback literacies as sociomaterial practice. *Critical Studies in Education*, 1–14. DOI: 10.1080/17508487.2020.1747099

Jeyaraj, J. J., & Harland, T. (2019). Linking critical pedagogy practice to higher education in Malaysia: Insights from English language teachers. *Asia Pacific Journal of Education*, *39*(1), 1–13. DOI: 10.1080/02188791.2019.1572590

Kumpulainen, K., & Kajamaa, A. (2020). Sociomaterial movements of students' engagement in a school's makerspace. *British Journal of Educational Technology, 51*(4), 1292–307. DOI: 10.1111/bjet.12932

Loo, D. B., & Sairattanain, J. (2021). Disrupting discourses of deficiency in English for academic purposes: Dialogic reflection with a critical friend. *Pedagogy, Culture & Society*, 1–17. DOI: 10.1080/14681366.2021.1947355

MacLeod, A., Cameron, P., Ajjawi, R., Kits, O., & Tummons, J. (2019). Actor-network theory and ethnography: Sociomaterial approaches to researching medical education. *Perspectives on Medical Education, 8*, 177–86. DOI: 10.1007/s40037-019-0513-6

Ozdem-Yilmaz, Y., & Bilican, K. (2020). Discovery learning – Jerome Bruner. In B. Akpan, & T. J. Kennedy (Eds.), *Science Education in Theory and Practice. Springer Texts in Education* (pp. 177–90). Springer, Cham. DOI: 10.1007/978-3-030-43620-9_13

Towns, S. G. (2020). Which word list should I teach? Using word lists to support textbook vocabulary instruction. *THAITESOL Journal, 33*(1), 20–35. https://eric.ed.gov/?id=EJ1257894

Tietjen, P., Ozkan Bekiroglu, S., Choi, K., Rook, M. M., & McDonald, S. P. (2021). Three sociomaterial framings for analysing emergent activity in future learning spaces. *Pedagogy, Culture & Society*, 1–20. DOI: 10.1080/14681366.2021.1881593

Wilby, J. (2020). Motivation, self-regulation, and writing achievement on a university foundation programme: A programme evaluation study. *Language Teaching Research*, 1–24. DOI: 10.1177/1362168820917323

Winkle-Wagner, R., & McCoy, D. L. (2016). Entering the (postgraduate) field: Underrepresented students' acquisition of cultural and social capital in graduate school preparation programs. *The Journal of Higher Education, 87*(2), 178–205. DOI: 10.1080/00221546.2016.11777399

Case Study: Staff-student Collaboration across Disciplines

Abegglen, S., Burns, T., & Sinfield, S. (2019). It's learning development, Jim – but not as we know it: Academic literacies in third-space. *Journal of Learning Development in Higher Education, 15*, Article 15. https://journal.aldinhe.ac.uk/index.php/jldhe/article/view/500

Auten, J. G., & Twigg, M. M. (2015). Teaching and learning SoTL: Preparing future faculty in a pedagogy course. *Teaching & Learning Inquiry: The ISSOTL Journal, 3*(1), 3–13. DOI: 10.2979/teachlearninqu.3.1.3

Bownes, J., Ramsay, S., & Struan, A. (2020). Let's talk about [X]: A reflection on a model for engaging undergraduate students in research communication. In S. Mawani, & A. Mukadam (Eds.), *Student empowerment in higher education: Reflecting on teaching practice and learner engagement: Vol. II* (pp. 351–65). Logos Verlag.

Boyle, J., Ramsay, S., & Struan, A. (2019). The academic writing skills programme: A model for technology-enhanced, blended delivery of an academic writing programme. *Journal of University Teaching & Learning Practice, 16*(4), 1–12.

Bury, S., & Sheese, R. (2016). Academic literacies as cornerstones in course design: A partnership to develop programming for faculty and teaching assistants. *Journal of University Teaching & Learning Practice, 13*(3). https://ro.uow.edu.au/jutlp/vol13/iss3/3

Chan, C. K. Y., & Luo, J. (2021). A four-dimensional conceptual framework for student assessment literacy in holistic competency development. *Assessment & Evaluation in Higher Education, 46*(3), 451–66. DOI: 10.1080/02602938.2020.1777388

Craney, C., McKay, T., Mazzeo, A., Morris, J., Prigodich, C., & de Groot, R. (2011). Cross-discipline perceptions of the undergraduate research experience. *The Journal of Higher Education, 82*(1), 92–113. DOI: 10.1080/00221546.2011.11779086

Donovan, C., & Erskine-Shaw, M. (2020). 'Maybe I can do this. Maybe I should be here': Evaluating an academic literacy, resilience and confidence programme. *Journal of Further and Higher Education, 44*(3), 326–40. DOI: 10.1080/0309877X.2018.1541972

Gaia, A. C., Corts, D. P., Tatum, H. E., & Allen, J. (2003). The GTA mentoring program: An interdisciplinary approach to developing future faculty as teacher-scholars. *College Teaching, 51*(2), 61–5.

Gennis, H., DiLorenzo, M., Riddell, R. P., Spiegel, R., Connolly, J., & Martin, J. (2020). Does exposure to university researchers improve undergraduate perceptions of research?: A quasi cluster-randomized controlled trial. *Innovations in Education and Teaching International, 57*(6), 655–67. DOI: 10.1080/14703297.2019.1654401

Hey-Cunningham, A. J., Ward, M. H., & Miller, E. J. (2021). Making the most of feedback for academic writing development in postgraduate research: Pilot of a combined programme for students and supervisors. *Innovations in Education and Teaching International, 58*(2), 182–94. DOI: 10.1080/14703297.2020.1714472

Hill, P. (2010). From deficiency to development: The evolution of academic skills provision at one UK university. *Journal of Learning Development in Higher Education, 2*, 1–19. DOI: 10.47408/jldhe.v0i2.54

Huffmyer, A. S., & Lemus, J. D. (2019). Graduate TA teaching behaviors impact student achievement in a research-based undergraduate science course. *Journal of College Science Teaching, 48*(3), 56–65.

Lea, M. R., & Street, B. V. (1998). Student writing in higher education: An academic literacies approach. *Studies in Higher Education, 23*(2), 157–72. DOI: 10.1080/03075079812331380364

Lea, M. R., & Street, B. V. (2006). The 'academic literacies' model: Theory and applications. *Theory into Practice, 45*(4), 368–77. DOI: 10.1207/s15430421tip4504_11

Mariani, M., Buckley, F., Reidy, T., & Witmer, R. (2013). Promoting student learning and scholarship through undergraduate research journals. *PS: Political Science & Politics, 46*(4), 830–5. DOI: 10.1017/S1049096513001133

McVitty, D. (2021). *From work-ready to world-ready – why breaking down knowledge silos is the next frontier in student development.* WonkHE. https://wonkhe.com/blogs/from-work-ready-to-world-ready-why-breaking-down-knowledge-silos-is-the-next-frontier-in-student-development/

Park, J. H., & Choi, H. J. (2009). Factors influencing adult learners' decision to drop out or persist in online learning. *Journal of Educational Technology & Society, 12*(4), 207–17.

Prieto, L. R., & Altmaier, E. M. (1994). The relationship of prior training and previous teaching experience to self-efficacy among graduate teaching assistants. *Research in Higher Education, 35*(4), 481–97.

Ridgway, J. S., Ligocki, I. Y., Horn, J. D., Szeyiler, E., & Breitenberger, C. A. (2017). Teaching assistant and faculty perceptions of ongoing, personalized TA professional development: Initial lessons and plans for the future. *Journal of College Science Teaching, 46*(5), 73–83.

Ryker, K., & McConnell, D. (2014). Can graduate teaching assistants teach inquiry-based geology labs effectively? *Journal of College Science Teaching, 44*(1), 56–63.

Stamp, N., Tan-Wilson, A., & Silva, A. (2015). Preparing graduate students and undergraduates for interdisciplinary research. *BioScience, 65*(4), 431–9. DOI: 10.1093/biosci/biv017

Struan, A. (2021). Active blended learning at scale: University-wide writing programmes. In B. C. P. Rodriguez, & A. Armellini (Eds.), *Cases on active blended learning in higher education* (pp. 106–21). IGI Global.

Yu, S. (2020). Giving genre-based peer feedback in academic writing: Sources of knowledge and skills, difficulties and challenges. *Assessment & Evaluation in Higher Education, 0*(0), 1–18. DOI: 10.1080/02602938.2020.1742872

Case Study: Researching Together

Bovill, C. (2017). A framework to explore roles within student–staff partnerships in higher education: Which students are partners, when and in what ways? *International Journal for Students as Partners, 1*(1). DOI: 10.15173/ijsap.v1i1.3062

Bovill, C., & Bulley, C. J. (2011). A model of active student participation in curriculum design: Exploring desirability and possibility. In C. Rust (Ed.), *Improving student learning (ISL) 18: Global theories and local practices: Institutional, disciplinary and cultural variations* (Series: Improving Student Learning, 18) (pp. 176–88). Oxford Brookes University, Oxford Centre for Staff and Learning Development.

Braun, V., & Clarke, V. (2006). Using thematic analysis in psychology. *Qualitative Research in Psychology, 3*(2), 77–101. DOI: 10.1191/1478088706qp063oa

Cook-Sather, A., Bovill, C., & Felton, P. (2014). *Engaging students as partners in learning and teaching: A guide for faculty*. Jossey-Bass.

Davidson, J. M., & Lyons, M. (2018). Undergraduates as researchers – the impact of active participation in research and conference presentation on psychology undergraduate identity and career aspirations. *Journal of Perspectives in Applied Academic Practice, 6*(1), 39–46. DOI: 10.14297/jpaap.v6i1.320

Gravett, K., Kinchin, I. M., & Winstone, N. E. (2020). 'More than customers': Conceptions of students as partners held by students, staff, and institutional leaders. *Studies in Higher Education, 45*(12), 2574–87. DOI: 10.1080/03075079.2019.1623769

Healey, M., Flint, A., & Harrington, K. (2014). *Engagement through partnership: Students as partners in learning and teaching in higher education*. The Higher Education Academy.

John, J., & Creighton, J. (2011). Researcher development: The impact of undergraduate research opportunity programmes on students in the UK. *Studies in Higher Education, 36*(7), 781–97. DOI: 10.1080/03075071003777708

Madan, C. R., & Teitge, B. D. (2013). The benefits of undergraduate research: The student's perspective. *The Mentor: An Academic Advising Journal, 15*. DOI: 10.26209/mj1561274

Marquis, E., Jayaratnam, A., Lei, T., & Mishra, A. (2019). Motivations, barriers, & understandings: How students at four universities perceive student-faculty partnership programs. *Higher Education Research & Development, 38*(6), 1240–54. DOI: 10.1080/07294360.2019.1638349

Martens, S. E., Meeuwissen, S. N. E., Dolmans, H. J. M., Bovill, C. & Könings, K. D. (2019). Student participation in the design of learning and teaching: Disentangling the terminology and approaches. *Medical Teacher Short Communication*, https://www.tandfonline.com/doi/full/10.1080/0142159X.2019.1615610.

5

Collaboration with Stakeholders

Introduction

The cooperative, humane university works against the tradition of the individualistic, competitive one (Barnett, 2004) and thus requires methods and methodologies that make space for the whole person – student and staff member: a collective 'third space' (Bhabha, 2012; Burns et al., 2019; Gutierrez, 2008) where, by 'being with' (Nancy, 2000), individuals start to come together and 'become' together. Or, as Soja (1996) said, a space that allows for collaborative praxes and habits enabling the formation of Communities of Practice (Lave & Wenger, 1991), that sustain, provoke, challenge, extend and support. Communities that encourage reflection, innovation and change – crucial capacities in addressing real-world issues. Issues which include addressing the barriers to collaboration: time and financial poverty, precarious contracts, lack of self-efficacy and/or institutional support.

In this section of *Collaboration in Higher Education*, we provide case studies where societal and academic culture come and work together for 'real' change. We uncover the ways in which habits of being and working together help those stakeholders inside and outside the university to embrace the uncertainty (Sinfield et al., 2019) of the precarious and often hostile practices of a neoliberal world and a marketized academia, and sustain our academic identities and our praxes in creative ways (Robinson, 2006).

The case studies focus on those partnerships that develop alongside the university where schools, external partners and other higher education institutions come together to meet real needs, and foster student learning and success. The authors demonstrate that in each case, the very collaborative processes in and with which they engaged, helped academics and students, communities and individuals, the public and private sectors, allies and opponents, work more powerfully together to achieve common goals. A key to success was for partners to find their way 'into' the idea and work together to share experience, practices and resources whilst working together to shift strategy (Huxham, 1996), often developing their approach to what 'counts' as academic practice as a result.

The Case Study Chapters

Tutors, Students, and Other Stakeholders at the Roundtable by Gabriella Rodolico, Deborah Simpson and Geoff Barret outlines how a multi-stakeholder project designed to increase appreciation of the nature of STEM created commitment, energy and community. A unique collaboration between university and schools created an engaging engineering project for primary and secondary pupils, their parents and staff. The 'working-together' approach enabled professional dialogue and development between and among STEM practitioners (technicians and academics), student teachers and the wider school community.

In *Healthcare Scientist Education,* Carol Ainley demonstrates how universities can collaborate to produce an excellent student experience. The chapter looks at how three universities came together to overcome traditional barriers to collaboration, working together to deliver science education to healthcare professionals for the benefit of both the students and the institutions. Ongoing, open dialogue where all partners have an equal voice has been key to this project's success.

Multi-partner Doctoral Training Collaborations by Donna Palmer, Rachel Van Krimpen and Susanna Ison discusses four types of collaboration which the authors have identified as underpinning the successful delivery of their collaborative, cross-institutional doctoral training programmes. The chapter highlights the innovative approaches they employed to initiate and maintain working partnerships between academic and non-academic stakeholders and the ways that they have shared knowledge, expertise, resources and facilities across their consortium to the benefit of students, lecturers and institutions alike.

Tutors, Students and Other Stakeholders at the Roundtable: A Matter of Equal Partnership

Gabriella Rodolico, Deborah Simpson and Geoff Barrett

- The development of STEM capacity in in-service and pre-service teachers can be achieved by collaborative projects that happen in the real world of the school.
- Academic and non-academic experts should be actively involved in collaborative processes with in-service and pre-service teachers and Initial Teacher Education tutors and other stakeholders to devise and develop innovative community projects to facilitate authentic learning.
- Community-based learning projects create practice where knowledge and experience can be exchanged in an ethos of equity and mutual enrichment.
- Multi-stakeholder projects model that teaching is best not as traditional 'pedagogy', but as the dialogic facilitation of communal learning.
- HE tutors should foster equal partnership with their students by actively involving them in their own learning, modelling a life-long professional development mindset.

Introduction

STEM education is considered an integral part of our future economic and social development (Scottish Government, 2017; Sharma & Yarlagadda, 2018); however, teachers entering the primary profession tend not to enter teacher education courses with a specific science background. Research shows that teachers are concerned about several barriers to their successful delivery of STEM subjects, such as lack of subject knowledge (Jones et al., 2021), pedagogical challenges of teaching science and lack of teacher support. Arguably, this could be overcome by promoting collaboration with peers as part of effective professional development (Margot & Kettler, 2019).

It is also plausible to think that a focus on the nature of STEM as a whole, rather than individual STEM subjects (Kelley & Knowles, 2016), will enable Initial Teacher Education (ITE) institutions to promote professional dialogue between and among STEM practitioners (technicians and academics) and student teachers – creating an equal partnership where the sharing of knowledge, as well as of learning and teaching experiences, could generate professional development opportunities and enhance student teachers' self-efficacy with respect to STEM delivery (Healey et al., 2016). It has been recommended that educators work together with industries and schools (Veenstra, 2014) to create hands-on activities which could enhance fundamental STEM skills (Ejiwale, 2013).

Building on this premise, in early 2020, Gabriella Rodolico, lecturer in Science Education at the School of Education, University of Glasgow, and one of the authors of this case study, resolved to address this issue via a new collegiate STEM project aimed to develop a more collaborative approach to STEM learning. Gabriella initiated the programme with a series of professional conversations across a team made up of academic and non-academic professionals (engineering and mathematics), Post Graduate Diploma in Education (PGDE) primary-teacher students and co-authors, Geoff and Deborah, and in-service teachers in mainstream and Additional Support for Needs (ASN) schools.

The team worked together to produce a hands-on remotely delivered STEM Challenge: *Build Your Own Sustainable House*. This project was undertaken by schools, teachers, parents/guardians and pupils to achieve the common goal of learning for Sustainability. Four schools engaged in the STEM challenge, supporting the theoretical aspects and the practical model building, through a series of lessons. These were managed at schools by the in-service and probationer teachers who engaged with pupils, and at home by Gabriella and the Project Engineer Lorna Bennet from the Sustainable Energy (ORE) Catapult who delivered a series of twilight sessions engaging pupils and parents/guardians.

The project's outcomes went far beyond expectations. In this short case study, we, the authors, reflect on the project's outcomes, its collaborative workings as well as the overwhelmingly positive participant feedback. Finally, we present recommendations on how better success in STEM education could be achieved when ideas are exchanged in an active collaborative process between Home-School-University and other stakeholders with pupils in the middle.

Ways of Working: Launching and Reflecting on the Collaborative Project

Recent studies highlight the benefits of Home-School collaboration in both primary and secondary schools. They underline how the interaction between parents and teachers, beyond parents' nights and homework, could promote pupils' autonomy and empower the students' agency (Vedeler, 2021). Our STEM project took a triangulated approach, bringing together Home-School-University – with the University element drawing on the benefits of HE outreach activities. Reimers and Marmolejo (2022) have demonstrated such outreach to be very effective in supporting schools through the production of learning resources and technical support (Lazareva, 2021). The project incorporated third-sector engineering expertise to produce a final hands-on resource to support teachers in developing a deeper understanding of the nature of STEM, and enhance the STEM literacy of their learners, for example, by understanding the engineering design process with a 'to engineering' mindset (MacLeod, 2017), that is, the ability to identify complex problems and generate elaborate practical solutions that meet human needs (Faikhamta, 2020).

As with all engineering projects the process involved collaborative experimentation and prototype development, initiated by an initial STEM challenge: *Build a Floating Turbine* which was jointly developed with the student teachers into the *Build Your Own House* and subsequently *Build Your Own Sustainable House*. The STEM challenge was to be delivered to a total of four schools: one Additional Support Needs (ASN) secondary school and three mainstream primary schools – following an initial pilot in one of the mainstream primary schools in the project.

The pilot was led by in-service teachers where further reflections would refine the delivery plan and extend the project to the ASN school and finally to the last two mainstream primary schools led by Geoff and Deborah. The idea was to build a step-by-step reflective process with progressive and professional conversations between expert and novice teachers as well as University tutors and other stakeholders. This included parents' and pupils' feedback in a scaffolded teacher learning community fashion (Gutierez, 2019). Based on this ethos of equal collaboration, in-service and probationary teachers became active authors of the project, driving those changes that only their professional judgement could suggest (Donaldson, 2014).

Evaluative Collaborator Voices: In-service Teachers

Feedback and teachers' reflections gathered through reflective journals, Zoom chats, Twitter and emails were very positive. In-service teachers from the pilot mainstream primary school commented:

> [This project] has allowed opportunities for learners to brainstorm and discuss in class and in groups the need to use renewable energy and prioritise sustainable building/ houses. […] This project was also successful in raising teachers' and pupils' awareness of the social science.

Teachers also reflected on the importance for pupils to engage with 'a variety of careers related to the social sciences, including research' and to be 'fully engaged' in collaborative learning strategies. Even more importantly, pupils also raised their awareness that women can be very successful in STEM – with Dr Rodolico and Miss Lorna Bennett as positive role models. Feedback also highlighted an unexpected long-term impact of the project as teachers planned:

> … to incorporate elements of this project into our planning for our primary Year 7 classes next year. The learning covered so far has been a valuable introduction that we can now extend.

Parents and pupils' feedback highlighted how enjoyable it was to work collaboratively to build the house and discuss the great variety of topics that this project covered. It also fostered their awareness of STEM and STEM careers: 'I know that STEM careers are critical. Glad to be able to share these tasks with my daughter.'

To facilitate inclusion, sessions were also recorded and offered in a flexible manner and some parents said,

> While I couldn't participate in the live sessions due to work commitments, I think there was a lot of value and learning gained by both my daughter and I and gave us some great quality time together while discussing some real-world issues in a child friendly way.

Teachers at the ASN schools concluded:

> Everyone had the opportunity to achieve. Without doubt, the best 'evaluation' came from the pupil who left school that night with a 'carry-out' pack of equipment curious to develop and extend his learning.

Evaluative Collaborator Voices: Geoff and Deborah's Reflections

The collaborative approach of the project was vital to its success, as Geoff and Deborah reflected:

> Without clear and open communication between teachers, tutors and parents/ guardians, the project would surely have floundered.

> By reflecting on the pilot session and the outcomes from the ASN school, it became clear to us, that some of the material needed further development to be tailored around the needs of our pupils. For example, at my primary school I had younger pupils whose motor skills necessitated additional support and differentiation of process, by completing a simpler circuit than what was used by the other schools (Serret & Earle, 2018). It was also important that parents/ guardians felt comfortable taking part with their child to the asynchronous and/or synchronous sessions as appropriate.

Much was learned from this experience. It was challenging to find the required alignment between theory and practice to embed the project within all other curriculum areas (Bernay et al., 2020). Therefore, the possibility to approach all the other stakeholders as peers was vital to our success.

Due to the disparate range of age and ability it also became necessary to adapt some of the language used. It was felt that, by engaging with more experienced primary teachers and university colleagues, Geoff and I, gained increased skills, knowledge, and confidence to make changes and adapt lessons as appropriate.

(Herbert & Hobbs, 2018; Wang & Wong, 2017)

Lastly, particularly for myself, the involvement of external partners and my University's tutor also gave the project a greater sense of gravitas among pupils, along with a palpable sense of pride because they were 'working with the University of Glasgow' and real people from the industry. The children in my class still talk about this experience now as well as colleagues who wish to build interdisciplinary learning opportunities around it.

Conclusion and Recommendations

This case study is an example of how better success in STEM education can be achieved when ideas are exchanged in an active collaborative process which is able to bring to life the meaning and nature of STEM with a balanced blending of experiences, expertise, knowledge and skills. This case study concludes with some recommendations:

1. Communication is essential throughout a truly collaborative project: scaffold dialogue, before, during and after the project to create and build the learning community.
2. Working collaboratively will give your team a wider range of abilities than you first thought: flexibility, adaptability, reflection.
3. Projects with a social justice agenda tend to provoke greater interest and commitment.

And Finally

As coordinator of this project, I would suggest team leaders harness the social capital and sense of community (Barber & King, 2016) that a multi-stakeholder project creates. In education itself, such an approach also models that authentic learning results not from transmissive pedagogy but via the dialogic facilitation of learning. I have realized how much this alternative way to work with students has generated a mutual enrichment, promoting my own professional development as well as that of my students and the wider school community. I am now working on further implementation of this strategy not only in my courses at the University of Glasgow, but also in several international workshops I am developing in collaboration with global, international universities.

Healthcare Scientist Education: Multi-stakeholder Cross-institutional Collaboration to Deliver Excellent Student Experience

Carol Ainley

- HE institutions working together can go against the nature of competition to effectively deliver an exemplary student experience.
- This chapter looks at how one group has overcome traditional barriers to collaboration and is working together successfully for the benefit of both the students and the institutions.
- Ongoing, open dialogue and ensuring all partners have an equal voice have been key to this project's success.

Introduction

Within the UK, healthcare is delivered via the National Health Service (NHS). Each of the devolved nations of the UK has its own government department to lead on the NHS delivery. In England, Health Education England (HEE) are responsible for the education and training of the workforce, with much of the 'education' aspect undertaken by HE institutions, often universities. Universities compete to deliver the academic (degree) components. In some cases, the cost of this education is provided by HEE and universities must tender for the right to deliver. In Greater Manchester, England, the University of Manchester, Manchester Metropolitan University and University of Salford joined together to form Manchester Academy for Healthcare Scientist Education, in order to tender together, rather than compete, to deliver a new set of educational programmes.

Context

The NHS and public health services in the UK employ over 50,000 healthcare scientists (National School of Healthcare Science n.d. (a)). These encompass different roles, but all 'play a vital role in the prevention, diagnosis and treatment of a huge number of medical conditions' (NHS Careers, n.d.). The role spans research, service transformation, diagnoses and rehabilitation (National School of Healthcare Science n.d. (a); NHS Careers n.d.). Historically, the career pathways, including training and education of these professions, were considered on an individual basis. In 2010, the UK government published 'Modernising Scientific Careers', a structure to provide a common career framework with common educational outcomes, aiming to future-proof these careers (Department of Health and Social Care, 2010). The National School of Healthcare Science (NSHCS) was established to develop training and educational pathways, working with employers to develop curricula which would produce scientists fit for purpose and practice (National School of Healthcare Science n.d. (b)). As is common in the UK, HEE invited tenders from educational providers to deliver on those pathways which were to be commissioned (Health Education England n.d.). The MSc Clinical Science is the educational aspect of the Scientist Training Programme (STP), leading to a career at clinical scientist level (National School of Healthcare Science n.d.(c)). There is an MSc Clinical Science (named route) for the different specialist areas and these were the first programmes offered for tender.

MAHSE Is Born

Greater Manchester is a region in the North West of England, known for its rivalries, be they in sport, music or between academic institutions (Pride of Manchester, 2021; Williams, 2021). When the tender was released for the first MSc Clinical Science programmes, a group of foresighted senior academics recognized that by pooling expertise and working together, bids from a consortium of Greater Manchester universities would be stronger than the sum of individual bids. The vision was to create a 'Community of Practice' (Wenger-Trayner, 2015; Wenger et al., 2002) for the education of NHS trainee healthcare scientists where taught programmes cross institutional boundaries to provide the trainees the best-possible education. What began as a small team of senior academics meeting privately in a coffee shop has expanded to a team of academics, clinicians, support staff, patient and public representatives, professional bodies and students/trainees, all working together with shared values and a common goal of delivering an excellent student experience.

The Manchester Academy for Healthcare Scientist Education (MAHSE) was established in 2012 with the aim of consolidating collaborations between The University of Manchester, Manchester Metropolitan University, The University of Salford and partner NHS employers to provide the best-possible experience for healthcare scientists.

The MAHSE Team

The approach to building the team of stakeholders across the partners was based on transparency and equity. It was recognized that each partner has their strength, with each bringing something unique to the collaborative. Not all contribute equally, but all are equal partners. Beyond the universities and employers, key stakeholders in the MAHSE community of practice include students, lay (patient) representatives, clinical leads, HEE and the NSHCS. These attend stakeholder board meetings biannually and executive boards annually. Further universities are now linked to the consortium as associates, delivering some teaching and assessment and inputting to the discussions about how to ensure the collaborative works to the favour of the student experience.

MAHSE has a core team to support activities; the initial team of two is now a Director, 2x Deputy Directors, MAHSE manager, 2x administration colleagues and 2x e-learning developers – reflecting growth in the programmes and the introduction of a taught doctoral level qualification. All posts within the MAHSE core team are recruited through a transparent competitive process, with interview panels comprising representatives from partners and stakeholders. The MAHSE Director and Deputy Directors ensure that there is support for the programmes and recognition of the value of the partnership within partner institutions; if an institution withdrew from the consortium, the ability to offer an excellent student experience would be reduced. The views of all partners are brought together under MAHSE, through regular meetings and workshops, to encourage further development and allow a distinct voice in negotiating with external bodies. The size of the MAHSE Community of Practice provides a depth and breadth of experience, supporting one another in our delivery and assessment. This has led to frequent invitations as members to national workgroups, implementation groups, curriculum review groups and networks that have set national policies and shaped the education of NHS trainees.

The MAHSE Working Practices

The MAHSE core team works across the universities to ensure that there is parity of education and equity of academic experience across the 20+ discipline-specific programmes of healthcare science, something that was lacking, even within individual institutions, prior to the establishment of MAHSE. The wider team, comprising in addition to the teaching teams, lay representatives and students, work together to deliver the experience, using meetings and workshops to share best practices. The collaborative approach provides flexibility and agility when developing new, or adapting existing, programmes, allowing for the strengths of each institution to be combined to provide the best experience. Each university has their own links with NHS employers within Greater Manchester and beyond, which allows students to be taught by collaborative stakeholders who are subject experts and individuals who are at the forefront of research and clinical innovation. Cross-discipline teaching (Appleby, 2019) has been encouraged, ensuring as little duplicated effort as possible for academics and clinicians, whilst providing the basis for a career in the NHS where multi-disciplinary team working is commonplace (NHS, 2018). This is further reflected in teaching, using clinical skills facilities for inter-disciplinary learning. Lay representatives attend teaching sessions, enhancing teaching delivery and student understanding of how to engage with patients and carers.

The Student Voice

Collaborations can work better when students are regarded as partners not consumers (Healey et al., 2014). The student voice is essential for the development and improvement of our programmes. There is robust student representation, with multiple opportunities for students to feedback to both programme teams and MAHSE, formally and informally. Thus, MAHSE can self-regulate the quality of programmes and equity of experience. Challenges raised through the student voice are addressed as a team, with discussion taking place amongst the appropriate stakeholders to ensure the best outcome. The nature of the consortium allows for open discussion to elicit improvements, even if this means moving learning and teaching resources from one university to another to increase the quality of experience, or influencing processes to ensure no student feels disadvantaged.

Technological Support

Cross-team and cross-institutional collaboration with external stakeholders has led to improved knowledge of resources available and increased innovation. The e-learning developer team members draw on their experience of their wider institutional support networks to provide dedicated professional support infrastructure to facilitate innovation in the use of technology. They work across the main partner universities, overcoming boundaries of access at non-employing universities. This approach increases access to training for teaching staff, increasing knowledge and experience and further sharing best practice.

The pedagogic approach used to facilitate interactive and active learning includes digital technologies and apps, which encourage collaboration amongst students and between lecturers and students. The collaboration has allowed us to build on previous experience at University of Manchester (Mooney et al., 2013), gifting students an iPad at the commencement of their studies. Using these in combination with commercially available apps for learning has facilitated the creation of dynamic interactive learning environments in class, allowing the lecturers to engage with students' learning and understanding during sessions permitting them to tailor the content and their delivery to create the optimum learning environment. Laboratory tours simulated at 360° help contextualize the students' learning and tackle real-life clinical scenarios in a supportive non-intimidating virtual learning environment (Bates, 2015). MAHSE have invested in equipment that is shared across institutions to support the development of such high-quality resources.

Further MAHSE Developments

As a result of the Francis Report in the UK (Francis, 2013), patient and public involvement has become a mandatory component of all HEE-funded academic programmes. The challenge facing the collaborative was how to embed lay representatives (and thus patient views) in the programmes in a meaningful rather than tokenistic way and one that enriched the learning experience of the students. We established a Patient Forum (MAHSE, n.d.), a semi-autonomous group chaired by elected lead lay representatives. Their remit is to take responsibility for the Patient Public Involvement (PPI) Strategy, share good practice and assist and support the programme teams to develop and embed PPI within all aspects of their programme. The Forum has developed a set of guiding principles for patient and public involvement within MAHSE, ensuring all students benefit from raised awareness of the 'patient' in their practice.

Transparent operational and financial structures are key to the success of the approach. Although MAHSE is 'hosted' at one university (for legal and accounting purposes), all receive the same income for their teaching. The MAHSE administrative team support partner institutions and trainees accessing teaching at multiple universities. They are a point of contact to ensure experience is to a high standard, despite variations in working between institutions. The team also support the development of documentation to ensure that where there are multiple institutions delivering one programme, none of those institutions has an unfair burden in the administration of the programme.

Benefits MAHSE Brought

The collaborative cross-institution approach with input from external stakeholders has afforded a number of benefits. Lay representatives, employers, NHS departments and students have had input to the delivery of academic material. Programme teams have been able to draw on academic and clinical expertise from seven universities and over forty individual employers to create innovative educational provision, students have been able to experience different learning environments provided by the partner HE institutions and partnership has facilitated the sharing of good practice between the MAHSE programmes and beyond.

MAHSE's innovative approach to the design and delivery of healthcare science education is considered the 'gold standard' by HEE and the NSHCS. Since its creation in 2012 MAHSE has received multiple commendations from accreditation panels, as well as awards for collaboration and for our patient forum (Advance HE, 2018).

MAHSE has allowed for improved student experience, improved outcomes and thus, by extension, an impact on the provision of the health service. This could not have been achieved without formal collaboration, removing the barrier of 'competitor' to allow full sharing of good practice which we now share more widely. MAHSE has influence on the direction of education for healthcare scientists, working with an increasing number of organizations to produce high-quality graduates and practitioners who understand the benefits of collaboration. These graduates will become the educators of the future, perpetuating this cycle of improvement through collaboration.

To ensure the success of a complex collaboration with several different partners and stakeholders, we have been on a learning curve. Key from the outset was the need for open, honest and non-judgemental conversations to identify what could be the best student experience. Keeping this communication open and developing, through meetings, workshops and board meetings, where we reflect and plan, has ensured that the collaborative has moved forwards. We may not always agree, but everyone has a voice and that voice is always delivered in a supportive manner, to overcome challenges and improve. Provided collaboration works to these ideals, we have shown it can be successful.

Multi-partner Doctoral Training Collaborations: More than the Sum of Their Parts

Donna Palmer, Rachel Van Krimpen and Susanna Ison

- This case study describes four types of collaboration which the authors have identified as underpinning successful delivery of collaborative doctoral training programmes.
- Outlined are examples of innovative approaches to collaborative doctoral training which have been employed to initiate and maintain working partnerships between academic and non-academic stakeholders.
- Examples are provided of how those involved in delivering collaborative doctoral training partnerships share knowledge, expertise, resources and facilities.

Introduction

Over the past twenty years there has been substantial progression in the delivery of doctoral study in UK HE institutions through multi-institutional partnerships (Budd et al., 2018; McAlpine, 2017). This shift towards collaborative doctoral provision demonstrates the evolving nature of the university (Barnett, 2000) and has been guided by funders including UK Research and Innovation (UKRI). There is emphasis on the development of doctoral graduates equipped with training and skills across the breadth and depth of their chosen field of study which prepares them for future careers in and beyond academia. This remit allows institutions to take different approaches to the design and delivery of doctoral research training programmes (Newbury, 2003).

Doctoral Training Partnerships (DTPs) act as a conduit of best practice across these collaborations and rely on significant administrative expertise, interpersonal skills and energy to maximize their effectiveness and to navigate the complexity inherent in multi-institutional collaboration. Drawing on examples from three different UKRI-funded DTPs covering the Arts and Humanities, Biological Sciences and Social Sciences, which are described in more detail below, this case study focuses on four types of collaboration which we have identified as underpinning successful delivery of these programmes:

1. Intra-university collaboration
2. Inter-university collaboration
3. External collaboration
4. Researcher collaboration.

Summary of the Partnerships

Midlands4Cities DTP (M4C)

Funded by the Arts and Humanities Research Council (AHRC), this partnership brings together eight universities from across the Midlands regions of the UK. With the addition of Coventry University and the University of Warwick, M4C grew out of Midlands3Cities and recruits up to 100 Arts and Humanities PhD researchers annually.

Midlands Graduate School DTP (MGS)

This Economic and Social Research Council (ESRC)-funded partnership was established in 2016 and recruits around sixty-five PhD students each year spanning social science disciplines. Led by University of Warwick, it brings together six universities from across the Midlands. Prior to 2017, Birmingham, Warwick and Nottingham Universities ran single institution doctoral training centres.

The Nottingham BBSRC DTP

Funded by the Biotechnology and Biological Sciences Research Council (BBSRC) and led by the University of Nottingham, this programme was a single institution programme from 2012 to 2019 before partnering with Nottingham Trent University (NTU) from 2020. It is a four-year PhD programme which recruits around fifty students per year in research areas spanning the biological sciences, including industry-linked projects.

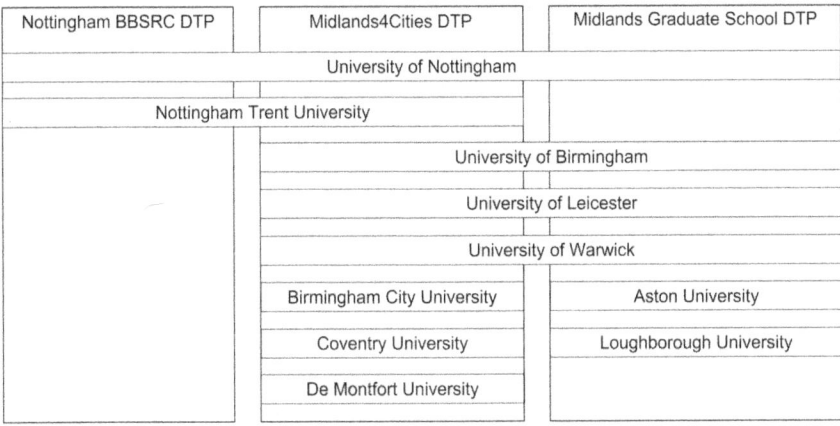

Figure 5.1 Illustration showing which institutions are involved in each of the three DTPs exemplified in this case study.

Types of Collaborations and Examples in Practice

Intra-university Collaborations

All the listed DTPs are multi-faculty and -school programmes, managed centrally within the University of Nottingham's Researcher Academy. Co-location of teams managing DTPs is an effective way to pool expertise within the institution. Managers of twenty-two cohort-based PhD programmes at the University of Nottingham benefit from membership of the Doctoral Training Programmes Managers' Network, a forum for the sharing of best practice, linked with wider university postgraduate researcher networks. It regularly results in cross-programme training development in areas including responsible research and innovation, and peer mentoring.

Many research themes addressed by these DTPs are interdisciplinary and lend themselves to be supported by PhD supervisory teams from multiple schools and faculties. MGS researchers are linked to specific training pathways, for example, 'Health and Wellbeing' draws expertise from disciplines such as Sociology, Social Policy, Health Sciences and Psychology. Approximately half of all PhD projects in the BBSRC DTP include cross-disciplinary supervision. These models allow researchers to access broader academic networks and schools to share the cost of co-funding interdisciplinary studentships.

Inter-university Collaborations

Access to Facilities and Expertise

Inter-university collaborations provide opportunities for researchers to access specialist facilities, including performance spaces or laboratory equipment, and collaborate to develop training based on partner specialisms. In the BBSRC DTP this includes bespoke introductory bioinformatics training led by NTU, and MGS researchers benefit from free access to a portfolio of Masters-level research methods modules. This is only made possible through the partnership as institutions contribute training from their own programmes and facilitate researchers registered at other institutions to attend. This requires substantial administrative support and expertise to align multiple institutional processes.

Technical Support for Inter-university Collaboration

Effective multi-institutional collaboration can be supported through effective IT solutions which help to provide consistency of experience for students regardless of their registered institution.

M4C utilizes a digital platform using Microsoft SharePoint. All M4C researchers, supervisors and administrators have access via their usual university login. The platform enables researchers to build an online profile, communicate and network with peers, access development opportunities and work collaboratively to develop workshops, symposia and conferences. The platform also offers easy access to all guidance documentation and supports progress monitoring.

In contrast, the BBSRC DTP has procured an app called Inkpath which is used by researchers across the consortium to manage their training and development and allows effective monitoring of engagement. Researcher engagement with the system is high, thanks to tailored training and an accessible mobile app interface.

External Collaborations

DTPs reach beyond the HE sector to include diverse collaborators, including industry and creative links of mutual benefit. This is not dissimilar to the concept of collaborative anchor institutions (Birch, 2013); however, the non-academic collaborators of DTPs are not necessarily located in the same geographical region. From a university perspective, these relationships broaden the training offering, strengthen strategic partnerships and may provide leverage for funding for research (both immediate and future). From the collaborator's perspective, they provide the opportunity to explore challenges through hosting a placement or co-supervising a project. They also allow collaborators to build their relationship with academia and can offer development opportunities for their own staff. A tangible outcome of these long-term collaborations is seen in employment outcomes – 8 per cent of the BBSRC DTP's first two graduating cohorts and 30 per cent of ESRC-funded researchers have been employed by their placement hosts.

Each DTP has a specific scheme to grow external collaborations through co-development of projects and co-supervision of studentships. For M4C and MGS, these projects rely on in-kind support, enabling organizations such as charities and non-government organizations to benefit from close links with academia. The BBSRC DTP offers engagements with low financial commitment to maximize inclusivity of potential collaborators. Further, each DTP offers a range of funded placement opportunities to students. Researchers benefit both personally and professionally by increasing their research network and working in another organization. Research benefits by interactions with new research groups, access to facilities and exposure to different expertise. For example, an MGS researcher was recently able to employ a novel technique to their research as a direct result of a placement, and the BBSRC DTP's partnership with the Research Complex at Harwell has seen researchers access cutting-edge scientific facilities.

External collaborations also support the governance of the programmes. M4C's Partner Advisory Group includes representatives from a mix of fifteen regional and national creative and cultural industries. They contribute to the strategic development of regional and national engagement, as well as training and professional development opportunities. Similarly, the BBSRC's External Advisory Board brings together expert voices in industry and policy engagement to support the strategic direction of the programme. A crucial role of these groups is to monitor the DTPs' training for fit with industry requirements.

Researcher Collaborations

Collaborating with Researchers to Develop the Programme

Effectively engaging with researchers at the heart of programme governance allows for the development of more effective collaboration across all the above three areas. It can guide the development of training programmes through consultation and co-development, which in turn facilitates collaboration between researchers. The researcher voice has strongly influenced the development of the BBSRC and MGS DTP's training programmes and has significantly improved feedback. The BBSRC DTP now offers a broader range of training options at a range of levels, to allow researchers to select relevant courses at the level they require, and MGS now facilitate peer learning opportunities in addition to the more traditional taught offering.

Supporting Researcher-researcher Collaboration

All three DTPs have specific schemes to support researcher-led initiatives, both formal and informal. For example, the MGS annual conference is wholly developed and hosted by researchers, and both MGS and M4C allow researchers to apply for funding to run workshops and events on topics of common interest. An interdisciplinary research network – Midlands Music Research Network – grew from inter-cohort collaboration at the M4C Research Festival. Music researchers recognized that their diverse approaches to music research held meaningful commonalities and identified a need for an active network to build lasting connections in this space. Widely available communication software and apps are frequently used by researchers to set up groups and maintain connections with each other. These opportunities diversify the training offering as well as providing significant professional development opportunities for the researchers involved in development and delivery.

Conclusion and Recommendations

The DTPs described here are collaborative by design and each operates within a unique co-created space. This space facilitates connections between the partner institution, members of staff and the doctoral researchers. Engaging each as active collaborators allows mutual benefits and responsibility for training to be shared. Researchers access facilities they would not ordinarily have the opportunity to, they are encouraged to engage with peers from different disciplines and can contribute to the design of the programmes. Students actively decide to pursue their PhD research as part of a collaborative doctoral training programme. The collaborative interactions enrich their doctoral experience and researchers are vocal in their praise for the breadth and depth of opportunities available to them:

> One of the best things about completing your PhD on a doctoral training programme is that it prepares you for many different careers, not just those in academia.
>
> (BBSRC DTP Researcher)

> The M4C community is a lively and inspiring network with plenty of initiatives and characterised by cooperation between institutions: the annual M4C Research Festival groups together the student cohorts and showcases the wide variety of doctoral projects underway, an event everyone looks forward to!
>
> (M4C DTP Researcher)

For academic members of staff, engaging with DTPs provides fruitful ground to pursue research interests and contributions to the development of others to be made:

> Thinking of my experience as a supervisor, I consider the ESRC DTP offers an excellent frame for a PhD studentship. I really like the emphasis there is on a PhD as a point not just to produce a good thesis, but also to develop the student's wider research skills for their career. I find this very refreshing. The DTP is also there as another point of support for me as a supervisor, and it makes me think more holistically as a supervisor as well.
>
> (MGS DTP Supervisor)

Non-academic staff, who support the aforementioned, benefit from engagement with their peers across the partnerships by creating support networks, sharing resources, practices and developing new ways of working. Hall (2020) notes that 'value' within the university is visualized as surplus or profit, but the true value seen in doctoral training partnerships is human – the structures support academic collaboration at all levels, whilst also providing professional services staff with opportunities to develop their networks and learn from one another.

We have presented a range of workable approaches to multi-partner collaboration and demonstrated how these collaborative efforts combine to offer more than the sum of their parts in the doctoral training sphere. In our experience, the key recommendations arising from this case study are to:

1. recognize multi-institutional collaborations as an innovative space and approach the challenges of working across different systems and cultures creatively to achieve success and
2. recognize the significant administrative burden of realizing effective multi-faceted, multi-institutional collaborations and resource collaborations appropriately to maximize outcomes.

References

Introduction

Barnett, R. (2004). The purposes of higher education and the changing face of academia. *London Review of Education, 2*(1), 61–73. DOI: 10.1080/1474846042000177483

Bhabha, H. K. (2012). *The location of culture*. Routledge.

Gutiérrez, K. D. (2008). Developing a sociocritical literacy in the third space. *Reading Research Quarterly, 43*(2), 148–64. DOI: 10.1598/RRQ.43.2.3

Huxham, C. (Ed.) (1996). *Creating collaborative advantage*. Sage.

Lave, J., & Wenger, E. (1991). *Situated learning: Legitimate peripheral participation*. Cambridge University Press.

Nancy, J. L. (2000). *Being singular plural*. Stanford University Press.

Robinson, K. (2006). *Do schools kill creativity*. TED Talk. https://www.ted.com/talks/sir_ken_robinson_do_schools_kill_creativity?language=en

Sinfield, S., Burns, T., & Abegglen, S. (2019). Exploration: Becoming playful – the power of a ludic module. In A. James, & C. Nerantzi (Eds.), *The power of play in higher education: Creativity in tertiary learning* (pp. 23–31). Palgrave Macmillan.

Soja, E. W. (1996). *Thirdspace: Journeys to Los Angeles and other real-and-imagined places.* Blackwell.

Case Study: Tutors, Students and Other Stakeholders at the Roundtable

Barber, W., & King, S. (2016). Teacher-student perspectives of invisible pedagogy: New directions in online problem-based learning environments. *Electronic Journal of e-Learning, 14*(4), 235–43.

Bernay, R., Stringer, P., Milne, J., & Jhagroo, J. (2020). Three models of effective school–university partnerships. *New Zealand Journal of Educational Studies, 55*(1), 133–48. DOI: 10.1007/s40841-020-00171-3

Donaldson, G. (2014). Teacher education and curriculum change in Scotland. *European Journal of Education, 49*(2), 178–91. DOI: 10.1111/ejed.12077

Ejiwale, J. A. (2013). Barriers to successful implementation of STEM education. *Journal of Education and Learning, 7*(2), 63–74. DOI: 10.11591/edulearn.v7i2.220

Faikhamta, C. (2020). Pre-service science teachers' views of the nature of STEM. *Science Education International, 31*(4), 356–66. DOI: 10.33828/sei.v31.i4.4

Gutierez, S. B. (2019). Teacher-practitioner research inquiry and sense making of their reflections on scaffolded collaborative lesson planning experience. *Asia-Pacific Science Education, 5*(1), 1–15. DOI: 10.1186/s41029-019-0043-x

Healey, M., Flint, A., & Harrington, K. (2016). Students as partners: Reflections on a conceptual model. *Teaching & Learning Inquiry, 4*(2). DOI: 10.20343/teachlearninqu.4.2.3

Herbert, S., & Hobbs, L. (2018). Pre-service teachers' views of school-based approaches to pre-service primary science teacher education. *Research in Science Education, 48*(4), 777–809.

Jones, L. C., McDermott, H. J., Tyrer, J. R., & Zanker, N. P. (2021). The effect of teacher's confidence on technology and engineering curriculum provision. *International Journal of Technology and Design Education, 31*(1), 117–37. DOI: 10.1007/s10798-019-09542-4

Kelley, T. R., & Knowles, J. G. (2016). A conceptual framework for integrated STEM education. *International Journal of STEM Education, 3*(1), 1–11. DOI: 10.1186/s40594-016-0046-z

Lazareva, A. (2021). University and school collaborations during a pandemic. Sustaining educational opportunity and reinventing education: A book review. *Journal of Language and Education, 7*(4), 198–203. DOI: 10.17323/jle.2021.13456

MacLeod, I. A. (2017). *To Engineer-strategies for solving complex problems.* The Institution of Engineers in Scotland. https://engineers.scot/publication/to-engineer

Margot, K. C., & Kettler, T. (2019). Teachers' perception of STEM integration and education: A systematic literature review. *International Journal of STEM Education, 6*(1), 1–16. DOI: 10.1186/s40594-018-0151-2

Reimers, F. M., & Marmolejo, F. J. (2022). Leading learning during a time of crisis. Higher education responses to the global pandemic of 2020. In F. M. Reimers, & F. J. Marmolejo (Eds.), *University and school collaborations during a pandemic: Sustaining educational opportunity and reinventing education* (pp. 1–31). Knowledge Studies in Higher Education, vol 8. Springer. DOI: 10.1007/978-3-030-82159-3_1

Scottish Government (2017). *Science, technology, engineering and mathematics: Education and training strategy*. https://www.gov.scot/publications/science-technology-engineering-mathematics-education-training-strategy-scotland/pages/3/

Serret, N., & Earle, S. (2018). *ASE guide to primary science education*. Association for Science Education.

Sharma, J., & Yarlagadda, P. K. (2018). Perspectives of 'STEM education and policies' for the development of a skilled workforce in Australia and India. *International Journal of Science Education, 40*(16), 1999–2022. DOI: 10.1080/09500693.2018.1517239

Vedeler, G. W. (2021). Practising school-home collaboration in upper secondary schools: To solve problems or to promote adolescents' autonomy? *Pedagogy, Culture & Society*, 1–19. DOI: 10.1080/14681366.2021.1923057

Veenstra, C. (2014). The collaborative role of industry in supporting STEM education. *The Journal for Quality and Participation, 37*(3), 27–9.

Wang, X., & Wong, J. L. (2017). How do primary school teachers develop knowledge by crossing boundaries in the school–university partnership? A case study in China. *Asia-Pacific Journal of Teacher Education, 45*(5), 487–504. DOI: 10.1080/1359866x.2016.1261392

Case Study: Healthcare Scientist Education

Advance HE (2018). *Manchester Academy for Healthcare Scientists Education*. Manchester Metropolitan University. https://www.advance-he.ac.uk/cate-team/manchester-academy-healthcare-scientist-education-manchester-metropolitan-university

Appleby, M. (2019). *What are the benefits of interdisciplinary study?* http://www.open.edu/openlearn/education/what-are-the-benefits-interdisciplinary-study

Bates, A. (2015). Teaching in a digital age. *BC Open Textbook Project*. https://opentextbc.ca/teachinginadigitalage/

Department of Health and Social Care (2010). An overview of modernising scientific careers. https://www.gov.uk/government/publications/an-overview-of-modernising-scientific-careers

Francis, R. (2013). Final report of the Mid Staffordshire NHS Foundation Trust public inquiry. *National Archives*. http://webarchive.nationalarchives.gov.uk/20150407084231/http://www.midstaffspublicinquiry.com/report

Healey, M., Flint, A., & Harrington, K. (2014). *Engagement through partnership: Students as partners in learning and teaching in higher education*. The Higher Education Academy.

Health Education England (n.d.). Our work. https://www.hee.nhs.uk/our-work

MAHSE (n.d.). Patient and public involvement. http://mahse.co.uk/for-the-public/patient-and-public-involvement/

Mooney, J., Byrne-Davis, L., Cappelli, T., Dexter, H., Taylor, M., Moffatt, L., & Lumsden, C. (2013). Implementing mobile learning with iPads in higher education: A large scale case study. In *Mobile learning: How mobile technologies can enhance the learning experience* (pp. 18–23). https://www.research.manchester.ac.uk/portal/en/publications/implementing-mobile-learning-with-ipads-in-higher-education(7dd7f755-97c6-4a1f-a17e-b26556e7a439)/export.html#expor

National School of Healthcare Science (n.d.a). Healthcare science. https://nshcs.hee.nhs.uk/healthcare-science/

National School of Healthcare Science (n.d.b). About us. https://nshcs.hee.nhs.uk/about/

National School of Healthcare Science (n.d.c). Scientist training programme. https://nshcs.hee.nhs.uk/programmes/stp/

NHS (2018). Making it happen- multi-disciplinary team (MDT) working. https://www.england.nhs.uk/publication/making-it-happen-multi-disciplinary-team-mdt-working/

NHS Careers (n.d.). Healthcare science. https://www.healthcareers.nhs.uk/explore-roles/healthcare-science

Pride of Manchester (2021). Top 100 Manchester bands. https://www.prideofmanchester.com/music/top100.htm

Wenger, E., McDermott, R., & Snyder, W. M. (2002). *Cultivating communities of practice: A guide to managing knowledge*. Harvard Business School Press.

Wenger-Trayner, E., & Wenger-Trayner, E. (2015). Communities of practice – a brief introduction. http://wenger-trayner.com/wp-content/uploads/2015/04/07-Brief-introduction-to-communities-of-practice.pdf

Williams, B. (2021). The rivalry between united and city. https://aboutmanchester.co.uk/the-rivalry-between-united-and-city

Case Study: Multi-partner Doctoral Training Collaborations

Barnett, R. (2000). University knowledge in an age of supercomplexity. *Higher Education, 40*, 409–22. DOI: 10.1023/A: 1004159513741

Birch, E., Perry, D. C., & Taylor Jr, H. L. (2013). Universities as anchor institutions. *Journal of Higher Education Outreach and Engagement, 17*(3), 7–16.

Budd, R., O'Connell, C., Yuan, T., & Ververi, O. (2018). *The DTC effect: ESRC doctoral training centres and the UK social science doctoral training landscape*. Liverpool Hope University Press.

Hall, R. (2000). The hopeless university: Intellectual work at the end of the end of history. *Postdigital Science and Education, 2*, 830–48. DOI: 10.1007/s42438-020-00158-9

McAlpine, L. (2017). Building on success? Future challenges for doctoral education globally. *Studies in Graduate and Postdoctoral Education, 8*(2), 66–77. DOI: 10.1108/SGPE-D-17-00035

Newbury, D. (2003). Doctoral education in design, the process of research degree study, and the trained researcher. *Art, Design & Communication in Higher Education, 1*(3), 149–59. DOI: 10.1386/adch.1.3.149

6

Creative and Digital Partnerships

Introduction

Working collaboratively requires people to come together, face-to-face or virtually. Arts and arts-based subject areas have always utilized creativity to connect, either within their own discipline area or with the wider public. Especially since the 'great interruption' (Conley & Massa, 2022) of Covid-19, faculty and students have had to be creative in finding new ways of working – and new ways of cooperating. Since the challenges of the pandemic the digital has flourished creatively, with programmes and courses pivoting online overnight. This, in a similar, yet different way, required creative responses from faculty and students alike: a 'ground up' development of innovative and supportive practice that has utterly transformed the way we might conceive learning, teaching and assessment.

This section highlights how arts-based, creative and emergent (digital) practices can transcend a focus on competitive individuality. Successful collaboration requires the use of the imagination to destabilize isolating, transactional notions of education itself. That is, to provoke curiosity (Schmitt & Lahroodi, 2008) and facilitate active, creative and 'owned' learning, we need to disrupt the 'taken for granted' perception that education is training, that knowledge is memorization and that 'study' involves the rote learning of fixed forms of knowledge (Burns et al., 2009). A creative approach to academic practice, both in-person and online, promotes the freedom to experiment and question (Huizenga, 1949) which helps students to navigate uncertainty, explore contradictory knowledge-claims and cross the academic threshold of 'phronesis': deliberation with no predetermined outcome (Abegglen et al., 2018; Meyer & Land, 2005; Molinari, 2017).

The case studies in this section demonstrate how to bring in play, curiosity and experimentation to scaffold more exploratory and emergent forms of collaborative practice. There is focus on the imagination educators need to integrate new creative ways of bringing students together, creating spaces and places for exchange, work and being with. The creative tools and methods discussed result in the breaking of stereotypes and the disruption of standard practices. Teamwork and working together do not necessarily come naturally, either to staff or to students, but it can be fostered in students by providing them with the tools and resources to flourish. Even more importantly, collaborative practice flourishes if we provide the space and agency for students to develop their own projects, work practices and voices. Creative partnership then is being creative in the way we come and work together but also embraces a more holistic approach to education and educational practice, something emergent, liberatory and transformational. As Pablo Picasso once said:

> There are painters who transform the sun to a yellow spot, but there are others who, with the help of their art and their intelligence, transform a yellow spot into sun.

The Case Study Chapters

In *Paper as Teacher* Briony Supple, Siobhán O'Neill, Alex Pentek and Guangbo Hao outline how faculty members from teaching and learning, an artist and a senior lecturer in Engineering used origami to challenge dominant teaching norms in HE. Origami, they argue, can bring a much-needed ethos of playful learning, curiosity and experimentation into HE. They model this via hands-on workshops in Engineering and with university lecturers to illustrate how their origami-based collaboration creates space for formulating new ideas and developing creative approaches to education.

With *Upheaval, Creativity and Student Partnerships,* Alina Georgeta Mag highlights the importance of a relational, collaborative pedagogy for creative learning and teaching. Re-designing practice for the pandemic, teaching methods were rethought, and opportunities created for students to continue their learning in a completely new online environment. The virtual *Creative Teachers' Cafe* and storytelling sessions created space, time and place for creative thinking that helped students to de-stress, bond and belong.

Transforming the Arts Curriculum in Practice by Jessica Slotte makes the case for *Supporting Collaboration*, a resource pack and active learning tool, designed to be used to introduce and support a more collaborative learning environment. Originally created with and for Design students, the resource pack is aimed at all Arts students to help them focus on what is possible through collaboration.

With *Connectivity as Transgressive Practice in Doctoral Research*, Kiu Sum discusses her PhD elephant and reveals how making virtual connections during a doctorate provided sustenance and support. Whilst the PhD myth propagates the notion of the isolated academic silently struggling, joining online communities helped her overcome her PhD challenges. Sharing experiences, helping the elephant dance with others, she argues, is essential to challenge and disrupt an academic culture that is isolating and individualistic.

Changing the Rules of the Game by Jennie Blake, Adam Cooke and Jasmine Nisic discusses the power of peer-to-peer digital networks and student-produced online resources to promote the voices and success of students from underrepresented groups. Their project has effectively harnessed, and acted as an advocate for, marginalized voices in HE. In the process it has contributed to the development of university-wide practice on engagement for successful learning that models collaborative practice that creatively includes staff-student partners.

In *Enhancing Digital Inclusivity*, Karen Arm argues that dismantling consumerist hierarchies inherent in 'student voice' work is essential for effective staff-student partnership initiatives. Her diverse collaborative team of Student Inclusive Curriculum Consultants worked within an academic development team to support staff with university-wide course enhancement and cultural change. Initiated to support the pivot to online LTA during the pandemic, the work is continuing and showcases how these partnerships can be successfully fostered remotely and online.

Paper as Teacher: Challenging Dominant Learning Norms in Higher Education through Collaborating in Origami

Briony Supple, Siobhán O'Neill, Alex Pentek and Guangbo Hao

- The practice of origami, or indeed any hands-on, collaborative, creative and dialogic approach to teaching and learning, enables a reconceptualization of power imbalances inherent within traditional educational norms by allowing learners individually and collaboratively to shine.
- Creative approaches also allow for the expansion of understanding into other disciplines – our case study highlights how origami achieves this through its combination of Engineering/Robotics Engineering and origami.
- Learning as playful and fun is a discourse which is missing often within HE, we argue this needs to change.

Introduction

This chapter is a collaborative case study between two academic faculty members from teaching and learning (Supple and O'Neill), an Artist (Pentek) and a Senior Lecturer in Engineering (Hao), which highlights the use of origami to challenge dominant teaching norms in HE. The chapter presents the theoretical and philosophical underpinnings of our work, followed by an outline of two collaboratively driven, practice-based examples of origami in (1) Engineering teaching for students and (2) a teaching and learning workshop for lecturers. Evaluation was undertaken via a short Google form survey shared with participants at the conclusion of the sessions. We begin with a discussion of how our work challenges dominant, individualistic, power imbalanced systems. Guided by our conceptual framework, we highlight how our collaboration pushes disciplinary boundaries and creates space for formulating new ideas about creative approaches to education. Our practice-based examples are micro-case studies which exemplify the praxis aspect of our collaboration.

It's Challenging: An Arts-based Model

The dominant systems still found in HE are based largely upon the outdated 'master-apprentice' model (Chabot et al., 2013): the lecturer as 'sage on the stage', and instruction and assessment which is heavily cognitively and linguistically biased (Troxler, 2015). Our collaboration challenges these dominant systems and practices. We are influenced by Piaget's (1973) notion that 'to understand is to invent', and Papert's ideas regarding Constructionism (Papert & Harel, 1991). We also draw on Vygotsky (1978) where learning happens 'in collaboration with more capable peers' (p. 86). Our work is also informed by inclusive practice in education (Basit & Tomlinson, 2012; Slee, 2011; Supple & Agbenyega, 2015), material methods (Woodward, 2020) and the power of play in HE (James & Nerantzi, 2019; Hao & Pentek, 2021).

The word 'art' has long been associated with skill; thus, the art of a subject can also mean the total skill or gestalt of that subject (Read, 2014) – encompassing the entire programme while remaining open to inspiration from outside fields of knowledge and expertise. 'Art' is therefore an invariably decentralized resource in the teaching of disciplines (Hao & Pentek, 2021). Arts-based practices can be the catalyst for co-constructing, rather than transmitting, knowledge via direct, hands-on, materials-led experience. Playful, materials-led experimentation contrasts with traditional, interpretive knowledge-based approaches often found in Engineering (Hao & Pentek, 2021).

The 'hands-on' workshops we created were designed to catalyse active learning across disciplinary boundaries as staff and students work together. The processes with which our participants engaged were designed to provide open spaces for collaborative exchanges; spark creativity through informal learning and curiosity-driven explorations; and facilitate experiential learning. This was especially pertinent for students and staff who may not have had opportunity to engage in learning through modelling, prototyping, etc. (Supple et al., 2021).

Building on arts-based practice and theory, we, as an interdisciplinary team, have learned much from each other, and our participants, and we continue to develop this learning through ongoing teaching and research collaborations. Table 6.1 illustrates the conceptual framework governing our work.

Table 6.1 Conceptual framework: Dominant systems vs arts-based practices.

Dominant systems (outdated)	Arts-based practices (future trend/modernized)
Assessment	
1. Failure is 'bad'	Failure is part of learning
2. Text-based	Flexible mediums of expression/materials
3. Focus on outcomes from learning over process	Focus on processes of learning over final outcomes
Collaboration	
4. Learning should be 'serious'	Learning as playful, fun and curiosity sparking
5. Disciplinary silos	multi/trans/interdisciplinary
6. Dendritic centralized power: the lecturer is the 'all knower'	Rhizomatic decentralized learning power dynamic. Collaboration/learn from others outside of the discipline/learn from students/peer-to-peer

For the purposes of this chapter we focus on sub-themes pertaining to 'Collaboration', discussed in more detail in the following sections.

Practice-based Examples

Origami and Robotics Engineering

The origami-led course in Robotics Engineering is collaboratively delivered by Artist, Pentek, and Senior Lecturer in Mechanical Engineering, Hao, and includes three parts: a two-hour lecture on the theory of origami and its engineering applications, and a 'warm up' folding session; and two intensive hands-on workshops of 2.5 hours each, focused on origami. These sessions are an integrated part of the existing timetable. The sessions begin with an outline of connections between Engineering and origami delivered by Pentek and Hao, and then Pentek demonstrates the origami folds to students as per Figure 6.1. Students are divided into teams and provided with a task, for example, to utilize the origami folds and create an object with the paper which can withstand weight or can contain water. These challenges encompass the application of origami folds with the mechanics and physics of Engineering. All teams are starting from the same foundation folds (such as the Miura and the Waterbomb fold). Each team is required to use at least two different folds in their final finished product combining creativity with innovation.

Figure 6.1 Folding demonstration (Image courtesy of Hao & Pentek, 2021).

Figure 6.2 Students working on Miura folding (Image courtesy of Hao & Pentek, 2021).

This application of origami works as a way of translating concepts in Kinematics and of investigating Statics. If the paper facets and folds are substituted with rigid links and revolute joints, students can access and play with the kinematic analysis intuitively via the medium of paper (Supple et al., 2021). Origami-based projects serve to displace the 'all-knowing' teacher and empower student learning through 'making'; thus, they are an integral part of the teaching and continuous assessment in the Advanced Robotics module (Hao & Pentek, 2021) and these approaches continue to be developed (Liang et al., 2021).

Pedagogic Workshop: Origami for Teaching and Learning

This hands-on pedagogic workshop was designed to inspire academics across disciplines to engage in the process of origami and to use this as a vehicle through which to reflect on their own teaching. An email was sent to all staff via the Teaching and Learning Vice President which invited participants to attend a virtual workshop via Zoom. The online workshop was attended by nine participants who were academics from across the University, and came from disciplines of Business Information Systems, Engineering, Dentistry, Food Science, Geography, Law, Chemistry and Architecture. The workshop took place at the height of the Covid-19 pandemic, and as such, a chance to connect with others was a huge motivation for some of the participants in joining.

The workshop design was predicated on emerging evidence supporting the use of materials-led approaches (also known as 'making') as a tool for teaching reflection (e.g. Hughes et al., 2018; Kjällander et al., 2018). The aims of the session can be seen in Figure 6.3.

At the start of the workshop, participants were introduced to some of the disciplinary applications for origami by both Pentek and Hao (such as via their work with Engineering students). Next, they were guided through elements of the creation of the Miura fold by Pentek. A live-video stream captured the folds by Pentek, with a camera which was angled on his hands so that participants could see what he was doing for the folds. This was supplemented by diagrams of the folds, shared on screen (see Figures 6.4 and 6.5). This was somewhat challenging as ideally, participants can see each other and share their work together as they go. We did stop and start and ask participants to hold up their work at different stages, but it lost the momentum which an in-person workshop would have allowed.

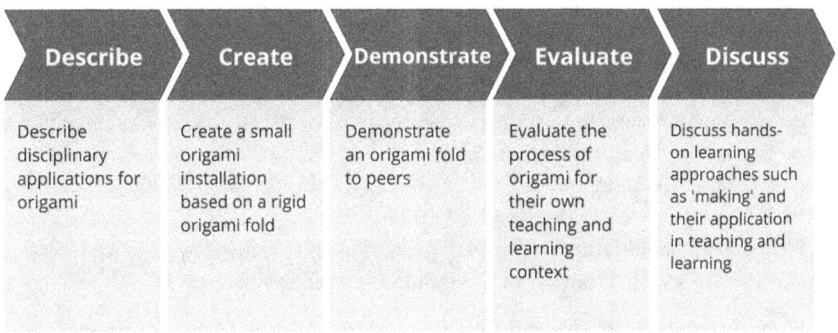

Figure 6.3 Workshop aims.

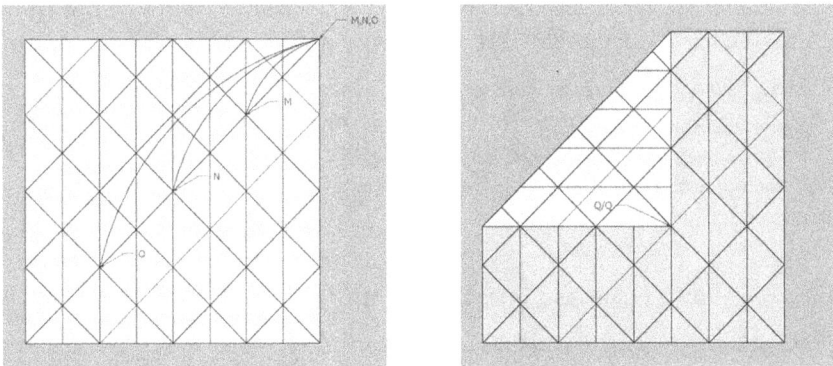

Figures 6.4 and 6.5 Supplemental diagrams by Pentek, showing fold points along a piece of paper.

Despite this, the workshop prompted participants to reflect: What could a humble piece of paper teach them about the processes of interdisciplinary learning? The 'Evaluate and Discuss' phase allowed participants to further engage in dialogues with other participants to reflect on the diversity of students within classroom settings, collaborative 'making' as student engagement and interdisciplinary co-teaching where teachers move away from 'lecturing' to 'guidance and support'.

Findings and Feedback

Feedback was sought from (a) students in the origami and Robotics Engineering sessions (Hao & Pentek, 2021) and (b) participants from the teaching and learning workshop. We categorize this evidence of our collaboration as per themes 4, 5 and 6 from our conceptual framework.

Theme 4: Learning as Playful, Fun and Curiosity Sparking

Hands-on learning is creative and playful; yet, 'play' is not often associated with HE contexts. However, the processes of play are inextricably linked to experimentation, design and encouraging 'flow' states (Csikszentmihalyi, 2011). This 'tension' is reflected in the answers given by students and staff:

Engineering students:

> I wanted to thank you for organising such an imaginative, original and very effective workshop. I learned a lot and thoroughly enjoyed it.

> I have learned lots of Origami techniques as well as stimulated my imagination from it.

Pedagogic workshop participants:

> It was a brilliant way to spend a couple of hours on a Monday, in between lecturing and working on assessments, I feel quite revitalised afterwards.

> I have few opportunities to work with my hands in my work. While I understand academia as a form of creative labour, there is something thrilling about putting myself in my students' shoes by learning something new and creating something in the process. It's great to feel the frustrations and satisfactions tied to the learning process.

Theme 5: Multi-, Trans- and Interdisciplinarity

Origami has been used for designing foldable structures and robots by engineers (Nishiyama, 2012; Zhakypov et al., 2018) and for 'teaching geometry, thinking skills, fractions, problem solving, and fun science' (Hao & Pentek, 2021, 1). Origami therefore naturally lends itself to being multi-, trans- and interdisciplinary – it can be used both as a way of learning functional mechanisms and facts as well as being a reflective lens into the meta-processes behind learning something new. This is illustrated by the following responses:

Engineering students:

> Before taking this workshop, I thought that origami is only about paper folding aimed to create something to play. I had never thought about the relationship between origami and robotics applications.

> It was a unique experience to have some hands-on training with origami folding patterns ... I found it very fascinating to do some easy folds, that patterned over a sheet of paper, [and how this] would greatly modify the mechanical properties of this paper.

Pedagogic workshop participants:

> The workshop also stimulated thoughts on possible teaching activities using origami for energy engineering examples.

> We often refer to origami in our teaching of both Architecture and Engineering students, and I feel there is an untapped potential interest for such workshops to be offered to students in both schools.

Theme 6: Decentralized Learning

Another important part of the collaborative nature of origami practice as we have fostered is that of decentralized learning – situations where participants learn from one another and work together, and the shift away from the all-knowing teacher to the power of learning within the group. Hands-on activities challenge learners to work with peers and 'develop their own questions ... discuss ideas, recognise and articulate problems that they meet along the way, look for solutions, evaluate progress, hypothesise, test and re-test ...' (Harris et al., 2016, p. 8). This is confirmed by the following participant replies:

Engineering students:

> There were also practical experiences in folding papers, and that experience increased the student involvement and understanding.

> In the last lesson, we were split in groups to figure out our origami structure and solicited to be creative. It was a good way to work together and share ideas.

Pedagogic workshop participants:

> I learnt a variety of practical and aesthetic uses for rigid origami as well as some new techniques for modelling paper. I also enjoyed hearing some interesting comments from other participants about how they could apply this type of workshop in their own disciplines and teaching modules.

Great to feel the swap from teacher to learner, it gave me a sense of freedom to be able to follow the instructions and do the work with my own hands.

Conclusions and Recommendations for Praxis

Our collaboration has resulted in using origami as: (1) a lab-based (design) tool to analyse and design robots within the discipline of Engineering and (2) a hands-on tool for reflections on learning and teaching approaches across disciplines. Together, we continue to build our collaborative practices and outputs – our aims going forward relate particularly to play and pedagogy. We aim to:

- Bring the language and ethos of 'playful learning', curiosity and experimentation into HE via further collaboratively driven, hands-on workshops. In doing so we want to encourage interdisciplinary learning by encouraging a focus on non-traditional notions of HE, and learning through process and experimentation. We encourage others to do the same.
- Leverage the rich interdisciplinary, materials-led potential of origami in order to inspire educators to create learning opportunities for their students (an ongoing focus by Liang et al., 2021).
- Develop tools to help educators design their curriculum to include interdisciplinary, hands-on learning opportunities.
- Continue to collaborate – we have learned much as practitioners, researchers and educators when planning workshops. We encourage others to seek out similar interdisciplinary networks to create 'rich' experiences and exchanges.

Upheaval, Creativity and Student Partnerships: A Case Study of Relational, Collaborative Pedagogy

Alina Georgeta Mag

- The case study highlights the importance of a relational, collaborative pedagogy for creative learning and teaching.
- Re-designing practice for the pandemic, teaching methods were rethought, and opportunities created for students to continue their learning in a completely new online environment.
- The online *Education Cafe* created space, time and place for creative thinking that helped students to de-stress, bond and belong.
- Sustaining individual well-being and cohort identity, online and face-to-face, develops self-efficacy and promotes academic success.
- The chapter argues that when being creative and attentive to the quality of the partnership relations with students, we can find the best solutions for an authentic educational training.

Introduction

In the context of the upheaval created worldwide by the Covid-19 pandemic, educational relationships remain of vital importance. HE teachers and students have gone through an intense period of new challenges, to which they have had to adapt at a rapid pace, and which have brought many changes in the way educational relationships can be constructed. The goal of this chapter is to discuss how staff in a Teacher Training department at an RO university responded creatively to the pandemic, and how they sustained a relationship approach to teaching and learning in the process.

Participation, Collaboration and Creativity

The development of creative personality is a goal of modern society (Robinson, 2015). Participation and collaboration are seen as the locus of creative action, orientating thoughts and behaviour towards novel solutions, strategies and outcomes (Cury, 2007; Schiavio et al., 2021). In the university context, therefore, creativity must be a constant in teaching and relating with students (Pânișoară, 2015) – based on strong relationships and mutual trust (Robu, 2008).

In the pivot to online teaching, HE was challenged to look for new solutions to keep students engaged, active and motivated to learn. Teachers looked for creative ways to connect with students. A quality partnership is directly related with effective and high-quality teaching and learning (Pânișoară, 2015; Schiavio et al., 2021) and successful academic education; arguably this has been neglected in this critical period (Malureanu et al., 2021). Yet, as this case study demonstrates, collaboration and partnership can be part of the solutions to address the challenges of the pandemic and beyond.

Teaching Involves a Collaborative Relationship with Students

In order for all students to achieve their full potential (Cretu, 2019), the traditional, transmissive approach to educational relationships and the teaching process must be replaced by one that allows all students to actively engage and participate. Creating a cooperative partnership between teachers and students through which to value diversity, learning and personal development can be the solution to this period of crisis (Schiavio et. al., 2021). These are times of 'supercomplexity' (Abegglen et al., 2020), and we must adapt and discover new ways of understanding the learning process, through new ways of building partnerships with students – face-to-face and in the virtual environment.

While teachers strive to adapt to new means of connection and communication, students expect not only innovative ways of teaching, but also ways of rebuilding relational partnerships. This is particularly true for those becoming teachers, who will be responsible for their own students when becoming professionals. They need to be able to 'connect'.

The Covid Effect

The pandemic has greatly affected everyone's way of life (Schiavio et al., 2021). Students now have more mental and emotional health issues that affect the way they think, feel and act (Cury, 2007; Robu, 2008). Thus, the mental and emotional health of students should be of paramount importance for all teachers. Although online education has several advantages, most students miss the human interaction in 'regular' classes. Recent research claims that success in life, performance in learning, and mental and emotional health depend on the effectiveness of educational relationships (Crețu, 2019; Gordon & Burch, 2011).

Confidence in itself develops from early ages (Malureanu et al., 2021) but during the pandemic each student went through many challenges and obstacles that challenged their level of self-confidence. Low self-esteem is now the most common symptom of learning and emotional problems among young people (Cury, 2007; Dumitrescu & Dumitrescu, 2005). In the current context of the pandemic not all students coped well with the pressure of facing the academic requirements (Schiavio et al., 2021), especially when isolated and alone at home, as opposed to cooperating and working collaboratively face-to-face. Stress can be experienced by any student with great intensity, being caused by the fear of not making mistakes, of not being disappointed, of being labelled (Cretu, 2019) but the pandemic has accelerated emotional ill-health.

Creative, innovative partnerships must be re-built through healthy teacher-student interactions, online during the pandemic, and then arguably be reinvented and reinterpreted as face-to-face teaching returns as the 'new normal'. This is not just a re-thinking of didactic pedagogy, but re-thinking pedagogy based on an emotional education with meaning and significance for educational partners. Teachers need to provide students with a warm, calm atmosphere and a 'quality' time in which they can enjoy all their attention, sharing pleasant and relaxing activities (Cury, 2007). Being creative can allow partners-in-learning to look at the positives of this difficult period, and this can create opportunities for better relationships (Robinson, 2015).

Examples from the Teacher Training Department

There is no one ideal method or recipe for building effective relationships with students. Inside the Teachers Training Department, at the University 'Lucian Blaga' of Sibiu, RO, the Pedagogy course and seminar had to be moved online, so we started looking for new ideas to support our students' needs and motivation. One innovation was our online seminar that was called *Creative Teachers' Cafe*. Amongst the stresses of the pandemic and virtual learning, we wanted to create a space where student teachers could speak more freely about ideas, where their minds could roam together unconstrained by the demands of assessment. Thus, in our Cafe, students were encouraged to imagine that seminar discussions were taking place in different, beautiful cafes, each week in another part of the world. We created a pleasant and innovative learning environment, in order to let students share, discuss and their minds wander. We asked them to reflect and speak freely about the teachers they held as models and the reasons they were inspired to teach. Because of this, online seminars became more attractive, and students involved showed more self-confidence during subsequent formal presentations about models of education practice.

Another example of good, creative practice is the partnership created with Master's students who were learning about inclusive education and school-based experts on inclusion. Online activities had to be created, as the schools were not allowed to receive students for face-to-face instruction. Online brainstorming sessions were organized to find new ways of achieving our goals. Thus, we invited voluntary educational partners with expertise in inclusion into a weekly, dialogue-focused discussion on 'practical solutions'. In each meeting we set the challenge of creating an online story, based on shared experiences about inclusion. The 'setting' of the creative story was developed by integrating *The Colour of the Day*, based on the *Thinking Hats* method – an interactive technique to stimulate creativity. Participants imagined that they wore hats of different colours, which led them to adapt their thinking style to the colour of the hat: *white* was focused on data and facts, *red* on emotions and intuitions, *black* on denial and pessimism, *yellow* on optimism, *green* on creativity and *blue* on leadership. These cooperative creative challenges led students not only to create imaginative stories but also to better communicate – with each other and, those present, the teachers and guests. Each meeting allowed students to feel more confident, more open to collaboration and more creative together, as partners.

Evaluation

In these pandemic times and beyond, young people need the chance to feel important, valued and 'intelligent'. Inspired by teachers who collaborate with them to provide an optimal relational environment for creativity and learning, they are more engaged when they are in connection with those who accept, respect and encourage them (Cozolino, 2014).

Creative collaboration in the university environment is of vital importance to build relationships and actively involve all students in their own education (Robinson, 2015). The emotions experienced by students in the context of the educational relationship are those that define the quality of the relationship. Students appreciate teachers with whom they have personalized, creatively constructed, quality relationships (Cretu, 2019).

It is desirable to constantly reflect on how well we relate to each student, on how well we manage to know what capacity each has. Here are concrete examples of reflective questions, developed from our own work with trainee teachers, for teachers who want to collaborate better with their students:

- How can we increase empathy to understand different students' circumstances?
- How can we learn about our students' backgrounds and make them feel included?
- Do we offer constant and objective encouragement?
- How often do we ask students for feedback on how they feel about our classes, how they feel about us?
- Do we give them enough opportunities to succeed?

Conclusion and Recommendations

During the pandemic we needed to innovate to develop community, creativity and self-efficacy online. Beyond the pandemic, we continue to need innovative and practical solutions, adapted to today's young people, to build a humane HE suitable for a supercomplex world.

Any educational activity will have a valuable additional impact if the teacher-student relations are positive and authentic. From the way we greet students at the beginning and end of the course, to the interest given to each relationship, we prove that we value not only the specialized content with which we all interact, but also all of our students, their unique personality and the cultural wealth each brings to the learning encounter. Through this relational and creative pedagogy, we collaborate to make a difference to each student through our attitude and care for them.

Thus, the university must be a space for authentic relationships, knowledge-building and trust. Interaction is the key to build relationships for collaboration. Students do not develop connection through hours spent in online courses, but through communication, questions, dialogue, direct experimentation and constant feedback. Therefore, how we, as educators, build our relationships and attitude towards them are so important. For university 'teacher training' to be effective, it requires practical approaches connected to 'real' life, to the different needs of learners, and imagination.

In conclusion, it is important to reflect on innovative ways to build educational partnerships in which the emphasis is on developing creative practice, cohort identity and belonging between and among staff and students. A relational pedagogy that personalizes relationships is sustained by careful knowledge of each student, where the needs and potential of the individual are valued within the collective of the class. Training university teachers for quality relationships must become a priority, regardless of the times. True pedagogues are those who master the 'art' of relationships, not just their field of expertise.

Supporting Collaboration: Transforming the Arts Curriculum in Practice

Jessica Slotte

- *Supporting Collaboration*, a resource pack and active learning tool, is designed to be used to introduce and support a more collaborative learning environment.
- Originally created with and for Design students, the resource pack is aimed at all students to help them focus on what is possible through collaboration.
- This case study reveals an important model of creative and emergent learning activities and space designed to cultivate lifelong collective practices.
- Students are the future, and their skills need to match the change and development of our societies and communities and beyond.

Introduction

This chapter discusses the motivation for and processes of developing *Supporting Collaboration* (SC), a resource pack and active learning tool designed to be used to seed and support a more collaborative learning environment in our Arts and Design university (Slotte, 2020). I was initially inspired to start the project from seeing the lack of student-to-student collaboration in our own university. The aim of this chapter is to make a case for why collaboration in UK HE is not only important, but vital, for the future of design and why SC could support those first steps towards a more inclusive and innovative future.

Supporting Collaboration

SC is a six-chapter 'Resource Pack' aimed at HE students, intended to support and help lay a solid foundation upon which collaborative practice can be built. The Pack is not meant to tell the students how to collaborate but rather focuses on how to support collaboration – whatever that collaboration may look like. The chapters of the Resource Pack are carefully constructed in a way that gives students a holistic understanding of the basics of teamwork and available resources to aid in building efficient, productive and fun collaborations. It aims at making itself the base, the supporting structure to a student's collaborative practice while being at university and beyond. Currently, the Resource Pack exists in pdf form to make it easy for students to access on any device.

The seeds of SC were sown in the second year of my BA (Hons) Design for Art Direction (DfAD) course at the University of the Arts London (UAL), when I sent out a questionnaire to my peers about their experiences of, and thoughts about, collaboration and group work. This was in response to being asked to make a presentation on thinking about collaboration and how that could feed into our future projects in the following year. The content of the Resource Pack was developed through this research. Development continued in practice through the Temporary Studio which was made for the Work in Progress show held by third-year students across the London College of Communication at UAL.

Rationale

As future designers and innovators, we are the ones who will need to find innovative ways to sustainably develop our societies and help communities thrive (Oblinger, 2018). I decided to build the Resource Pack to support collaboration-driven learning in students, wanting them to experience the power and joy of successful collaborative practices, and positively impact how they view collaboration and group work. Student responses to collaboration and group work revealed a need to develop students' 'tools' for effective collaboration. Collaboration does not come naturally, it is necessary to build successful collaborative practices in university for us all to be able to work together successfully. Knowing how to collaborate efficiently and compassionately is an essential skill, not just for study but in any work we do after university (Moravec, 2019).

When analysing the student questionnaires, three pitfalls became evident: (1) most projects (if not all) are individually assessed, (2) student unwillingness to collaborate and lastly (3) lack of networking across courses and years to find other students to collaborate with. Responses revealed a lack of understanding of how to organize a group for effective collaboration and there was no understanding of what drives a collaboration forward. Every project needs a driving force at its core: all participants or collaborative partners need a shared vision and a sense of commitment. This is crucial for a collaborative project's productivity and success.

When being a student myself and asked to undertake group work, no strategies were introduced to help me ease into this way of working. Cooperation and collaboration were not supported as part of our institution's curriculum design and pedagogic processes, even though it clearly is included and expected. Therefore, it became evident that we needed to take the initiative to develop these skills ourselves. Understanding the value of each other in creative collaboration is essential for a collaborative, sustainable and innovative future. Because when we as human beings do not know something, we fill in the blanks, which leads to leaving out someone else's experience, needs or ideas – and the joint project may fail.

The Pack Itself

The Resource Pack addresses issues like *Physical Implications of Collaboration* that describes pitfalls students can fall into during the first meetings. *Digital Collaboration & Workflow* – a sub-chapter and a continuation of the first – was written specifically with the restrictions of the pandemic in mind and addresses how to work together virtually. This led to *Finding Common Ground and What Happens If You Can't* which talks about questions and advice on what to explain or emphasize when first starting out with a group, to get communication rolling. Through research it also became evident that collaboration worked better when everyone is on the same page about their expectations of the outcome and their grades, which is why the chapter *Ascertain the Goals* pinpoints strategies and questions for working out the group's individual and collective goals. *Enabling the Project* touches upon ego and how to let go of your original ideas to improve your project or collaboration through reflection while *Connecting to Other People's Ideas* follows the theme of reflecting on your own ideas by reflecting on other peoples' ideas and ultimately finding your own point of view in a collective. Lastly, *How Collaboration Is Rewarded & Assessed* discusses the big question of how we can navigate collaboration in an environment that prioritizes individual submissions.

Learning through Collaboration

Ellen Mara De Wachter (2017), an arts and culture writer, discusses how the ways we conceptualize collaboration affects the way we think about it. Defining collaboration can help students navigate their collaborative journey. The purpose is for students to be able to focus on what is possible through collaboration. Moreover, as Gibbs (1988, 9) 'it is not sufficient to have an experience in order to learn. Without reflecting on this experience it may quickly be forgotten, or its learning potential lost'. Thus, if we want students to value the potential benefits that collaboration might bring them, we need to create spaces where they can think through what they have done, why and how, in order to make the learning conscious. Thus, even if submitting work individually, when we reflect on our collaborations we can get a positive learning benefit from it.

These arguments build the theoretical background of the Resource Pack, which argues that we need not just students to engage with the topic but also lecturers, professors and the institution itself for collaboration to be successful. 'Support is an enabling tool, whether that be a person, an environment, or a specific physical device, or a combination of these' (Slater, cited in Condorelli, 2009, 80). Through strategically enabling collaboration, we create an environment that takes some of the pressure off the individual and makes space for effective and affective collaborative learning.

Evaluation in Practice

As said above, the SC resources developed were refined in practice through the Temporary Studio (TP), where collaborative-work-in-progress was showcased. The TP was a space where we, the students, hosted lectures, workshops and talks. Subjects ranged from illustration, digital collaboration and multi-disciplinary design to rave culture. It was a space where we could share the issues, practices and skills we were developing and interested in while working on our presentation and collaboration skills. The studio space also showcased our work including an entire wall full of our research so that others could get a glimpse of what inspired and informed us. Furthermore, the TP was designed to evolve and change, like projects usually do. The learning space represented experimentation and 'work in progress'. Working out loud highlighted for us the students' crucial skills that do not necessarily make it to the classrooms and gave us the opportunity to make our design education our own. As students and learners, we had craved for opportunities to collaborate on our own terms.

This collaborative working in and through the curriculum led me to further refine the SC. The experience of the TP changed the pre-conceptions of collaboration while flagging up how successful co-creation may be integrated into and through the curriculum. TP demonstrated the power of emergent learning spaces, and students apprehended the power of this. My argument is that if students are actively supported in creative collaborative challenges and given the tools to engage powerfully together, they can become change agents of their own learning:

> [We] need a whole generation with the capacities for creative thinking and for thriving in a collaborative culture ... People are not born with inherent innovation skills, but they can learn them. They can acquire the social skills to work in diverse, multidisciplinary teams, and learn adaptability and leadership.
> (Council on Competitiveness, 2005)

Conclusion

The hope for SC is that it could work as a pedagogical tool and act as a catalyst for transformational and liberatory opportunities, creating space for collaboration within design education – somewhere it is woefully lacking at this time. SC is a small step towards allowing students to come together – to make collaboration fun again by addressing issues that usually exhaust the fun out of it. It is designed as a 'pocketbook' that students could reference whenever necessary. We grow through collaboration and it is essential not just for study, but life. As Morten Hansen's (2009), a Norwegian-American professor whose research focuses on social networks and collaboration, says: 'If people knew how to collaborate well, the world would simply work better' (140).

Connectivity as Transgressive Practice in Doctoral Research: Making the Elephant Dance

Kiu Sum

- Making new connections during a doctorate provides opportunities for new collaborations and pushes academic boundaries.
- To overcome PhD challenges is not to only accept them and move on, but rather, work with them and share that experience with others in the community.
- Participating in online communities offers an alternative approach to seeking input and inspiration from those not directly influencing your PhD.
- The elephant needs to dance because the current academic culture is isolating and individualistic.

Introduction

In this reflective, auto-ethnographic case study, I share my experience of dealing with the PhD 'elephant'. Academia is isolating and individualistic, and nowhere more so perhaps than when undertaking doctoral studies. In my reflections, I reveal the importance of connectivity for survival, where connectivity is inherently a 'transgressive practice' in HE. Jecks (2013) defines this as an act of boundary-crossing or constraint-defying, and crossing those boundaries and connecting with others benefitted my academic experience and also arguably the wider community. The isolating Covid-19 pandemic revealed the PhD 'elephant in the room', making connectivity even more urgent and important. This chapter argues that collaboration is about pushing against academic boundaries, going beyond subject knowledge to explore what collegial transgressions might enable and how they empower those at the margins through multi- and interdisciplinary collaborations.

Background

Eat the Elephant one bite at a time (Unknown).

I have been thinking about how I will survive my PhD journey. At times, the enthusiasm I once had feels like it is slowly slipping through my fingers. It is like being lost in a forest, and everywhere you navigate, this six-tonne greyish black shadow rustles the leaves on the surrounding trees. Doctoral researchers, like myself, face several challenges as they carve themselves out, proving they have the stamina to take on the PhD elephant. Committing several years to graduate school is not a light decision; doing the same research for years can be infuriating. The elephant is always in the room, following and staring at you, wondering how and if you will ever defeat it. Googling no longer works when the size of the elephant overshadows your self-belief. It is like consuming food – even the most delicious food will get tiring after a time. Likewise, putting all your energy into this one elephant will drain you, leaving a bad taste after enough bites. Here, this elephant represents the whole PhD experience, from the actual research project, the weight of expectations and peer pressure, whether from supervisors, fellow doctorate researchers or my personal self. But also to me, it represents the relationship-building with others that I realized I needed to sustain me – whether it was with those who immediately influence my PhD work or those lingering at the end of a long rope of connectivity, offering words of encouragement and wisdom, reinforcing motivation, revealing opportunities or at times waiting to see what will happen. To survive my PhD journey is not just finding the answer to my research question but also maintaining those mutual support and encouragement relationships.

Obstacles such as lack of motivation, self-confidence and focus, poor time management, limited support, fear of failure, and missing relevant experience can either make or break the success and completion of a doctorate (Lau, 2019; Mantai, 2015; Nori et al., 2020). Thus, finding like-minded people, my 'tribe', by joining a community (or more), participating with the wider academic network, and getting the support and feedback needed to facilitate the progress and advancement on this journey helped me deal with the elephant one bite at a time.

Finding Solutions: Making the Elephant Public

While working on my PhD elephant, I discovered that no one particular work experience could set you up directly to survive a PhD. Yet, my diverse experiences helped me realize the elephant I was looking for. The skills I have cultivated in several different spheres certainly helped me 'befriend' my elephant and not perceive it as a burden. Accepting the elephant helped me use my enthusiasm to connect with and collaborate with others – the tigers and giraffes further afield. Therefore, a lesson learnt by reflecting on my relationship with my elephant is not about subjecting myself to what I 'should' be doing but celebrating what I am doing and what I am trying to achieve. Barriers are there not to steer you off course, but invitations to leap over, boundaries to cross, stretching your capabilities to discover the more expansive educational spaces beyond. Here, the elephant's role is to nudge me to go beyond my comfort zone, to provoke new ideas and discussions and, along the way, discover the motivation to learn to communicate research that could be of relevance to other disciplines through mutual collaborations.

The next step to finding my solution was taking the opportunity to face my elephant using what appeared to be extra-academic approaches – harnessing social media. This ensured my development is not only through traditional methods such as the already-established institutional-based network but by innovatively connecting with others online. For example, a speaker in a career workshop shared their personal experience on the benefits of using technology to search areas where other individuals had similar interests – e.g. through professional organizations. With this inspiration, a simple message on social media (Twitter and LinkedIn) opened opportunities for further discussions, making my doctorate journey less isolating and more interactive than one initially imagined. I never quite knew what hashtags were initially used for. However, stumbling on a few suggested hashtags and accounts, I soon discovered information in innovative ways, often observing real-time activities in other related areas.

I discovered how walking around with my elephant became a coping strategy, helping me to overcome the isolating PhD barriers. I took the plunge by revealing my elephant experience on social networks, taking it outside the typical academic environment and talking about it – first, sharing it tentatively with those in my discipline and whose experience resonated with mine. With confidence, I took it to another level, conversing with others in academic social networks on HE-related topics. Thus sharing a student's perspective on progressing through my PhD became a connective experience. I understood that my 'student voice' position empowered me to 'break the ice' and be accepted for who I was in a community. Eventually, this digital online connectivity has evolved from observing the discussions from a distance, inspired by those with more experience in the community, to have the courage and confidence to discover my story. Regular active participation led to subsequent collaborations within the community.

Taking the elephant outside and online allowed me to engage in my work creatively and find new networks that are somewhat indirectly related to my PhD. These online communities of practice or personal learning networks have been around for a long time. However, the extraordinary Covid-19 pandemic has revealed to many more of us the online power to creatively transform not just teaching and learning, but also our research practice.

Establishing the Elephant Online

Though my initial struggle to find my identity amongst the already-established online community was frightening, the realization that technology can unexpectedly help reach others was eye-opening. For instance, taking the first step and pushing myself outside my comfort zone and having the courage to engage in online conversations about my elephant was more encouraging than I thought. Of course, like everyone, I had that imposter syndrome (all the time), not knowing what other people, professionals, may think – where in this society, everyone is very conscious that anything posted virtually could be interpreted or judged without understanding the full context. But through this engagement, I realized that everyone has their own elephant with them – whether other doctoral researchers who are also struggling with the process or other academics struggling to disseminate their work – there existed a veritable 'memory' of potential friends and allies. Thus 'preparing students for a more globalised and connected world' is not just a mantra but a reality for doctoral students collaborating together online. Together, we become a memory of elephants, a tower of giraffes and an ambush of tigers, increasing discipline awareness and sustaining motivation and engagement across many subject areas.

The Importance of Connection

Multi-disciplinary collaboration has been a key lesson. Having an aspiration to learn and become an expert within my one research area is impossible without acknowledging the relevance, applications and connections to other people and other related areas.

Connectivity and online connectivity is inherently a transgressive practice in HE and beyond. Sharing my story and experiences facilitated many discussions, leading to online collaborations with colleagues beyond my existing network. For example, participating in online conferences from the other side of the world during the pandemic has enabled my discovery of other researchers in a similar research area. Despite being in different geographical locations, there was this opportunity to connect and compare our PhD elephants, sharing our struggles and challenges, leading to peer support and motivation. Closer to home and curious about different hashtags, I regularly stumble across relevant subject area posts. It is fascinating to see what activities people are involved with, discovering far more than you thought, uncovering the many potential connections when others are 'live tweeting'.

Online connectivity is undoubtedly an asset leading to forward-thinking discussions and collaborations. As a doctoral researcher, a virtual network facilitates confidence to share knowledge and practices with the wider community, growing your support network, especially during uncertain times and the sudden shift to remote working. Furthermore, the discovery of hashtags provides pathways to unexpected resources and opportunities, meeting like-minded people through organized synchronous and asynchronous activities. Navigating a PhD elephant is challenging. However, online connectivity and subsequent collaborations could help break down imposter syndrome barriers, especially when approaching people at conferences could sometimes be intimidating.

Recommendations

The experiences of online connectivity and collaboration from a doctoral researcher's perspective are transferable to any learner in HE. It is the value of making connections with others beyond your existing network, highlighting the multi-disciplinary aspects of working in person or remotely. It is the sharing of best practices experienced by like-minded individuals, knowing what works and what does not, without relying on textbook answers. It is the opportunity to be innovative and creative, engaging with new ways of thinking that could easily be transferred, transforming how we could strategically facilitate a more globalized and connected world, breaking barriers down for a more collaborative community. It is about having a thick skin like an elephant, being authentic to your intentions and goals, simultaneously trusting the process as you make choices and mould your experience.

Conclusion

The PhD elephant will always be with me. But living in a digital era where human interaction could benefit the positiveness, productivities and achievement of goals, the unprecedented pandemic has changed many people's perception of connectivity and collaborations. The quick answer to deal with the elephant is, supposedly, to eat it entirely in one go. However, the more strategic way of coping with stress and imposter syndrome is to walk with, talk with and share the elephant, bit by bit, valuing the knowing and becoming the process of making connections, sharing stories. Though this is only a short chapter, life after a PhD elephant will nevertheless lead to exciting, new and unexpected ventures. As such, the application of virtual connections and collaborations empowers the existing community and lays the foundations together with colleagues from multi-disciplines to engage and create spaces to achieve shared knowledge, stories, poems to elaborate our goals and visions – and of course, the Elephant.

Changing the Rules of the Game: A Staff-student Digital Support Network

Jennie Blake, Adam Cooke and Jasmine Nisic

- Digital networks facilitated by peers who understand the lived experience of HE for students from underrepresented backgrounds offer a valuable addition to a spectrum of university support and multiplicity of relations.
- This pilot project has acted as an advocate for underrepresented voices and contributed to university-wide practice on engagement for successful learning across WP activities and modelled collaborative practice to include staff-student partners.
- Collaborative staff-student projects are well placed to be both proactive and reactive with respect to student needs in challenging contexts.

Introduction: Library Peer Network

Universities struggle to create the necessary structures and programmes that allow students from WP backgrounds (see Kikabhai, 2018) to access systems in the same manner as those from privileged groups, leading to attainment and retention gaps (Brooman & Darwent, 2013; Jones, 2017; Stevenson et al., 2010). As part of the University of Manchester's response to the Covid-19 pandemic and its efforts to recognize and moderate the effect of transitioning to life at university, the library developed a digital community space to support students deemed 'at risk' – of failing, withdrawing and/or not realizing their potential. The Library Peer Network (LPN) operates collaboratively as a staff-supported and student-facilitated invitation-only Microsoft Teams space for students from a range of underrepresented cohorts, identified through their admissions data including specific socio-economic and transition routes. Additionally, the team created resources in an open online publication (Library Peer Network, 2022) centred around the lived experiences of students from underrepresented and disadvantaged communities as well as academic and information literacy support. Around two thousand students were identified through their admissions data to be targeted by the project of which 15 per cent of students accepted the invite to join the support space. The open access publication (Library Peer Network, 2021) receives over one thousand visits per month.

In this chapter we present our model of student support for students from underrepresented backgrounds, facilitated through peer-to-peer framework and online support network. Students employed by the Library were the public 'face' of the network and were supported by other staff at the University Library to create bespoke digital resources, deliver empathetic support and model best practice in the face of adverse circumstances. We reflect on key lessons learnt and consider the development of the project from a pilot start-up to one that is embedded in University support structures.

WP at the University of Manchester

The University of Manchester has one of the largest intakes of students in the UK and has an above-average number of students from underrepresented backgrounds (University of Manchester, 2020a). The University's Access and Participation Plan recognizes the changes needed to ensure better access to, success at and progression from university (University of Manchester, 2020b). Students from WP backgrounds, as identified through their socio-economic, ethnicity and disability status, do not progress to university or achieve the same degree outcomes as their peers (Stone, 2022; Thomas, 2020).

The LPN extends the staff-student partnerships established as part of the University Library's Student Team (ST), where the students work in staff-student roles to support teaching and learning programmes in the Library (see Library Student Team, 2022). Recognizing that WP students were likely to be more affected by the impacts of the global pandemic exacerbating existing barriers to learning such as tensions in class (Archer et al., 2005), identity (Reay et al., 2010) and language (Bruce et al., 2016), the Library secured additional funding to extend the ST's roles into online peer support. Library teaching focuses on collaborative, collective and connective models in a student led space (Bell, 2011; Giroux, 2010). Therefore, the LPN is an additional layer of support for students who are less likely than their peers to have the support networks and the social, cultural and economic capital (Clark & Hordósy, 2018; Hordósy & Clark, 2018) to enact the accepted habitus of elite HE in the UK (Reay et al., 2009). The LPN has identified and met a need for personalized support that had not previously been effectively provided through non-targeted peer support programmes. The aims of the project were threefold:

- Support the creation of reciprocal networks for students to access peer-led expertise in all areas of university life including academic and pastoral support.
- Provide access to a series of resources and talks to unlock social and cultural capital, with a particular focus on academic transition to higher education and longer-term employability.
- Allow student participants to grow confidence and self-efficacy, challenging imposter syndrome and recognizing their exceptional abilities and potential for success.

To achieve these aims, collaborative planning, using a theory of change, developed a tiered approach to the support with an open set of online resources produced by the students and hosted via a Medium publication (Library Peer Network, 2021), faculty-specific channels in Teams and individual peer mentors within the ST for participants to reach out to. This approach was considered the best way to utilize the wider ST expertise to write and record collaborative resources whilst offering their academic and personal backgrounds as mentors. There is extensive research on the efficacy of peer learning and collaborative co-creation of learning environments and materials (Bovill et al., 2011a). While not all ST members are from underrepresented backgrounds, the majority of those supporting LPN are. This system attempted to recognize that participants would benefit from support tailored around their existing university experience with a faculty, school and course structure (Bovill et al., 2011b), led by those who most closely connected to, their own experience, fellow students.

Rules of the Game

The Library's ST produced original content firstly centred around transition support, habitus and 'rules of the game' (Reay et al., 2010) and later, collaboratively with participants, developed written and audio support on academic skills and employability through a collection of blogs and podcasts. The Library ST also acted as a point of contact for students, sending regular Teams chats and signposting wider support where necessary. This proved to be the most intensive and impactful part of the project with some strong support relationships being formed. The ST was able to spot crises before they matured, find the gaps in support and signpost where needed.

The ST view was that they, as a team of WP staff-students, and the students in the project were competing with their peers from a position of disadvantage. The 'rules' of how to act, be, do were not explained and the 'game' of succeeding at University was inherently unfair (Devlin & McKay, 2018). All the collaborative work was intended to make clear the rules and ensure participating students were equipped with the knowledge, expertise and confidence to 'participate'. A resource that explores this is a reflective podcast recorded between the LPN team and a student who came to the University through supported access programmes. The student talks powerfully about their uneasiness about their WP status, being singled out as 'in need', the challenge of acceptance and imposter syndrome (Library Peer Network, 2022). It is exactly this sort of experience that led us to springboard from a WP-targeted network to create the open resource.

Engagement and Impact

The LPN was specifically targeted at WP students, and whilst this attracted some push back, as per the podcast discussed, the project placed student voice and collaboration at its centre and specifically elevated the voices of students from underrepresented cohorts (Dawson et al., 2013) making a significant contribution to WP discourse across the institution. The LPN became an advocate for underrepresented voices and an accessible route through which colleagues across the University could disseminate information and receive feedback from otherwise marginalized voices: a partnership model (Bovill et al., 2015) recognizing marginalized voices and sharing powerful collective experiences (hooks, 1994). This is reflected in the following comment:

> As an individual who herself has overcome significant barriers to her education in a challenging school system in a challenging area, I became the first in my family to attend University and be awarded the highest grading of degrees at undergraduate and postgraduate level from The University of Manchester. Support and scholarship funding from the Dick Camplin Education Trust (DCET, 2021) provided a framework through which to transfer my experiences of support to the LPN. My first-hand accounts of balancing my studies ensured that the team's approach was one of inclusivity and empathy. We have enabled students to build the confidence to seek the help that will enable them to become what has always been within them – successful.
>
> (Jas Nisic, Library Peer Network)

Concluding Reflections

The project emerged in a moment of crisis where education and student support had to be moved online and harnessed the opportunities of the digital to bring staff and students, but especially students together. The opportunity to have a student collective leading the way, many of whom identify as being from WP backgrounds, gave staff and student interactions an authenticity and validity and harnessing more empathy in contrast to top-down, university-wide correspondence.

The project successfully became part of the embedded offer across the University and influenced transition materials for students who have not yet joined. The project is currently being developed for post-pandemic circumstances, emerging as smaller Faculty-orientated networks with the Library ST offering centralized academic and information literacy support.

The collaborative project continues to try to centre marginalized voices. We therefore consider appropriate to leave the final words of this case study to a participant:

> The LPN has been a bit of a lifeline this year, all the opportunities it's given me and having someone to talk to and having someone to relate to on things like working part-time and being a role model for your siblings made the first semester less isolating. Add that to being nudged out of my comfort zone to apply to things in the second semester like scholarships and internships (which I didn't even know were a thing until this year). I didn't realise how valuable it was for me to have someone from the same background to just vent to and guide me to make the most out of my first year and out of my uni experience. Now I really want to make the most of my time here instead of just trying to do well academically because I know I deserve to be here.
>
> (LPN Student, Materials Science and Engineering)

Enhancing Digital Inclusivity: Powerful Partnership with Students

Karen Arm

- Working in partnership with a collaborative team of Student Inclusive Curriculum Consultants in a centralized academic development team can help support university-wide course enhancement and cultural change.
- Dismantling consumerist hierarchies inherent in student voice work is essential to effective partnership working in Faculties.
- Partnering with diverse students is pivotal to ensuring learning, teaching and assessment are inclusive.
- Student and staff collaboration in HE can be successfully fostered remotely and online.

Introduction: Students as Partners

At Solent University, we are strategically committed to working in partnership with students to enrich learning and teaching (Cook-Sather et al., 2014). We do not want our students to be passive recipients of teaching but rather active learners who work collaboratively with staff to co-produce knowledge (Naidoo et al., 2011). Yet partnership working on the frontline often gets subsumed by 'You said, We listened' student 'voice' campaigns and can sometimes get used as a management tool (Lygo-Baker et al., 2019). These one-directional feedback processes can create a culture of despondency amongst academics – making them feel like service providers trying to please their customers rather than educators (Anonymous Academic, 2015). As a centralized team of education developers tasked with university-wide course enhancement, we have been concerned by these trends in our academic community and have been asking ourselves: How can we work effectively with students in genuine partnership to support strategic learning and teaching agendas (Dunne et al., 2011)?

Whilst we were preoccupying ourselves with this question, Covid-19 hit the UK. The country went into lockdown and there was an emergency pivot to digital learning and teaching in universities. This shone a spotlight on the importance of inclusive pedagogy in ways that it had not done before:

> Sector conversations are highlighting concerns, particularly about the impact of Covid-19 on our most disadvantaged and vulnerable students. And the fear is we will erase the good work and progress that has been made in terms of widening access, success and outcomes if we don't care.
> (Nona McDuff, Pro Vice Chancellor, Students and Teaching, Solent University Internal News Bulletin, 2020)

Course teams needed to take urgent action to ensure that all students remained connected to their studies, their lecturers and their peers, and had an easy-to-navigate learning journey which was inclusive and accessible. Academics could no longer rely on their tried and tested methods of face-to-face teaching to achieve this. They needed to reach out to students to understand how connected learning could be best facilitated in this new and – for many – unfamiliar digital world (Syska, 2021). In this way the pandemic created an opportunity to dismantle the consumerist hierarchies that had been lingering in existing partnership working, and for staff and students to work in genuine partnership to build an inclusive online learning and teaching environment together. This chapter outlines how Solent University successfully worked with students, in partnership, to manage this change.

The Student Inclusive Curriculum Consultancy Project

In June 2020 we recruited six students to the position of 'Inclusive Curriculum Consultant' to work centrally in the Solent Learning and Teaching Institute. These positions were paid, and contracts ran for six months before the employment opportunity was opened to others (as per Burns et al., 2019). The purpose of the role was to work collaboratively with members of academic staff to help them consider how their newly developed online modules could be made inclusive and accessible to all learners. The students came from a variety of disciplinary backgrounds, with interests in equality and diversity, but no previous experience of academic development. Following an intensive training period aimed at building a cohesive and cooperative team, the students co-constructed a list of reflective prompts to use for reviewing the inclusivity, accessibility and usability of online modules, from diverse learner perspectives (differentiated by race, gender, class, age, dis/ability, circumstances, etc.). The prompts enshrined Solent University's commitment to providing an Inclusive

Curriculum that is (1) accessible, (2) enables learners to see themselves reflected in it and (3) equips students to work in a global and diverse world (McDuff et al., 2020). At the heart of this strategic mission is the importance of staff working in partnership with students to co-create, review and enhance learning and teaching.

For each module, the student team recorded their reflections on a feedback sheet identifying three strengths, three weaknesses and three recommendations for improvement to create a more inclusive, accessible and usable module. This feedback was sent to the module leader for action and then integrated into academic planning and enhancement activities at a programme level. The entire process took place virtually, in online meetings and other collaborative digital spaces (i.e. shared documents and discussion forums). In many cases, student feedback was followed with tailored pedagogic advice and technical support from Academic Development and Learning Technologies staff to support the course teams in implementing the students' suggested actions. This provided a welcomed opportunity for educational developers to forge greater collaborative networks in Faculties through the students' enhancement recommendations. Further professional development on inclusive pedagogy, co-facilitated and designed by the students, was also offered to course teams as part of the process (e.g. on racial equality in learning and teaching).

Evaluation

In the 2020/21 academic year, our collaborative team of Student Inclusive Curriculum Consultants supported academic colleagues to review and enhance the inclusivity of their digital learning and teaching practice in over 235 online modules across all Faculties. Typical enhancements included:

- Ensuring learning resources and case studies represent varied and diverse voices (different faiths, nationalities, cultures, ethnicities, genders, etc.).
- Ensuring all images used in the module and teaching materials represent our diverse student population – not just young, white, able-bodied people.
- Adding subtitles and/or transcripts on all videos (and editing these to match the spoken word).
- Using colours and fonts that increase accessibility for every student, especially those with dyslexia.
- Including infographics and chunking text into short paragraphs with headings to help make it easily digestible.
- Offering a variety of learning resources in different formats to suit multiple learning preferences.
- Using student-friendly and inclusive communications throughout the module. Avoiding stereotypes and binary language.
- Providing a dedicated space to discuss mental health/learning disabilities and signposting students to the dedicated university services.
- Making online face-to-face sessions informal and welcoming through active learning strategies so all students feel comfortable to participate.

- Offering opportunities for students from different backgrounds to interact and work with each other through group work and/or co-creation activities.
- Recording live (online) teaching sessions where possible and making them available to all students to increase accessibility of learning.

Feedback from students on the inclusivity and accessibility of the Solent Online Learning environment has been overwhelmingly positive as demonstrated in our internal Student Experience Module Surveys across both semesters in 2020/21 (19,616 responses in total):

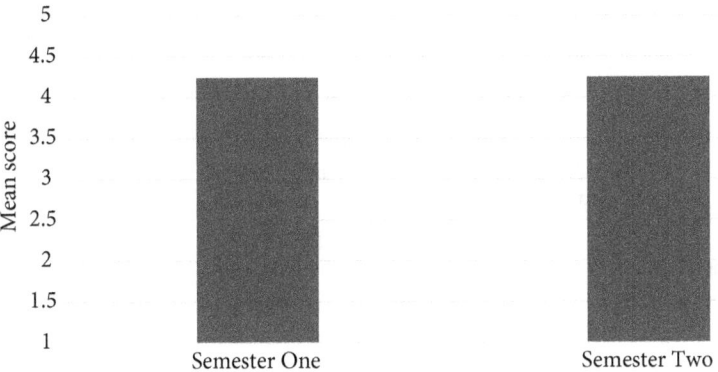

Figure 6.6 Mean scores for the survey question – 'To what extent do you agree with the following statement? The online learning environment and content is accessible': 1 = Definitely disagree, 5 = Definitely agree (n=10,699).

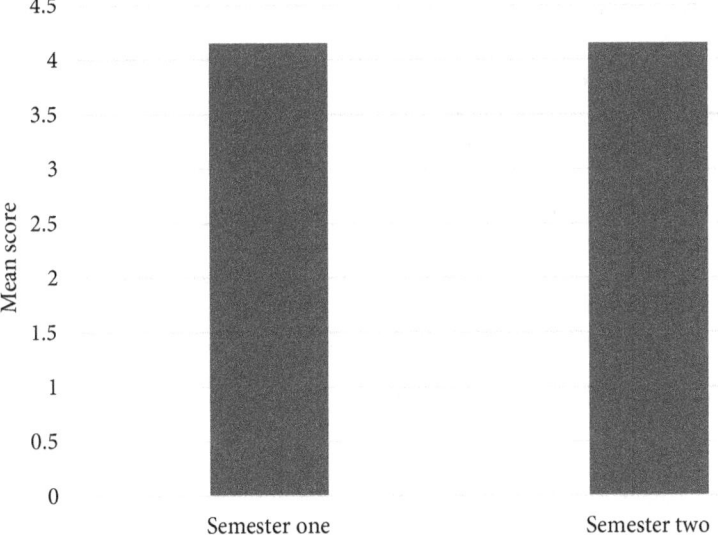

Figure 6.7 Mean scores for the survey question – 'To what extent do you agree with the following statement? The online learning environment and content is inclusive': 1 = Definitely disagree, 5 = Definitely agree (n=8,917).

Commenting on the value of working in partnership with staff to successfully manage the shift to online learning, our Student Inclusive Curriculum Consultants said:

> Throughout my work as an Inclusive Curriculum Consultant, I've come to truly appreciate how input from students is necessary to understand the direction education needs to follow. By collaborating with students you'll be ensuring that the content is easy to understand, is digestible, and that information consolidation is possible across all subject matter. It also gives course teams an opportunity to work in partnership with students, keeping essential communication channels open. Solent University is already seeing the benefits from the work we have been undertaking with module pages, students have expressed their appreciation of all the work that has gone into Solent Online Learning Environment in the recent months.

> Being a Student Inclusive Curriculum Consultant is being part of the change. Is being part of a group of individuals who work together to make higher education inclusive, available to all. It's being at the top of new ideas, new ways of teaching, new ways of learning. As a group we had the challenge of working while a pandemic breaks outside. Students were sent home to study remotely which means the course modules have been adapted for online delivery. Our job has been to make sure that teaching is fully accessible and inclusive to all learners.

Partnership: A Lasting Legacy

The success of the Student Inclusive Curriculum Consultancy initiative has created a legacy of centrally led partnership working at Solent University. Whilst the project was initially created to support the emergency pivot to online learning and teaching in 2020/21, the University is continuing to work in partnership with an expanded and increasingly diverse Student Inclusive Curriculum Consultancy team to support strategic learning and teaching agendas going forward (e.g. the implementation of an Inclusive Curriculum Framework and pedagogic enhancement actions aimed at eradicating our Black, Asian and Minority Ethnic awarding gap – McMaster, 2021). Good inclusive online teaching practice identified in the 2020/21 Student Inclusive Curriculum Consultant module review process is, and will continue to be, shared across Solent University via a series of student-authored professional development resources for staff. Indeed, academics have expressed their appreciation for this student input and are using it to inform the design of student-centred and inclusive online teaching for the next iteration of their modules. As one colleague explains:

> Thank you for the extremely useful and wonderful feedback provided by your team on my module design. I put a great deal of effort into making the module as inclusive and diverse as possible. Even despite that I found that your team provided many additional suggestions which I can incorporate in the next academic year. The process was fun and collaborative. I think your team provides an absolutely great resource and thank you very much for offering it.

Whilst initially met with some suspicion by staff, the Curriculum Consultancy Project has helped to build greater academic trust in working in partnership with students. Our project has exemplified the value of dismantling power hierarchies inherent in student voice partnership models (de Bie et al., 2021) and illustrated the potential for working in genuine and meaningful partnership with students to actively create inclusive online pedagogy. Furthermore, we have demonstrated the possibility of this collaboration taking place entirely in virtual spaces through online team meetings, discussion forums and shared documents (Ntem et al., 2020). We are delighted that our project has become a catalyst for more online co-creation initiatives within course contexts at the University, such as student/staff forums, digital employability events and exhibitions of student work. Going forward we will continue to encourage course teams to work more closely in partnership with their students – both in the digital and the physical world – to consider tangible ways of enhancing the inclusivity of learning and teaching practice to meet the needs of our increasingly diverse student body.

References

Introduction

Abegglen, S., Burns, T., & Sinfield. S. (2018). Drawing as a way of knowing: Visual practices as the route to becoming academic. *Canadian Journal for Studies in Discourse and Writing/Rédactologie*, 28, 173–85. DOI: 10.31468/cjsdwr.600

Conley, B., & Massa, R. (2022, 28 February). The great interruption. Inside Higher Ed. https://www.insidehighered.com/admissions/views/2022/02/28/enrollment-changes-colleges-are-feeling-are-much-more-covid-19#:~:text=According%20to%20the%20National%20Student,just%20over%20a%20million%20students

Huizinga, J. (1949). *Homo ludens: A study of the play-element in culture*. Routledge & Kegan Paul.

Meyer, J. H. F., & Land, R. (2005). Threshold concepts and troublesome knowledge (2): Epistemological considerations and a conceptual framework for teaching and learning. *Higher Education*, 49(3), 373–88. DOI: 10.1007/s10734-004-6779-5

Molinari, J. (2017). What makes our writing academic? ReGenring17 Conference. Nottingham Trent University, Nottingham, 21 June.

Schmitt, F. F., & Lahroodi, R. (2008). The epistemic value of curiosity. *Educational Theory*, 58(2), 125–48. DOI: 10.1111/j.1741-5446.2008.00281.x

Sinfield, S., Holley, D., & Burns, T. (2009). A journey into silence: Students, stakeholders and the impact of a strategic governmental policy document in the UK. *Social Responsibility Journal*, 5(4), 566–74. DOI: 10.1108/17471110910995401

Case Study: Paper as Teacher

Basit, T. N., & Tomlinson, S. (2012). *Social inclusion and higher education*. Policy Press.

Chabot, J., Cramer, F., Rutten, P., & Troxler, P. (2013). *Reinventing the art school, 21st century*. Willem de Kooning Academie.

Csikszentmihalyi, M. (2011). *Flow: The psychology of optimal experience*. HarperCollins.

Hao, G., & Pentek, A. (2021). Art into engineering: Demonstrating how origami creativity can inform robotics education. *The 10th International Conference on Engineering Education for Sustainable Development (EESD2021)*, 14–16 June 2021, Cork, Ireland.

Harris, E., Winterbottom, M., Xanthoudaki, M., Calcagnini, S., & De Puer, I. (2016). Tinkering: A practitioner guide for developing and implementing tinkering activities. *Erasmus +*. https://epale.ec.europa.eu/en/resource-centre/content/tinkering-practitioner-guide-developing-and-implementing-tinkering

Hughes, J., Morrison, L., & Dobos, L. (2018). Re-making teacher professional development. In G. Craddock, C. Doran, L. McNutt, & D. Rice (Eds.), *Transforming our world through design, diversity and education* (pp. 602–8). IOS Press. DOI: 10.3233/978-1-61499-923-2-602

James, A., & Nerantzi, C. (Eds.) (2019). *The power of play in higher education: Creativity in tertiary learning*. Springer.

Kjällander, S., Åkerfeldt, A., Mannila, L., & Parnes, P. (2018). Makerspaces across settings: Didactic design for programming in formal and informal teacher education in the Nordic countries. *Journal of Digital Learning in Teacher Education*, 34(1). DOI: 10.1080/21532974.2017.1387831

Liang, H., Hao, G., Olszewski, O. Z., & Pentek, A. (2021). The design of a twisting origami robot inspired by resch triangular tessellation. *5th IEEE/IFToMM International Conference on Reconfigurable Mechanisms and Robots (ReMAR 2021)*, 12–14 July 2021, Toronto, Canada.

Nishiyama, Y. (2012). Miura folding: Applying origami to space exploration. *International Journal of Pure and Applied Mathematics*, 79(2), 269–79. http://ijpam.eu/contents/2012-79-2/8/8.pdf

Papert, S., & Harel, I. (1991). Situating constructionism. In S. Papert, & I. Harel (Eds.), *Constructionism* (pp. 1–11). Ablex Publishing Corporation.

Piaget, J. (1973). *To understand is to invent*. Grossman.

Read, H. (2014). *Education through art*. Faber & Faber.

Slee, R. (2011). *The irregular school: Exclusion, schooling and inclusive education*. Taylor & Francis.

Supple, B., & Agbenyega, J. S. (2015). Reframing the self in an international learning context: Experiences of international students with a disability. *Current Issues in Education*, 18(1), 1–13. https://cie.asu.edu/ojs/index.php/cieatasu/article/view/1333

Supple, B., O'Neill, S., Hao, G., & Pentek, A. (2021). Beyond paper folding: Origami and focused play to enhance interdisciplinary learning and teaching in universities. *AISHE-J: The All Ireland Journal of Teaching & Learning in Higher Education*, 3. https://ojs.aishe.org/index.php/aishe-j/article/view/591/943

Troxler, P. (2015). *Beyond consenting nerds: Lateral design patterns for new manufacturing*. Hogeschool Rotterdam.

Vygotsky, L. S. (1978). *Mind in society: The development of higher psychological processes*. Harvard University Press.

Woodward, S. (2020). *Material methods: Researching and thinking with things*. Sage.

Zhakypov, Z., Heremans, F., Billard, A., & Paik, J. (2018). An origami-inspired reconfigurable suction gripper for picking objects with variable shape and size. *IEEE Robotics and Automation Letters*, 3(4), 2894–901. https://ieeexplore.ieee.org/stamp/stamp.jsp?arnumber=8385192

Case Study: Upheaval, Creativity and Student Partnerships

Abegglen, S., Burns, T., Maier, S., & Sinfield, S. (2020). Supercomplexity: Acknowledging students' lives in the 21st century university. *Innovative Practice in Higher Education*, 4(1), 21–24.

Cozolino, L. (2014). *Predarea bazată pe atașament*. Trei.
Crețu, D. (2019). *Predarea și învățarea în învățământul superior. Aspecte teoretice și practice*. Universitară.
Cury, A. (2007). *Părinți străluciți, profesori fascinanți*. For You.
Dumitrescu, M., & Și Dumitrescu, S. (2005). *Educația pentru sănătatea mentală și emoțională – ghid metodologic pentru pregătirea cadrelor didactice*. Arves.
Gordon, T., & Burch, N. (2011). *Profesorul eficient. Programul Gordon pentru îmbunătățirea relației cu elevii*. Trei.
Malureanu, A., Pânișoară, G., & Lazar, I. (2021). The relationship between self-confidence, self-efficacy, grit, usefulness, and ease of use of elearning platforms in corporate training during the Covid-19 pandemic. *Sustainability, 13*, 6633. DOI: 10.3390/su13126633
Pânișoară, I. O. (2015). *Profesorul de succes – 59 de principii de pedagogie practică*. Polirom.
Robinson, K. (2015). *Școli creative. Revoluția de la bază a sistemului*. Publica.
Robu, M. (2008). *Empatia în educație. Necesități pedagogice moderne. Ghid pentru cadrele didactice din învățământul preuniversitar*. Didactica Publishing House.
Schiavio, A., Biasutti, M., & Philippe, R. A. (2021). Creative pedagogies in the time of pandemic: A case study with conservatory students. *Music Education Research, 23*. DOI: 10.1080/14613808.2021.1881054

Case Study: Supporting Collaboration

Condorelli, C. (2009). *Support structures*. Sternberg Press.
Council on Competitiveness (2005). *Innovate America national innovation initiative summit and report*. https://www.compete.org/storage/images/uploads/File/PDF%20Files/NII_Innovate_America.pdf
De Wachter, E. M. (2017). *Co-art: Artists on creative collaboration*. Phaidon Press Limited.
Gibbs, G. (1988). *Learning by doing: A guide to teaching and learning methods*. Further Education Unit, Oxford Polytechnic.
Hansen, M. (2009). *Collaboration*. Harvard Business Press.
Moravec, J. W. (Ed.) (2019). *Emerging education futures: Experiences and visions from the field*. Education Futures.
Oblinger, D. G. (2018, August 2). What will AI and robotics mean for UK? *eCampus News*. https://www.ecampusnews.com/2018/08/02/what-will-ai-and-robotics-mean-for-higher-education/2/
Slotte, J. (2020). *Supporting collaboration*. https://jessicaslotte.squarespace.com/work/supportingcollaboration
University of Birmingham (2015). *A short guide to reflective writing*. https://intranet.birmingham.ac.uk/as/libraryservices/library/asc/documents/public/Short-Guide-Reflective-Writing.pdf

Case Study: Connectivity as Transgressive Practice in Doctoral Research

Jenks, C. (2013). Transgression: The concept. *Architectural Design, 83*(6), 20–3. DOI: 10.1002/ad.1669
Lau, R. W. K. (2019). You are not your PhD: Managing stress during doctoral candidature. In L. Pretorius, L. Macaulay, & B. Cahusac de Caux (Eds.), *Wellbeing in doctoral education* (pp. 47–58). Springer.

Mantai, L. (2015). Feeling like a researcher: Experiences of early doctoral students in Australia. *Studies in Higher Education*, 1–15. DOI: 10.1080/03075079.2015.1067603

Nori, H., Peura, M. H., & Jauhiainen, A. (2020). From imposter syndrome to heroic tales: Doctoral students' backgrounds, study aims, and experiences. *International Journal of Doctoral Studies*, *15*, 517–39. DOI: 10.28945/4637

Case Study: Changing the Rules of the Game

Archer, L., Hutchings, M., & Ross, A. (2005). *Higher education and social class: Issues of exclusion and inclusion*. Routledge.

Bell, F. (2011). Connectivism: Its place in theory-informed research and innovation in technology-enabled learning. *The International Review of Research in Open and Distributed Learning*, *12*(3), 98. DOI: 10.19173/irrodl.v12i3.902

Bovill, C., Bulley, C., & Morss, K. (2011). Engaging and empowering first-year students through curriculum design: perspectives from the literature. *Teaching in Higher Education*, *16*(2), 197–209. DOI: 10.1080/13562517.2010.515024

Bovill, C., Cook-Sather, A., & Felten, P. (2011). Students as co-creators of teaching approaches, course design, and curricula: Implications for academic developers. *International Journal for Academic Development*, *16*(2), 133–45. DOI: 10.1080/1360144x.2011.568690

Bovill, C., Cook-Sather, A., Felten, P., Millard, L., & Moore-Cherry, N. (2015). Addressing potential challenges in co-creating learning and teaching: Overcoming resistance, navigating institutional norms and ensuring inclusivity in student–staff partnerships. *Higher Education*, *71*(2), 195–208. DOI: 10.1007/s10734-015-9896-4

Brooman, S., & Darwent, S. (2013). Measuring the beginning: A quantitative study of the transition to higher education. *Studies in Higher Education*, *39*(9), 1523–41. DOI: 10.1080/03075079.2013.801428

Bruce, M., Rees, S., & Wilson, J. (2016). Language issues facing non-traditional students: Some problems and solutions. In C. Marshall, S. Nolan, & D. Newton (Eds.), *Widening participation, higher education and non-traditional students* (1st ed., pp. 41–55). Palgrave Macmillan.

Clark, T., & Hordósy, R. (2018). Social identification, widening participation and higher education: Experiencing similarity and difference in an English red brick university. *Sociological Research Online*, *24*(3), 353–69. DOI: 10.1177/1360780418811971

Dawson, P., Charman, K., & Kilpatrick, S. (2013). The new higher education reality: What is an appropriate model to address the widening participation agenda? *Higher Education Research & Development*, *32*(5), 706–21. DOI: 10.1080/07294360.2013.776520

DCET (2021). *About*. The Dick Camplin Education Trust. https://www.dcet.org.uk/about

Devlin, M., & McKay, J. (2018). Teaching inclusively online in a massified university system. *Widening Participation and Lifelong Learning*, *20*(1), 146–66. DOI: 10.5456/wpll.20.1.146

Giroux, H. (2010). Rethinking education as the practice of freedom: Paulo Freire and the promise of critical pedagogy. *Policy Futures in Education*, *8*(6), 715–21. DOI: 10.2304/pfie.2010.8.6.715

hooks, b. (1994). *Teaching to transgress: Education as the practice of freedom*. Routledge.

Hordósy, R., & Clark, T. (2018). Student budgets and widening participation: Comparative experiences of finance in low and higher income undergraduates at a northern red brick university. *Social Policy & Administration*, *53*(5), 761–75. DOI: 10.1111/spol.12410

Jones, S. (2017). Expectation vs experience: Might transition gaps predict undergraduate students' outcome gaps? *Journal of Further and Higher Education, 42*(7), 908–21. DOI: 10.1080/0309877x.2017.1323195

Jones, S., & Harvey, M. (2017). A distributed leadership change process model for higher education. *Journal of Higher Education Policy and Management, 39*(2), 126–39. DOI: 10.1080/1360080x.2017.1276661

Kikabhai, N. (2018). The rhetoric of widening participation. In N. Kikabhai (Ed.), *The rhetoric of widening participation in higher education and its impact* (pp. 147–83). Springer. DOI: 10.1007/978-3-319-75966-1_6

Library Peer Network (2021). *Library peer network – Medium.* Medium. https://medium.com/library-peer-network

Library Peer Network (2022a). *LPodcast'N #7: MAP/MDAS special + overcoming impostor syndrome + the culture shock of starting at ….* Medium. https://medium.com/library-peer-network/lpodcastn-7-map-mdas-special-overcoming-impostor-syndrome-the-culture-shock-of-starting-at-210861a15dab

Library Student Team (2022b). *Who are the student team?* Medium. https://studentteam.medium.com/who-are-the-student-team-34ebdb5ae467

Reay, D., Crozier, G., & Clayton, J. (2009). Strangers in paradise? *Sociology, 43*(6), 1103–21. DOI: 10.1177/0038038509345700

Reay, D., Crozier, G., & Clayton, J. (2010). 'Fitting in' or 'standing out': Working-class students in UK higher education. *British Educational Research Journal, 36*(1), 107–24. DOI: 10.1080/01411920902878925

Stevenson, J., Clegg, S., & Lefever, R. (2010). The discourse of widening participation and its critics: An institutional case study. *London Review of Education, 8*(2), 105–15. DOI: 10.1080/14748460.2010.487328

Stone, C. (2022). Improving student engagement, retention and success in online learning. In M. Shah, S. Kift, & L. Thomas (Eds.), *Student retention and success in higher education* (pp. 167–89). Palgrave Macmillan. DOI: 10.1007/978-3-030-80045-1_9

Thomas, L. (2020). Excellent outcomes for all students: A whole system approach to widening participation and student success in England. *Student Success, 11*(1), 1–11. https://doi.org/10.5204/ssj.v11i1.1455

University of Manchester (2020a). *The University of Manchester access and participation plan 2020-21 to 2024-25* [ebook]. University of Manchester. https://documents.manchester.ac.uk/display.aspx?DocID=44186

University of Manchester (2020b). *Widening participation annual report 2020* [ebook]. University of Manchester. https://documents.manchester.ac.uk/display.aspx?DocID=4294

Wainwright, E., Chappell, A., & McHugh, E. (2019). Widening participation and a student 'success' assemblage: The materialities and mobilities of university. *Population, Space and Place, 26*(3). DOI: 10.1002/psp.2291

Case Study: Enhancing Digital Inclusivity

Anonymous Academic (2015, December 18). My students have paid £9000 and now they think they own me. *The Guardian.* https://www.theguardian.com/higher-education-network/2015/dec/18/my-students-have-paid-9000-and-now-they-they-own-me

Burns, T., Sinfield, S., & Abegglen, S. (2019). Third space partnerships with students: Becoming educational together. *International Journal for Students as Partners, 3*(1), 60–8.

Cook-Sather, A. Bovill, C., & Felten, P. (2014). *Engaging students as partners in learning and teaching: A guide for Faculty*. Jossey Bass.

de Bie, A., Marquis, E., Cook-Sather, A., & Luqueno, L. P. (2021). *Promoting equity and justice through pedagogical partnership*. Stylus Publishers.

Dunne, E., Zandstra, R., Brown, T., & Nurser, T. (2011). *Students as change agents: New ways of engaging with learning and teaching in higher education*. Escalate. http://escalate.ac.uk/downloads/8242.pdf

Lygo-Baker, S., Kinchin, M., & Winstone, N. (2019). *Engaging student voices in higher education: Diverse perspectives and expectations in partnership*. Palgrave Macmillan.

McDuff, N., Hughes, A., Tatam, J., Morrow, E., & Ross, F. (2020). Improving equality of opportunity in higher education through the adoption of an inclusive curriculum framework. *Widening Participation and Lifelong Learning*, 22(2), 83–121.

McMaster, N. C. (2021). *Ethnicity awarding gaps in UK higher education in 2019/20*. AdvanceHE. https://www.advance-he.ac.uk/knowledge-hub/ethnicity-awarding-gaps-uk-higher-education-201920

Naidoo, R., Shankar, A., & Veer, E. (2011). The consumerist turn in higher education: Policy aspirations and outcomes. *Journal of Marketing Management*, 27(11–12), 1142–62.

Ntem, A., Nguyen, E., Rafferty, C., Kwan, C., & Benlahcene, A. (2020). Students as partners in crisis? Student co-editors' perspectives on COVID-19, values, and the shift to virtual spaces. *International Journal for Students as Partners*, 4(2). https://mulpress.mcmaster.ca/ijsap/article/view/4432

Syska, A. (2021). Compendium of innovative practice: Learning development in a time of disruption. Editorial. *Journal of Learning Development in Higher Education*. Special Issue 22. https://journal.aldinhe.ac.uk/index.php/jldhe/article/view/850/575

7

Decolonizing Relationships and Partnerships for Social Justice

Introduction

Education is often posited as a route to social justice and equality. However, as history shows, educational institutions are far from inclusive (Abegglen & Bustillos, 2021) and education, rather than facilitating equity, serves to reproduce society as it is with all its injustices (Althusser, 2012). Since the late 1990s in the UK, HE was supposed to operate a conscious anti-racist widening participation agenda, actively reaching out to, and recruiting those traditionally excluded from or unwelcome within traditional university spaces. Critical commentators have noted that rather than develop a more inclusive HE with a wider vocabulary and more creative practices, what has emerged is a more exclusive HE (Molinari, 2022) with some universities, courses and students more highly valued than others:

> The point is that by celebrating your 'otherness' without addressing the historical circumstances that created that 'other' as an inferior in the wider public arena, you run the risk of becoming embroiled in a fruitless tautological endeavour, such as debating whether 'all lives matter'.
>
> (Henry, 2021, 32)

Critics such as Noble (2003) argue that hand in hand with the promoted 'opening up' of HE has been the increasing commodification, bureaucratization and micromanaging of its processes and practices, with course development and pedagogic decision-making the first casualties. For the lecturer in this climate, teaching becomes the management-directed assemblance of the course into packages of decontextualized 'things': learning outcomes, syllabi, lessons and exams. The outcome is offered for sale in the marketplace if sufficient numbers of students are willing to subscribe, and if their future salaries are predicted to meet government-defined acceptable levels (Office for Students, 2022). Thus, teachers become producers, students become consumers and their relationship takes on not 'education, but a shadow of education, an assemblance of pieces without a whole' (Noble, 2003, 4).

More recently, academia has been shaken by the reverberations of Indigenous activism and the Black Lives Matter movement, leading to renewed calls for anti-racist practice and to 'decolonize the curriculum' for equity, and to acknowledge diversity in all its facets and forms. This has seeded opportunities for reflection, introspection and action. Whilst diversity and inclusion will differ according to geographic contexts, and 'decolonizing' has multiple meanings (from challenging the normalcy of empire, to enabling all students to see themselves within the curriculum, to creating active pedagogy that ensures all students are framed as actors and agents within their own learning process), universities as a whole and academics individually and collectively have been spurred to reimagine curriculum, pedagogy and practice in response to these additional and very urgent provocations.

In this section we include chapters that explore and discuss the various ways in which the practitioners have attempted to address historical and more recently created injustices within HE and thus to 'decolonize' relationships as they collaborate for action for social justice.

The Case Study Chapters

In *Coming in Together*, Ryan Arthur and Nahid Huda discuss their 'decolonizing' induction process designed to disrupt negative assumptions made about students. Their collaborative approach reveals the power of authentic dialogic activities that acknowledge students' socio-cultural histories. They argue that these cooperative learning activities need to be continued in and through the curriculum if, rather than passive enculturation, we are to facilitate openness to and engagement in 'emergent' academic processes.

With *Unite and Unrule!* Cybele Atme, Pauline Bon, Mila de Graaf, Daniel Haudenschild, Mieke Lopes Cardozo, Melina Merdanovic and Eleonore Nouel discuss their self-organized Masters course: Critical Development and Diversity Explorations that sits within International Development Studies. Seeded by an occupation in 2015 that called for a radical reimagining of the university itself, they moved on as a collective to experiment with co-creation as means to develop a more creative, innovative and collaborative space to enact (in)direct transformations in the larger HE system. Inspired by insights from critical, contemplative, social justice and relational pedagogy, they highlight two interrelated features of their co-creation approach to developing transgressive learning spaces: relational learning beyond individualism, and reflective and self-directed learning beyond competition – with an informative example of their practice that is adaptable for many HE contexts.

In *Honest Conversations about 'Race' and Racisim* Anthony Kalume and Jess Moriarty raise the issue of institutionlized racism in HE and explain how their anti-racist cultural project was designed to create the space, place, networks and research necessary to design an innovative, community-based module to challenge and change negative experiences and dominant discourses around Black and Minority Ethnic (staff and) students in HE. In the process of their collaboration, Anthony and Jess created a cultural project in which it was possible to have open and honest conversations about 'race' and racism, and the practices (and allyship) crucial to dismantling institutionalized racism in HE.

In *Love, Respect, Esteem*, Vikki Hill and Louise Taylor offer two examples of student partnership projects that address educational inequalities in relation to transition, attainment and belonging. The projects, that focused on challenging and changing racial inequity of outcome and treatment in HE, were designed iteratively with students over time, a collaborative approach that challenged power hierarchies and built relationships for change. They applied Honneth's Theory of Recognition as a framework to explain and argue for the relational complexities of the approach taken in their projects – both with respect to project design and to implementation as well as the outcomes achieved. Love, respect and esteem appear essential to develop equal and successful partnerships.

With *Inclusive Learning and Teaching in Higher Education*, Uzma A. Siddiqui reveals how collaboration between teachers and students can enhance engagement and participation amongst a socially and culturally diverse cohort of Health and Social Care students, thereby promoting social justice through co-creation. Seeking to address a lack of student participation and engagement with course content, a pilot session was redesigned with students, adopting a collaborative approach where students led the session and teachers acted as co-learners/facilitators. Evaluation indicated increased teacher-student communication, higher level of engagement with the subject material and inclusive student-student interaction through improved participation amongst a diverse student cohort. Student-teacher collaboration as curriculum partners is strongly recommended as a way of realizing students' added value in designing their own learning and increasing all students' engagement.

Tess Czerski, Jana Finke, Cybele Atme and Mieke Lopes Cardozo give us a practical example of *Teaching for Equality and the Politics of Feminist and Decolonial Education*. The course was created through the collaboration of junior and senior colleagues to contest normalized and normative notions of education and de-centre dominant teaching practices and curriculum. The pedagogic space was designed to move all participants from polarized debate to collaboration for change – via the collective lenses of the student 'education change' interventions. The authors acknowledge that transgressive practices can create discomfort for all concerned and emphasize the need to revert to practices of care and responsibility within the whole classroom, by both students and teachers/facilitators.

Coming in Together: Staff-student Collaboration in a 'Decolonizing' Induction Process

Ryan Arthur and Nahid Huda

- Current induction programmes and processes are rooted in assumptions made about students as 'lacking' and needing guidance. Arguably, this can lead to remedial or monologic approaches when planning induction sessions.
- Our collaborative approach reveals the power of authentic dialogic induction activities that invite students to immerse themselves in the learning process.

> - The significance of students' socio-cultural histories is important in establishing a welcoming and inclusive learning environment that is relevant to all participants.
> - Inviting students to collaborate and co-construct knowledge via dialogic learning activities facilitates openness to and engagement in 'emergent' academic processes – rather than passive enculturation.

Introduction

Every year, universities welcome a new cohort of students. The first stop on their 'voyage of University discovery' is usually a 'welcome day', which is part of the wider 'orientation process' or 'induction process' (Cock et al., 2008). The induction process is a 'ubiquitous intervention' by universities designed to help new students adjust to their degree programme (Cock et al., 2008, 37; Richardson & Tate, 2013). They are widely recognized as being a 'valuable instrument in the integration process' (Cock et al., 2008, 37; Richardson & Tate, 2013). However, this 'integration' is a one-way street. Welcome events often epitomize 'banking', that is, those who deliver these events 'issue communiqués and make deposits which the students patiently receive' (Freire, 1996, 53). This was the case in the post-1992 university where the authors delivered their collaborative induction session. The observations of the authors were confirmed by Curran (2016) who evaluated the induction process in the same university. He found a similar scenario in which students felt that the university said to them: 'This is us – get used to it!'

To 'de-colonize' our pedagogy and practice, such a scenario needed to be 'disrupted' and redesigned to accommodate our predominantly non-traditional students. If WP is to fulfil its promises, rather than changing the student, we must change. We must start by creating a sense of belonging from the moment students first enter the university (Cook & Leckey, 1999; Cock et al., 2008; Curran, 2016; Read et al., 2003). This chapter outlines the power of a different, dialogic induction where the various processes are welcoming and collaborative.

The Dialogic Welcome Day

The Welcome Day was a four-hour single event partitioned into three distinct sessions: identity, motivation and unveiling. This event was an expression of 'dialogic learning', where insight and understandings emerge through the process of dialogue in a learning environment (Mezirow, 1985; Savin-Baden, 2007), where staff work with students to draw upon their lived experiences to make concepts and ideas accessible, and where the students 'then use that experience to make sense for themselves and to explore further issues' (Savin-Baden, 2008, 54).

To create a dialogic environment, there are no specific 'how to steps' because creating dialogue is not a 'mere technique ... This would make dialogue a technique for manipulation rather than illumination' (Freire & Shor, 1987, 13). Instead, dialogic environments are created by putting the object to be known 'on the table between the two subjects of knowing. They meet around it and through it for mutual inquiry' (Freire & Shor, 1987, 14). This means, we, as the instructors, took part in the tasks with as much enthusiasm as the students in order to 'relearn the objects through studying them with the students' (Freire & Shor, 1987, 14).

Regulations around the Covid-19 pandemic required us to deliver the Welcome Day online. Though delivering this event face-to-face is the ideal scenario for dialogic engagement, the online space can be equally powerful. However, it is not without its difficulties; student engagement can be determined by the challenge of the 'digital divide' (Boyd, 2016; ONS, 2019), in our case, much time was spent introducing students to Blackboard Collaborate platform and resolving any technical issues that the students encountered. Yet, our alternative induction session proved to be empowering and illuminating.

In the following we outline the three Welcome Day sessions delivered and discuss the impact they had.

Identity

'Identity Texts' (Cummins & Early, 2011) are creative expressions that showcase the influence of cultural background on the individual in a new social setting,

> Identity Texts challenge hegemonic societal trends by bringing learners' cultural backgrounds to the foreground, and drawing attention to the multiple facets of life experiences which shape interactions in learning environments.
> (Cummins, 2009; Cummins & Early, 2011; Zaidi et al., 2016, 2)

This first session offered a creative exercise where students and instructors relayed 'their stories'. Aware that students were not familiar with the notion of Identity Texts, a brief explanation was given, supported with additional resources in the form of exemplars and suggestions presented in an e-handbook. The students were given time to create their pieces and upload them on Padlet – a digital sharing platform. Students elaborated on their Identity Texts in energetic group discussion. Initial caution in discussing their writing dissipated as we encouraged students with conversational prompts, facilitated by our reading the pieces as they were posted. This allowed for a specificity when addressing questions to students, which, in turn, affirmed the value of each contribution. There followed a rich retelling of personal histories, addressing themes such as 'What represents me?' 'How does my history shape me?' 'What defines me?' As students became comfortable with the idea of holding a dialogic space, further themes emerged centred on shared qualities, such as compassion, empathy, care and working with others. Thus, a 'grounding' of students' experiences had been established, preparing all participants to explore their motivations to learn.

Motivation

Motivation should not be regarded as a one-dimensional construct; instead, motivation is complex, multi-dimensional and transient (Kember et al., 2008; Nowell, 2017). It is viewed as a significant factor in the transition into university. In particular, the first six months of the first year is seen as the period to embed interventions that 'monitor' and 'enhance' motivations to learn (Edgar et al., 2019). It seemed appropriate to devise an exercise that introduced students to the concept of motivation and facilitate an exploration into their own motivations to learn. Thus we created an affirmative model of motivation, rather than further reinforcing a predominantly deficit model.

In our session, students were given time to consider what their key motivations were, initiated by a personal, internal dialogue. Students were encouraged to set the parameters for this exercise, acknowledging themselves as actors invested in the activity. The quality of responses from students evidenced a reflective stance, critically aware of how different motivators resonated with their identities and personal contexts, and how these could be located within wider, public spheres. These contributions showed a cognisance amongst all participants of the different positions and voices that can exist in one space, thus priming students for an exploration into the final session 'unveiling' the hidden curriculum.

Unveiling

Besides talking about course and study programmes in the induction, it is crucial to reveal and name the hidden curriculum. As Neve and Collett (2018, 2) state, 'the hidden curriculum may also be a useful tool for triggering debate about issues such as power, patient centredness, personal resilience and career stereotypes in medicine'. This not only creates awareness amongst the student body about its existence, it also allows staff to develop an understanding of its potential impact. To this point, Freire notes that the educator remakes their 'cognoscibility' through the 'cognoscibility' of the students. 'That is the ability of the educator to know the object is remade every time through the students' own ability for knowing, for developing critical comprehension in themselves' (Freire & Shor, 1987, 14).

Engagement with this topic was structured through interactive approaches where the starting point was, again, students' experiences. With respect to teaching and learning, a series of questions and quizzes were used to scaffold the discussion. Students' responses were mediated via chat streams and unmuting their mikes. This provided a 'sand pit' for students to explore ambiguities, weigh up assumptions and voice opinions, thereby developing an understanding of the hidden curriculum through co-construction. As facilitators, we were keen not to diminish any of the voices present and actively engaged with all the contributions made. A key outcome of this open, free-flowing discussion was the abandonment of the fear of getting it wrong and an acceptance of emergence. Students became confident enough to put forward their ideas knowing that they may be contested, something we hope they can utilize throughout their study.

Evaluation

Feedback was taken directly after the induction sessions with confidence emerging as a central theme. For students, confidence was expressed in terms of recognizing that their perspectives have a place in any discourse and the possibility that these might be open to challenge should not dissuade them from contributing to discussions. One student observed:

> It's easy to get very shy about what you're gonna say or what you're thinking, whether it's right or wrong. Just have confidence in what you want to say.

Confidence was also expressed in how students might engage in learning. At the beginning of the sessions, students were tentative. However, there was a noticeable change throughout the day as the combination of scaffolded tasks, preparation time given and a dialogic space to share contributions permitted students to actively collaborate in the co-construction of knowledge. Arguably, the sessions facilitated a learning process removed from traditionally passive approaches (Angelo, 1993) and students acknowledged this:

> I think the overall session was a complete icebreaker, introducing us to different ways of doing things and that we have the support when we are not sure and that's really important.

The capacity for self-reflection was also evident. Students felt they had been given the space to explore aspects of their lives and articulate how their socio-cultural backgrounds might shape their futures (Gutierrez, 2018):

> I feel more confident about my motivations and values ... I wasn't sure what drives me – what my characteristics, values and motivations were, but this whole exercise has helped me to understand myself better.

Overall, the students were able to use the induction to synthesize their experiences and prepare a grounded understanding of themselves as learners embarking upon the next phase of their learning.

Limitations

Despite the overwhelming positive feedback by students, two key limitations were identified. First, student participation was determined by the challenge of the 'digital divide'. No matter how well-designed the Welcome Day was, the lack of technology and internet access and the missing digital expertise frustrated its aim for some.

Secondly, our induction was a 'one off'. Students were afforded the opportunity to engage in a dialogic discourse; yet, how much of this will be replicated in other learning spaces they encounter is questionable. If students are left to acculturate to traditional transmissive forms of learning and teaching which take little account of their socio-cultural backgrounds (Lea & Street, 1998), then an isolated academic epiphany will not change the elitist and exclusionary status quo.

These limitations can only be tackled with a root and branch transformation of pedagogy and practice that extends beyond the induction of students. Arguably a way forward is a commitment to education for social justice curricula and practices that sustain the dialogic teaching and learning process into, through and across the curriculum. We argue for a collaborative approach where learning, and staff development practitioners work alongside discipline academics to reimagine their practices. Discipline staff need to be given time, space and support to devise strategies and activities suited to their contexts and to integrate into the curriculum space. Students require time to experiment, practise and tweak their ideas. This would demonstrate a commitment by institutions to integrate dialogic, collaborative pedagogical practice within learning environments.

Conclusion

Delivering induction sessions differently has demonstrated that opportunities for students to engage must be crafted in ways that allow them to do so. This 'invitation' must be supported with scaffolds that ensure all students can participate and actively immerse themselves into the learning process. Collaboration offers a vehicle for this to happen and, if mediated through dialogic spaces, ensures that students and staff can carve out a positive learning experience together.

Unite and Unrule! Reflections of a Co-created Pedagogy for Transformation

Cybele Atme, Pauline Bon, Mila de Graaf, Daniel Haudenschild, Mieke Lopes Cardozo, Melina Merdanovic and Eleonore Nouel

- As a collective, we experimented with co-creation as means to develop a more creative, innovative and collaborative space in order to inspire (in)direct transformations in the larger HE system we study and work in.
- Our approach to co-creation, as a specific form of collaboration, is inspired by insights from critical, contemplative, social justice and relational pedagogy based on design principles derived from regenerative development.
- In this case study, we highlight two interrelated features of our co-creation approach to developing transgressive learning spaces: (1) relational learning beyond individualism and (2) from competition towards reflective and self-directed learning.

Introduction: Planting the Seeds of Collective Self-organizing

The occupation of the University of Amsterdam's (UvA) main administrative building, Maagdenhuis, and the banner reading 'No Democratisation without Decolonisation' in spring 2015 signalled two key demands of the protesting students and staff. They demanded equal access, democratic participation and more transparency from the university management, while a second demand was aimed at decolonizing knowledge (The University of Colour, 2018). The movement mandated the new Diversity Commission chaired by Prof. Dr. Gloria Wekker to investigate the state of the University, which resulted in the publication of concrete recommendations for democratic and decolonial practices (Wekker et al., 2016).

Inspired by this spirit, a handful of Master students and a lecturer at the UvA's International Development Studies (IDS) programme started self-organizing the Critical Development and Diversity Explorations (CDDE) initiative to collaboratively explore alternative pedagogies for social justice-inspired and transgressive learning. The CDDE initiative was initiated in 2017 as an attempt to 'unrule' student-teacher asymmetries, address epistemological hierarchies and overcome institutional barriers to develop a more collaborative and holistic learning space. We are a growing collective which started with ten and has grown into a group of thirty-two (former) Master students and an initiator and lecturer(s) who are organizing the seminar-style CDDE 'course', which is open to Master students in the IDS programme. CDDE student members are recognized for their CDDE membership and can include a number of study credits within their Portfolio, a 'free' space within the IDS curriculum. The initiator and lecturer was awarded a teaching innovation grant which freed up time to develop this initiative during the initial three years. Over the past five years of the CDDE journey, we experienced and un-learned together, while also influencing tangible changes in teaching and learning practices within the IDS teaching programme, and increasingly in other academic and professional contexts where CDDE alumni continue to design CDDE-inspired work.

Our broader objective is to contribute towards imagining and enacting a transgressive (hooks, 1994; Wals, 2015) and collaborative alternative to the neoliberal HE model. On the one hand, we seek as a collective to counter a managerialist, competitive, market-oriented and Westernized HE culture (Springer, 2016). On the other hand, through CDDE we aim to co-create a creative, revitalizing and critical space to cultivate a pluriversality of knowledges along with a cross-hierarchical learning community based on an ethics of care (Mountz et al., 2015) and slow scholarship (Berg & Seeber, 2013). Inspired by Regenerative Development and Design (Mang & Haggard, 2016), and infused with contemplative pedagogies and practices (Berila, 2016), CDDE co-creates an innovative space to develop personal self-reflection and development as individual and collective 'change agents', in order to inspire (in)direct transformations in the larger HE system we study and work in. Extending the notion of relational pedagogy into community building has its foundations in the work of Nell Noddings (Bingham & Sidorkin, 2004; Biesta et al., 2004), Humberto Maturana and Paulo Freire (Souza et al., 2019). In this chapter, we reflect on our collaborative and co-creative practices and experiences of the CDDE initiative to create a transgressive and more inclusive learning space within the university.

Enacting Transgressive Education through Co-creation

We translated our aim into practice through our agency-oriented, cross-hierarchical and co-created 'course' design. Co-creation, as a specific form of collaboration, is considered a key approach to relational pedagogy (Bovill, 2020; Souza et al., 2019) and serves as a way to integrate (individual and collective) contemplative practices into collective spaces of anti-oppressive learning (Berila, 2016). We highlight two interrelated features of our co-creation approach to developing transgressive learning spaces: (1) relational learning beyond individualism and (2) from competition towards reflective and self-directed learning.

Relational Learning beyond Individualism

Through co-creation, community building and engagement with an ethics of care, we learned how to think of education as a collective, relational process (Bingham & Sidorkin, 2004; Mountz et al., 2015), rather than a pre-fixed route to a predefined destination. With teams of students and the lecturer, we collaboratively co-create each of our bi-weekly sessions. The themes for each session are brainstormed together at the beginning of the semester. Then, small teams prepare the content and activities for a particular session, which are further refined and co-facilitated. We found that the key in the co-creation processes is taking time to collectively and inclusively make decisions: a '[d]ecision-making process is a consensus-based dialogue, rather than democratic voting. The extra effort this takes is worth it in terms of making people feel included'. As expressed by one CDDE member:

> I learned how challenging it is to take everyone's opinion/wishes into planning while also being pragmatic of possibilities and time constraints. I do believe we managed that well and that everyone's preferences were included.

In this learning community, we hold each other and ourselves accountable and have a sense of responsibility towards each other. As a lecturer, this process creates a very different dynamic:

> I prepare for and leave these sessions with students more energised and enriched with resources and insights I would not have experienced in more traditionally organised classes, and I too benefit from the sense of community which is established, there is a shared sense of care which is not always present in academia.

From Competition to Inclusive and Self-directed Learning

Co-created sessions often include contemplative practices in combination with social justice pedagogies, which enables a reflection on our education process. Through self-directed learning and both introspective and collaborative reflection exercises, we aim to enhance our agency with regard to our individual learning trajectories, as well as a shared purpose for the CDDE community to support broader systemic transformation within and possibly beyond the department. Through meditation, journaling and sharing our experiences, we learnt to channel empathy towards each other but also towards ourselves. Instead of focusing on competition in our HE space (Naidoo, 2018; 2016), we have been motivated by our sense of community. Inspired by the integration of regenerative design and living systems thinking frameworks (Mang & Haggard, 2016), our reflective frameworks focused on enhancing 'internal locus of control' and 'external consideration' as practices of introspective personal development. This dimension was addressed by a CDDE member:

> For me, CDDE is a way to connect the academic to the personal. It is a space where I am learning to enjoy education again. I have always been very passionate about education, but I often experience stress and anxiety. Our focus on contemplation, embodiment, and sharing spaces have helped me to reconnect to my surroundings and be more present and mindful.

Through practices of embodied knowledge, we focus on 'walking the talk' of what a feminist decolonizing learning process might look like, by recognizing and employing a pluriverse of knowledges in and beyond the classroom (Kothari, 2006; Kothari et al., 2019; Sultana, 2019). One of our sessions in 2019 was themed on storytelling as a form of knowledge. During this session, each of us shared an experience of marginalization at university (that they experienced or heard). At the end of the exercise, we reflected together on the common elements in the stories and the axis of oppression. By exploring the politics of ontology and epistemology, we identified how power operates at the university and specifically in a complex and interdisciplinary field like IDS (Harcourt, 2017). For us, the alternative practices of (forum) theatre, music, poetry, yoga, storytelling and so forth are a way to engage with the pluriverse of knowledges. These contemplative and creative methods have enriched a sense of inclusivity in the way we co-create our learning journey. For instance, by consciously designing the atmosphere for collaborative and empathetic work in CDDE sessions, co-creation teams would often include a piece of poetry, a song or visual art in the opening part of the session for the members to wake up to a more creative, mindful interaction and reflection.

For example, in a session we co-created between a group of the student members and the lecturer on intersectional feminism and climate justice, when the group entered the room we had a painting by Bolivian artist Mamani Mamani on the screen called 'La Pacha Mama' (Mother Earth), and played some Andean music as we all settled in. We then started seated in a circle with a grounding and visualization exercise, using breath techniques and visualizing what 'mother earth' means for us, followed by some structured journal writing on the theme of the session. After this wake-up, we had a conversation about intersectionality as represented in feminist literature, after which we listened collectively to a historically recorded speech by the American nineteenth-century women's rights activist Sojourner Truth and watched a short video by Kimberley Crenshaw on intersectionality. We then connected these feminist reflections to the theme of climate justice and present-day debates. We went outside for a walk around the university campus in small groups to work on a 'counter-mapping' exercise, which allowed groups to reflect on and draw out a counter-hegemonic picture of real-life examples in the way the university environment (mis)represents issues of intersectional and climate justice (including the build environment, food offerings and more discursive expressions such as posters or observed interactions). We then closed the session by engaging with each other's counter-maps, and ended with a brief guided breathing exercise and journaling moment. Post-session, we captured notes of what we worked on, and asked all participants to reflect briefly in an online post-session survey to capture key insights, to inform our continued work and analysis, resulting in ongoing projects such as this one.

Drawing Some Conclusions: To Unite and Unrule?

After five years of collaboratively organizing the CDDE space in various forms, we carefully navigated between personal autonomy, the neoliberal academy and our project goals, as well as shifting constellations in our collective – not least shifting from in-person to online engagements due to the Covid-19 pandemic. One of our key motivations lies in our shared desire to create a sense of community, ownership and transformative space, while this brings up the challenge of becoming integrated into the mainstream institutional university culture in less-valued ways or being showcased as another 'diversity' success (Ahmed, 2012). Nevertheless, we inspired tangible changes in the IDS programmes at the UvA, including integrating aspects of the co-creation pedagogical approaches into several Bachelor and Master courses, and more attention paid to research ethics, reflectiveness on positionality and the importance of (introspective) reflection and inquiry to develop students' capability to (re)connect to their unique learning trajectory and purpose.

Another tension we successfully navigated concerned the sustaining of the community space over multiple years and generations of students. Each year, CDDE has reinvented itself based on that year's unique make-up of members while building on experiences and insights gained from the past. Together, we are committed to disseminating insights and approaches we gained. This means uniting energies as students and lecturers alike to co-create inclusive, transformative and transgressive learning spaces in HE, to individually and collectively un-rule existing education structures and connected patterns of thinking, being and acting from competition to collaboration.

CDDE has inspired us to explore the re-appropriation of the classroom space as one of movement and connection, rather than fixed 'banking education' (Giroux, 2010). By (re)claiming space and challenging hierarchies in the classroom, we explore what it means to transgress traditional institutional boundaries. In CDDE, we co-created the content and pedagogical design of the sessions, shared food and built friendships beyond the classroom.

Acknowledgements

We would like to thank all the people who were involved in the CDDE initiative over the years to build a community of care for transformative, social justice inspired learning, as without them this work would not have been possible. We are thankful for the financial support by a Comenius grant (grant number 405.17865.009) for innovative teaching practices that Mieke Lopes Cardozo received, and institutional encouragement of supportive colleagues in IDS. In addition to the respective authors' input, we wish to thank Annet Kragt (also CDDE member) for her editorial support.

Honest Conversations about 'Race' and Racism: Innovative Decolonizing Practice

Anthony Kalume and Jess Moriarty

- Creating a culture in which it is possible to have open and honest conversations about race and racism is understood as crucial to dismantling institutionalized racism in HE.
- This anti-racist project was a cultural collaboration between HE and community partners where the goal was to develop a new anti-racist module. All parties were equally valued in the process and via the co-authored research outputs.
- The collaborative project aimed to challenge and change negative experiences and dominant discourses around BAME (staff and) students in HE.

Please note that this chapter uses Black Asian Minority Ethnic (BAME) as this is the term used in much education research on this topic, but we respect that it is not a term that many people would use to describe themselves and apologize that we are unable to be more specific in terms of 'race' and ethnicity within this piece.

Introduction – The Clothes on Our Backs

The 'Clothes on Our Backs' was a collaborative project between Diversity Lewes (DL, 2015), a charity set up to challenge racism in the South East of the UK. DL, the University of Brighton (UoB) and Brighton Museum aimed to respond to findings from a National Union of Students' (NUS) report that identified continuing, unresolved issues around Black Asian Minority Ethnic (BAME) student participation within HE. Forty-two per cent of BAME students who took the survey stated that they did not believe their curriculum reflected issues of diversity, equality and discrimination, and a third (34 per cent) stated that institutions often 'did not take into account diverse backgrounds and views' (NUS and Universities UK Report, 2020, 4).

In the UK, universities are deeply gendered and racialized (Emejulu, 2017), and a later report from the NUS (NUS, 2019) identified four key areas for HE to urgently address:

1. a need for strong BAME leadership;
2. creating a culture in which it is possible to have open and honest conversations about race and racism;
3. developing racially diverse and inclusive environments and communities; and
4. getting the evidence and understanding what it means and understanding what works.

Further highlighted were problems regarding the number of modules being devised by white tutors for BAME students who already doubted institutional commitment to diversity and inclusion (NUS, 2019).

Our cross-racial collaboration aimed to offer a method of co-creation that acknowledges, and also seeks to resist and change, dominant inequalities that exist in HE (Bell & Phall, 2018; Facer & Enright, 2016). We hope that the insights into our experiences will provide thought and inspiration for other colleagues working on pedagogy that aspires to:

- challenge and change negative experiences and dominant discourses in HE;
- value community partners as equal in the process;
- explore methodologies that permit personal and evocative storytelling in academic work in multi-disciplinary initiatives; and
- are sustainable once the project (and or funding) ends.

Method

In the following, we outline Anthony's story, Director of DL, to provide insight into the collaborative workings of our project as an autoethnographic approach. We move on to tell the story of Anthony and Jess' collaboration, a collaborative autoethnography (CAE).

We adopted an autoethnographic approach as it is personal and connected to the social group under study (Moriarty, 2019) and our project of democratizing academic discourse to make it more inclusive (Canagarajah, 2002). People are often drawn to autoethnography because it enables 'a better conversation in the face of all the barriers and boundaries' (Ellis & Bochner, 2000, 748).

CAE has implications for issues of power and control within the field of academic research (Bell & Phall, 2017; Chang et al., 2016). Our approach advocates a way of conducting and disseminating research that we have developed and written together. This way of working allowed for our collective exploration of our subjectivity and facilitated power-sharing between us as co-researchers and co-authors.

As co-authors we argue that this approach has deepened our collaboration, enabling us to have discussions around institutionalized racism and personal storytelling that have informed dissemination about this project at conferences and via co-authored texts (Kalume & Moriarty, 2022, forthcoming).

Anthony Kalume: My Story

Anthony is not only the Chair of DL but also a Visiting Lecturer at the UoB. In this double role, and with his familiarity of Black students' 'struggles' in HE, he came together with Jess Moriarty to form a collaborative between LD, Brighton University and Museum. The aim was to harness their resources to raise awareness of racism by hosting community events in neutral spaces.

One of the activities revolved around Khangas (see Figure 7.1), as Anthony explains: As part of my work with DL, I was invited by The Royal Pavilion Trust (RPT) Museum to share my knowledge and expertise on Khangas, polka-dotted handkerchiefs (Lêsos) supplied by the Portuguese merchants who came to Africa in search of slaves and trade (Rawley & Behrendt, 2005). The Gardens and Galleries of Brighton Museums had within their collection a variety of Khangas which came to my attention when officiating during the Fashion Cities Africa (The Royal Pavilion, 2016). The project looked at four cities on the African continent Lagos, Nairobi, Casablanca and Johannesburg, where local contemporary designers were commissioned to deliver fashion items that would respond to trends amongst African people and the diaspora (Pool, 2016). The Brighton Museum asked DL to join the collecting panel who designed, collated and delivered the exhibition (Kalume, 2019a) and this meant that a working relationship of mutual trust and respect had already been established when the collaboration for the 'Clothes on our Backs' began.

By the beginning of January 2019, I had carried out some initial research in Kenya on the various aspects of using the Khanga (Hanby, 1984). At this point, I approached my friend and colleague Ednah Chepkirui from the American University Kenya, and

Figure 7.1 Khanga. Anthony Kalume shares the history of the Khanga at Brighton Museum (image credits: Willie Robb).

Figure 7.2 Khanga exhibit. Anthony Kalume giving a talk on the Khanga exhibit at Brighton Museum (image credits: Willie Robb).

Dr Jess Moriarty from the UoB on the feasibility of developing a project exploring identity through my own research on Khangas. DL had worked together with Jess on a Creative Writing module and also completed a Heritage Lottery Funded project called *Celebrating African Caribbean's in Sussex Past and Present* in 2015 (Kalume, 2019b) developing mutual trust that has enabled us to work together as equal partners.

There is something essentially collaborative and cooperative about the Khanga: the way that the Khanga is used as a means of communicating a personal story and connecting people together speaks to Jess' work on autoethnography and a focus on storytelling as a way of connecting people that is also an emphasis in my own practice of collaborating on transdisciplinary projects to raise understanding and awareness around Black people in Sussex. I have known Jess for many years and appreciate her ability to give feedback, her humour and her commitment to diversity and social justice, which is perhaps why we work so well together and value each other as friends. The project's intention meant that a workshop based around the Khanga seemed an ideal way of developing connections and telling and sharing stories that could help us develop pedagogy.

Anthony Kalume and Jess Moriarty: Our Story

Our collaborative partnership: CUPP issued a call for projects that developed research and knowledge exchange between the university and community partner(s). The Ignite funding scheme kindly accepted our proposal that aimed to:

- establish a collaboration between DL, the UoB and Brighton Museum that is built on mutual respect and trust;
- engage members of the BAME community in Sussex and students and staff at the university to work on archival material housed at Brighton Museum;
- devise a series of creative workshops that used the Khanga as a source of inspiration for poems, textiles and prose;
- collect feedback from workshop participants to inform the development of a new module in the School of Humanities and Social Science at the UoB that looks at archival material and creative practice and draws on the expertise of BAME artists and tutors; and
- disseminate findings via workshops and co-authored texts that value each partner as equal.

The workshops would focus on identity and clothing, in particular how the Khangas contain symbols and messages that relate to autobiographical experiences including empowering sayings and statements. The workshops were to help participants devise texts about their identity that they could then inscribe (using textiles and print) into garments that had significant meaning to them. The outputs generated (see Figure 7.2) by the workshops would then be used in an exhibition in Black History Month at the Brighton Dome and at the UoB that would seek to engage more people from inside and outside the university with the project.

We agreed to use the workshops to identify staff, students and community partners who would collaborate on devising a new module, focused on creative practice and archives, that built on concepts of diversity and inclusion. The module would develop teaching and learning that might inspire existing students and also engage members of the wider BAME community with the University.

Outcomes and Issues

Brighton Museum was incredibly supportive, allowing us to expand our collaboration with external stakeholders, beyond the university and DL members. We were allowed unique access to their Khanga archive (see Figure 7.3) which provided a real focal point for the workshops we ran and engaged the wider Sussex community with the exhibit. As a result of the events, we were able to build an extensive mailing list and host several networking events at the university where BAME scholars discussed decolonizing and developing the curriculum.

We wanted to develop a collaboration that would facilitate better conversations around diversity in HE and use the Khangas at Brighton Museum to connect Black people with the UoB – as students and members of staff. The project also explored how conversation and storytelling can produce liberatory research for cultural and social change. Our research and the workshops indicated that a module housed at Brighton Museum and run by local BAME experts was feasible and desirable but recruiting experts needs resourcing and sustainable support from the institution.

The main challenge facing the project was that we were only funded to run the initial workshops, and without additional funding to pay people for their time and travel, we were unable to set an agenda to take forward the module development.

Arguably a further challenge was that without this resourcing, the idea of Jess (who is white) writing a module for a BAME tutor to teach would go against our research and our beliefs. Part of the Race Equality Charter insists that BAME tutors lead such teaching. We had no desire to perpetuate the racism evident in HE and undermine the BAME expertise we had engaged with the project.

Conclusion

Our research identified racism as an institutionalized issue within HE that needs challenging and resisting. The initial motivations for the project were to collaborate within and outwith the University to take forward an anti-racist cultural project that would transform into an innovative anti-racist module to be delivered in the Brighton Museum.

The DL 'Clothes on our Backs' project was the seedbed of research for that potential module and harnessed the talents of a multi-disciplinary BAME network of scholars from Law, Educations, Arts, Social Sciences and Humanities. This collaboration did create anti-racist opportunities to develop new modules, new research, and a new and evolving community of BAME academics and scholars.

However, a key issue with this project was sustainability, and once the project ended, there was no scaffold in place to develop a new module led by Black experts. Jess, a

Figure 7.3 Khanga workshop. Workshop at Brighton Museum using the Khanga exhibit as a source of inspiration for creative work (image credits: Willie Robb).

white academic, was embarrassed at the thought of continuing as solitary project lead. The collaboration meant that we were able to talk about and problematize this issue but we did not and could not resolve it. Essentially, we need more Black leaders in HE to do this work so that people like Jess can continue to be an ally but not a leader on a project challenging racism in HE. Our fear is that until change is supported, racism and white privilege will continue to limit and reduce HE, undermining not just our education system but also our humanity.

Acknowledgements

With thanks to the Ignite Fund at the UoB for funding this project and to staff at Brighton Museum for taking part in the collaboration and supporting this work so generously. With further thanks to Willie Robb for allowing us to use his images of the project for which he received consent from all those photographed.

Love, Respect, Esteem: Collaborative Student Partnerships for Social Justice

Vikki Hill and Louise Taylor

- We present two collaborative student partnership projects that address educational inequalities in relation to transition, attainment and belonging.
- Honneth's Theory of Recognition is applied as a framework to examine the relational complexities in our partnership projects.
- Socially just partnerships can be designed to recognize love, respect and esteem.
- We propose collaborative approaches that challenge power hierarchies and build relationships for change.

Introduction

In our chapter, we present two collaborative student partnership projects that aim to address educational inequalities in relation to transition, attainment and belonging at London College of Communication (LCC), University of the Arts London (UAL). As authors of the paper and project leads, we recognize the activism of colleagues across the institution in shaping the development of anti-racist and socially just pedagogies and partnerships. We present *Peer Mentoring* and *Creative Mindsets* (UAL, 2021a) as two collaborative case studies that are closely aligned in practice and ambition to foster a sense of belonging in first-year students as they transition to university. We then conceptualize our understanding of student partnership and draw upon Honneth's

Theory of Recognition to consider love, respect and esteem as a social justice framework to reconcile the complexities within our context (Power, 2011). Finally, we offer reflections as implications for future development of both Peer Mentoring and Creative Mindsets and for partnership work in the HE sector.

The Context

Based in South London, LCC is one of six colleges that make up UAL. It is renowned for creative communication education and industry-focused courses in Design, Media and Screen. Student partnerships are embedded as key approaches to teaching and learning across the college, and the university's Anti-racism action plan (UAL, 2021b) has strengthened this position. It states that UAL will develop partnerships with students and the Student Union (Arts SU) to address ethnicity awarding differentials that exist and persist across the HE sector, between home white students and home students of colour. The plan pledges significant change to systems, processes and culture and a commitment to dismantle systemic racism across all levels of the institution.

The Projects

Peer Mentoring was established in 2014 to support students as they 'settle in' to university life and encourages the exchange of knowledge and experiences between students at different levels. It adopts a model where mentees in year-one are matched with mentors in the second or final year of their course. The project is informed by developmental approaches to mentoring that emphasize the mutuality of learning and the personal and professional development of both parties (Clutterbuck, 2008). The aim is to develop a sense of community where mentors and mentees benefit from making connections with a wider support network across different levels of study. Mentors receive payment for their work and are employed through the university's creative recruitment agency. Training focuses on defining the mentor/mentee relationship and the development of communication skills. Unlike traditional mentoring in which mentees are positioned as 'novice' (Colley, 2001), developmental mentoring encourages students to engage in an ongoing partnership in which both parties benefit. This form of collaboration challenges unequal power relations by flattening hierarchies between participants.

Creative Mindsets was developed in 2017 as part of the Office for Students, 'Addressing Barriers to Student Success Programme' *Changing Mindsets*, that was designed to eliminate persistent and disproportional inequalities experienced by Black, Asian and Minority Ethnic students in HE (Mahmud & Gagnon, 2020; Singh, 2009). *Creative Mindsets* combines social and psychological approaches to develop growth mindsets (Dweck, 2006) in students and staff to reduce racial bias (Devine, 2012; Good et al., 2008) through a programme of co-facilitated workshops led by a team of students, alumni and the project lead (Hill & Simpson, 2020). The workshops are dialogic and offer space for staff and students to consider unexamined biases and devise strategies to change practices and behaviours. The student team were appointed on hourly paid contracts and attended workshops on mindset theory, anti-racism, intercultural communication and teaching in arts HE to build trust and to collectively devise approaches to deliver forty-five workshops to 2,400 students. In 2020, the project moved to an asynchronous delivery hosted on the UAL Academic Support Online platform with scheduled synchronous sessions co-facilitated by students and staff.

Recognizing Partnerships

In the process of reflecting on our student partnership projects we interrogate inherent tensions and complexities in reimagining our collaborative and relational practices. Bovill (2013) states that the key condition for partnerships is that, along with choice and meaningful learning, the 'student-tutor relationship is facilitatory, collaborative and based on dialogue; and that the learner is viewed as a knowledgeable and critical partner in learning' (p. 99). Relational student-staff identities are constructed when values of mutual respect, reciprocity and shared responsibility are centred (Cook-Sather et al., 2014). A focus on the relational can be transgressive as it challenges normative market-driven approaches that characterize the field of HE as 'impersonal', individualistic and 'objective'. Our partnership projects tried to expand traditional pedagogical approaches, as students engage from positions of power, resistance and agency (Dei, 2016) to co-produce knowledge (Freire, 1970).

Of particular importance to our work is the goal of social justice – a contested and complex term which resists a single definition (Fraser & Honneth, 2003). As Fraser (cited in Lovell, 2007) points out, disputes about justice frequently extend beyond traditional framing, leaving not only the substance of justice in dispute, but also the frame itself. In our reflection we draw upon Honneth's relational, interdisciplinary approach to critical theory to locate recognition as fundamental to social justice. Honneth (2014) argues that justice is a form of mutuality embodied in both the interactions and identity formation of both self and others. McArthur (2018) states that 'mutual recognition is always about both self-realisation and social inclusion' (p. 55) and these intersubjective practices are of particular importance within student-staff and student-to-student partnerships.

Below we consider Honneth's (2014) three aspects of recognition – love, respect and esteem – that combine to form his notion of social justice and use this as a framework in which to examine some of the complexities in our partnership projects.

Love

Honneth (1997) conceptualizes love recognition as unconditional concern where an individual's needs and desires are of value to another. Drawing upon the tradition of moral philosophy, love recognition is about care of the other. In *Peer Mentoring*, this is expressed through building effective communication and cooperation in the relationship between mentor and mentee – the ability to recognize divergent experiences and identify with each other through curiosity and dialogue (Sennett, 2012). Mentees have highlighted a high level of support available from mentors who they describe as 'a much-needed support system' and 'very kind and reassuring', as well as an increased confidence (Taylor, 2021): 'It has helped me communicate better with people I don't know.' In our podcast on *Creative Mindsets*, that captured student voices and experiences, students spoke of how their self-confidence grew when they learnt about the commonality of their experiences (Simpson et al., 2020) in the workshops they were trained to facilitate: 'realising this [racial bias] is a thing that other people go through and I finally know how to word it'. Each of these projects demonstrates the transformative potential of working collaboratively for both the individual and the wider learning community, where difference and mutuality are recognized and valued.

Respect

For Honneth (1997), respect recognition is about legal rights as moral accountability. The importance of understanding the law and affording others the same rights is the essence of Honneth's approach to universal equality and social justice. In the facilitator training for *Creative Mindsets*, we frame discussions around the Equality Act 2010 (an Act of Parliament of the UK with the primary purpose of consolidating, updating and supplementing the numerous prior Acts and Regulations) to further understand intersectionality of protected characteristics, to develop racial literacy and to identify systemic barriers within HE. The students we engage as partners in both our projects are employed and paid through UAL Arts Temps that aims to be a social enterprise recruitment agency built upon ethical and inclusive practices. Although Colley (2002) warns of the capitalist exchange-value of human relationships, the recognition of the role provided by the formal processes of employment and training, and the guarantee of a real living wage, is key to successful collaboration in these projects. These formal processes contribute towards a 'respect for autonomy (that) also includes rights that make possible the exercise of autonomy' (van Leeuwen, 2007, 183).

Esteem

Honneth proposes esteem as 'heavily dependent on collectively shared values and goals' (van Leeuwen, 2007, 183). This form of recognition has a duality in that it refers to both the social and individual and grows from what Honneth (1996) also defines as 'solidarity' with others. McArthur (2018) writes, 'Self-esteem is fostered when our abilities and actions are regarded as socially useful and are recognized as such' (p. 57). The developmental approach to peer mentoring emphasizes the relational experience as social good and traditional power relations (in which the mentor is positioned as expert) are challenged. In the *Creative Mindsets* project, students and alumni spoke of how they learnt from each other when co-facilitating both student and staff-facing workshops on bias. One student partner commented:

> I was aware of observing teaching methods, knowing they would develop my own pedagogical practices for future projects. The workshops encouraged active learning as a facilitator.
>
> (Team Member in Hill et al., forthcoming, 2022)

This relational, problem-posing pedagogy positions the construction of knowledge through 'invention and re-invention, through the restless, impatient, continuing, hopeful inquiry human beings pursue in the world, with the world, and with each other' (Freire, 1970, 45).

Implications for Practice

In our case studies we have drawn upon Honneth's Theory of Recognition to consider how the relational practices of love, respect and esteem can offer tools to analyse and reflect upon partnership projects designed to achieve social justice aims. Honneth (2014) reminds us that social structures are required to achieve recognition between individuals, and that we must examine existing conditions that obstruct and can instead provoke misrecognition, particularly within competitive and individualistic cultures of HE. For both *Peer Mentoring* and *Creative Mindset*s, we have identified recommendations to contest existing norms and assumptions about partnership projects (Healy et al., 2014; Mercer-Mapstone, 2018) and to foster social justice across the curriculum. The first is to acknowledge the emotional labour associated with creating relational practices that are premised by love and care, and to design institutional policies and practice to support this. The second is to ensure formal employment processes sustain and nourish respect and that precarious working conditions for student and staff partners are addressed. Finally, institutions should construct equitable teaching and learning environments so that non-hierarchical collaborative partnership projects are embedded into the core curriculum delivery. As project leads, we consider in what ways collaborative partnership projects can challenge patterns of misrecognition and support strategic social justice aims as we continue to question – who is valued within our institutions as worthy of love, respect and esteem?

Inclusive Learning and Teaching in Higher Education: Students as Co-creators in Course Re-design

Uzma A. Siddiqui

- This case study provides a real-world example of how collaboration between teachers and students can enhance inclusivity and involvement amongst a diverse cohort of learners, thereby promoting social justice through education.
- Seeking to address the lack of student participation and engagement with course content, a pilot session within a Health and Social Care course was redesigned adopting a collaborative approach where students led the session and teachers acted as co-learners/facilitators.
- Students were engaged with the deep transformative process of reflection, critical thinking and problem-solving, thus creating conditions for dialogue

> amongst students that would encourage their epistemological curiosity and promote free and critical learning.
> - The pilot session was evaluated using observations and feedback questionnaires from students and teachers. The evaluation indicated increased teacher-student communication, higher level of engagement with the subject material and inclusive student-student interaction through improved participation amongst a diverse student cohort.
> - Student-teacher collaboration as curriculum partners is strongly recommended as a way of realizing students' added value in designing their own learning and increasing student engagement.

Introduction

Collaboration has a key place in the Health and Social Care provision in HE. While Kuh (2005) suggests what students learn at university matters more to their success and development than where they study, shaping future practice in the social professions through partnership is core. Diverse social care graduates bring valuable cultural wealth to the health care of a diverse population (The Office for National Statistics, 2017). To promote this, universities can offer programmes that do not just develop subject knowledge, but that tend to the holistic development of their students. Particularly, encouraging students in collaborative practice as part of increasing cultural awareness and acceptance is key. Such collaborative practice can extend to the student networks that will sustain students postgraduation and into which widening participation students are not automatically plugged. Keeping partnership for social justice in mind, this case study explores the co-creation of a pilot session, to inform future curriculum re-design, with students at a post-92 inner-city university in the UK.

Context

Our university is committed to inclusive education and fair outcomes for all students (see Education for Social Justice Framework, ESJF, 2021) as juxtaposed with the traditionally competitive approach in HE. Hockings et al. (2010, 1) provides a core definition of inclusive curriculum:

> Inclusive learning and teaching [L&T] in HE refers to the ways in which pedagogy, curricula and assessment are designed and delivered to engage students in learning that is meaningful, relevant, and accessible to all. It embraces a view of the individual and individual difference as the source of diversity that can enrich the lives and learning of others.

This was acknowledged when developing a pilot session for a student cohort composed of highly diverse, mature students largely from lower socio-economic backgrounds and ethnic minorities, and some with certain disabilities. A session for the Urban Health module from final year Health and Social Care (H&SC) course was redesigned using a dialogic and collaborative L&T approach rather than didactic techniques, creating conditions for dialogue amongst students encouraging their epistemological curiosity and promoting free and critical learning, as suggested by Freire (1970). This approach involved students leading the session and teachers acting as co-learners. The pilot session was evaluated through observations and feedback questionnaires from students and teachers.

Collaboration for Inclusive Curriculum and Pedagogy

It is essential to restlessly reinvent both HE and the 'skills' necessary to succeed in HE in these super-complex times. An example would be how all participants – tutors and students – successfully participated in online L&T amidst the Covid-19 pandemic. By creatively utilizing technology (digital skills), emotional intelligence, resilience and adaptability (life-skills), it was possible to fight against all the odds and persevere (Luthera & Mackenzie, 2021).

This reinvention required addressing the needs of the marginalized and excluded. Marginalization and exclusion from traditional HE cultures, curricula and communities lead to underachievement (Ainscow, 1999). Hockings (2010) emphasizes that HE learning environments should change, i.e. by taking account of and appreciating students' differing attributes, developing all students within mainstream curriculum, pedagogy and assessment – promoting inter-dependent learning and development rather than sending students off to be 'fixed' or to additional support services. Moreover, as Abegglen, Burns and Sinfield (2016) recommend a collaborative approach to pedagogy and practice helps students take control of their learning, through being involved in dialogic group discussions, followed by reflection and de-briefing. Thus, a collaborative approach is required where learning occurs through co-construction/co-creation of knowledge (Trowler, 2010) – even online, in times of crisis.

The Pilot Project

The pilot session for the Urban Health module was collaboratively redesigned, involving students as co-creators, adopting more innovative and creative methods (McIntosh & Warren, 2013) which would not only inspire student learning but would also challenge, stimulate and excite enough to improve overall student engagement.

Students split into self-selected groups of five, devising together the 'pilot session' with mutual consensus. A three-hour whole-class session was developed – with ice breaker and in workshop format. Its aim was to build confidence and trust amongst students as they were transitioning from monologic teaching to student-led learning. This required participation from everyone.

Each part of the workshop was led by a different group. There was a student-led (Group 1) subject-specific discussion on personal/work-related scenarios, with reflection time and a break. In the second part of the session an article recommended as per module handbook was selected (by Group 2), discussed and analysed using a creative activity called 'Text Mapping' (Abegglen et al., 2019). In the last part of the session, Group 3 opted to show a short video relevant to the session topic and then conducted a discussion, followed by a recap of the session by the teacher and time for students to debrief within their groups to reflect on their learning and future improvements. All group activities were delivered to the whole class where the teacher's role was to advise/guide, scaffold and facilitate.

Throughout this three-hour workshop session, the student-led approach focused on creative strategies designed to better prepare students for their complex/specialized roles after graduating. Students were engaged with the deep transformative process of reflection, critical thinking and problem-solving, as suggested by Hockings (2010). Following an experiential/learner-centred approach, the teacher's role was identified as one of a co-learner and a facilitator, where knowledge emerged as being interpersonal derived from interaction among students, the (selected) text and teacher. To facilitate student learning and fostering deeper rather than surface approaches, it was deemed necessary that knowledge was culturally, socially and politically conditioned where the students were supported to make the learning their own (Toohey, 1999).

Evaluation

The session was evaluated based on Kirkpatrick's (1994) model. A qualitative approach was followed for collating information in the form of both informal and formal appraisal.

Student Observations/Reactions

Prior to the pilot session, student attendance had declined. Approximately 20 per cent of students would arrive late/leave early. Together with an increase in the use of mobile phones, this led to unfruitful sessions indicating a lack of interest and declining student engagement. After implementation of the student-led pilot, student feedback indicated not only a difference in attitudes but also broader learning gain:

- Seventy-six per cent of attendees noted the quality of the teaching session was enhanced and, where previously no-one had the courage to engage in academic dialogue, let alone openly with the tutor, 84 per cent indicated their teacher-student communication was enhanced, thus indicating that collaboration amongst diverse cohorts improves engagement per se.
- Eighty-eight per cent felt scope of creative engagement was enhanced because of collaborating within a diverse cohort.
- Everyone indicated a higher level of engagement with the subject material; they were more attentive and gave satisfactory feedback.
- Sixteen per cent noted their initial apprehension with moving from a teacher-centred approach to student-centred one – with mandatory participation; however, icebreakers helped them ease into the new session format.

Tutors' Responses

Teachers involved in the delivery of the module were also invited to provide feedback on the pilot session to support the collaborative approach to curriculum redevelopment. Their comments highlighted that

> the effectiveness of working closely and in collaboration with students to raise perception of a better service will help improve the University's National Student Survey score.
>
> It's always beneficial to rethink and evaluate one's own teaching and learning approach to develop inclusive teaching practices.

The findings above were further interrogated through a short questionnaire, utilizing a 'Stop, Start, Continue' framework adopted from Hoon et al. (2015). Teachers' reflections on specific practices included:

- Making the pre-session reading mandatory for all attendees (*Continue*).
- To promote inclusivity and encourage shy students, icebreakers should be employed (*Start*).
- Students felt that it was better when the lecturer did not prompt individuals to participate (*Stop*) but rather opened the discussion to the whole room or groups promoting collaboration (*Continue*).
- Future sessions would be recorded and made available to students via VLE (*Start*) for better service and post-session support.

Recommendations and Implications

Collaborative teaching creates conditions for dialogue amongst students and encourages their epistemological curiosity, while promoting free and critical learning (Freire, 1970). Going forward more teachers should act as facilitators/co-learners realizing that students' cultural wealth brings added value and participation to the classroom. Thus, they must ensure that the diversity of students is taken into consideration. Instead of tutor-led monologues, the sessions should be 'interactive workshops' focusing on dialogic discussions around 'evidence' and knowledge-claims. Collaboration can be enhanced through authentic group work in bespoke sessions that are student-led. To prepare the education systems and institutions for the future, the Organisation for Economic Co-operation and Development (OECD, 2018) has suggested that empowering individuals to develop knowledge, skills, attitudes and values today will help them to contribute to an inclusive and sustainable future. This is particularly important for those in Health and Social Care who are responsible for the well-being of others. For this, a more integrated and interconnected pedagogic approach is required to empower students to participate, understand the needs and desires of others, and to problem-solve and share ideas which will help reduce the awarding gap. This recommendation is pivotal to empowering teachers to co-facilitate with students creating inclusive L&T practices that encourage effective collaboration amongst a wider learning community.

Teaching for Equality and the Politics of Feminist and Decolonial Education: From Polarized Debate to Collaborations for Change

Tess Czerski, Jana Finke, Cybele Atme and Mieke Lopes Cardozo

- The course *Teaching for Equality?: The Politics of Feminist and Decolonial Education* was created through the collaboration of junior and senior colleagues of our faculty at the University of Amsterdam to move from polarized debate to collaboration for change.
- In collaborative courses we can de-centre dominant teaching practices and the curriculum. This creates space for turning critical theory, in this case decolonial and feminist pedagogy, into practice.
- Co-creation and collaboration can lead to discomfort, which requires always reverting to practices of care and responsibility within the whole classroom, by both students and teachers/facilitators.

Introduction

The course *Teaching for Equality?: The Politics of Feminist and Decolonial Education* was created through the collaboration of junior and senior colleagues of our faculty at the University of Amsterdam. The course encourages a collective effort for analysis and imagination on how to foster education equality in our university, and in society. It emerged from discussions among students and teachers about tensions between our educational practice, the feminist and decolonial theories of our courses, and the politico-institutional realities of the (neoliberal) university (Diversity Commission UvA, 2016; Icaza & de Jong, 2018; Rizvi, 2017). The course responds to experiences with educational inequalities by centring the following question: to what extent and how can students and teachers collaborate towards (educational) equality (for conceptualizations, see Lynch & Baker, 2005; hooks, 1994)? We strive to answer this by putting feminist and decolonial theories into practice, regarding the context described above. In this chapter we reflect on our collaborative effort to teach and learn from and with students, teachers and activists, focusing on the core assignment: the education intervention. In the conclusion, we reflect on the wider applicability of such an intervention exercise in the university classroom.

Educational Intervention

The elective course is part of the social science *Gender & Sexuality Studies* minor and is open to Bachelor students of all disciplines. It consists of eleven two-hour interactive seminars across two months, facilitated by a teacher and guest lecturers. At the heart of the course is the notion that mitigating inequality in education is a collaborative effort. To put that into practice this course is co-created with students in a way that destabilizes the norm of prescriptive teaching. Each session introduces a new theme, e.g. feminist and decolonial pedagogies and student activism (Freire, 1968; hooks, 1994, 2003; Merry, 2020; The University of Colour, 2019). The teacher-facilitators decide on the themes and literature in the course, but actively encourage students to provide input on the course content through class conversations and assignments. To cater to diverse learning strategies, students have the option to engage with academic and non-academic written, oral and visual material. Next to a reflection assignment, where students critically reflect on their own and a peer's experience with education inequality, collaboration centres around the course's core assignment: the 'education intervention'. Following Giroux (2003) and Freire (1968), this course sought to move away from the hierarchical relationship between teacher and students so that both become participants in the classroom.

The 'education intervention' encourages students to take the lead in their educational process by envisioning, together with other classroom participants, how to foster equality in or through education. They are challenged to engage with the feminist and decolonial (ideal) perspectives in the course material, to co-create their own format for a class session, and then to deliver it. The intervention consists of three parts, which allow students to step-by-step build up their collaborative potential through group work and peer feedback:

1. *Student Discussion Leaders*: Three discussion leaders per session co-create a classroom exercise of about thirty minutes relating to the session's theme, putting together creative ideas for course material and possible guest speakers. Participants and the teacher would often discuss their ideas for the session beforehand in a meeting and over email to create a coherent session.
2. *Education Intervention Presentation*: In the final three sessions of the course, groups of two to three students prepare an education intervention tackling (education) inequality to implement in the classroom. Students share preparation materials with the class (e.g. academic articles, podcasts, exercises). After that, the class gives dialogic feedback in the light of the theory and the practical and institutional limitations.
3. *Intervention Reflection Essay*: Emerging from the class discussion and feedback, students individually write a 1,500-word paper where they contextualize, reflect on and redevelop their intervention addressing its limitations while taking the theory and the politico-institutional context into account.

Reflections on and for Educational Praxis

Transgressing Institutional Realities
'Teaching for Equality's' collaborative step-by-step set-up transgresses (hooks, 1994) the classical 'banking model of education' (Freire, 1968) dominant in educational institutions. The course was seeded by junior staff; some just transitioned from student to teacher, and co-created with senior colleagues, activists and educators

who co-facilitate it with the students and their 'education interventions'. Through this collaborative process, the role of the teacher shifted from 'teacher as information sharer' to 'teacher as intellectual' (Giroux, 2003), who engaged with and learned from the students' reflections and interventions.

Transgression may be experienced as disturbing by teachers and students (hooks, 1994; see also hooks, 2003; Freire, 1968) and whilst some students relished the room for creativity, something they are often not offered in other courses, others found it stressful and intimidating. Straying from traditional 'academic' norms and forms can make 'success' uncertain. For example, the student with dyslexia who argued for the inclusion of non-written materials in courses to facilitate the learning experience of students with dyslexia went on to present their assignment in the more traditional academic, written format, despite encouragement by the teacher to present their ideas in an alternative format.

The course itself, while enriching and exciting, was challenging in diverse ways for teachers. In our case, it required additional care and engagement outside class hours, adding to emotional labour and work pressure. Further, grading students' work felt increasingly contradictory to the course's aim. Yet, the course provided room to turn the challenges into new possibilities. One group of students, critiquing the hierarchical student-teacher relationship in grading, presented a peer-to-peer grading form focusing on progress and process that they tested with the class. The exercise led to a thoughtful discussion about grading. Although the class agreed that grades lead to stress and inequality in the classroom (many shared personal experiences around this issue), some wondered how peer-to-peer grading, or no grading, would affect participation and motivation. For some, it felt freeing, but others did not feel as incentivived to participate without the extrinsic motivation of receiving grades. This intervention group subsequently integrated the class's feedback on the complexity of assessment via a podcast (Mala Iyer) and a magazine spread (Quinty Hopman).

In the end, the class discussion led them to propose letting students themselves decide on how and whether to be graded on assignments. Even though it was not possible to change the actual way in which students were graded in the course, this collaborative intervention created a safe and open space wherein both students and teachers were able to dialogue about possible alternatives. In the process, teachers became more aware of diverse drivers of motivation and participation. Teachers were also able to express their frustrations towards the institutional limitations, which also made students more mindful of the teacher's agency.

Political Tensions and Care

The course has revealed political tensions that we encounter in and around university. Working through these tensions requires collaborative care work, which should be not only the responsibility of the teacher but shared by all participants (Berila, 2016; hooks, 1994; Mehta, 2019). In our course we sought to create a space for collective engagement with inherently political critical theories of decolonial and feminist pedagogy – valuing personal experience as knowledge (hooks, 1994). At the same time, we consciously chose to discuss politico-institutional realities and (un)conscious biases which might interfere with the ideals of the abovementioned theories, thereby purposefully disturbing the notion of the classroom as a 'safe space' (Ludlow, 2004).

The contrast between the possibilities within our classroom and the hierarchical structures 'outside', in the institution, could be disheartening to students. However, by envisioning collaborative interventions, we can meet those challenges with excitement, hope and care for each other (hooks, 2003, referring to Freire). During the discussion of an education intervention by students Lynne Kavishe, Rozan Snoek and colleague, the classroom carefully and collaboratively formulated ways to include both discomfort and excitement in addressing political tensions. These students conducted an exercise, wherein artworks served as the starting point to discuss emotions around racism and mental health in response to 'colourblind' approaches in the Dutch education system (Herve, 2018; Sijpenhof, 2020). Afterward, the class offered sensitive feedback for the intervention's further development. They pointed to the risk of white students participating in the exercise consuming the traumas of students of marginalized positionalities (Mehta, 2019). They suggested including artworks expressing joy to do full justice to lived experiences. In their reflection essays, the creators took this feedback into account and suggested the inclusion of new images for the intervention, but also reflected on the possibility of explicitly discussing the consumption of trauma in their intervention. The whole class collaborated to centre experience knowledge and emotions, thereby creating a 'contested space' (Ludlow, 2004) in which tensions can be met with care.

Conclusion

To what extent and how then can students and teachers collaborate towards (educational) equality in a course like the one we introduced in this chapter? The education intervention described in the three steps above offers students and teachers a sense of agency and shared responsibility – for action (Freire, 1968). The format encourages collaborative self-reflection, social scientific analysis of complex inequalities and imagination inspired by critical theory to conceive creative interventions to tackle them. Most students actively tried to consider the real politico-institutional settings in which their intervention would take place and its accompanying limits. One could take the interventions one step further by asking students to try them outside the 'bubble' of the classroom. This may further support participants to implement their idea(l)s in their future (educational) careers, putting visions into practice.

We created the course to critically analyse how our education is embedded in (discourses of) inequalities, but also to collaborate as teachers and students and imagine how to work towards equality to bring about real educational change. We believe that similar educational inequalities are faced in many institutions across the world and that this format can be useful in many different educational contexts. One can also decouple the format from the topic of education and use it to bring critical theory into practice in other social science courses. Instead of an 'educational intervention' students could come up with an NGO or governmental intervention, being asked to take theoretical principles and common ideal(s) (such as equality) into account.

Through critical peer and self-reflection, we learn that such interventions are always 'work in progress', requiring resources of time, energy and care, but when students and teachers collaborate, they generate excitement.

Acknowledgements

Thank you to all students who have followed and co-created Teaching for Equality, and in particular those who were so kind to share their work with us for this chapter: Tongyu Gu, Jannah Diekerhof, Floor Langen, Quinty Hopman, Sam Jones, Rozan Snoek, Mala Iyer and Lynne Kavishe. Also, thanks to our proofreaders for their valuable feedback and new perspectives: Hannah Bragdon and Isa Buenfil-Van Rijs (Amsterdam United).

References

Introduction

Althusser, L. (2012). Ideology and ideological state apparatuses (notes towards an investigation). In M. G. Durham, & D. M. Kellner (Eds.), *Media and cultural studies. Keyworks* (pp. 80–8). Wiley-Blackwell.

Bustillos, J. A., & Abegglen, S. (2021). Issues of gender, 'race' and social class in education. In S. Isaacs (Ed.), *Social problems in the UK: An introduction* (2nd ed., pp. 86–110). Routledge.

Henry, W. L. (2021). Black lives matter, decolonisation and the legacy of African enslavement. In S. Isaacs (Ed.), *Social problems in the UK: An introduction* (2nd ed., pp. 25–42). Routledge.

Molinari, J. (2022). *What makes writing academic: Rethinking theory for practice.* Bloomsbury.

Noble, D. (2003). Digital diploma mills. In B. Johnson, P. Kavanagh, & K. Mattson (Eds.), *Steal this university* (pp. 39–54). Routledge.

Office for Students (2022). *OfS sets out plans to crack down on poor quality courses.* https://www.officeforstudents.org.uk/news-blog-and-events/press-and-media/ofs-sets-out-plans-to-crack-down-on-poor-quality-courses/

Case Study: Coming in Together

Angelo, T. (1993). A 'teacher's dozen': Fourteen general, research-based principles for improving higher learning in our classrooms. *AAHE Bulletin, 45*(8), 3–13.

Boyd, D. (2016). What would Paulo Freire think of Blackboard: Critical pedagogy in an age of online learning. *International Journal of Critical Pedagogy, 7*(1), 165–86.

Cock, D., Nixon, S., Walker, C., Mitchell, E., Walsh, B., & Zaitseva, E. (2008). Understanding student engagement: Evaluation of an intensive five-week transition programme. *CETL Journal: Innovations in Practice, 1*(1), 36–43.

Cook, A., & Leckey, J. (1999). Do expectations meet reality? A survey of change in the first year student opinion. *Journal of Further and Higher Education, 23*(2), 157–71. DOI: 10.1080/0309877990230201

Cummins, J. (2009). Pedagogies of choice: Challenging coercive relations of power in classrooms and communities. *International Journal of Bilingual Education and Bilingualism, 12*(3), 261–71. DOI: 10.1080/13670050903003751

Cummins, J., & Early, M. (2011). Identity texts: The collaborative creation of power in multilingual schools. *Trentham Books.* DOI: 10.1002/ tesq.241

Curran, J. (2016). *An investigation into student sense of belonging at a post-1992 university* [doctoral dissertation, London Metropolitan University]. British Library EThOS.

Edgar, S., Carr, S. E., Connaughton, J., & Celenza, A. (2019). Student motivation to learn: Is self-belief the key to transition and first year performance in an undergraduate health professions program? *BMC Medical Education, 19,* 111. DOI: 10.1186/s12909-019-1539-5

Freire, P. (1996). *Pedagogy of the oppressed*. Penguin.

Freire, P. (2014). *Pedagogy of commitment* (D. Brookshaw & A. Oliveira, Trans.). Paradigm Publishers.

Gale, T., & Parker, S. (2012). Navigating change: A typology of student transition in higher education. *Studies in Higher Education, 39*(5), 734–53. DOI: 10.1080/03075079.2012.721351

Gutierrez, K. (2018). Developing a socio-critical literacy in the third space. *Reading Research Quarterly, 43*(2), 148–64. DOI: 10.1080/03075079812331380364

Kember, K., Hong, C., & Ho, A. (2008). Characterizing the motivational orientation of students in higher education: A naturalistic study in three Hong Kong universities. *British Journal of Educational Psychology, 78*(2), 313–29. DOI: 10.1348/000709907X220581

Lea, M. R., & Street, B. V. (1998). Student writing in higher education: An academic literacies approach. *Studies in Higher Education, 23*(2), 157–72. DOI: 10.1080/03075079812331380364

Mezirow, J. (1985). A critical theory of self-directed learning. *New Directions for Adult and Continuing Education, 32*(1), 3–24. DOI: 10.1002/ace.36719852504

Neve, H., & Collett, T. (2018). Empowering students with the hidden curriculum. *The Clinical Teacher, 15*(6), 494–9. DOI: 10.1111/tct.12736

Nowell, C. (2017). The influence of motivational orientation on the satisfaction of university students. *Teaching in Higher Education, 22*(7), 855–66. DOI: 10.1080/13562517.2017.1319811

ONS (2019). *Exploring the UK's digital divide*. https://www.ons.gov.uk/peoplepopulationandcommunity/householdcharacteristics/homeinternetandsocialmediausage/articles/exploringtheuksdigitaldivide/2019-03-04

Read, B., Archer, L., & Leathwood, C. (2003). Challenging cultures? Student conceptions of 'belonging' and 'isolation' at a post-1992 university. *Studies in Higher Education, 28*(3), 261–77. DOI: 10.1080/03075070309290

Richardson, M., & Tate, S. (2013). Improving the transition to university: Introducing student voices into the formal induction process for new geography undergraduates. *Journal of Geography in Higher Education, 37*(4), 611–18. DOI: 10.1080/03098265.2013.769092

Savin-Baden, M. (2007). *Learning spaces: Creating opportunities for knowledge creation in academic life*. Open University Press.

Shor, I., & Freire, P. (1987). What is the 'dialogical method' of teaching? *Journal of Education, 169*(3), 11–31. DOI: 10.1177/002205748716900303

Zaidi, Z., Verstegen, D., Naqvi, R., Dornan, T., & Morahan, P. (2016). Identity text: An educational intervention to foster cultural interaction. *Medical Education Online, 21*(1), 331–5. DOI: 10.3402/meo.v21.33135

Zapata, G., & Ribota, A. (2020). The instructional benefits of identity texts and learning by design for learner motivation in required second language classes. *Pedagogies: An International Journal, 16*(1), 1–18. DOI: 10.1080/1554480X.2020.1738937

Case Study: Unite and Unrule! Reflections of a Co-created Pedagogy for Transformation

Ahmed, S. (2012). *On being included: Racism and diversity in institutional life*. Duke University Press.

Berila, B. (2016). *Integrating mindfulness into anti-oppression pedagogy*. Social Justice in Higher Education. Routledge.

Berg, M., & Seeber, B. K. (2013). The slow professor: Challenging the culture of speed in the academy. *Transformative Dialogues: Teaching & Learning Journal, 6*(3), 1–7.

Biesta, G., Bingham, C., Margonis, F., Sidorkin, A., Hutchinson, J., McDaniel, B. L., & Pijanowski, C. M. (2004). Manifesto of relational pedagogy: Meeting to learn, learning to meet. *No Education without Relation*, 5–7. https://www.researchgate.net/publication/280572543_Manifesto_of_relational_pedagogy_Meeting_to_learn_learning_to_meet

Bingham, C., & Sidorkin, A. M. (2004). *No education without relation*. Lang Publishers.

Bovill, C. (2020). *Co-creating learning and teaching: Towards relational pedagogy in higher education*. Critical Publishing.

Giroux, H. A. (2010). Rethinking education as the practice of freedom: Paulo Freire and the promise of critical pedagogy. *Policy Futures in Education, 8*(6), 715–21. https://journals.sagepub.com/doi/pdf/10.2304/pfie.2010.8.6.715

Harcourt, W. (2017). The making and unmaking of development: Using post-development as a tool in teaching development studies. *Third World Quarterly, 38*(12), 2703–18. DOI: 10.1080/01436597.2017.1315300

hooks, b. (1994). *Teaching to transgress*. Routledge.

Kothari, A., Salleh, A., Escobar, A., Demaria, F., & Acosta, A. (2019). *Pluriverse: A post-development dictionary*. Tulika Books.

Kothari, U. (2006). An agenda for thinking about 'race' in development. *Progress in Development Studies, 6*(1), 9–23. DOI: 10.1191%2F1464993406ps124oa

Mang, P., & Haggard, B. (2016). *Regenerative development and design, a framework for evolving sustainability*. Wiley.

Mountz, A., Bonds, A., Mansfield, B., Loyd, J., Hyndman, J., Walton-Roberts, M., Basu, R., Whitson, R., Hawkins, R., Hamilton, T., & Curran, W. (2015). For slow scholarship: A feminist politics of resistance through collective action in the neoliberal university. *ACME: An International Journal for Critical Geographies, 14*(4), 1235–59. https://acme-journal.org/index.php/acme/article/view/1058

Naidoo, R. (Host). (21 July 2016). Competition in higher education (No. 20) [Audio podcast episode]. In *FreshEd with Will Brehm*. FreshEd, Inc. https://freshedpodcast.com/rajaninaidoo/

Naidoo, R. (2018). The competition fetish in higher education: Shamans, mind snares and consequences. *European Educational Research Journal, 17*(5), 605–20. DOI: 10.1177%2F1474904118784839

Springer, S. (2016). Learning through the soles of our feet: Unschooling, anarchism, and the geography of childhood. In S. Springer, M. Lopes de Souza, & R. J. White (Eds.), *The radicalization of pedagogy: Anarchism, geography, and the spirit of revolt* (pp. 247–65). Rowman & Littlefield.

Souza, D. T., Wals, A. E. J., & Jacobi, P. R. (2019). Learning-based transformations towards sustainability: A relational approach based on Humberto Maturana and Paulo Freire. *Environmental Education Research*, *25*(11), 1605–19. DOI: 10.1080/13504622.2019.1641183

Sultana, F. (2019). Decolonizing development education and the pursuit of social justice. *Human Geography*, *12*(3), 31–46. https://www.farhanasultana.com/wp-content/uploads/2019/12/Farhana-SultanaDecolonizing-Development-Education-and-the-Pursuit-of-Social-Justice.pdf

The University of Colour (Awethu, A., Balk, T., van der Scheer, I. B., van Meyeren, E., Martis, A., & Nguyễn, N. C.) (2019). From the hollow of the lion: A testimony of revolt at the University of Amsterdam. In M. F. Weiner, & A. Carmona Báez (Eds.), *Smash the pillars: Decoloniality and the imaginary of color in the Dutch Kingdom* (pp. 17–29). Lexington Books.

Wals, A. E. J. (2015). Beyond unreasonable doubt. In *Education and learning for socio-ecological sustainability in the Anthropocene*. Wageningen University.

Wekker, G., Slootman, M. W., Icaza Garza, R., Jansen, H., & Vázquez, R. (2016). *Let's do diversity: Report of the University of Amsterdam Diversity Commission*. http://hdl.handle.net/1765/95261

Case Study: Honest Conversations about 'Race' and Racism

Bell, D. M., & Pahl, K. (2018). Co-production: Towards a utopian approach. *International Journal of Social Research Methodology*, *21*(1), 105–17. DOI: 10.1080/13645579.2017.1348581

Canagarajah, A. S. (2002). *A geopolitics of academic writing*. University of Pittsburgh Press.

Chang, H., Ngunjiri, F. W., & Hernandez, K. C. (2013). *Collaborative autoethnography*. Left Coast Press.

Diversity Lewes (2015). Celebrating African Caribbean's in Sussex past and present. *The Lewes Print Centre*. https://issuu.com/tonykalume/docs/booklet_layout

Ellis, C., & Bochner, A. P. (2000). Autoethnography, personal narrative, reflexivity: Researcher as subject. In N. Denzin, & Y. Lincoln (Eds.), *The Sage handbook of qualitative research* (2nd ed., pp. 733–68). Sage.

Emejulu, A. (2017). Feminism for the 99%: Towards a populist feminism?: Can feminism for the 99% succeed as a new kind of populism? *Soundings: A Journal of Politics and Culture*, *66*, 63–7.

Facer, K., & Enright, B. (2016). *Creating living knowledge*. University of Bristol.

Hanby, J. (1984) *Khangas: 101 uses*. Indiana University.

Kalume, A. (2019a). Khanga: Heritage, historic and cultural aspects [unpublished manuscript]. Diversity Lewes.

Kalume, A. (2019b). *Celebrating African Caribbeans in Sussex past and present*. Sharing Heritage Press. https://independent.academia.edu/TonyKalume

Kalume, T., & Moriarty, J. (2022, forthcoming). The clothes on our back: A collaborative project to diversify the curriculum in higher education. In K. Aughterson, & J. Moriarty E (Eds.), *Performance and communities*. Intellect Books.

Moriarty, J. (2019). *Autoethographies from the neoliberal academy*. Routledge.

Muir, H. (31 August 2010). Diverse Britain: Talking about racism in Lewes. *The Guardian*. https://www.theguardian.com/uk/2010/aug/31/diverse-britain-racism-lewes-sussex?CMP=share_btn_link

National Union of Students, & Universities UK (2019, May). Black, Asian and minority ethnic student attainment at UK universities: #Closingthegap. *Universities UK*. https://www.universitiesuk.ac.uk/policy-and-analysis/reports/Documents/2019/bame-student-attainment-uk-universities-closingthe-gap.pdf

National Union of Students, & Universities UK (28 September 2020). *Race for equality: A report on the experiences of Black students in further and higher education 2011*. https://www.nusconnect.org.uk/resources/race-for-equality-a-report-on-the-experiences-of-black-students-in-further-and-higher-education-2011

Pool, H. A. (Ed.) (2016). *Fashion cities*. Intellect.

Rawley, J. A., & Behrendt, S. D. (2005). *The transatlantic slave trade: A History*. U of Nebraska Press.

Smith, D. J. (8 August 2010). England's green and prejudiced land. *The Times*. https://www.thetimes.co.uk/article/england-s-green-and-prejudiced-land-8mt2zbx282v

Case Study: Love, Respect, Esteem

Bovill, C. (2013). Students and staff co-creating curricula – a new trend or an old idea we never got around to implementing? In C. Rust (Ed.), *Improving student learning through research and scholarship: 20 years of ISL* (pp. 96–108). The Oxford Centre for Staff and Educational Development.

Clutterbuck, D. (2008). What's happening in coaching and mentoring? And what is the difference between them? *Development and Learning in Organizations: An International Journal, 22*(4), 8–10. DOI: 10.1108/14777280810886364

Colley, H. (2001). Righting rewritings of the myth of mentor: A critical perspective on career guidance mentoring. *British Journal of Guidance & Counselling, 29*(2), 177–97. DOI: 10.1080/03069880020047120

Cook-Sather, A., Bovill, C., & Felten, P. (2014). *Engaging students as partners in learning and teaching: A guide for faculty*. Josey-Bass.

Dei, G. (2016). Decolonizing the university: The challenges and possibilities of inclusive education. *Socialist Studies* (St. Albert), *11*(1). DOI: https://doi.org/10.18740/S4WW31

Devine, P. G. (2012). Long-term reduction in implicit race bias: A prejudice habit-breaking intervention. *Journal of Experimental Social Psychology, 48*(6), 1267–78. DOI: 10.1016/j.jesp.2012.06.003

Dweck, C. S. (2006). *Mindset: The new psychology of success*. Random House.

Fraser, N., & Honneth, A. (2003). *Redistribution or recognition?* Verso.

Freire, P. (1970). *Pedagogy of the oppressed*. Seabury.

Good, C., Aronson, J., & Harder, J. A. (2008). Problems in the pipeline: Stereotype threat and women's achievement in high-level math courses. *Journal of Applied Developmental Psychology, 29*(1), 17–28. DOI: 10.1016/j.appdev.2007.10.004

Healey, M., Flint, A., & Harrington, K. (2014). *Engagement through partnership: Students as partners in learning and teaching in higher education*. Higher Education Academy. https://www.heacademy.ac.uk/sites/default/files/resources/engagement_through_partnership.pdf

Hill, V., & Simpson, J. (2020). *Creative mindsets facilitators handbook*. UAL. https://www.arts.ac.uk/__data/assets/pdf_file/0023/203288/Creative-Mindsets-Handbook-PDF-3.2MB.pdf

Hill, V., Bunting, L., & Arboine, J. (2020). *Fostering belonging and compassionate pedagogy*. AEM and Attainment Resources. UAL. https://www.arts.ac.uk/__data/assets/pdf_file/0019/223417/AEM3_FBCP.pdf

Hill, V., Clayton, E., Cound, C., Okobi, E., & Stan, A. (forthcoming, 2022). *A participatory action research project to explore whether the student members of University of the Arts (UAL) Creative Mindsets Team perceived a change in their own mindsets through becoming facilitators.* SPARK, UAL.

Honneth, A. (1996). *The struggle for recognition. The moral grammar of social conflicts.* Polity Press.

Honneth, A. (1997). Recognition and moral obligation. *Social Research*, 64(1), Spring 97, 16–35. http://www.jstor.org/stable/40971157

Honneth, A. (2014). *The I in we: Studies in the theory of recognition.* Polity Press.

Lovell, T. (2007). *(Mis)recognition, social inequality and social justice: Nancy Fraser and Pierre Bourdieu.* Taylor & Francis Group.

Mahmud, A., & Gagnon, J. (2020). Racial disparities in student outcomes in British higher education: Examining mindsets and bias. *Teaching in Higher Education.* DOI: 10.1080/13562517.2020.1796619

Mercer-Mapstone, L., Marquis, E., & McConnell, C. (2018). The 'partnership identity' in higher education: Moving from 'us' and 'them' to 'we' in student-staff partnership. *Student Engagement in Higher Education Journal*, 2(1), 12–29. https://sehej.raise-network.com/raise/article/view/Mercer-Mapstone

Power, S. (2012). From redistribution to recognition to representation: Social injustice and the changing politics of education. *Globalisation, Societies and Education*, 10(4), 473–92. DOI: 10.1080/14767724.2012.735154

Sennett, R. (2012). *Together: The rituals, pleasures and politics of cooperation.* Yale University Press.

Simpson, J., Hill, V., & Riggs, G. (2020). Bias and belonging in the creative arts studio. *Interrogating Spaces* [audio podcast episode]. https://interrogatingspaces.buzzsprout.com/683798/3045604-creative-mindsets-bias-and-belonging-in-the-creative-arts-studio

Singh, G. (2009). *Black and minority ethnic (BME) students' participation in higher education. Improving retention and success: A synthesis of research evidence.* Higher Education Academy. https://www.advance-he.ac.uk/knowledge-hub/black-and-minority-ethnic-bme-students-participation-higher-education-improving

Taylor, L. (2021). Peer mentoring works? Towards an understanding of mentoring in higher education. Unpublished.

UAL (2021a). *UAL creative mindsets.* https://ualcreativemindsets.myblog.arts.ac.uk/

UAL (2021b, April). Anti-racism action plan summary. https://www.arts.ac.uk/__data/assets/pdf_file/0044/288998/UAL-Anti-Racism-Action-Plan-Summary-02-June-21.pdf

van Leeuwen, B. (2007). A formal recognition of social attachments: Expanding Axel Honneth's theory of recognition. *Inquiry*, 50(2), 180–205. DOI: 10.1080/00201740701239897

Case Study: Inclusive Learning and Teaching in Higher Education

Abegglen, S. Burns, T., & Sinfield, S. (2016). The power of freedom: Setting up a multimodal exhibition with undergraduate students to foster their learning and help them to achieve. *Journal of Peer Learning*, 9, 1–9. http://ro.uow.edu.au/ajpl/?utm_source=ro.uow.edu.au%2Fajpl%2Fvol9%2Fiss1%2F2&utm_medium=PDF&utm_campaign=PDFCoverPages

Abegglen, S., Burns, T., Middlebrook, D., & Sinfield, S. (2019). Unrolling the text: Using scrolls to facilitate academic reading. *Journal of Learning Development in Higher Education, 14*. DOI: 10.47408/jldhe.v0i14.467

Ainscow, M. (1999). *Understanding the development of inclusive schools*. Falmer.

Bovill, C., Cook-Sather, A., & Felten, P. (2011). Students as co-creators of teaching approaches, course design and curricula: Implications for academic developers. *International Journal for Academic Development, 16*(2), 133–45.

Freire, P. (1970). *Pedagogy of the oppressed*. Continuum Books.

Gervedink Nijhuis, C. (2019). *Culturally sensitive curriculum development*. In J. Pieters, J. Voogt, & N. Pareja Roblin (Eds.), *Collaborative curriculum design for sustainable innovation and teacher learning*. Springer. DOI: 10.1007/978-3-030-20062-6_5

Harrington, K. Sinfield, S., & Burns, T. (2016). *Student engagement*. In H. Pokorony, & D. Warren (Eds.), *Enhancing teaching practice in higher education* (pp. 106–24). Sage.

The HE Academy (2011). *The UK professional standards framework for teaching and supporting learning in HE*. http://www.heacademy.ac.uk/system/files/downloads/ukpsf_2011_english.pdf

Hockings, C. (2010). *Inclusive learning and teaching in HE: A synthesis of research*. HE Academy. https://www.heacademy.ac.uk/system/… /inclusive_teaching_and_learning_in_he_1.do

Hoon, A., Oliver, E. J., Szpakowska, K., & Newton, P. (2015). Use of the 'stop, start, continue' method is associated with the production of constructive qualitative feedback by students in higher education. *Assessment and Evaluation in Higher Education, 40*(5), 755–67. DOI: 10.1080/02602938.2014.956282

Jenkins, A., Breen, R., & Lindsay, R. (2005). *Reshaping teaching in higher education*. Taylor and Francis.

Kirkpatrick, D. L. (1994). *Evaluating training programs: The four levels*. Berrett-Koehler.

Kuh, G. D. (2005). *Promoting student success: What campus leaders can do*. National Survey of Student Engagement.

Liedtka, J., & Mintzberg, H. (2006). Time for design. *Design Management Review, 17*(2), 10–18. DOI: 10.1111/j.1948-7169.2006.tb00034

London Metropolitan University (2010). *How can the policy emphasis on blended learning help to enhance digital literacies for students and staff?* https://wiki.brookes.ac.uk/display/slidacases/London+Metropolitan

London Metropolitan University (2012). *Assessment framework*. http://www.londonmet.ac.uk/celt/learning-teaching-assessment/university-frameworks.cfm

London Metropolitan University (2021/22). *London Metropolitan University Education for Social Justice (ESJ) Framework*. https://www.londonmet.ac.uk/media/london-metropolitan-university/london-met-documents/professional-service-departments/quality-enhancement-unit/quality-manual/course-development-and-design/forms-and-templates/AQD011-ESJF-Template.docx

Luthera, P., & Mackenzie, S. (2021). *2021 World Economic Forum*. https://www.weforum.org/agenda/2020/03/4-ways-covid-19-education-future-generations/

Markwell, D. (2007). *The challenge of student engagement*. Keynote address at the Teaching and Learning Forum. University of Western Australia, 30–31 January.

McIntosh, P., & Warren, D. (2013). *Case studies in using the arts in teaching and learning in HE*. The University of Chicago Press Books.

National Improvement Hub (NIH) (2019). *CIRCLE resource to support inclusive learning and collaborative working (primary and secondary)*. Education Scotland. https://education.gov.scot/improvement/learning-resources/circle-resource-to-support-inclusive-learning-and-collaborative-working/

NHS Employers (2021). *Responding to the needs of a diverse workforce and community during Covid-19*. https://www.nhsemployers.org/case-studies/responding-needs-diverse-workforce-and-community-during-covid-19

OECD (2016). *Innovating education and educating for innovation: The power of digital technologies and skill*. OECD Publishing. DOI: 10.1787/9789264265097-en

OECD (2018). *The future of education and skills Education 2030*. OECD Publishing. http://www.oecd.org/education/2030/oecd-education-2030-position-paper.pdf

Office of National Statistics (2017). *Overview of the UK population: July 2017*. https://www.ons.gov.uk/peoplepopulationandcommunity/populationandmigration/populationestimates/articles/overviewoftheukpopulation/july2017

The UK Quality Code for Higher Education (2018). Programme monitoring and review. http://www.qaa.ac.uk/Publications/InformationAndGuidance/Pages/quality-code-B8.aspx

Toohey, S. (1999). *Designing courses for HE*. The Society for Research into HE & Open University Press.

Trompenaars, F., & Hampden-Turner, C. (1997). *Riding the waves of culture: Understanding cultural diversity in business*. Nicholas Brearley.

Trowler, V. (2010). *Student engagement literature review*. Department of Educational.

University College London (2019). *Four ways to work in partnership with your students in 2019–20*. https://www.ucl.ac.uk/teaching-learning/news/2019/oct/four-ways-work-partnership-your-students-2019-20

Case Study: Teaching for Equality and the Politics of Feminist and Decolonial Education

Berila, B. (2016). *Integrating mindfulness into anti-oppression pedagogy*. Social Justice in Higher Education. Routledge.

Diversity Commission UvA (2016). *Let's do diversity*. University of Amsterdam. https://www.uva.nl/en/content/news/news/2016/10/diversity-committee-presents-final-report.html

Freire, P. (1968). *Pedagogy of the oppressed*. Penguin Books.

Giroux, H. (2003). Teachers as transformative intellectuals. In A.S. Canestrari, & Marlowe, B. A. (Eds.), *Educational foundations: An anthology of critical readings* (pp. 205–12). Sage.

Herve, A. (19 December 2018) *Philomena essed: Everyday racism and cultural cloning in education* [video]. YouTube. https://www.youtube.com/watch?v=dL6WN_ONepk

hooks, b. (1994). *Teaching to transgress: Education as the practice of freedom*. Routledge.

hooks, b. (2003). *Teaching community: A pedagogy of hope*. Routledge.

Icaza, R., & de Jong, S. (2018). Introduction: Decolonization and feminisms in global teaching and learning – a radical space of possibility. In R. Icaza, S., de Jong, & O. U. Rutazibwa (Eds.), *Decolonization and feminisms in global teaching and learning – a radical space of possibility* (pp. xv–xxxiv). At Gender Teaching Series. Routledge.

Ludlow, J. (2004). From safe space to contested space in the feminist classroom. *Transformations: The Journal of Inclusive Scholarship and Pedagogy XV*, *1*(40), 40–56. http://www.jstor.org/stable/10.5325/trajincschped.15.1.0040

Lynch, K., & Baker, J. (2005). Equality in education: An equality of condition perspective. *Theory and Research in Education*, *3*(2), 131–64. DOI: 10.1177/1477878505053298

Mehta, A. (2019). Teaching gender, race, sexuality: Reflections on feminist pedagogy. *Kohl: A Journal for Body and Gender Research*, *5*(1), 23–30. https://kohljournal.press/reflections-feminist-pedagogy

Merry, M. (2020). Justice and education. In M. Merry (Ed.), *Educational justice* (pp. 21–52). Springer International Publishing.

Rizvi, F. (2017, February). *Globalization and the neoliberal imaginary of educational reform*. UNESCO Education Research and Foresight Working Paper. http://unesdoc.unesco.org/images/0024/002473/247328e.pdf

Sijpenhof, M. L. (2020). A transformation of racist discourse? Colour-blind racism and biological racism in Dutch secondary schooling (1968–2017). *International Journal on the History of Education*, *56*(1–2), 51–69. DOI: 10.1080/00309230.2019.1616787

The University of Colour (Awethu!, A., Balk, T., van der Scheer, I. B., van Meyeren, E., Martis, A., & Nguyễn, N. C.) (2019). From the hollow of the lion: A testimony of revolt at the University of Amsterdam. In Weiner, M. F., & Carmona Báez, A. (Eds.), *Smash the pillars: Decoloniality and the Imaginary of color in the Dutch Kingdom* (pp. 17–29). Lexington Books.

8

Reflections on Collaboration

Introduction

Reflection on practice often draws on John Dewey (1933), Graham Gibbs (1988) and Donald Schön (1983) who urge us to make the time to reflect in and on action, making conscious what we have done and why, and working out how to do things better next time. This is particularly important in collaborative educational practice where we seek sustainable relationships rather than one-off projects. Arguably, such reflection is the most important source of personal professional development and improvement, as Schön (1983, 61) puts it:

> Through reflection, [we] can surface and criticize the tacit understandings that have grown up around the repetitive experiences of a specialized practice, and can make new sense of the situations of uncertainty or uniqueness which [we] may allow [ourselves] to experience.

A useful tool with respect to reflecting on multi-agency partnerships, partnerships with students and other partners, is Arnstein's ladder (1969). This seminal model considers partnership from manipulation to 'citizen control', with degrees of participatory power and agency increasing up the rungs of the ladder. This is imperative where there might be an unequal distribution of power across the actors: staff working with students, more experienced academics working with those who are less experienced, universities working with community organizations. Authentic collaboration is not about taking control, it is dialogue, recognition and acceptance of the other, with benefits for all. Critical reflection allows us to pay attention to the practical values and theories which inform the partnerships and partnership actions, illuminating them usefully, and leading to the development of fresh and powerful insights and actions.

The reflections offered in this section represent reflective practices that create powerful agency for those positioned as 'outsiders' in academic discourse. All illustrate instances where power has been meaningfully shared to bring more voices into the conversation – with recommendations for the reader with respect to adapting practices for their own diverse contexts.

The Case Study Chapters

Together by Hélène Pulker and Chrissi Nerantzi reports on an open educational picture book created by a self-forming group of international staff and students collaboratively working together. It highlights key features of successful collaborative practice: openness, honesty and inclusivity; listening carefully to all voices and perspectives; bonding as a team and clarifying working practices; keeping communication clear, open and transparent.

In *Autoethnography, Academic Identity, Creativity*, Emma Gillaspy and Anna Hunter reflect on how the creative collaborative approaches they have used to explore identity formation encouraged authentic academic identities to emerge in new staff. The two examples demonstrate how participants 'have grown wings' through the collaborative inclusive conversations in 'safe spaces'. Both examples involved working with 'outsider' academics, reflecting on academic development through collaborative conversation that sparked new ideas to drive sector-wide change.

Values-driven collaborative writing offers an opportunity for communities to share ownership of and responsibility for the writing, editing and reviewing process in a democratic, non-hierarchical environment. In *Working Together* the ALDinHE research vCoP reflects on the potential of collaborative writing for community building through the democratic co-construction of knowledge. The 'team sport' model of collaboration developed by this particular vCoP could be used by other groups both to address questions in the changing HE landscape and to model a more humane HE in the process.

Manuela Barczewski, Keith Beckles and Simone Maier's professional practices were bolstered through the very human relationships that they built as PGCert students. In *Humane Relationships*, they outline how their own trust relationships helped them to support their students. The authors offer a model of how creative practitioners can work collectively to share creative ideas and expertise to democratically develop new knowledge. They stress the need for staff to be given time and spaces to learn how to collaborate with each other.

With *Coaching for Collaborative Autonomy*, Monika Hřebačková, Martin Štefl, Jana Zvěřinová and Tanja Vesala-Varttala reflect on their collaborative European project that created an online English language course built around collaboration and co-creation. The course was integrated into real university courses and attracted ECTS credits. Working in culturally heterogeneous multi-disciplinary groups, student teams problem-solved issues of sustainability, and developed their language skills while actively reflecting on the processes of their collaborative working methods. The authors make light touch suggestions for how to harness non-directive coaching and Learning Journals in the process.

Together: The Story of Collaborating to Create the Open Picture Book

Hélène Pulker and Chrissi Nerantzi

- This case study reports on an open educational product, a picture book, collaboratively created by a self-forming group of international staff and students.
- The case study highlights the following points for such international collaborations:
  - be open and inclusive in your approach to collaboration and avoid making judgement;
  - listen carefully and listen to all voices and perspectives. Everybody has something valuable to contribute;
  - agree working practices and individual contributions and build time for team members to get to know each other;
  - remember that clear and transparent communication is vital; and
  - be flexible in your role as a leader and team member and be prepared to troubleshoot and come up with alternative solutions to bring your project to fruition.

Introduction

Collaborative working is an increasingly necessary part of academic life (Walsh & Kahn, 2009). Traditionally, university culture supported individual research and scholarship; however, working collaboratively whilst it may present challenges – networking, digital and social skills – offers sustaining and sustainable working spaces and practices. In informal learning, collaboration and openness are often the norm (Nascimbeni, 2020). This case study reports on an informal collaborative working experience of a group of distributed HE researchers, including doctoral students, as well as a High School student, an undergraduate student and a professional artist, who came together to create a picture book on the values of open education. The case study provides some background to the picture book project whilst the focus of the chapter is an analysis of this collaboration, using narrative inquiry. It concludes with some recommendations for collaborative staff/student working in HE.

Project Background

The Global Open Educational Resources (OER) Graduate Network (GO-GN) is a network of doctoral students around the world whose research projects focus on open education: resources, practices, pedagogy, policy and MOOCs. Offering a range of training activities and opportunities to share ideas has connected students and alumni and facilitated self-forming working groups created around common research methodologies or topics of shared interest (Weller et al., 2019). The picture book team is an example of such a self-forming group. With a fellowship from the GO-GN, secured by the project leader, a group of open educators and researchers located in four different continents formed to co-create a story about open education.

Together (Nerantzi et al., 2021) was written and illustrated collaboratively over six months, during the heart of the pandemic (Covid-19), using exclusively the open web and digital tools. The book aimed to raise awareness of open education and what it enables. It was widely shared on the Zenodo platform, including with primary and HE classrooms. The final book is now, thanks to the open education community, available in over twenty languages. An openly licensed drawing programme Doodlefan was also created to accompany the book and extend engagement with the story.

The team included academics, doctoral students and consultants with a variety of roles in a variety of institutions. With the exception of a High School art student, an undergraduate student and a professional artist who were invited to support the illustrations of the story, the team members were GO-GN alumni and HE academics or doctoral students. Although coming from various backgrounds and working in different countries and cultures, the shared values and aspirations about open education helped bring the picture book project to fruition.

Throughout the project, the international team communicated and collaborated via seven live meetings in Skype, Zoom and MS Teams as well as through emails, Twitter DM group and Google Drive. The team's individual and collective journeys were captured through publicly available blog posts, which form the data for this case study.

Together, the Collaborative Open Picture Book

For the story-writing phase of the project, we used a 'seed survey' to gather ideas and input from the wider open education community, also helping us avoid stereotypes. The team was split into two sub-groups. This helped us be more focused and make progress more quickly in the writing process. The challenge was to come up with a viable story that would speak to a cross-generational readership. We had decided to weave the story using animal characters and, in the spirit of OER, snippets of other stories. We also decided to use open licence exhibition pieces from the Rijksmuseum in Amsterdam, seeing this as an opportunity to model the reuse of OER. Throughout the creative process we continued to seek feedback from within and outside the team.

While the first sub-team wrote the skeleton of the story, the second sub-team finalized the story and decided on characters and further details. Once the writing process was completed, the project leader (Nerantzi & Mathers, 2021) together with the High School student did the illustrations, based on the collaborative storyboard developed. During the process, the team reached out to colleagues to get feedback on drafts; their critical comments and suggestions were extremely important to refine and polish our story and find a clear direction.

Collaborative Blogging as a Reflective Learning Tool

To learn from the project process and evaluate outcomes, team members used narrative inquiry to systematically gather, analyse and represent their experiences. Narrative inquiry is an umbrella term that captures personal and human dimensions of experience over time and takes account of the relationship between individual experience and cultural context (Clandini & Connelly, 2000). The emphasis is on co-construction of meaning between the participants.

Collective blogs were set up that allowed all project participants to reflect with contributors undertaking concurrent writing, peer review and feedback. Blogging as a team helped us to showcase our thinking processes and share our reflections, ideas, thoughts, feelings, concerns and knowledge, in the open and as they were experienced (Etherington, 2004). The team wrote four blogs collaboratively, at four crucial times of the journey. Each blog had a specific team leader, intention and a time frame.

- Blog post 1 had a focus on the seed survey and the metaphors we used that emerged from this. In this post the team shared the findings from this survey (Roberts et al., 2020).
- Blog post 2 was a reflection on the rationale for joining this team project. It is written with great honesty and openness, and illustrates the joy and fears at the same time about this mammoth task ahead (Pulker et al., 2020).
- Blog post 3 was devised after we had written the story and we used this milestone as an opportunity to reflect on how we connected with the story we co-authored. Our reflections reveal our special individual and collective relationships with this and our personal interpretation and connection (Corti et al., 2021).
- Blog post 4 was an opportunity at the end of the project to look back at what we had achieved and what helped us get there. The focus is how we worked together, collaborated on the different aspects of the book and what enabled us to succeed (Pulker et al., 2021).

The next section provides an analysis of the fourth and final blog: *A Collaboration Like No Other, Reflections by the Team as the GO-GN Picture Book Is Coming to an End* which specifically provides insights into authors' perceptions of collaborative working and what they have learnt from it (Pulker et al., 2021).

Findings and Discussion

A thematic analysis of the narrative inquiries of the final blog (Braun & Clarke, 2006) highlights three key findings:

Openness and Inclusion

All members of the team agreed that the collaboration would be open, inclusive and transparent from the outset, as these are the underpinning values of open education, and in this context, it is understood that no voice is more or less powerful than any others. This provided opportunities for diverse perspectives (Rourke & Coleman, 2009) throughout the project. Team members displayed a clear sense of mutual respect and suspended judgement between themselves. One academic member commented:

> The most enjoyable aspect of our collaboration is the freedom we felt in being allowed to openly share our ideas, our suggestions, our critics. We all welcomed them and took them into account before making choices.

Communication and Listening

The geographical spread of the team members situated in different time zones meant that synchronous meetings were extremely hard to organize. Nevertheless, thanks to collaborators' flexibility and agility, seven live meetings were able to take place. Not all members were present at each meeting but careful planning across the time zones enabled key people to attend when necessary, so that decisions could be made efficiently and in a timely fashion. Due to the project's tight working schedules, the rapid and constant flow of communication via Twitter and Google Drive felt overwhelming at times. However, thanks to team members' listening skills, openness and tolerance, timely decisions were made, and the project progressed through the milestones, even if not smoothly. As an academic member pointed out: 'What worked was being open to, and respectful of each other's ideas. Along with the different skills and perspectives we all contributed.'

Participation and Leadership

Contributions to the blog and particularly the fourth blog post revealed that each member of the team took part in the project willingly and with great enthusiasm. All members were engaged, committed to the same goal and motivated to achieve the set goal. Everyone also participated because they felt appreciated. For example, one academic member pointed out: 'The easiest aspect was certainly the passion we shared: nobody had to push anybody, we embraced our parts.' Team members contributed when possible, using their expertise while developing new skills and areas of interest. At the same time, work or study pressures were evident and self-care was important. However, there was no conflict or criticism when somebody could not respond or take part in a specific activity:

> There is no need to be 'on' all the time. The group has impetus, and it is ok to rely on the collective. You don't need to do everything, and asking questions is actually good!

As also shown in other studies, this collaboration was experienced as immersive and rewarding (Nerantzi, 2017):

> Completing a collaborative global project in the time of Covid-19 helped me better understand what was going on beyond the four walls of my house. […] This collaboration provided me with well needed human interaction and connections in a difficult time.

What proved to be useful was clear and inclusive project leadership (Wuffli, 2016), across a diverse, international collaboration. Team members were able to question and challenge aspects of the project openly and respectfully. The ongoing peer review led to knowledge sharing (Bogers, 2012) and continuous improvement of the story as a result. Even when there were serious doubts about the project at times, the leader was able to move the team on and responded to critical feedback with diligence and finesse:

> Thanks to our frank conversations, the fact that we suspended judgement and appreciated each other made a huge difference, I feel. This did by no means mean that we were not critical, but the criticality was focused on what we were doing, not the other person!

Conclusion

The picture book project *Together* engaged an international team in an imaginative and creative collaboration that embodied and reinforced our strong beliefs in the values of open education. The team navigated unknown territories and ambiguity, appreciated otherness and diversity of views and perspectives, and co-created a positive experience and an output that is truly cooperative.

Throughout this project, we reflected on how we worked together, our values, beliefs, habits, struggles and achievements (Etherington, 2002). Active participation in blogging reinforced the reflective learning cycle and led to deeper learning, new insights and better learning skills (Gibbs, 1988). One team member reflected: 'What I did learn about myself is that collaboration requires less talk, and more listening.'

As this project reaffirms, authentic collaborative projects require trust and openness, high levels of ethical and critical engagement, mutual and sincere communication, reflexive engagement throughout, and tolerance of ambiguity. Motivation and outcome should also be carefully considered when developing such collaborations in and across HE. A project like this could be considered in a range of learning, teaching and assessment situations with educators and students to experience inclusive collaboration that harnesses diverse voices and perspectives and fosters creative explorations and stimulates learning.

Autoethnography, Academic Identity, Creativity: Transitionary Tales from Practice to Teaching and beyond

Emma Gillaspy and Anna Hunter

- Creative collaborative approaches encourage authentic academic identities to emerge.
- Collaborative inclusive conversations in 'safe spaces' create much-needed peer support networks in HE.
- Reflecting on academic development through collaborative conversation sparks new ideas to drive sector-wide change.

Introduction

This chapter is a collaborative reflection on how each author adopted a different but linked creative approach to exploring emergent academic identity, one, with those who are 'becoming' teachers – the other with those who are exploring their academic identities. In bringing together these distinct yet complementary narratives, we have found synergies across our academic development praxes and sparked ideas for future practice. We hope our stories stimulate engagement in such collaborative activities to encourage reflection on, and development of, professional identity amongst our diverse readers. Academic identity is complex, multiple and always-shifting (Quigley, 2011). This fluidity carries great potential in terms of allowing academics to move between roles; however, the conflicting pressures to develop as a facilitator, researcher and leader can also result in ontological insecurity and imposter syndrome (Knights & Clarke, 2014; Parkman, 2016). This is particularly true for academics from working-class or practice-based backgrounds who may be navigating the challenges of a dual professionalism and the destabilizing effect of moving from an expert in one field to a novice in another (Smart & Loads, 2017).

Case Study 1: Using Collaborative Collage Making to Explore Academic Identity: Becoming Teachers

Staff at the University of Central Lancashire who are new to teaching in HE typically enrol on one of the taught Continuing Professional Development (CPD) programmes offered to help them enhance their skills and knowledge in teaching and learning. These range from CPD-only programmes to formal postgraduate qualifications; one thing they all have in common however is that many new academic staff embark on these courses with little or no sense of their own academic identity. Colleagues in this position reported feelings of dislocation between past and present selves, as if they needed to forget who they had been previously in order to succeed in their present incarnation.

In order to facilitate engagement with these diverse identities, in the early stages of all our taught programmes, staff are invited to take part in a collage-making activity as a prompt to reflectively explore what teaching and learning means to them. Working collaboratively in small groups, participants use pre-selected materials to produce a shared group collage in response to the title 'What teaching and learning means to me'.

Abegglen, Burns and Sinfield (2021) articulate the value to participants of different potential approaches to collage making, specifically the conscious and unconscious acts of the collage maker in choosing and placing images. For this exercise, source materials were provided by the facilitator, which in itself was a conscious choice designed to promote deeper engagement with the visual metaphors elicited in the act of selecting images. The source material provided was copies of the *Times Higher Education* magazine, which was chosen for its availability, visual qualities and education-related content. Having trialled the exercise at the 2017 Staff and Educational Development Association (SEDA) conference, participant feedback indicated that when dealing with images chosen from sources that are not of their own choosing participants need to think more carefully about how they can construct metaphors to explain their experiences of teaching, based on the images available to them.

The results are often deeply revealing, as the collaborative identification of visual metaphors leads to the uncovering of shared experiences, facilitating the development of a Community of Practice (Wenger, 1998) of novice educators. Coming from a place of disparate, often conflicted and conflicting professional identities, the collage artists can claim a new, shared identity forged in the here and now, and out of the creative process. The collage itself becomes a vehicle by which participants are able to tell their own, individual stories about *becoming teachers*, whilst the collaborative effort and shared experience of storytelling allow some of the more difficult narratives to surface. For example, the act of choosing and ascribing meaning to images for the collage creates a safe space in which participants can say 'this image represents something that I've found difficult'; 'yes, me too'. The collaborative focus on the images and what they represent creates a filter for the sharing of lived experience, allowing individual narratives of identity-formation to emerge through the creative collaborative act. To view an example of one such collage, see Hunter and O'Brien (2019).

Some participants have said they found the experience uncomfortable at first, as it challenged their assumptions of teaching and learning in HE, believing collages 'aren't academic enough' and the creative approach is too childish or playful to learn anything significant from. Those that pushed through that discomfort have commented that the collage-making process enabled them to form a bond within their groups based on shared experiences and recognize the power of the dialogic in enhancing learning. This in turn caused them to feel less isolated in the early days of their academic careers.

All participants are invited to return individually to their collaborative collages later on in the course, for further reflection on how they, and their teaching practices, have developed. Some have taken this a step further, using the collage as part of an autoethnographic account of their development as teachers (Hunter & O'Brien, 2019). A number have now adopted collage making into their own teaching, as a means of fostering collaboration and group identity formation (Hunter, 2020) with their students.

The transformative outcomes of the collage activity led the author to identify the possibilities of visual autoethnography as a means of capturing and developing the ideas arising from this work. As this research began to take shape, the two authors came together to discuss the potential for a creative autoethnographic activity as the vehicle to explore academic identity within another community: early career academics from a working-class background. From this starting point, Emma Gillaspy developed the project detailed in Case Study 2.

Case Study 2: Fostering Academic Belonging through Conversation

The second case study illustrates how a collaborative autoethnography approach (Chang et al., 2013) can promote belonging in academia. In this empirical research project, seven female educators at the University of Central Lancashire investigated how working-class roots shaped their academic values and identities (Gillaspy et al., 2022). The group followed an iterative cycle of individual and collective multimedia data collection and analysis to build on each other's academic identity stories and create meaning for themselves and the wider academe. The result of this project was not just a clearer sense of individual and collective academic identity but a realization of belonging in academia and a celebration of collaborative 'otherness' from a group of self-identified marginalized academics (Edwards-Smith et al., 2021).

Several elements were critical to the unexpected level of success of this project. This project began with a *call to action*. Each member of the team shared a visceral and personal connection to the theme of working-class academics. As a result, the team who came together to collaborate on this project were highly committed, both to the project itself and to the wider purpose of celebrating voices of underrepresented academic groups (Wilson et al., 2020).

The development of *trust* was critical in this project as has been documented in other collaborative autoethnography research (Lapadat, 2017). Trust created a developmental space where individuals in the team could expose their vulnerabilities without fear of judgement. As a result, the group felt able to share openly their honest reflections and memories, safe in the knowledge that these would not be exposed more widely unless the whole group agreed. This shared understanding and authenticity resulted in deepening both individual and collective reflective and reflexive practice.

Space and time for *storytelling* were created throughout this project which provided valuable insight on both the theory and practice of teaching (Spooner-Lane et al., 2008). Conducted entirely during a pandemic, the group embraced the flexibility of digital tools such as Padlets for data collection which encouraged meaningful reflective practice congruent with the preferences of the individuals in the group. For example, some collaborators chose to create diagrams or reflect using imagery, whilst others recorded video diaries or wrote blogs. Consequently, when the group came together regularly in live online sessions to tell their stories, the multimedia reflections could be articulated in greater depth whilst the rest of the team encouraged, challenged and deepened thinking through the use of open, coaching-style questions (Whitmore, 2017).

The collaborative, holistic and co-coaching approach to *peer support* meant that those new to research felt supported throughout and had a positive first experience of the research and publication process. The outcome of this developmental approach was identification of and increased confidence in individual strengths and authentic academic identities. The project team collaboratively agreed 'We have grown wings in our research and teaching ambitions' (Gillaspy et al., 2022).

Lessons Learnt

A shared interest in collaborative creative activities and autoethnographic approaches brought the two authors together to explore the outcomes of their separate projects. Through collaborative reflection we identified common themes and outcomes. In both activities showcased within this chapter, using creative materials and flexible tools enabled collaborative non-verbal ways of knowing to emerge which are resonant with individual core values and beliefs. Lessons drawn from these experiences include the importance of adopting a flexible approach to working with academics around their identity-formation and thinking carefully about how we can create spaces that allow authentic identities to emerge. In both of these instances, the use of creative and collaborative media has been pivotal and a conduit that has afforded flexibility within the process; this flexibility has then allowed participants to create their own safe space within which they can begin to explore nascent identities.

Academics at any stage of their career, but especially in the early years, often begin from a position of 'deficit' and 'imposter', focusing on what is missing from their skillset or how little they feel like 'proper' academics. This deficit model is unfortunately prevalent across HE within marginalized groups where pressure to assimilate can be the norm (Shukie, 2020). We hope the stories shared in this chapter illustrate that taking a strengths-based 'Appreciative Inquiry' coaching approach through collaborative reflection can build confidence in, and ownership of, academic identity. Working holistically and creatively with groups encourages the identification of congruence, authenticity and individualism in academic identity (Gillaspy, 2020), celebrating the collective strengths of the diverse academe.

Academia is traditionally an individualistic, competitive endeavour which is highly stressful with excessive workloads and multiple competing pressures (Persson, 2017) resulting in escalating poor mental health and staff insecurity (Morrish & Priaulx, 2020). The examples shared in this chapter show that collaborative conversations and creative exchange build academic confidence through surfacing, refining and celebrating the known and unknown aspects of individual and collective academic identity. Collaborating creatively with peers fosters emergent and authentic thoughts and feelings in much-needed 'safe spaces' in high stress environments, deepening support networks and resulting in a stronger sense of belonging to the profession.

Ultimately, this chapter aims to showcase the value of collaborative conversation, creativity and storytelling in the understanding and activation of self. The authors would like to thank all those academics who have worked with us on exploring their academic identities, it has been a pleasure observing their transitionary tales.

Working Together: Reflections on a Non-hierarchical Approach to Collaborative Writing

Karen Welton, Kiu Sum, Victoria Rafferty, Jane Nodder, Ralitsa Kantcheva, Ian Johnson, Paul Chin, Silvina Bishopp-Martin and Ed Bickle

The authors are a group of geographically dispersed UK HE Learning Developers interested in research-related topics. Due to Covid-19, the ability to meet in person at the annual 2020 ALDinHE conference was thwarted, resulting in the evolution of a research Virtual Community of Practice (vCoP).

- Collaborative writing offers an opportunity for communities to share ownership of and responsibility for the writing, editing and reviewing process in a democratic, non-hierarchical environment. Such activity can foster the overall growth and development of the community.
- Organizing collaborative writing as a shared, democratic responsibility, without a traditional leader figure, smoothed out concerns among the contributors about their previous writing experience, the validity of their ideas and their written input.
- Writing collaboratively, rather than alone, produced effects on contributors which were akin to participating in a team sport; it spurred individual contributions, encouraged self-selected responsibilities and acted as a safety net.
- The model of collaboration developed by this particular vCoP could be used by other groups to address questions in the changing HE landscape that are relevant to them, and plan activities to strengthen their vCoP's group identity, especially now that technological advances have opened up additional opportunities for communities to engage in collaborative writing for creating scholarly knowledge.

Introduction

The process of writing is a cornerstone for academia, reflecting values such as rigour, critique and engagement (Mountz et al., 2015). Academic writing is typically valorized as an individual endeavour, but with the advancement of technology such as synchronous online writing platforms, opportunities to construct scholarly knowledge collaboratively have multiplied (Nykopp et al., 2019). Collaborative writing (CW) involves 'sharing the responsibility for and the ownership of the entire text produced' (Storch, 2019, 40), factors that have certainly been enhanced by developing technologies. CW differs from cooperative writing, which involves a division of labour with each individual being assigned to, or completing, a discrete sub-task (Storch, 2019).

This chapter discusses the reflections of ten authors from a UK-based research virtual Community of Practice (vCoP) on the challenges and positives encountered during the CW of a research journal article using a shared Google Document.

Literature Review: Collaborative Writing

Existing literature identifies a number of approaches to CW, including: in-sequence writing, in parallel, one-for-all, multi-mode and reaction writing (Lingard, 2021). Although this categorization suggests CW is a multi-modal dynamic process, generally the progression of CW is linear (Lowry et al., 2004). Hynninen (2018) discusses the creation of a series of synchronous writing clinics in order to produce a collaborative academic publication within the field of computer science. Within that group, the research leader assigned specific tasks to colleagues, with more experienced researchers offering comments on the text. Hynninen's (2018) account suggests that their approach combines horizontal and stratified-division writing, where members have particular roles to perform.

In a similar vein, Ness et al. (2014) created a writing group in order to develop a body of academic literature relating to the authors' teaching practices within the field of nursing. Their approach involved the rotation of the first author between members, with each stage of the writing process being distributed evenly. The first author was then responsible for final editing and submission. Similarly, Collett et al. (2020) discussed their experiences of CW for publication; through face-to-face and online writing sessions the three academics shared and rotated roles such as leader, editor, mentor, indicating that such an approach helped with the cohesion of the group.

From the beginning the aspiration of our vCoP was to be democratic with a shared ownership of and responsibility for the whole writing, reviewing, editing and revising process.

Method

The writing of the original article (Bickle et al., 2021) involved a mixture of synchronous and asynchronous writing sessions. The synchronous sessions included live online discussions interspersed with periods of quiet writing. After completing the research article, the authors reflected on their CW journey, via a further synchronous writing session, recording their responses to two provocation questions: Q1. What challenges did the democratic experience of writing collaboratively present for you?; Q2. What were the positive elements of writing collaboratively? Responses from the authors were numbered A1–10 for transparency. The reflections discussed below are from all ten members of this vCoP, but one member self-excluded from this author list, due to competing time commitments.

Evaluating the vCoP Method

Through a meta-reflection, the research vCoP authors identified how the purely non-hierarchical approach they had taken to CW – creating their research journal article with no leading contributor(s) or initial division of writing tasks – had been pivotal to the quality of their experience. The democratic nature of construction evolved organically, enabling the ten authors to have an 'equal say, and all suggestions were carefully considered and discussed' (Q2.A1), thus demonstrating the 'level of respect that was shown for each other's writing – nothing was deleted or changed' (Q2.A3) without consultation between the whole group – either synchronously via verbal discussions, or asynchronously 'via suggestions or comments' (Q2.A3) on the Google Document. Despite the variation in their previous academic writing experiences, this non-hierarchical process enabled the 'opportunity of drawing out the skills and experiences of individuals and seeing how others work when writing the same topic but from a different perspective' (Q2.A6).

One author noted how they 'really felt like part of a team during this collaborative process, and the discussions we had as a group made me feel like I was contributing to the piece as a whole' (Q2.A3), whilst another compared it with 'a team sport [...] being spurred on by it [... but also enjoying] the sense of a security net' (Q2.A9).

The non-hierarchical nature also emanated a strong sense of responsibility – 'a personal pressure to complete bits for meetings out of a sense of responsibility to the group' (Q1.A6). There was 'the feeling of not being alone, [and it] sped up the rate at which I did things and wrote – like a team sport not wanting to let others down' (Q2 A7), while also 'knowing that things wouldn't come tumbling down when turning your back onto the project for a bit was really comforting – and very helpful for writing' (Q2.A9). This intentional focus on equitable inclusion built up a high level of trust between the authors with 'everyone's willingness to put their things out there for comment and criticism' (Q2.A7), and a 'general willingness to let people get on with things and give them a try, rather than worrying about what could go wrong beforehand' (Q2.A7).

The 'lack of hierarchy compared, say, with the supervisor/student type relationship' (Q2.A1), and the absence of predetermined roles, such as those noted in the literature above, provided a level playing field that encouraged peer support. One author noted feeling 'very supported when writing as this was a fairly new experience for me and an area which I had requested some mentoring for' (Q2.A3), whilst more experienced writers who were used to having sole ownership of a text found 'let[ting] go of a thought or a text and then see[ing] it in a new light when coming back because others have worked on it in between' (Q2.A9), a very positive aspect of this non-hierarchical CW process. This level of teamwork led to the feeling of never being 'stuck or blocked; there was always someone there to support you and collaborate with' (Q2.A10).

There were some elements of nervousness, which was an interesting phenomenon since many authors were already-experienced and published academic writers; '[I] worr[ied] a lot at the beginning about saying the wrong thing' (Q1.A1); 'scary to put your own draft work "out there"' (Q1.A5); 'I was apprehensive about the structure of my sentences, the grammar, the spelling, and also what will my writing reveal about me both professionally and personally' (Q1.A9); 'I felt worried about getting things wrong or doing things in a way that did not fit with everyone else's ideas of writing for publication' (Q1.A2). Perhaps these apprehensions occurred due to the act of sharing the writing process, versus the lone-working which is more commonplace in academic writing endeavours (Lowry et al., 2004).

The literature also discusses how CW can foster elements of professional development, such as extending the learners' knowledge of the topic and/or writing process, learning from peers and combining perspectives to ascertain a shared goal (Abrams, 2019; Šuković & Milanović, 2021; Storch, 2019; Thorpe & Garside, 2017). It is clear that the non-hierarchical CW process provided the opportunity for professional development. The vCoP authors reported how it was 'very helpful and insightful to experience the different writing styles of others and opened my views on how I might write in the future' (Q2.A1); 'the different styles of writing and approaches to writing [...] was interesting to see, in real time' (Q2.A2); a positive element was 'everyone's writing styles and [...] gain[ing] an understanding of what writing for publication entailed from a range of perspectives' (Q2.A3).

Variation in writing styles was also noted as challenging for some of the authors: 'my writing style was quite different to many of the other contributors and I was concerned about this' (Q1.A2); 'merging styles of writing' (Q1.A3); 'how my "voice" fitted with other voices' (Q1.A4); 'getting used to the writing styles of different people' (Q1.A6); 'different styles and approaches to writing' (Q1.A7). Although some expressed concerns about 'how one consistent voice could be achieved for the whole paper' (Q1.A4), and 'how would we be able to agree and move forward' (Q1.A7), such concerns soon disappeared as the true benefits emerged as the 'sense of belonging from the community turn[ed] the perceived challenges into positive experiences' (Q2.A6). These comments might suggest, more widely, the need to carefully consider the purpose, focus and author constitution of collaborations. Such considerations could include not only the different styles of collaborating authors but also the varying norms in different disciplines and academic fields (Lee, 2001). However, as our own group evolved organically from a research group with a mentoring aim, these considerations need not be seen as essential to all CW endeavours.

Conclusion

From our meta-reflection we conclude that a democratic, non-hierarchical environment enhances the effectiveness of collaborative writing activities in a research vCoP, and perhaps more widely for academics across the disciplines who are also committed to co-creating a more humane and democratic HE. The opportunity to present, discuss and evaluate a variety of perspectives, freely and democratically, promotes the truly collaborative nature of both the content creation and the writing processes from start to finish. Therefore, this chapter evidences the importance of not only seeking out opportunities to collaborate with immediate colleagues but also networking beyond an individual's immediate institutional context in their wider field of academic practice in collaborative writing *per se* and thus also of modelling the opportunities and power provided in collegiality and cooperation. We recommend that any CW endeavours should be undertaken following a democratic and non-hierarchical approach to achieve a truly joint authorship of the co-created text.

Humane Relationships: Reflections on Dialogue and Collaboration in a Foundation Art, Architecture and Design Course

Manuela Barczewski, Keith Beckles and Simone Maier

- The authors' professional practices were bolstered, enhanced and even enabled through the very human relationships that they built as they studied together as students of the PGCert.
- Learning to bond, belong and collaborate in real, human ways enabled the authors to form an authentic Community of Practice (CoP).
- When the pandemic struck, the authors drew on their relationships of trust and human bonds to honestly interrogate their own behaviours, worries and concerns, and this in turn helped to support students and create creative, collaborative Learning & Teaching (L&T) spaces.
- The authors offer a model to their students of how creative practitioners can work collectively to share creative skills, ideas and expertise to democratically develop new knowledge.
- To allow for a CoP to develop, the authors advocate for tutors to have time and spaces in which to learn how to collaborate with each other and develop human relationships that in turn bolstered, enhanced and even enabled their L&T practices.

Introduction

This chapter focuses on the importance of the development of human and humane relationships between academic staff and that this needs to be developed consciously in and between staff. We argue that courses for staff development, like our University's Postgraduate Certificate in Learning and Teaching in HE (PGCert), should model, build and enable collaborative teaching and learning practice. Our PGCert makes space for collaborative practice in action, promoting the power of collegiality and the CoP (Smith, 2009; Wenger-Trayner, 2015) and encouraging staff to experience the process of 'becoming' with each other (del Carmen Salazar, 2013). We outline our own teaching context and the role that the PGCert played in our collaborative professional and practical development. We make recommendations for collegiate L&T practice via our case study example of our own collaborative practices.

Context

We, the authors of this chapter, teach together at London Metropolitan University's School of Art, Architecture and Design (AAD) to deliver the Level 3 Foundation Course. London Metropolitan University was established as a post-1992 institution (Archer, 2003) and maintains a focus on Education for Social Justice (ESJ) which results in the recruitment of largely non-traditional students with complex backgrounds (Abegglen et al., 2020). Successful completion of the course enables students to progress on to one of seventeen Bachelor of Arts offered by the AAD or to apply to other UKHE art schools. The course thus serves as a 'diagnostic' environment for students, to affirm that their making is 'worthy' of developing and to 'test' which creative discipline they choose to progress in to. Unlike many UKHE courses that are required to focus on employability, our course emphasizes 'belonging', helping students find a 'fit' within the AAD's epistemic community through the validation of prior knowledge and their nascent creative practices.

Developing Humane Relationships

In 2018-20 we, the authors of this chapter, studied together towards our Fellowship of Advance HE (formerly known as the Higher Education Academy) via our PGCert. Removed from the immediate pressures of the L&T environment we had an opportunity to get to know, learn from and collaborate with other members of staff and with each other, thus building humane relationships that recognized and value each other's contributions as part of a collective endeavour. Facilitating Student Learning (FSL), the first module of our PGCert, proved to be a particularly important space in which we were guided to learn with and from each other, the teaching team and the other academic staff attending FSL to cultivate a toolkit of resources that we could use to build positive L&T environments for the collaborative co-construction of knowledge. As participants on the FSL module, we the authors collectively developed our pedagogies while also gaining an understanding and mutual respect for what turned out to be a shared belief in the socially just potential of Arts education. We are now able to offer a model to our students of how creative practitioners can work collectively to share creative skills and develop each other's contributions (Gutiérrez, 2008) to democratically develop new knowledge. As we continue to work together our humane relationships strengthen, providing a source of motivation, and adding to our sense of accomplishment as professionals of a wider academic community.

Based on our experience, it seems possible that other creative academics/professionals may also find value in making space for collaboration and human connection in their L&T practice, for themselves and their student learners, and thus we outline how we have developed two studio modules of the Foundation art, architecture and design course.

How We Worked Together: Collaborative Practice in Action

Throughout 2020–1 we taught together and worked alongside three more senior colleagues to pivot online the delivery of the Foundation course. Like most UKHE courses during the (Covid-19) lockdowns, we first moved online and then to a blended learning pedagogy. This required us to adjust from campus-based, large studio L&T, to delivering our studio modules first online and then in small face-to-face 'bubbles' supported by a single tutor. Further Covid-19 disruptions in early 2021 necessitated us moving L&T to split delivery, for which some students remained online while others came back onto campus. Two of us continued to deliver the studio-based modules in face-to-face bubbles while one tutor remained online. To help retain confidence in our pedagogies we frequently discussed the delivery of the curriculum under these new conditions, working through the ways that our pedagogic dynamics had been disrupted by the pivot to online and then blended delivery.

We all aim to support active learning spaces in which students can work in partnership with lecturers and peers but found that with the back and forth of online and in-person teaching, studios had become less collaborative and democratic, with the pedagogic hierarchies between staff, and between tutors and students shifting. There was the sense that students required more staff guidance than usual. As tutors, we recognized that online education was curtailing spaces for 'emergence' and 'creative conflicts'. From our collaborative PGCert experience, we knew open discursive spaces to be essential to both the students' educational experience and the maintenance of our own humane relationships. Without space to reflect with each other and thereafter adjust our L&T, the pandemic conditions would have led to a diminished awareness of the importance of collaboration in creative practices. Attempting to address this we frequently had to remind ourselves that the co-construction of knowledge means accepting silences as critical thinking time, both for our students and for ourselves (Giroux, 2010).

Our ongoing collaborative dialogue allowed us to find adequate language (Orr & Shreeve, 2018) to discuss the situation we all found ourselves in, making space for creative ideas to emerge, finding different ways for the students to engage with the L&T. We found that moving online introduced

> blocking, freezing, blurring, jerkiness and out-of-sync audio […] confound perception and scramble subtle social cues. Our brains strain to fill in the gaps and make sense of the disorder, which makes us feel vaguely disturbed, uneasy and tired without quite knowing why.
>
> (Murphy, 2020)

As a CoP we discussed and fundamentally adjusted our teaching approach, introducing additional asynchronous online spaces for use by both the F2F and online students. Our Padlets and Miro boards allowed students to display work, leave comments, connect, collaborate and develop their creative work with each other and with us. To facilitate the creative exchange, we encouraged peer-to-peer engagement, asking the students to post comments, thoughts and questions to each other to create a sense of belonging as they developed their work in these different settings.

Evaluation: Human Bonds as the Cornerstone of Humane Relationships

Looking back, the pandemic conditions impacted our L&T practice. Moving online, then to a face-to-face and blended studio delivery, made us increasingly aware of the importance of connection to each other and our students. The basis for this built our joint experience as co-educators and co-learners. Our pedagogies evolved through our ongoing dialogic collaboration and the dialogic encounters we facilitated between our students (Bahktin, 1981). We created spaces and places for students to connect and be with each other, to both display, comment upon and validate each other's work. These spaces proved to be successful and have since become an integral part of our ongoing inclusive pedagogy that strives to provide opportunities to both staff and students to think critically, pose problems and engage in a culture of questioning where everyone has a say in the modes of knowledge-claims and identities at play in and across the curriculum. When students are provided with such L&T spaces, there is a surge in energy and a strong sense of collective knowledge fabrication. Conversation – in the context of the powerful trust relationships that we had built in and from FSL – is the best way to respond to and reflect on super-complex L&T challenges. It was through discussion that we came to recognize issues at play in our pandemic practice and together we brainstormed ways to better scaffold students' creative practices in online L&T spaces. As a result of our experiences, we fervently encourage staff to develop their humane relationships as a means to support and sustain their creative L&T practice as they scaffold cooperative learning.

Concluding Recommendations

During the challenges of the past two years, we, the authors, have set aside time to discuss and evaluate our pedagogy and continue to build the bonds and respect between us. As a result of making a space for reflection and collaboration, we have continued to develop the humane relationships that we initially established during professional pedagogic development. Via sharing ideas, knowledge and our different skills, we found ways to create creative, collaborative spaces. As a result of our experiences, we advocate for teaching staff to have time and space to collaborate with each other, to share creative skills to improve the quality of the L&T and ensure an inclusive critical pedagogy in which everyone, tutors and students, has a say in the creation of new knowledge.

Coaching for Collaborative Autonomy: A Reflection on an Inter-university Course

Monika Hřebačková, Martin Štefl, Jana Zvěřinová and Tanja Vesala-Varttala

- As part of a project focusing on language coaching, a team of European HE teachers and educators organized an online course built around collaboration and co-creation.
- The inter-university course was open to thirty-five international bachelor and master students asking them to produce outputs related to sustainability and product marketing to develop their language and transversal skills online.
- Working in culturally heterogeneous multi-disciplinary student teams presupposes a good deal of collaborative autonomy as well as the ability to give and receive non-directive feedback.
- Reflecting on the collaborative process through Learning Journals and coaching tools facilitated the development of collaborative autonomy and cross-cultural inter-dependent learning.

Introduction

To remain relevant beyond the Covid-19 pandemic, HE institutions need to reflect on their approaches to Digital Education and effectively complement the newly reinvented educational environments. Teaching online does not just change teaching and learning but offers opportunities to transform teachers from transmitters of knowledge into co-creators, facilitating collaborative learning as coaches, mentors and evaluators (Richardson, 2003).

Aiming to fortify collaborative autonomy in English for Specific Purposes (ESP) learning and teaching, a European team of researchers have been developing interdisciplinary, collaborative, coach-oriented language teaching tools, methods and resources as part of Erasmus+ project CORALL. The CORALL project is a transnational initiative developed as a strategic partnership to support students in becoming effective multi-cultural collaborators, and well-oriented, reflective and inter-dependent learners. It also informs HE teachers on how to harness coaching skills to develop students' autonomous language and transversal skills online, whilst encouraging students' reflection about the learning process (Kleppin & Spänkuch, 2012). This chapter discusses how a team of European HE academics and educators organized an online course built around collaboration and co-creation to develop students' skills such as cross-cultural communication and critical collaborative autonomy.

Coaching and Collaboration

The CORALL project is a cross-European project, with many different partners/partner institutions. The CORALL team organized a nine-week inter-university collaborative course KREA (an abbreviation derived from a Scandinavian word for creativity, *kreativitet*) inviting thirty-five international bachelor and master students to participate. The course was integrated into students' language curricula, offering up to five ECTS credits, and was promoted among the students of partnering universities as a unique opportunity to collaborate and network internationally whilst practising English in a multi-cultural academic/professional community. Interested students were selected based on their motivation letters.

In practice, the course participants collaborated to produce outputs related to sustainability and product marketing. Teams of four to five students were coached by international teacher-coaches who facilitated a dialogue with the intention to involve students in problem solving through effective questioning and listening. The coaches did not give directive feedback but used specific coaching tools – e.g. questioning, mirroring, journaling, framing – to facilitate students' collaborative journey. The teachers came from subjects including marketing, project management, and language teaching, and had been trained as coaches as part of the project. The aim was to develop students' critical collaborative autonomy, defined as the process of 'assuming control of one's language learning within a community' (Myskow et al., 2018, 361), whilst also making them reflect on the collaborative process, and learn from it.

Collaboration as the Cog in the Engine of Team Performance

The course responded to current issues of sustainability and aimed at developing collaboration where students co-constructed meaning as members of a group (Kesser & Bikowski, 2010). Collaboratively, student teams focused on sustainability challenges of chocolate production by co-creating digital marketing solutions (Instagram Story videos) to inspire sustainable consumer purchasing decisions. As the course featured culturally heterogeneous multi-national teams, effective collaboration was of utmost importance.

Although students recognized the importance of collaboration in the co-creation process, some were reluctant in certain circumstances. One of the issues that surfaced was breaking the myth that getting input from people automatically means reaching a consensus. This was addressed by emphasizing that team collaboration is more about pursuing new ways of working and developing ideas and different perspectives to gain better/shared solutions and to learn from one another.

The course supported collaborative behaviour in the strong belief that a team's success or failure at collaborating reflects the philosophy of its leaders (Gratton & Erickshon, 2017). Here the proposition is that professional teams do well when leaders invest in supporting social relationships, demonstrate collaborative behaviour and create a 'gift culture' in which trainees experience interactions with leaders and colleagues as something valuable and generously offered – a gift.

Below we will focus on strong learning moments that were frequently reflected upon in the participants' Learning Journals and should be of interest to educators planning similar collaborative projects.

Collaboration, Autonomy and Learning Journals

Collaborative learning presupposes some degree of learner autonomy, especially when it comes to the type of autonomy which allows 'speakers' to interact within a group (Myskow et al., 2018). Learning languages involves students in some sort of collaboration, thus here, autonomy in learning does not equal learning individually. Therefore, the course focused on four key principles of collaborative autonomous learning: maximum peer interactions, equal opportunities to participate, individual accountability and positive interdependence. The teacher-coaches helped teams feel comfortable in the culture of their learning environment through socializing, facilitating collaborative choices and observing each other's learning styles. While students examined how to use what they learnt to benefit the team and progress towards their shared goal, stepping beyond individual empowerment was important.

As journaling is generally recognized as an effective coaching tool promoting student autonomy (Langer, 2002; Ning et al., 2011; Veiene et al., 2020), students were encouraged to reflect on their experiences in Learning Journals (LJs), noting their reflection as autonomous learners and as members of a multi-cultural interdisciplinary team. This further scaffolded the sense of a community of learning and underscored the value of collaborative process and team dynamic.

Participants also received multiple rounds of strictly non-directive feedback from their teacher-coaches, further fostering collaborative co-creation and partnering between lecturers and students. Students' LJs thus became a linchpin of collaborative autonomous learning by reflecting, engaging students in observation, speculation and awareness-raising, especially in relation to collaboration and their status as language speakers and learners.

Upon securing an agreement of all involved students, we analysed the challenges reported in the LJs to understand the role of learner autonomy in collaboration within online interdisciplinary teams in more detail. Key findings were shared and discussed with the students during the last course session.

Collaboration and Evaluation

The coaches' experience and the participants' LJs revealed takeaways which are crucial for anyone planning a collaborative project with a constructivist mindset. From the socio-cultural perspective (Oxford, 2003, 2015; Sudhershan, 2012), the students seemed to agree that the experience made them realize that autonomous collaboration is a complex dynamic process and that the non-directive feedback they received allowed them to reveal and tackle their own attitudes to collaboration, collaborative successes and related frustrations. They also realized that non-directive feedback requires their active reflection in order to help them in their effort – this coaching dialogue needs to be engaged prior to (if possible) and throughout any collaboration. Our experience thus confirms the principles of the multi-disciplinary teaming model (Edmondson & Harvey, 2018, 347–60) which demonstrates that multi-disciplinary collaborations tend to work as a complex adaptive system, allowing collaborators to go beyond traditional systems thinking.

Both students and teacher-coaches learnt that working collaboratively presupposes collaborative autonomy and that bottlenecks emerging in collaborative settings – including shyness to communicate, express thoughts or feelings, and a lack of knowledge and trust in the power of an individual to drive change – can be best mitigated through collaborative effort. Awareness of these bottlenecks is of key importance to educators planning collaborative projects.

To address these issues, teachers planning to work with students collaboratively and/or as coaches need to motivate both individual students and student teams by providing supportive yet non-directive feedback and by encouraging reassuring peer feedback, creating an atmosphere of critical collaborative autonomy 'characterised not by independence but by interdependence' (Little et al., 2002, 7).

To promote collaborative autonomy, teacher-coaches have to clearly frame student/teacher roles and be very clear about what they can and cannot do – not giving directive feedback might surprise many students. However, they should be directive when explaining the conditions and/or rules of the collaboration, for instance, explain what happens if one of the team members drops out or actively encourage peer feedback, but remain strictly non-directive in providing feedback on the students' work. With this sort of clarity, a good deal of frustration on both sides can be avoided. These observations reflect the idea of 'autonomy-supportive teachers', who are ready and able to 'promote intrinsic motivation by understanding learners' perspectives' (Némethová, 2020, 154).

Conclusion and Recommendations

The CORALL project enabled the development of a unique nine-week inter-university collaborative course. The experiences collected throughout the course confirmed that collaborative work in intercultural interdisciplinary teams offers an opportunity to develop co-creativity and collaboratively innovate but also explains common lexis and the accuracy of communication. Making students individually and collaboratively reflect on their intercultural experience means making them aware of and appreciate positive cultural difference: people 'not only know different things, but also know things differently' (Dougherty, 1992, quoted in Edmondson & Harvey, 2018, 352); they may look at the same phenomenon and each see different opportunities and/or challenges. This repeatedly surfaced in project-related discussion groups and the follow-up findings, including students' LJs. The project findings communicate important implications for educators who wish to embed coaching oriented collaborative autonomous learning in HE teaching during and beyond the Covid-19 pandemic, emphasizing the social and transformative character of collaborative autonomy, which 'not only transforms individuals, [but] also [...] the social situations and structures in which they are participants' (Benson, 1996, 34; see also Benson, 2001).

Acknowledgements

The authors would like to thank all CORALL partners involved in activities and research mentioned.

References

Introduction

Arnstein, S. R. (1969). A ladder of citizen participation. *Journal of the American Planning Association, 35*(4), 216–24.

Dewey, J. (1933). *How we think*. University of Wisconsin Press.

Gibbs, G. (1988). *Learning by doing: A guide to teaching and learning methods*. Further Education Unit.

Schön, D. A. (1983). *The reflective practitioner: How professionals think in action*. Basic Books.

Case Study: *Together*

Bodgers, M. (2012). Knowledge sharing in open innovation: An overview of theoretical perspectives on collaborative innovation. In C. de Pablos Heredero, & D. López (Eds.), *Open innovation in firms and public administrations: Technologies for value creation* (pp. 1–14). IGI Global. DOI: 10.4018/978-1-61350-341-6.ch001

Braun, V., & Clarke, V. (2006). Using thematic analysis in psychology. *Qualitative Research in Psychology, 3*(2), 77–101. DOI: 10.1191/1478088706qp063oa

Clandinin, D. J., & Connelly, F. M. (2000). *Narrative inquiry: Experience and story in qualitative research*. Jossey-Bass.

Corti, P., Pulker, H., Nerantzi, C., Bentley, P., Fransman, G., & Roberts, V. (12 February 2021). *Our story and our connection to it ... GO-GN blog*. http://go-gn.net/research/our-story-and-our/

Etherington, K. (2002). Working together: Editing a book as narrative methodology. *Journal of Psychotherapy Research, 2*(3), 167–76.

Etherington, K. (2004). *Becoming a reflexive researcher: Using our selves in research*. Jessica Kingsley.

Etherington, K. (2007). Ethical research in reflexive relationships. *Qualitative Inquiry, 13*(5), 599–616. DOI: 10.1177/1077800407301175

Gibbs, G. (1988). *Learning by doing: A guide to teaching and learning methods*. Further Education Unit.

Nascimbeni, F. (2020). Empowering university educators for contemporary open and networked teaching. In D. Burgos (Ed.), *Radical solutions and open science – An open approach to boost higher education* (pp. 123–34). Springer Open.

Nerantzi, C. (2017). *Towards a framework for cross-boundary collaborative open learning in cross-institutional academic development* [PhD thesis]. Edinburgh Napier University.

Nerantzi, C., & Mathers, B. (21 January 2021). *To illustrate or not to illustrate? Bryan mentoring Chrissi for the open picture book, a GOGN Fellowship project*. GO-GN blog. http://go-gn.net/research/to-illustrate-or-not-to/

Nerantzi, C., Pulker, H., Bentley, P., Corti, P., Roberts, V., Fransman, G., Frank, O., & Mathers, B. (2021). *Together* (Versions 1, 2). Zenodo. https://doi.org/10.5281/zenodo.4703978

Pulker, H., Bentley, P., Fransman, G., Roberts, V., Nerantzi, C., Corti, P., Frank, O., & Mathers, B. (7 April 2021). *A collaboration like no other, reflections by the team as the GOGN picture book project is coming to an end*. GO-GN blog. http://go-gn.net/research/a-collaboration-like-no-other/

Pulker, H., Bentley, P., Corti, P., Fransman, G., Roberts, V., & Nerantzi, C. (18 November 2020). *Why on earth did I join this project?* GO-GN blog. http://go-gn.net/research/why-on-earth/

Roberts, V., Nerantzi, C., Corti, P., Pulker, H., Bentley, P., & Fransman, G. (10 December 2020). *The seeds in our data basket, reporting findings, no penguins found ...* GO-GN blog. http://go-gn.net/research/the-seeds-in-our-data-basket/

Rogers, Y., & Ellis, J. (1994). Distributed cognition: An alternative framework for analysing and explaining collaborative working. *Journal of Information Technology*, 9(2), 119–28.

Rourke, A. J., & Coleman, K. S. (2009). An emancipating space: Reflective and collaborative blogging. *Same places, different spaces*. Proceedings Ascilite Auckland 2009. http://www.ascilite.org.au/conferences/auckland09/procs/rourke.pdf

Walsh, L., & Kahn, P. E. (2009). *Collaborative working in higher education: The social academy*. Routledge.

Weller, M., Farrow, R., & Pitt, R. (2019). GO-GN: Lessons in building an open research community. In Pan Commonwealth Forum 9 (PCF9), 9–12 September 2019. Edinburgh, Scotland, Commonwealth of Learning.

Wuffli, P. A. (2016) Introduction: A framework for inclusive leadership. In: P. A. Wuffli (Ed.), *Inclusive leadership: A framework for the global era* (pp. 1–8). Springer. DOI: 10.1007/978-3-319-23561-5_1

Case Study: Autoethnography, Academic Identity, Creativity

Abegglen, S., Burns, T., & Sinfield, S. (2021). Dialogic montage: Reflecting on playful practice in higher education. *The Journal of Play in Adulthood*, 3(2), 82–95. DOI: 10.5920/jpa.843

Chang, H., Ngunjiri, F. W., & Hernandez, K. A. C. (2013). *Collaborative autoethnography*. Left Coast Press.

Edwards-Smith, A., Gillaspy, E., & Routh, F. (2021). *Embracing 'otherness' through belonging: Experiences of engaging in a research project as female working class educators* [paper presentation]. Researcher Education and Development Scholarship (REDS) Conference. https://conferences.leeds.ac.uk/reds/

Gillaspy, E. (2020). Developing the congruent academic through an integrated coaching approach. *International Journal for Academic Development, 25*(3), 285–9. DOI: 10.1080/1360144X.2019.1593175

Gillaspy, E., Routh, F., Edwards-Smith, A., Pywell, S., Luckett, A., Cottam, S., & Gerrard, S. (in press, 2022). *Hard graft: Collaborative exploration of working class stories in shaping female educator identities*. PRISM.

Hunter, A., & O'Brien, K. W. (2019). Seeing and sticking, being and becoming: The kaleidoscopic impact of a creative intervention. *Student Engagement in Higher Education Journal, 2*(3), 214–21. https://sehej.raise-network.com/raise/article/view/853

Hunter, A. (2020). Snapshots of selfhood: Curating academic identity through visual autoethnography. *International Journal for Academic Development, 25*(4), 310–23. DOI: 10.1080/1360144X.2020.1755865

Knights, D., & Clarke, C. A. (2014). It's a bittersweet symphony, this life: Fragile academic selves and insecure identities at work. *Organization Studies, 35*(3), 335–57.

Lapadat, J. C. (2017). Ethics in autoethnography and collaborative autoethnography. *Qualitative Inquiry, 23*(8), 589–603. DOI: 10.1177/1077800417704462

Morrish, L., & Priaulx, N. (2020). *Pressure vessels II: An update on mental health among higher education staff in the UK*. Hepi Occasional Paper 23. Higher Education Policy Institute (HEPI). https://www.hepi.ac.uk/2020/04/30/pressure-vessels-ii-an-update-on-mental-health-among-higher-education-staff-in-the-uk/

Parkman, A. (2016). The imposter phenomenon in higher education: Incidence and impact. *Journal of Higher Education Theory and Practice, 16*(1), 51.

Persson, R. S. (2017). *Distress or satisfaction?: Talent management in higher education worldwide*. The International Centre for Innovation in Education (ICIE). http://hj.diva-portal.org/smash/record.jsf?pid=diva2%3A1121027&dswid=-5400

Quigley, S. (2011). Academic identity: A modern perspective. *Educate, 11*(1), 20–30.

Shukie, P. (2020, October). Let's do it. Let's do it now. *Working Class Academics Conference Blog*. https://workingclass-academics.co.uk/lets-do-it-lets-do-it-now-by-peter-shukie/

Smart, F., & Loads, D. (2017). Poetic transcription with a twist: Supporting early career academics through liminal spaces. *International Journal of Academic Development, 22*(2), 134–43.

Spooner-Lane, R., Henderson, D., Price, R., & Hill, G. (2008). Practice to theory: Co-supervision stories. *International Journal of Research Supervision, 1*(1), 39–51.

Wenger, E. (1998). *Communities of practice: Learning, meaning and identity*. Cambridge University Press.

Whitmore, J. (2017). *Coaching for performance: The principles and practice of coaching and leadership* (5th ed.). Nicholas Brealey Publishing.

Wilson, A., Reay, D., Morrin, K., & Abrahams, J. (2020). 'The still-moving position' of the 'working-class' feminist academic: Dealing with disloyalty, dislocation and discomfort. *Discourse: Studies in the Cultural Politics of Education, 42*(1), 30–44. DOI: 10.1080/01596306.2020.1767936

Case Study: Working Together

Abrams, Z. I. (2019). Collaborative writing and text quality in Google Docs. *Language Learning and Technology, 23*(2), 22–42. DOI: 10125/44681

Bickle, E., Bishopp-Martin, S., Canton, U., Chin, P., Johnson, I., Kantcheva, R., Nodder, J., Rafferty, V., Sum, K., & Welton, K. (2021). Emerging from the third space chrysalis: Experiences in a non-hierarchical, collaborative research community of practice. *Journal of University Teaching & Learning Practice*, *18*(7), 135–58. DOI: 10.53761/1.18.7.09

Collett, K., van den Berg, C. & Verster, B. (2020). Sympoiesis 'becoming with and through each other': Exploring collaborative writing as emergent academics. *Critical Studies in Teaching and Learning*, *8*(Special Issue), 168–85. https://doi.org/10.14426/cristal.v8iSI.266

Hynninen, N. (2018). Impact of digital tools on the research writing process: A case study of collaborative writing in computer science. *Discourse, Context and Media*, *24*, 16–23. DOI: 10.1016/j.dcm.2018.01.005

Lee, D. Y. W. (2001). Genres, registers, text types, domains and styles: Clarifying the concepts and navigating a path through the BNC jungle. *Language Learning and Technology*, *5*(3), 37–72. http://llt.msu.edu/vol5num3/lee/

Lingard, L. (2021). Collaborative writing: Strategies and activities for writing productively together. *Perspectives on Medical Education*, *10*(3), 163–6. DOI: 10.1007/s40037-021-00668-7

Lowry, P. B., Curtis, A., & Lowry, M. R. (2004). Building a taxonomy and nomenclature of collaborative writing to improve interdisciplinary research and practice. *Journal of Business Communication*, *41*(1), 66–99. DOI: 10.1177/0021943603259363

Mountz, A., Bonds, A., Mansfield, B., Loyd, J., Hyndman, J., Walton-Roberts, M., Basu, R., Whitson, R., Hawkins, R., Hamilton, T., & Curran, W. (2015). For slow scholarship: A feminist politics of resistance through collective action in the neoliberal university. *Acme*, *14*(4), 1235–59. https://acme-journal.org/index.php/acme/article/view/1058

Ness, V., Duffy, K., McCallum, J., & Price, L. (2014). Getting published: Reflections of a collaborative writing group. *Nurse Education Today*, *34*(1), 1–5. DOI: 10.1016/j.nedt.2013.03.019

Nykopp, M., Marttunen, M., & Erkens, G. (2019). Coordinating collaborative writing in an online environment. *Journal of Computing in Higher Education*, *31*(3), 536–56. DOI: 10.1007/s12528-018-9203-3

Storch, N. (2019). Collaborative writing. *Language Teaching*, *52*(1), 40–59. DOI: 10.1017/S0261444818000320

Šuković, T., & Milanović, J. (2021). Academic growth through collaborative writing. In J. Filipović, G. Goetz, & A. Jovanović (Eds.), *Teaching and learning to co-create* (pp. 89–98). Palgrave Macmillan. https://link.springer.com/chapter/10.1007/978-3-030-72718-5_7

Thorpe, A., & Garside, D. (2017). (Co)meta-reflection as a method for the professional development of academic middle leaders in higher education. *Management in Education*, *31*(3), 111–17. DOI: 10.1177/0892020617711195

Case Study: Humane Relationships

Abegglen, S., Burns, T., Maier, S., & Sinfield, S. (2020). Supercomplexity: Acknowledging students' lives in the 21st century university. *Journal of Innovative Practice in Higher Education*, *4*(1), 20–38. http://journals.staffs.ac.uk/index.php/ipihe/article/view/195

Archer, L., Hutchings, M., & Ross, A. (2003). *Higher education and social class: Issues of exclusion and inclusion London*. Routledge Farmer.

Bakhtin, M. (1981). *The dialogic imagination: Four essays*: University of Texas Press.
Del Carmen Salazar, M. (2013). A humanizing pedagogy: Reinventing the principles and practice of education as a journey toward liberation. *Review of Research in Education, 37*(1), 121–48. DOI: 10.3102/0091732X12464032
Gutiérrez, K. D. (2008). Developing a socio-critical literacy in the third space. *Reading Research Quarterly, 43*(2), 148–64. http://lchc.ucsd.edu/mca/Mail/xmcamail.2014-12.dir/pdftsnR0mXbcJ.pdf
Giroux, H. A. (23 November 2010). *Lessons to be learned from Paulo Freire as education is being taken over by the mega rich*. Truthout. https://truthout.org/articles/lessons-to-be-learned-from-paulo-freire-as-education-is-being-taken-over-by-the-mega-rich/
Murphy, K. (29 April 2020). Why Zoom is terrible: There's a reason video apps make you feel awkward and unfulfilled. *New York Times*. https://www.nytimes.com/2020/04/29/sunday-review/zoom-video-conference.html
Orr, S., & Shreeve, A. (2018). *Art and design pedagogy in higher education: Knowledge, values and ambiguity in the creative curriculum*. Routledge. https://www.taylorfrancis.com/books/mono/10.4324/9781315415130/art-design-pedagogy-higher-education-susan-orr-alison-shreeve
Smith, M. K. (2003, 2009). Jean Lave, Etienne Wenger and communities of practice. *The encyclopedia of pedagogy and informal education*. https://infed.org/mobi/jean-lave-etienne-wenger-and-communities-of-practice/
Wenger-Trayner, E., & Wenger-Trayner, B. (2015). *Communities of practice: A brief introduction*. http://wenger-trayner.com/introduction-to-communities-of-practice/

Case Study: Coaching for Collaborative Autonomy

Benson, P. (1996). Concepts of autonomy in language learning. In R. Pemberton, E. Li, W. Or, & H. D. Pierson (Eds.), *Taking control: Autonomy in language learning* (pp. 27–34). Hong Kong University Press.
Benson, P. (1997). The philosophy and politics of learner autonomy. In P. Benson, & P. Voller (Eds.), *Autonomy and independence in language learning* (pp. 18–34). Longman.
Benson, P. (2001). *Teaching and researching autonomy in language learning*. Longman.
'CORALL' Project (n.d.). *About the project*. https://corallprojecteu.wixsite.com/presentation/about-the-project
Dougherty, D. (1992). Interpretive barriers to successful product innovation in large firms. *Organization Science, 3*, 179–202.
Edmondson, A. C., & Harvey, J. F. (2018). Cross-boundary teaming for innovation. *Human Resource Management Review, 28*(4), 347–60. DOI: 10.1016/j.hrmr.2017.03.002
Gratton, L., & Erickshon, T. J. (2017). Collaboration and teams: Eight ways to build collaborative teams. *Harward Business Review, 11*. https://hbr.org/2007/11/eight-ways-to-build-collaborative-teams
Kleppin, K., & Spänkuch, E. (2012). Sprachlern-coaching. Reflexionsangebote für das eigene Fremdsprachenlernen. *Fremdsprache Deutsch, 46*, 41–9. DOI: 10.37307/j.2194-1823.2012.46.09
Kessler, G., & Bikowski, D. (2010). Developing collaborative autonomous learning abilities in computer mediated language learning: Attention to meaning among students in wiki space. *Computer Assisted Language Learning, 23*, 41–58. DOI: 10.1080/09588220903467335

Langer, A. M. (2002). Reflecting on practice: Using learning journals in higher and continuing education. *Teaching in Higher Education*, *7*(3), 337–51. DOI: 10.1080/13562510220144824

Little, D. (2002). General introduction. In D. Little, J. Ridley, & E. Ushioda (Eds.), *Towards greater learner autonomy in the foreign language classroom* (pp. 15–22). Authentik.

Myskow, G., Bennett, P. A., Yoshimura, H., Gruendel, K., Marutani, T., Hano, K., & Li, T. (2018). Fostering collaborative autonomy: The roles of cooperative and collaborative learning. *Relay Journal*, *1*(2), 360–81. https://kuis.kandagaigo.ac.jp/relayjournal/issues/sep18/myskow_et_al/

Ning, D., Lew, M., & Schmidt, H. G. (2011). Writing to learn: Can reflection journals be used to promote self-reflection and learning? *Higher Education Research & Development*, *30*(4), 519–32. DOI: 10.1080/07294360.2010.512627

Némethova, I. (2020). Autonomy and motivation in language learning and teaching. *CASALC Review*, *10*(1). DOI: 10.5817/CASALC2020-1-12

Oxford, R. L. (2003). Toward a more systematic model of L2 learner autonomy. In D. Palfreyman, & R. C. Smith (Eds.), *Learner autonomy across cultures: Language education perspectives* (pp. 75–91). Palgrave Macmillan.

Oxford, R. L. (2015). Expanded perspectives on autonomous learners. *Innovation in Language Learning and Teaching*, *9*(1), 51–71. DOI: 10.1080/17501229.2014.995765

Richardson, V. (2003). Constructivist pedagogy. *Teachers College Record*, *105*(9), 1623–40. DOI: 10.1046/j.1467-9620.2003.00303.x

Sudhershan, A. (2012). *Fostering autonomy in intercultural language learning in the foreign language classroom: A case study of international students learning English at a higher education institution in Ireland*. [doctoral thesis, Dublin City University]. https://libguides.ioe.ac.uk/c.php?g=482485&p=3299852

Veine, S., Kalvig Anderson, M., Haugland Andersen, N., Espenes, C. T., Søyland, T. B, Wallin, P., & Reams, J. (2020). Reflection as a core student learning activity in higher education – insights from nearly two decades of academic development. *International Journal for Academic Development*, *25*(2), 147–61. DOI: 10.1080/1360144X.2019.1659797

Afterword: Collaboration, Community-building and 'Brokering'

Debbie Holley

In this Afterword, Professor Debbie Holley reflects on her own rich professional practice which across the years has involved working with students as partners, collaborating with staff and external stakeholders and innovative and creative (digital) practice. Debbie offers a powerful collaboration from the very beginning of her teaching career, and one from the Covid-19 pandemic. This personal reflective narrative draws together the themes of the book as a whole in a very human and accessible way, providing additional insights and inspiration on how readers can enhance their own practice.

Reflections on Collaboration: An Opening

As Professor of Learning Innovation at Bournemouth University, UK, I lead on innovation in research, teaching and professional practice within the Faculty of Health and Social Sciences. Joining academia from industry I approach much of my work as an academic outsider, sustained through friends, allies and networks. I have had an interesting and varied inter-disciplinary journey: working in a Business School; being a Reader in a Teacher Training department; running a central education unit; and now working with colleagues in Nursing Sciences. To build community through collaboration has been the essence of my work, and this chapter shares examples of what I term 'brokerage' (Outram, 2009).

Actively engaging with others means co-creating and sharing, and also participating as equal partners. We all have something to offer. At the heart of my teaching practice is 'working with others' – in particular with students – to motivate and include them in a meaningful dialogue. Speaking but also really listening as we act together. This encompasses the blend between learning inside the classroom, learning within professional practice placements, and scaffolding informal learning outside the university. It is also at the heart of the various research projects in which I have been involved across the years – collaborating with diverse colleagues to produce innovative practice and resources for students. I extend this collaboration, taking real pleasure in sharing educational networks and resources with peers and fellow practitioners, developing their 'circles of influence' as they progress on their own career paths.

When hearing about *Collaboration in Higher Education* – as a book and a wider project in which the editors have engaged – I thought how strongly this reflects my values, and values are an essential part of what it means to be an educator in these challenging times (see Advance HE UKPSF, n.d., the benchmark for educational excellence). The book highlights how staff work with staff – and with students, how students connect with other students, how universities partner with other universities and beyond, and how staff and students connect with other stakeholders. In this *Afterword*, I map my own collaborative journey as an educator and professional, linking it to wider arguments of an HE system that has been increasingly marketized and commodified, becoming more individualistic and competitive, rather than a collaborative or collegiate endeavour. This HE rarely responds positively to the challenges – or opportunities – of Digital Education and WP. I begin therefore with a brief outline of my journey into academia that was always fuelled by my passion for the 'other'. The key message is the importance of 'connection' in challenging university environments, before arguing for more liberatory practice through the collaborative: the genuine value of HE.

The Business School

My first academic post was within a Business School at a post-92 inner city university dedicated to WP and seeking to improve the experiences of 'non-traditional' students. My pedagogic approach was – and still is – to establish a learning environment within which all students can collaborate – inside and outside the classroom. This journey begins pre-entry, continues in induction and goes beyond the first year. Positive initial student experiences are central to retention and completion – they can change lives.

With a predominance of WP students at the university, most combining complex home/work/study lives, our students were offered a skills-based module to help orientate them to HE and academic success. This HE orientation module was often equally loathed by staff and students alike and it was important to reimagine our version into something challenging, creative and inspiring. I also wanted the course to blend face-to-face, online and extramural activities designed to pique student curiosity and motivate them to learn how to learn as they navigated their first assessment challenge together. This not only supported and empowered students but also connected them with each other. Student curiosity was for example raised when, instead of a printed module guide, they were offered a business card in the genre of a 'Cluedo' board, which seeded the blend of formal classroom, informal group and online activities that supported the development of cohort identity and active, interactive learning and teamwork.

Further, the assessment strategies and tasks were adapted so students could work together to showcase their learning (see Biggs, 1996, principles of constructive alignment). The final assessment further piqued student curiosity, requiring a visit to the Tate Modern (London, UK), based on which they had to cooperatively design and present an art-based artefact to the rest of the class. This was a new, joint learning experience for many students, most of whom had little of what academia considers cultural capital (Bourdieu, 1986):

> Before coming to class, I had never heard of the Tate Modern or Salvador Dali. I really didn't want to go and visit the gallery, but when I got there, I was amazed ... there's a whole world I knew nothing about. Now, coincidently, I hear about the Tate Modern in the newspapers ... and I also read a novel that mentioned Salvador Dali. It was probably there all the time. This made me wonder how many other things just go right over my head because I don't know about them.

The shift from a teacher-centred to a student-centred set of learning activities transformed the unit. I worked with thirty-five staff to redesign the HE Orientation module for 1,000+ students experiencing narratives of difficulty, isolation and compromise in the 'new cold climate' of HE (Sinfield et al., 2004). We moved large lectures to smaller tutorial groups and engaged students in creative, collaborative, problem-based learning. All this required a shift in staff attitudes. Encountering staff more used to traditional models of delivery as well as those unwilling to deliver 'remedial' programmes to students, I designed and led staff development sessions for colleagues, bringing them on board with the project that collaboratively reinvented the learning, teaching and assessment practices of a previously unloved 'study skills' module:

> It was such a joy working with a member of staff who wanted to redesign teaching, learning and assessment for student empowerment.

> I loved the creativity, who would have thought a first-year skills unit would now include a staff and student trip to the Tate Modern!

The values underpinning my work with staff and students in the Business School are reflected in the body of work in this book and can particularly be found in the section on *Decolonising Relationships and Partnership for Social Justice*. The case studies, as with this example, reveal educational development as collegiate practice. They bring together new, radical collaborative approaches to teaching and learning, uncovering the development of collaborative pedagogy that enabled authors, students and external entities to position themselves powerfully within academic discourse. These chapters actively connect their ostensibly isolated stories into powerful narratives of inclusion. As with my own experience some twenty years before, other examples constitute staff and students co-designing previously unloved modules and courses into creative and invigorating capstone projects that have impact beyond individuals and university programmes, rippling out locally, nationally and globally.

Digital Collaboration: Learning Technology, Connection and Humanity

There is a Zulu proverb called Ubuntu that says: 'I am a person through other people. My humanity is tied to yours.' Archbishop Desmond Tutu explained it this way: 'One of the sayings in our country is Ubuntu – the essence of being human.

Ubuntu speaks particularly about the fact that you can't exist as a human being in isolation. It speaks about our interconnectedness ... We think of ourselves far too frequently as just individuals, separated from one another, whereas you are connected and what you do affects the whole world.'

(Archbishop Desmond Tutu from Metz, 2017)

HE is always changing but in 2020 everything changed radically with the emergence of the Covid-19 pandemic that moved university teaching, learning and assessment online, overnight. Whilst previously the 'digital revolution' was driven by policy and management, and thus perhaps was treated with caution (see for example Morley & Carmichael, 2020), suddenly there was a distributed network of academics playing, experimenting and challenging what Digital Education could and should be. There are now many examples of how wonderfully designed, collaborative and shared technologies offer students those liberatory places and spaces we wish for them, without the 'technostress' baggage that our standard/normative practices often unknowingly design in (Holley & Biggins, 2021).

This was crowd-sourced experimentation for empowering technology enhanced learning at its best: building a vision from the ground up. Unfettered by the limitations of policy drivers and strategic goals, academics just had to get on and do it, and share it. For example, the Covid-19 Higher Education Literature Database (CHELD) became an open access repository for 138 manuscripts published between 1 January 2020 and 30 June 2020 (Butler-Henderson et al., 2020; 2021). This collection set out to map an emergent field and capture the contributions academics were making to our understanding that Covid-19 brought about the real potential of Digital Education, and to highlight cross-cutting themes. This open-access sharing of 'best practice' and current research brought not only researchers together but academics more generally: a network was created (Castells, 2004; Wenger, 1997).

This rapid and collegiate response to the digital reality and innovation launched by the pandemic is exemplified within my work in Nursing Sciences. Here we also needed to move our dedicated nursing academics, and our students, online 'in a hurry' and this ahead of the rest of the University. In this medical emergency, our student nurses were in demand, with requests to graduate and enter the workforce – immediately. The potential conflict was that high-quality nursing teaching that is typically developmental, taking place over time and in various collaborative ways was 'fast tracked'. Despite the challenging situation and calls for changing our training, we wanted to maintain high teaching standards for the students – those nurses – to ensure exceptionally high quality for their patients. Our staff pride themselves on delivering a high level of content knowledge and skills to trainee nurses, with an approach very much in Wenger's (1997) Community of Practice model and founded on a 'humanization' curriculum led by BU Nursing academics (Todres et al., 2009).

The faculty learning technologist and I collaborated to identify potential solutions. We wanted to offer a safe hybrid 'place' where staff could come together overcoming their own apprehension through collaboration and 'place-binding' at the intersection of the paths people create and follow in their daily lives (Ingold, 2011, in Ellis & Goodyear, 2016; and also Cook & Holley, 2022). Thus the daily *Coronavirus Teachinar* was launched. The *Teachinar* adopted a radio chat show format, with participants free to listen, share or contribute – and again, at a place and time of their own choosing – to podcasts and recordings designed to share good digital practice and enable access to critical information. A different kind of collaborative network was born. Pandemic, or no pandemic, technologies offer us different options, and this very much echoes the *Creative and Digital Partnerships* section, with students and faculty supporting each other online, building community for well-being and sharing stories and histories of success and resilience. The interconnectiveness of a network developing, flowing humanely, especially in a time of crisis, embodies the ethos of Ubuntu, the humanity towards others – something we all need to consider when working with others.

Concluding Thoughts

Learning is often presented as an individualistic and even competitive pursuit, much like university teaching, and a wholesale switch to online can exacerbate this. However, learning and teaching with others, no matter the circumstances, is empowering when collaboration is the starting point. My ethos is both student- and staff-centred: I celebrate students (and staff as students) and what they bring. I aim to empower students in and out of the classroom; my practice considers lifelong learning as a process supported by practice that lights a spark in the heart of the learner. I work with colleagues to develop communities of practice across the university and beyond: my urge to network and act in a collegiate manner brings together learning developers, discipline academics, librarians, technicians, members of the public and other 'stakeholders' to co-create spaces to co-explore with students, and for all of us to travel the journey together.

As exemplified by the stories of hope in *Collaboration in Higher Education,* the 'brave new university' would benefit from exploring its own practices through a collaborative lens. There is potential when we work together, when practice emerges from ground up experimentation, when we embrace collaborative multimodal interaction and mixed social networks, and all with a truly student-centred focus. The supercomplexity of the world, of our students' lives and of the problems that we need to face and tackle together requires a humanizing approach to 'scaling at speed' (Holley et al., 2020) requiring:

- Staff collaborations to enhance teaching and learning
- Students as partners
- Collaborations with stakeholders
- Creative and digital partnerships
- Decolonizing relationships
- Reflections on collaboration.

Exactly what this inspiring book offers to its readers – illuminated and highlighted by all the case studies and shared through the local, national and international mutual learning projects they represent. This book clearly articulates the ways in which we can all – student community, discipline staff, learning developers, technologists, artists and beyond – come together to reframe these as spaces of agency and power.

Collaboration is always important in teaching in a humane context; we are interdependent beings. It is especially important to nurture collaborative working practices when developing teaching and learning online. As mentor, the advice I offer students and staff 'on becoming' an academic can be summarized as:

You learn how to become academic over time and through the range of practices that you engage with through your time in university, developing competencies that you only become aware of and recognise at the end of that journey.

References

Advance HE (n.d.). UK Professional Standards Framework (PSF). https://www.advance-he.ac.uk/guidance/teaching-and-learning/ukpsf

Biggs, J. (1996). Enhancing teaching through constructive alignment. *Higher Education, 32*, 347–64. DOI: 10.1007/BF00138871

Bourdieu, P. (1986). The forms of capital. Trans. R. Nice. In J. Richardson (Ed.), *Handbook of theory and research for the sociology of education* (pp. 241–58). Greenwood Press.

Butler-Henderson, K., Crawford, J., Rudolph, J., Lalani, K., & Sabu, K. M. (2020). Covid-19 in higher education literature database (CHELD V1): An open access systematic literature review database with coding rules. *Journal of Applied Learning & Teaching, 3*(2), 1–6. DOI: 10.37074/jalt.2020.3.2.11

Butler-Henderson, K., Tan, S., Lalani, K., Mandapam, S. K., Kemp, T., Rudolph, J., & Crawford, J. (2021). Update of the Covid-19 higher education literature database (CHELD V2). *Journal of Applied Learning & Teaching, 4*(1), 1–4. DOI: 10.37074/jalt.2021.4.1.22

Castells, M. (2004). *The network society: A cross-cultural perspective*. Edward Elgar Publishing, Incorporated.

Cook, J., & Holley, D. (2022). Covid-19 lock-down: Hybrid learning cases using the lens of the zone of possibility. In E. Gil, Y. Mor, Y. Dimitriadis, & C. Koppe (Eds.), *Hybrid learning spaces*. Springer. http://eprints.bournemouth.ac.uk/35528/

Ellis, R.A., & Goodyear, P. (2016). Models of learning space: Integrating research on space, place and learning in higher education. *Review of Education, 4*(2), 149–91.

Holley, D. & Biggins, D. (2021). *Wellbeing: The chasm between students' expectations and institutional provision* [blog]. #Take5, #65. https://lmutake5.wordpress.com/2021/11/25/take5-65-wellbeing-the-chasm-between-students-expectations-and-institutional-provision/

Holley, D., Donaldson, I., & Moran, J. (2020). *A humanising response to scaling at speed*. Shaping academic practice for the new decade, 18th Annual Academic Practice and Technology (APT), 6 July 2020.

Morley, D., & Carmichael, H. (2020). Engagement in socio constructivist online learning to support personalisation and borderless education. *Student Engagement in Higher Education Journal, 3*(1), 115–32. https://sehej.raise-network.com/raise/article/view/1004

Metz, T. (4 October 2017). What Archbishop Tutu's ubuntu credo teaches the world about justice and harmony. *The Conversation*. https://theconversation.com/what-archbishop-tutus-ubuntu-credo-teaches-the-world-about-justice-and-harmony-84730

Outram, S. (2009). Revisiting dissemination. *SEDA, 10*(3), 1–5. https://www.seda.ac.uk/wp-content/uploads/2020/09/Educational-Developments-10.3.pdf

Sinfield, S., Burns, T., & Holley, D. (2004). Outsiders looking in or insiders looking out? Widening Participation in a post 1992 University. In J. Satterthwaite, A. Atkinson, & W. Martin (Eds.), *The disciplining of education: New languages of power and resistance* (pp. 137–52). Trentham Books.

Todres, L., Galvin, K. T., & Holloway, I. (2009). The humanization of healthcare: A value framework for qualitative research. *International Journal of Qualitative Studies on Health and Well-being, 4*(2), 68–77. DOI: 10.1080/17482620802646204

Wenger, E. (1997). *Learning, meaning and identity. Communities of practice.* Cambridge University Press.

Index

Abegglen, S. 189, 213
ABP. *See* Architecture Building and
    Planning (ABP)
academic literacies model 93, 96–7
academic observations 65–8
academic writing 39–42, 49–50, 88–9, 93,
    216, 218–19
Actor Network Theory 88
Adapt to Postgrad (ATP)
    79–81
Additional Support Needs (ASN) 111–13
adventure 8–29
Ainley, C. 110, 115
Allan, Q. 34, 39–40
Anand, P. 34, 57
*Approaching Blended Learning through
    Teaching Team Collaboration*
    (Herbert, Lynch and Murshed) 34,
    52–7
*Arabian nights: A Caravan of Moroccan
    Dreams* (Shah) 49
Architecture Building and Planning (ABP)
    44–6, 48
Arm, K. 131, 154
Arnstein, S. R. 205
art 132
Art, Architecture and Design (AAD) 221
Arthur, R. 166–7
Arts and Humanities Research Council
    (AHRC) 121
arts-based practices 132
Ashley, T. 35, 62
Association for Learning Development in
    Higher Education (ALDinHE) 49,
    206, 216
Atme, C. 166–7, 172, 192
ATP. *See Adapt to Postgrad* (ATP)
Australia (AU) 57–61
*Autoethnography, Academic Identity,
    Creativity* (Gillaspy and Hunter)
    206, 212–15

Barclay, L. 34, 49
Barczewski, M. 206, 220
Barret, G. 109–14
Beckles, K. 206, 220
Bennett, L. 113
Bickle, E. 216
Biotechnology and Biological Sciences
    Research Council (BBSRC) 121–4
Bishop, J. 35, 62
Bishopp-Martin, S. 216
Bittner, S. 34, 49
Black Asian Minority Ethnic (BAME)
    177–8, 181–2
Black History Month 181
Black Lives Matter movement 69, 165
Blake, J. 130, 150
blended learning project 34, 52–7, 222
blogging 209
Bon, P. 166, 172
Bovill, C. 100–1, 185
Braun, V. 99
Brazant, K. 34–5
Brighton Museum 177, 179–83
Bringing Research to Life (Barclay, Bittner
    and Reck) 34, 49–52
British Association of Social Work
    (BASW) 36
Build Your Own House 112
Build Your Own Sustainable House 111–12
Built Environment Learning and Teaching
    (BEL+T) group 44–8
Bulley, C. J. 101
Burns, T. 189, 213
Business School 234–6

Cardozo, M. L. 166–7, 172, 177, 192
*Celebrating African Caribbean's in Sussex
    Past and Present* 180
Changing the Rules of the Game (Blake,
    Cooke and Nisic) 130, 150–4
Chin, P. 216

Clarke, S. 24
Clarke, V. 99
'Clothes on Our Backs' 177–9, 182
coaching 45, 206, 215
Coaching for Collaborative Autonomy (Hřebačková, Štefl, Zvěřinová and Vesala-Varttala) 206, 224–8
co-creation 55, 63, 77, 95, 145, 152, 157, 159, 166–7, 172, 174–6, 178, 188–9, 192, 206, 224–6
cognoscibility 170
Cohen, J. I. 85
collaboration 1–3, 238–9
   approach 45–6
   coaching and 225
   and evaluation 226–7
   inclusive curriculum and pedagogy 189
   LAs and FL 41–2
   participants 47–8
   potential 98
   process of 7
   on student learning 42
   student-staff 81–2, 85, 87, 93–7
   supporting 143
   team and 94, 225–6
   types of 120, 122–4
Collaboration for Academic Literacies Development and Enriched Inter-professional Relationships (Allan, McWilliams and Raleigh) 34, 39–43
collaborative autoethnography (CAE) 178, 214
collaborative learning 37, 91, 113, 130, 142–3, 145, 224, 226
collaborative teaching model 55–6
collaborative vocabulary learning 89
collaborative writing (CW) 206, 216–20
collective self-organizing 173
Collett, K. 217
Collett, T. 170
Colley, H. 186
Coming in Together (Arthur and Huda) 166–72
communication and listening 210
community 33
   BAME 181
   CDDE 175
   M4C 124

community-based learning 62–4, 110
Community of Practice (CoP) 33, 39, 62, 116, 213, 220, 222–3, 237
confidence 42, 56, 61, 66, 78, 81, 87–8, 93, 100–1, 114, 140–1, 148–9, 152–3, 171, 185–6, 189, 215, 222
Connectivity as Transgressive Practice in Doctoral Research (Sum) 130, 146–50
Connolly, H. 35, 62
Continuing Professional Development (CPD) 21, 212
conversation 2–4, 17, 45, 47, 54, 81–2, 87, 94–5, 148, 155, 166, 175, 177, 181, 193, 206, 211, 214–15, 223
Cooke, A. 130, 150
Cook-Sather, A. 77, 100
Co-producing a Skills-based Programme (Soccio and Tregloan) 34, 43–8
co-production 66, 77
CORALL project 224–5, 227
Covid-19 Higher Education Literature Database (CHELD) 237
Covid-19 pandemic 4, 8, 46, 69, 80–1, 85, 95, 129, 134, 139–40, 142, 146, 148, 151, 155, 169, 176, 189, 208, 211, 222, 224, 228, 237
Creative Mindsets 183–7
Creative Teachers' Cafe 130, 140
creativity 36–7, 62–3, 66, 129–30, 132–3, 139, 141–2, 194, 215, 225, 236
Crenshaw, K. 175
Critical Development and Diversity Explorations (CDDE) 173–7
critical reflection 36–7, 96, 205
Cross-disciplinary Collaborations for Sustainable Futures, and a Vital and Relevant Academic Community (Pritchard, Connolly, Egbe, Saeudy, Rowinski, Bishop, Ashley and Worsfold) 35, 62–9
cross-institutional 58–9, 61, 110, 115–19
Curran, J. 168
Czerski, T. 167, 192

decentralized learning 137–8
decision-making process 36, 77, 87, 165, 174
decolonization 3, 88, 166–73, 175, 177–83, 192–6

Developing 21st Century Skills through Meaningful Cross-institutional Collaborative International Community Service Projects (Anand and Tsz Kit Lui) 34, 57–61
De Wachter, E. M. 144
Dewey, J. 205
dialogic learning 89, 168
dialogic pedagogy 37
Dick Camplin Education Trust (DCET) 153
diversity 64, 78, 81, 83, 86–7, 136, 139, 155, 166, 173, 176–8, 180–1, 188, 191–2, 211
Diversity Lewes (DL) 177–82
Doctoral Training Partnerships (DTPs) 120–5
dominant systems 132
Duncan, H. 51

Economic and Social Research Council (ESRC) 121, 123, 125
educational intervention 192–3, 195
Education for Social Justice (ESJ) 221
education intervention presentation 193
education transformations 65–6
Egbe, A. 35, 62
embedded literacy 40
emotion-focused coping (EFC) 90
English for Specific Purposes (ESP) 224
English language 54
Enhancing Digital Inclusivity (Arm) 131, 154–9
Enhancing the Wider Postgraduate Experience (Jones, Kurtin, Liu and Southwell) 78–83
Equalities Act (2010) 84
Equality and Diversity (E&D) project 83–8
equity 57, 110, 116–18, 165–7, 187, 218
escape room collaboration 8–29
esteem 167, 186–7
evaluation 59–60, 65, 86–7, 99, 131, 141, 145, 156–8, 167, 171, 190–1, 223, 226–7
External Advisory Board 123
external collaborations 123

face-to-face learning 55–6, 99, 129, 139–41, 155, 169, 217, 222–3, 235
Facilitating Student Learning (FSL) 221

faculty lecturers (FLs) 39–43
feminism 167, 175, 192–6
Finke, J. 167, 192
4 P principle 49, 52
Fraser, N. 185
Frazier, S. 78, 83
Freire, P. 170, 173, 189, 193

Gardiner, M. 78, 97
genre approach 39
Gibbs, G. 145, 205
Gillaspy, E. 206, 212
Giroux, H. A. 193
Global Open Educational Resources (OER) Graduate Network (GO-GN) 207–8
Graaf, M. d. 166, 172
Graduate Teaching Assistants (GTAs) 78, 93–6
Greater Manchester 115–17
group work activities 58

Hall, R. 125
hands-on workshops 111–12, 130–4, 136–8
Hannaford, E. D. 78, 93
Hansen, M. 146
Hao, G. 130–1, 133
Hardie, S. M. 78, 97
Haudenschild, D. 166, 172
Health and Social Care (H&SC) 167, 187–9, 191
Healthcare Scientist Education (Ainley) 110, 115–19
Health Education England (HEE) 115–16, 118–19
Henneman, E. A. 85
Herbert, K. 34, 52
Heritage Lottery Funded project 180
hidden curriculum 170
Higher Education Achievement Record (HEAR) 99
Hill, V. 166, 183
Hockings, C. 188–90
holistic approach 64–5, 130
Holley, D. 234
Holmwood, J. 66
Home-School-University 111–12

Honest Conversations about 'Race' and Racism (Kalume and Moriarty) 166, 177–83
Hong Kong (HK) 57–61
Honneth, A. 167, 183–7
Hoon, A. 191
horizontal learning 63
Hřebačková, M. 206, 224
Huda, N. 166–7
Humane Relationships (Barczewski, Beckles and Maier) 206, 220–3
Hunter, A. 206, 212–13
Hynninen, N. 217

identity 4, 45, 100, 142, 148, 169, 181, 185, 206, 212–16
Imagining Ivy Williams (Weait) 50
inclusive and self-directed learning 174–6
Inclusive Learning and Teaching in Higher Education (Siddiqui) 167, 187–91
inclusivity 3, 44, 48, 53, 78, 82–4, 123, 131–2, 141, 143, 153–9, 165, 167–8, 173–6, 178, 186–9, 191, 206–7, 211, 223
individual learning 47–8, 174
induction process 166–72
innovation 58, 95, 109, 117–18, 120, 122, 133, 140, 145, 173, 234, 237
interdisciplinary 36, 39, 93, 95–7, 114, 122, 124, 132, 136–8, 146, 175, 185, 224, 226–7
inter-disciplinary group 51, 96, 132
International Development Studies (IDS) 173
inter-university collaborations 122–3
intervention reflection essay 193
intra-university collaborations 122
Ison, S. 110, 120

Javanbakht, N. 78, 88
Jenks, C. 146
Johnson, I. 216
Jones, A. M. 78–9
justice 3, 63, 114, 165–7, 172–7, 180, 183–8, 195

Kalume, T. 166, 177, 179–81
Kantcheva, R. 216
Kerr, H. 78, 83
Khangas 179–82

Kirkpatrick, D. L. 190
Knowles, J. 78, 83
Korbmacher, M. 78, 97
Kragt, A. 177
KREA course 225
Krimpen, R. V. 110, 120
Kuh, G. D. 188
Kurtin, D. L. 78–9

learning advisors (LAs) 39–43
Learning Development (LD) 93–6
Learning Journals (LJs) 226
Learning Management System (LMS) 45–6, 53
learning & teaching (L&T) practices 188–9, 191, 220–3
Lee, J. L. 85
Library Peer Network (LPN) 151–4
Library Student Team 151–3
limitation 92, 171–2, 193–4, 237
Liu, T. 78–9
London College of Communication (LCC) 183–4
Loo, D. B. 78, 88
Love, Respect, Esteem (Hill and Taylor) 166–7, 183–7
Lynch, J. 34, 52

McArthur, G. 185–6
McWilliams, R. 34, 39–40
Mag, A. G. 130, 138
Maier, S. 206, 220
Mamani Mamani, R. 175
Manchester Academy for Healthcare Scientist Education (MAHSE) 116–19
Mantell, A. 36
Marmolejo, F. J. 112
Masters of Professional Accounting (MPA) 53
Merdanovic, M. 166, 172
meta-reflection 81, 218–19
Microsoft Teams 94–5
Midlands4Cities DTP (M4C) 121–4
Midlands Graduate School DTP (MGS) 121–4
Moriarty, J. 166, 177, 180–1
motivation 8, 20, 41, 54, 67, 86, 91–2, 98–9, 134, 140, 143, 147–9, 168–71, 176, 182, 194, 211, 221, 225, 227

MSc Clinical Science 116
Multi-partner Doctoral Training Collaborations (Palmer, Krimpen and Ison) 110, 120–5
Murshed, H. 34, 52

narrative inquiry 207, 209
National Health Service (NHS) 115–17, 119
National School of Healthcare Science (NSHCS) 116, 119
National Union of Student (NUS) 177–8
Nerantzi, C. 206–7
Ness, V. 217
Neve, H. 170
Ngadi, J. 78, 97
Nisic, J. 130, 150
Noble, D. 165
Nodder, J. 216
non-governmental organisation (NGO) 34, 57–61, 65, 195
Nottingham Trent University (NTU) 121–2
Nouel, E. 166, 172

O'Brien, M. C. 78, 93, 213
O'Neill, S. 130–1
online connectivity 148–9
openness and inclusion 210
Organisation for Economic Co-operation and Development (OECD) 61, 191
origami 130–1, 133–8

Palmer, D. 110, 120
Paper as Teacher (Supple, O'Neill, Pentek and Hao) 130–8
participant feedback 81, 111, 213
participation 56, 68, 97–100, 139, 148, 167, 171, 210–11
Partner Advisory Group 123
partners 1–4, 57, 60–1, 65, 77–101, 109–10, 114–19, 123, 130, 140–1, 144, 154–5, 180–1, 185–8, 225, 235
partnership 2–4, 33, 40–1, 43, 45, 47–8, 63, 77–83, 85, 87, 93, 97–101, 110–11, 117, 119–23, 125, 130–1, 138–42, 153–9, 166–7, 180, 183–5, 187–8, 205, 222, 224
Paterson, V. 78, 83
patient forum 118–19

Patient Public Involvement (PPI) Strategy 118
pedagogic workshop 134–7
Peer Mentoring 183–7
peer-to-peer learning (P2P) partnerships 45, 47–8
Pentek, A. 130–1, 133, 135
PhD elephant 130, 146–50
Piaget, J. 132
Picasso, P. 130
pilot project 150, 189–90
political tensions and care 194–5
Postgraduate Certificate in Education (PGCert) 206, 220–2
postgraduate-taught (PGT) study 79–80
Pritchard, D. J. 35, 62
problem-based learning (PBL) 85–6
Professional Development (PD) 34, 44–6, 48
Prosser, D. 78, 83
Pulker, H. 206–7

Rafferty, V. 216
Raleigh, S. 34, 39
rationale 143–4
Reck, A. -K. 34, 49
reflection 1–3, 8, 36–7, 43, 45, 47–8, 59, 80–1, 91–2, 109, 112–14, 138, 153–4, 172–7, 184–5, 190, 193–6, 205–28
Regenerative Development and Design 173
Reimers, F. M. 112
relational learning beyond individualism 174
relationships 3, 28, 33–4, 41–3, 45, 50, 52, 54, 61, 66, 77–8, 88, 101, 123, 137, 139–42, 147, 152, 166–7, 179, 184–6, 193–4, 205–6, 209, 218, 220–3
researcher collaborations 123–4
Researching Together (Wright, Korbmacher, Gardiner, Ngadi, Shahid and Hardie) 78, 97–101
Research Volunteer Scheme (RVS) 97–101
resource pack 51, 130, 142–5
respect 41, 56, 62, 78, 85, 111, 141, 167, 170, 179, 186–7, 205, 210, 218, 221, 223
Robotics Engineering 133–4, 136

Rodolico, G. 109–11, 113
Rong, Z. 78, 88
Rowinski, P. 35, 62
Ryan, L. 78, 83

Saeudy, M. 35, 62
Schön, D. 205
School of Life Sciences (SoLS) 83–4, 86–7
Schuman, S. 85
Science, Technology, Engineering and Maths (STEM) 83, 109–14
Scragg, T. 36
self-directed learning 34, 42, 52, 54–7, 166, 172, 174–6
self-esteem 140, 186–7
Sessional Staff Engagement (SSE) 44–5
Shahid, A. 78, 97
Shah, T. 49
Siddiqui, U. A. 167, 187
Silver Sessional 34, 45–8
Simpson, D. 109–14
Sinfield, S. 189, 213
Slotte, J. 130, 142
Soccio, P. 34, 43
social learning 38, 43, 45, 48, 62, 64
social work
    critical 36–7
    programmes 36
    students 35–7
Social Work England 36
socio-material approach 88–9, 92
Solent Online Learning Environment 157–8
Solent University 154–5, 158
Southwell, A. 78–9
Speaking of Vocabulary (Loo, Javanbakht, Rong and Wang) 78, 88–92
Staff and Educational Development Association (SEDA) 213
staff partners 80–2
Staff-student Collaboration across Disciplines (Struan, O'Brien, Hannaford and Taylor) 78, 93–7
stakeholder 3, 85, 109–20, 235
Štefl, M. 206, 224
STEM. *See* Science, Technology, Engineering and Maths (STEM)
Stop, Start, Continue framework 191
storytelling 49–52, 130, 175, 178, 180–1, 213–15
Struan, A. 78, 93

student
    contributions 90
    discussion leaders 193
    exemplar texts 40–1, 43
    learning 39–40, 42–3, 50, 52, 55, 63, 66, 109, 134, 189–90
    partners 77, 80–2
Student Inclusive Curriculum Consultancy 131, 154–9
Students as Co-creators of an Inclusive Equality and Diversity Teaching Resource (Szelics, Frazier, Kerr, Knowles, Prosser, Ryan, Paterson, Veitch and White) 78, 83–8
StudentShapers scheme 80
student-staff collaboration 80–2, 85, 87
student-staff partnership 78–81, 83, 97–101
student team (ST) 151–3, 156, 184, 206, 225, 227
Subject Convenor (SC) 54
subject teaching teams 52–7
Sum, K. 130, 146, 216
supercomplexity 7, 33, 139
supervision 86, 122
Supple, B. 130–1
Supporting Collaboration (SC) 130, 142–6
Sustainability Forum (SF) 62–8
Szelics, A. 78, 83

Taylor, L. 166, 183
Taylor, S. J. 78, 93
Teacher Training department 139–41, 234
Teaching for Equality and the Politics of Feminist and Decolonial Education (Czerski, Finke, Atme and Cardozo) 167, 192–6
team sport model 206, 216, 218
Temporary Studio (TP) 143, 145
Text Mapping 190
Theory of Recognition (Honneth) 167, 183–4, 187
Thirkell, E. 17
Thompson, R. P. 49
Together (Pulker and Nerantzi) 206–11
Tracey, D. 34–5
Transforming the Arts Curriculum in Practice (Slotte) 130, 142–6
transgression 146, 193–4
transgressive education 174–6

Tregloan, K. 34, 43
trust 214
Truth, S. 175
Tsz Kit Lui, B. 34, 57
Tutors, Students, and Other Stakeholders at the Roundtable (Rodolico, Simpson and Barret) 109–14

Ubuntu 236–8
UK Research and Innovation (UKRI) 120
UNESCO 62
Unite and Unrule! (Atme, Bon, Graaf, Haudenschild, Cardozo, Merdanovic and Nouel) 166, 172–7
University of Amsterdam (UvA) 173, 192
University of Brighton (UoB) 177, 179–81, 183
University of Glasgow (UoG) 78, 83, 85–7, 111, 114
University of Manchester 118, 151–3
University of the Arts London (UAL) 143, 183–6
unveiling 170
Upheaval, Creativity and Student Partnerships (Mag) 130, 138–42

Veitch, N. 78, 83
Vesala-Varttala, T. 206, 224
virtual Community of Practice (vCoP) 206, 216–19
Vygotsky, L. S. 132

Wang, X. 78, 88
Weait, M. 50
Wekker, G. 173
Welcome Day 168–9, 171
Welton, K. 216
White, S. 78, 83
Widening Participation (WP) 63, 150–3, 168, 235
Williams, I. 50
Working Together (Welton, Sum, Rafferty, Nodder, Kantcheva, Johnson, Chin, Bishopp-Martin and Bickle) 206, 216–20
Worsfold, N. 35, 62
Wright, L. 78, 97
Writing Retreats in Social Work (Brazant and Tracey) 34–9

Zvěřinová, J. 206, 224

www.ingramcontent.com/pod-product-compliance
Lightning Source LLC
Chambersburg PA
CBHW071811300426
44116CB00009B/1271